IMPRISONING THE ENEMY

IMPRISONING THE ENEMY

How 12 million Axis POWs were held in captivity during WW2 and after

NIKOLAOS THEOTOKIS

Pen & Sword
MILITARY
AN IMPRINT OF PEN & SWORD BOOKS LTD.
YORKSHIRE - PHILADELPHIA

First published in Great Britain in 2024 by
PEN AND SWORD MILITARY
An imprint of
Pen & Sword Books Limited
Yorkshire – Philadelphia

Copyright © Nikolaos Theotokis, 2024

ISBN 978 1 03610 001 8

The right of Nikolaos Theotokis to be identified as Author of this work has been asserted by him in accordance with the Copyright, Designs and Patents Act 1988.

A CIP catalogue record for this book is available from the British Library.

All rights reserved. No part of this book may be reproduced or transmitted in any form or by any means, electronic or mechanical including photocopying, recording or by any information storage and retrieval system, without permission from the Publisher in writing.

Typeset in Times New Roman 9.5/11.5 by
SJmagic DESIGN SERVICES, India.
Printed and bound in the UK by CPI Group (UK) Ltd.

Pen & Sword Books Limited incorporates the imprints of Atlas, Archaeology, Aviation, Discovery, Family History, Fiction, History, Maritime, Military, Military Classics, Politics, Select, Transport, True Crime, Air World, Frontline Publishing, Leo Cooper, Remember When, Seaforth Publishing, The Praetorian Press, Wharncliffe Local History, Wharncliffe Transport, Wharncliffe True Crime and White Owl.

For a complete list of Pen & Sword titles please contact
PEN & SWORD BOOKS LIMITED
George House, Units 12 & 13, Beevor Street, Off Pontefract Road,
Barnsley, South Yorkshire, S71 1HN, England
E-mail: enquiries@pen-and-sword.co.uk
Website: www.pen-and-sword.co.uk

or

PEN AND SWORD BOOKS
1950 Lawrence Rd, Havertown, PA 19083, USA
E-mail: uspen-and-sword@casematepublishers.com
Website: www.penandswordbooks.com

Contents

Introduction vi

PART ONE – DETAINEES (I) 1

Germans 2
Nazi leaders – Top brass – Committed suicide – High-ranking officers –
Surrendered (I) – Surrendered (II) – War Criminals – Detained (I) – Committed
suicide (II) – POW massacres – Naval commanders – Luftwaffe commanders –
Surrendered (III) – Handed over – Women pilots – Paratrooper commanders –
Civilian massacres (I) – Civilian massacres (II) – Mobile killing squads – Civilian
massacres (III) – Hitler's inner circle – Concentration camp officials – Nazi
doctors – Female guards – Female prisoners of war

Italians 90
Mussolini: the slain – Italian atrocities

Japanese 115
Tokyo, Yokohama and Guam trials – Manila trials – British military
tribunals – Australian military tribunals – Dutch military tribunals –
Saigon trials – Chinese and Soviet military tribunals – Never charged –
The Fugu plan – The Imperial family – The 'Mata Hari of the Far East'

PART TWO – DETAINEES (II) 141
Romanians – Hungarians – Spaniards – Conscripted

Pro-Axis puppet governments 152
Croatians – Slovenians – Serbian anti-communists – Albanians – Greeks

Volunteers and collaborators (I) 161
French – Belgians – Dutch – Danes – Norwegians – British and
Commonwealth collaborators and spies

Volunteers and collaborators (II) 173
Russians – Ukrainians – Georgians – Caucasians – Armenians – Estonians –
Latvians – Lithuanians – Arabs – Indians – Chinese – White Russians – Koreans

PART THREE – RELEASE AND REPATRIATION 193

Bibliography and Recommended Reading 198
Notes 207
Index 235

INTRODUCTION

People across the globe are quite familiar with the harsh treatment of Allied prisoners of war (POWs) by their captors during the Second World War. It can partly be attributed to the repeated showing, over the past sixty-five years or so, of TV series like *Colditz* and of commercially successful movies, including *The Bridge on the River Kwai* (1957), *The Great Escape* (1963), Merry Christmas Mr Lawrence (1982) and *Unbroken* (2014). At the same time, it is also hard to find a TV or a film dealing with German, Italian or Japanese POWs. This is also the case in publishing, where such biographies remain rare to this day even though hundreds of thousands of military men from the three Axis nations (Germany, Italy and Japan), including POWs from co-belligerent countries (Romania and Hungary mostly), as well as pro-Axis volunteers from all over the world, were detained in camps established and run by the Allies in Europe, in North America, in Africa, in Asia and in Australia and New Zealand. Axis POWs were also held in neutral countries such as Switzerland and the Republic of Ireland. The Axis and co-belligerent military personnel in Allied captivity during the war or immediately after the German and the Japanese capitulation in mid-1945 numbered almost 12 million people (roughly the population of Belgium or Portugal in 2022). Of these POWs, about one third were detained in the Soviet Union. Another problem is that few camps remain intact in any form. Most of these, particularly in the United Kingdom, passed into private ownership after the war and either reverted to whatever they had been before or were put to new commercial use. One of the many exceptions was Eden POW camp near Malton, in North Yorkshire. This did time as an agricultural holiday camp after the war and was earmarked as the site of a crisp factory before the owner was persuaded to turn it into a museum.[1]

A few thousand of the 500,000 women who had volunteered as uniformed auxiliaries in the German armed forces were detained and interrogated in the final stages of the war in Vilvoorde, north of Brussels, in Belgium by the British Army and in Recklinghausen in North Rhine-Westphalia in Germany by the US Army. Among them were several 'brown nurses', so called because of the colour of their uniform, who were committed Nazi women. Most of the 3,700 women who served as overseers or attendants in Nazi concentration camps were eventually arrested by the Allies. They were brought to trial in Germany and Poland accused of crimes against humanity. At least fifteen of them were sentenced to death. They were executed by hanging between December 1945 and September 1947.[2] One of them, Elsa Ehrich, an SS helferin (female guard) organised and ran a Nazi brothel in Majdanek concentration camp in 1943, using inmates as sex workers. No wife of any Nazi high-ranking official was put in jail after the war with the exception of Hermann Göring's, Emma ('Emmy') Sonnemann, a stage actress from Hamburg, and Heinrich Himmler's wife and daughter. Sonnemann was sentenced to

INTRODUCTION

one year in jail by a German denazification court. After her release, she found that 30 per cent of her property had been confiscated by the post-war West German authorities.[3] Margarete and Gudrun, the wife and the daughter of Heinrich Himmler, head of the notorious SS (Schutzstaffel) and responsible for the killing of more than 6 million Jews, were held in various POW camps by the US Army until their release in November 1946.[4] In East Germany, the wives of several military officers were arrested by the communist authorities and punished for their collaboration with the Nazis. A famous alpine ski racer, Belgian-born Christel Cranz, a gold medal winner in the 1936 Winter Olympics, was forced to do farm work for eleven months.[5] At the time, her husband, Luftwaffe Major Adolf Borchers, was in Russian captivity. Cranz fled to the American occupation zone in 1947. Her husband, whom she married in 1943, was repatriated from the Soviet Union in 1955. Hitler's secretaries were interrogated after the German surrender by Allied officers and spent some time in detention. One of them, Else Krüger, who left the bunker after Führer's suicide, later married her interrogator, a British Army intelligence officer, and both settled in Wallasey, near Liverpool, in north-west England.[6]

Axis prisoners of war were held in custody by their captors during the Second World War for a range of legitimate and illegitimate reasons. They had to be isolated from friendly troops still in the field. While the definition of POW applied to soldiers, it also came to encompass civilians who may not have been part of an organised military unit, but were suspected of having loyalty to the enemy. The United States imprisoned about 110,000 Japanese immigrants and Japanese American citizens for most of the war and ruined them financially.[7] It also detained or exchanged 14,000 enemy aliens from Germany, Italy, Hungary, Romania and Bulgaria from a pool of almost one million suspects. Numerous POWs, normally officers, were prosecuted and eventually punished for war crimes or crimes against humanity. Prisoners, particularly officers, were used by their captors to discover military and political intelligence. They were also indoctrinated in new political beliefs, as happened to Axis and co-belligerent personnel held not only during the war but also well after 1945 in POW and labour camps in the Soviet Union and Communist China.[8]

International laws govern the fair treatment of people detained in POW camps, and mistreatment of prisoners is therefore considered a war crime. There are claims that conditions in POW camps in Canada often tended to be better than the conditions in the barracks Canadian troops were kept in.[9] The treatment of POWs was supposedly governed by the Geneva Convention, a document formulated in 1929 in Switzerland and signed by the major Western countries, including Great Britain, United States, Germany and Italy. The Soviet Union and the Empire of Japan were not among the signatories and their treatment of both military prisoners and civilian detainees during the war was some of the worst. The literature covering the Kanchanaburi death camp on the River Kwai, Changi Jail in Singapore, the Bataan March and so on have particularly foul places in the long history of man's inhumanity to man.[10] Cold-blooded torture and routine execution of prisoners seem to have been standard procedure in Japanese POW camps. Sinking lifeboats carrying Western survivors was also common practice in the Pacific.[11] Although the bombings of Hiroshima and Nagasaki were not among them, some war crimes were committed by the Allied on captured Axis military personnel. During the Battle of the Pyawbwe, in Burma, in April 1945, between twenty and fifty wounded Japanese soldiers had rocks dropped on them in cold blood by elements of a

Commonwealth (Indian) unit.[12] Wounded German soldiers who fell into the hands of Yugoslav guerrillas near Belgrade in late 1944 were fatally tortured by impalement.[13] On 7 June 1945 an SS officer, Senior Colonel Oscar Dirlewanger, was beaten to death by guards at a POW camp at Altshausen, near Ravensburg, in Baden-Württemberg.[14] A day later, at Neudorf, in north-western Czechoslovakia, Reichsführer Karl Hanke, who had recently replaced Heinrich Himmler as supreme commander of the Schutzstaffel (SS), was beaten to death by Czech partisans after his capture.[15]

Article 2 of the Geneva Convention stated: 'POWs are in the power of the hostile government, but not of the individuals or the formation which captured them. They shall at all times be humanely treated and protected, particularly against acts of violence, from insults and from public curiosity. Measures of reprisal against them are forbidden.' The armies of the Western Allies were under strict orders to treat Axis prisoners in line with the Geneva Convention – something with which they generally occurred. The Convention stipulated that prisoners should not be forced to work while in captivity. Given a choice, however, many Italian and German POWs (including low-ranking officers who also volunteered) in Great Britain and the United States chose to work rather than sit around in the camp and do nothing. They were employed in farms harvesting, in the construction sector rebuilding homes or clearing bomb damage. Winston Churchill was even advised by Stalin in Yalta to exploit Axis POWs in the post-war period as forced labour and as a form of reparation. The Western Allies could agree to that to a certain extent, but the British prime minister had other plans for the approximately 2 million German soldiers who were in British and Commonwealth custody. Representing a 'huge strategic reserve', these men could fight along British forces in case of an invasion of Western Europe by the Red Army.[16] Churchill expressed his views on this matter during a public speech at Woodford, Essex, on 23 November 1954.[17] After the surrender of Nazi Germany in May 1945, the POW status of German prisoners was maintained and they were used as labourers in countries including Great Britain and France. Many died when they were forced to clear (Wehrmacht-laid) wartime minefields in Norway, Denmark and France.[18] After the Japanese surrender, Western Allied forces rushed to their occupation zones to halt the growth of native independence movements.[19] In Indonesia and Indochina, Japanese prisoners were armed by the British and the French armies and took part voluntarily in the fighting against communist guerrillas.[20] When Japan surrendered, more than 2½ million armed Japanese were stranded in several East Asian countries. Anglo-American expeditionary forces had to rush to these countries in order to rescue Allied POWs and arrest those responsible for the death or torture of 40 per cent of those held.[21] The Japanese had moved 20,000 Commonwealth and American prisoners to Japan to keep them away from potential liberators.[22] Furthermore, the surrendered troops had to be shipped to Japan as quickly as possible before wars of revenge broke out all over Asia. In Hong Kong, for example, a Chinese mob assaulted the disarmed Japanese as they marched to ships and killed hundreds without using firearms.[23]

After their countries' capitulation, surrendered regular German and Japanese soldiers were only held briefly by the Western Allies, but officers, including generals, were detained for an average of two years. The last 10,000 Germans in Soviet captivity were released and repatriated in late 1955 – more than two years after Joseph Stalin's death.[24] The last of the Japanese POWs held in Communist China were freed as late as March 1964.

PART ONE
DETAINEES (I)

A few thousand officers of the German, Italian and Japanese armed forces, as well as several prominent contemporaries from Nazi Germany's 'satellite' countries including Hungary and Romania, were captured by or surrendered to Allied troops, during the war. They were only a portion of the about 12 million Axis prisoners of war, who were detained in Great Britain, Canada, the United States, the Union of Soviet Socialist Republics (USSR or Soviet Union) and other parts of the world.

GERMANS

Rudolf Hess, Adolf Hitler's deputy since 1933, was the first of Nazi Germany's highest-ranking officials to be imprisoned by the Allies. On 10 May 1941 he flew solo to Scotland in a twin-engine Messerschmitt Bf 110 fighter-bomber. He was discovered by a local ploughman after landing by parachute in a field south of Glasgow. Hess was initially taken by Home Guardsmen to Busby, in East Renfrewshire, and by midnight he was transferred to a police station at Giffnock, in the Central Lowlands. On 11 May he was taken to Maryhill Barracks, in Glasgow, where his injuries suffered in the parachute landing were treated.[1] During interrogation, he claimed that he was on a 'mission of humanity', aiming at stopping the war between Great Britain and Nazi Germany.[2] Hess was held in Buchanan Castle, in Stirlingshire, before being transferred to the Tower of London. Mytchett Place, a fortified mansion in Surrey, some 30 miles (48km) south-east of London, was his next place of detention. He stayed there for the next thirteen months.[3] On 16 June 1942, Hess attempted suicide by jumping over the railing of a staircase. His left leg was fractured in the fall. Ten days later, he was transferred to Maindiff Court Hospital, near Abergavenny, in Monmouthshire, where he was hospitalised under guard for several months. Hess was treated mostly as a mental patient. On 4 February 1945 he made a second suicide attempt, when he stabbed himself with a bread knife. On 10 October 1945 Hess appeared before the International Military Tribunal in Nuremberg, as a war criminal.[4] He was tried with the first group of twenty-three defendants, from November 1945 to October 1946. They were charged with conspiracy against peace, war crimes and crimes against humanity in violation of international laws governing warfare.[5] Hess, found guilty, was given a life sentence. He was found dead in his cell in Spandau prison, in Berlin, on 17 August 1987, aged 93.

Nazi Leaders

After the German surrender, in Court Room 600 of the Palace of Justice (Justizpalast), in Nuremberg, the International Military Tribunal sought to prosecute the most important surviving leaders of Nazi Germany in the political, military and economic sphere. The judges were two Americans (Francis Biddle and John Parker), one Briton (Sir Geoffrey Lawrence), one Soviet (Ion Nikitchenko) and two Frenchmen (Henri Donnedieu de Vabres and Robert Falco). The indictment was (a) participation in a common plan and conspiracy for the accomplishment of a crime against peace, (b) planning, initiating and waging wars of aggression and other crimes against peace, (c) participation in war crimes, and (d) crimes against humanity. Ten of these leaders were sentenced to death by hanging. They were: Field Marshal of the Reich (Reichsmarschall) Hermann Göring, Field Marshal Wilhelm Keitel, Colonel General (Generaloberst) Alfred Jodl, Ernst Kaltenbrunner, Joachim von Ribbentrop, Alfred Rosenberg, Hans Frank, Wilhelm Frick, Arthur Seyss-Inquart, Friedrich 'Fritz' Sauckel and Julius Streicher. Martin Bormann was sentenced to death in absentia. In the same trial, which lasted from 20 November 1945 until 1 October 1946 (218 days), three defendants were sentenced to life imprisonment. These were Rudolf Hess, Admiral Erich Raeder and Walter Funk. Four of the defendants received long prison terms: Baldur von Schirach and Albert Speer were sentenced to twenty years, Konstantin von Neurath to fifteen years and Grand Admiral Karl Dönitz to ten years in jail. Of the twenty-four defendants, three were acquitted. These were Hans Fritzsche, Hjalmar Schacht and Franz von Papen. One defendant, Gustav Krupp von Bohlen und Halbach, was neither acquitted nor found guilty. Another defendant, Robert Ley, was not tried because he committed suicide on 25 October 1945 – before the trial began in Nuremberg.

Reichsmarschall Göring was the highest-ranking Nazi official to be tried at Nuremberg.[6] He was taken prisoner on 6 May 1945 near Radstadt, in the Austrian state of Salzburg, after his surrender to elements of the US 36th Infantry Division. He was detained with the Nazi elite in Camp Ashcan, a well-guarded hotel, at Mondorf-les-Bains, in Luxemburg, until their trial.[7] Göring made an appeal asking to be shot as a soldier instead of being hanged as a common criminal but the court refused. He committed suicide with a potassium cyanide capsule the night before his scheduled execution.[8]

Field Marshal Keitel, the chain-smoking head of Hitler's strategic decision-making body of the Wehrmacht (Oberkommando der Wehrmacht or OKW), signed a number of criminal orders and directives that led to numerous war crimes. The notorious statement that the Second World War had nothing to do with soldierly chivalry or the regulations of the Geneva Conventions was attributed to Keitel.[9] He placed great trust on what he perceived to be Hitler's genius.[10] Keitel was arrested on 13 May 1945. After Hitler's suicide, Keitel followed Grand Admiral Karl Dönitz, who formed an acting Reich government near Flensburg on 5 May 1945. On 8–9 May the German delegation with Keitel was flown to Berlin, where they signed the total surrender of the German armed forces at the Soviet headquarters. Keitel was executed by hanging on 16 October 1946.

Generaloberst Jodl was chief of operations of the Wehrmacht High Command. He signed the German instrument of surrender on 7 May 1945 in Reims, France, on behalf of the OKW.[11] He was arrested with the rest of the Flensburg government by British troops on 23 May 1945. His house in Muivik, a few miles from Flensburg, was raided by elements of British Army's Cheshire Regiment. Twelve Grade 1 prisoners were taken in the area on 23 May, including Keitel and Jodl. Jodl was transferred to Ashcan and at Nuremberg he was indicted on all charges. The principal charge against him related to his signature of the criminal Commando Order and Commissar Order.[12] Found guilty of all charges, he was sentenced to death and hanged, at Nuremberg prison, on 16 October 1946.[13]

Austrian-born Kaltenbrunner, a lawyer by profession, rose to the rank of general of the SS prior to his appointment as chief of the Reich Security Office (RSHA).[14] In mid-April 1945, he was appointed commander-in-chief of the remaining German forces in southern Europe. Kaltenbrunner was the highest-ranking SS leader to be tried at Nuremberg. He was arrested by elements of the US 80th Infantry Division in the Totes Mountains, in south-eastern Austria. During the Nuremberg trials, he was wheeled

IMPRISONING THE ENEMY

into court, having suffered a brain haemorrhage during interrogation. On 1 October 1946 Kaltenbrunner was sentenced to death by hanging for atrocities committed during his tenure as chief of RSHA with Gestapo and the SS security branches being under his command from January 1943 to April 1945.[15] On 16 October he was executed, aged 43.

Former businessman von Ribbentrop served as Nazi Germany's minister of Foreign Affairs from 1938 to 1945. After Hitler's suicide, he went into hiding until his arrest on 14 June 1945 in Hamburg by a Belgian trooper of a British Special Air Service (SAS) squadron.[16] During the Nuremberg trials, von Ribbentrop was held directly responsible for atrocities carried out by German troops in occupied Denmark and in Vichy France since officials in both countries reported to him. He was sentenced to death and executed on 16 October, aged 53.

The hangings of those who received the death sentence in Nuremberg began with von Ribbentrop.[17] German Alfred Rosenberg, who was born in Tallinn, the capital of present-day Estonia, played a decisive role in shaping Nazi ideology. He also served as head of the Reich ministry for the Eastern occupied countries from 1941 to 1945. Rosenberg was captured by Allied troops on 19 May 1945 in Flensburg-Mürwik, in northern Germany.[18] At Nuremberg, he was found guilty of all counts and sentenced to death by hanging. He was executed on 16 October 1946, aged 53. Next to be hanged, right after Rosenberg, was Frick. He was Third Reich's minister of the interior (1933–43) and governor-general of the Protectorate of Bohemia and Moravia (1943–45). Frick's main task as minister of the interior was to organise the state bureaucracy and the administration of the occupied countries according to the Nazi ideology. Sentenced to death as a war criminal, he was executed, aged 69.

Frank, a politician and lawyer, served as governor-general of German-occupied Poland. He was captured by US troops on 4 May 1945 in southern Bavaria.[19] As a prisoner, he attempted suicide twice. Frank was indicted of war crimes at Nuremberg and sentenced to be hanged. He was executed on 16 October 1946, aged 46.

Seyss-Inquart, an Austrian Nazi politician, became chancellor of Austria prior to his country's annexation by the German Reich. He was a member of the Schultzstaffel (SS) and held the rank of obergruppenführer (lieutenant general). In 1940 Seyss-Inquart was appointed governor-general of the occupied Netherlands and in April 1945 he replaced von Ribbentrop as foreign minister. He was arrested in Hamburg in November 1945 by elements of British Army's Royal Welsh Fusiliers Regiment.[20] Convicted of war crimes and sentenced to death, Seyss-Inquart was hanged, aged 54.

Sauckel, a Nazi politician and former merchant seaman, was also a member of the Schultzstaffel (SS), holding the rank of obergruppenführer (lieutenant general). Appointed to implement a slave labour programme as General Plenipotentiary for Labour Development in 1942, he was granted extraordinary powers over both civil and military authorities in the occupied territories. Forced civilian and prisoner of war labour was introduced and developed. Sauckel was arrested in Salzburg by members of US Army's Counterintelligence Corps on 12 May 1945.

The last to be hanged in Nuremberg prison was Streicher. A member of the Reichstag and publisher of Nazi propaganda, including the virtually anti-Semitic newspaper *Der Stürmer*, he was arrested on 24 May 1945 in Waidring, a town in southern Austria, by elements of the US 101st Airborne Division.[21] Streicher was indicted of crimes against humanity in the Nuremberg trials and sentenced to death by hanging. He was executed on 16 October, aged 61. The remains of the executed Nazi officials, as well as Göring's, were cremated at Ostfriedhof and the ashes were scattered in the Wenzbach River, near Munich, to prevent the establishment of a permanent burial site that might be enshrined by nationalist groups.[22]

Raeder and Funk were sentenced (along with Hess) to life imprisonment. Grand Admiral (Grossadmiral) Erich Raeder commanded the German Navy (Kriegsmarine) until his resignation, in January 1943. He was captured by the Red Army on 23 June 1945 and was briefly imprisoned in Moscow.[23] At the Nuremberg Trials, Raeder was convicted of war crimes and sentenced to life imprisonment. He was released from Spandau prison on health grounds on 26 September 1955.[24] Raeder died in Kiel on 6 November 1960, aged 84.

Funk served as Reich minister of Economic Affairs (1938–45). He was arrested by the US Army on 11 May 1945 and sent to Camp Ashcan, in Luxemburg. During the Nuremberg Trials he was convicted of war crimes and sentenced to life imprisonment. Funk was released from Spandau prison because of ill health on 16 May 1957. He died of diabetes in Düsseldorf on 31 May 1960, aged 69.

The defendants who received various prison terms in Nuremberg were von Schirach (twenty years), Speer (twenty years), von Neurath (fifty years) and Dönitz (ten years). Nazi politician and SA-Overgruppenführer (lieutenant general) von Schirach served as Reich governor in Vienna. He was arrested in May 1945, in Schwaz, western Austria, by elements of US Army's 103rd Counterintelligence Corps. He was found guilty in Nuremberg of the deportation of Viennese Jews to extermination camps in Poland. He was released from prison after serving his full term. Von Schirach died of coronary thrombosis on 8 August 1974, in Kröv, western Germany, aged 74.

Speer served also his full term in prison. He was the Reich minister of Armaments and War Production (1942–45). Speer was arrested by British troops on 23 May 1945, near Flensburg and was convicted of war crimes during the Nuremberg Trials. He was released from Spandau prison on 30 September 1966. Speer suffered a stroke on 1 September 1981 in London, aged 76. He was there to participate in a BBC *Newsnight* programme.

Von Neurath, a diplomat, was Germany's foreign minister from 1932 until 1936. Between 1941 and 1943 he served as Reich Protector of Bohemia and Moravia. At Nuremberg, von Neurath was condemned for crimes against humanity and sentenced to ten years in prison. He received an early release from Spandau on 6 November 1954 after suffering a stroke in his prison cell. Von Neurath died in Enzweihingen, near Stuttgart, on 14 August 1956, aged 83.

Dönitz commanded Nazi Germany's navy between January 1943 and May 1945. He also briefly became president of the Third Reich following Hitler's suicide. Dönitz was arrested on 23 May by British troops near Flensburg and was later indicted at the Nuremberg Trials as a major war criminal.[25] Found guilty of committing crimes against peace and against the laws of war, he was sentenced to ten years in jail.[26] He was released on 1 October 1956 from Spandau prison. The third grand admiral (grossadmiral) in German history died in a small village (Aumühle) in north-west Federal Germany, on 24 December 1980, aged 89.

Three of the defendants, Papen, Schacht and Fritzsche, were acquitted by the International Military Tribunal. Von Papen was Chancellor of Germany in 1932. Between

1933 and 1934, he served as vice-chancellor under Hitler. Von Papen was arrested in his home on 12 April 1945 by elements of the US 194th Glider Infantry Regiment.

Schacht served as president of the Reichsbank until January 1939 and as minister without portfolio until 1943. Fritzsche was a popular radio commentator and director in the Nazi propaganda ministry. He surrendered to the Red Army in Berlin on 1 May 1945 and was detained in Lubyanka Prison in Moscow until his transfer to Nuremberg for trial.

Hitler and Goebbels had committed suicide and therefore could not be tried. Bormann, Adolf Hitler's closest aide and the successor to Hess as Nazi deputy leader, was sentenced to death in absentia by the International Military Tribunal in Nuremberg. He had committed suicide by biting a cyanide capsule to avoid capture by Soviet soldiers, near Lehrter Station, on 2 May 1945, while trying to flee Berlin on foot.[27] In 1963, German authorities were informed that Soviet soldiers had ordered a civilian to dig on that spot for the burial of two bodies.[28] Moscow never admitted finding Bormann's body but his remains were later found on 7 December 1972 during excavations. The remains were identified as Bormann's in 1998, following genetic testing on fragments of the skull.[29] These were cremated and the ashes were scattered in the Baltic Sea on 16 August 1999.

Himmler, another leading member of the Nazi Party of Germany, also died by his own hand. The founder and head of the SS (Reichsführer-SS), who set up the concentration camps during the Third Reich, was rounded up on 21 May 1945 by British soldiers at a checkpoint in Bremervörde, near Bremen, in northern Germany.[30] His intention must have been to escape since he had shaved off his characteristic moustache and adopted the disguise of a black patch over his left eye.[31] Himmler carried forged identity papers, issued under the name of Sergeant Heinrich Hitzinger. He was taken, two days later, to 031 Civilian Interrogation Camp at Lüneburg. Himmler's identity was shortly discovered by the officer in charge, Captain Tom Selvester, who had the ill-looking captive immediately stripped and searched for concealed poison phials. While being thoroughly examined by a doctor later at the headquarters of the British Second Army in Lüneburg, he bit a small capsule hidden between two of his teeth and then swallowed a potassium cyanide pill. For fifteen minutes there were frantic but unsuccessful efforts to save Himmler's life by the use of stomach pumps and artificial respiration.[32] His body was buried in an unmarked grave near Lüneburg. The grave's location is unknown.

Ley took his life in his prison cell on 24 October 1945, almost a year before the conclusion of the Nuremberg trials. The Reich commissioner for social housing and construction from November 1940 until May 1945 had been arrested in his pyjamas, in a house in the village of Schleching in southern Bavaria on 22 May 1945 by elements of the US 101st Airborne Division.[33] Ley strangled himself to death using a noose made by tearing a towel into stripes fastened to the toilet pipe in his prison cell.[34]

Austrian-Hungarian-born Edmund Glaise-Horstenau was arrested on 5 May 1945 by US troops. He was Austria's last Vice-Chancellor before the Anschluss, the annexation of his country into Nazi Germany on 13 March 1938, whom Hitler appointed in 1941 as Plenipotentiary General in Croatia, then part of the German-occupied Yugoslavia. Fearing extradition to Josip Broz Tito's communist regime in Belgrade, 64-year-old Glaise-Horstenau committed suicide on 20 July 1964 in a POW camp at Langwasser, near Nuremberg.

Only twenty-one top Nazis were eventually brought to trial,[35] and those who were committed were a select few that were central to Nazi organisations.[36] The Nuremberg trials were only concerned with the concentration camps as evidence for war crimes and crimes against humanity committed by the Third Reich leadership.[37] The tribunal declared in 1946 the Gestapo, the Waffen-SS and Sicherheitsdienst or SD, the SS intelligence section, to be inherently criminal organisations of the Nazi Party and consequently guilty of crimes against humanity.[38] Hundreds of concentration camp officials, most of them SS personnel, were tried in post-war West Germany and Poland. These trials were held in Lüneburg, near Hamburg (Bergen-Belsen Trials, September–November 1945), Dachau (Dachau/Mauthousen-Gusen Trials, March–May 1946), Hamburg (Ravensbrük Trials, 1946–48), Bonn and Cologne (Chełmno Trials, 1962–65), Munich (Belzec Trial, 1963–65), Düsseldorf (Treblinka Trials, 1964–65) and Hagen, near Dortmund (Sobibor Trial, 1965). The first of the Majdanek trials was held in Łublin, in Poland. The first of the Chełmno trials was held in Łódź, in Poland. In Poland, concentration camp personnel, including SS officers, were tried in Łublin (Majdanek trials, 1944–81) and Gdańsk/Toruń (Stutthof trials, 1946–47) The Majdanek trials were the longest, spanning thirty-seven years. Several lesser-known trials were also held to punish military officers for murdering surrendered Allied military personnel, for mistreating prisoners of war or for murdering civilians as a reprisal for the activity of resistance fighters in German-occupied territories.[39] Examples of military officers tried in subsequent proceedings before American tribunals were the Milch case, the Hostages case and the High Command case.

Top brass

Hundreds of high-ranking officers of Nazi Germany's armed forces were taken prisoner by the Allies during and immediately after the end war in Europe, including the only Field Marshal of the Reich (Hermann Göring) and eighteen of Nazi Germany's twenty-four field marshals (generalfeldmarschall). One field marshal, Walter Model, avoided capture by committing suicide. He commanded Army Group North on the Eastern Front. On 17 August 1944 he was appointed overall commander of the German forces in the West. On 21 April 1945, in a forest near Duisburg in Western Germany, 54-year-old Model shot himself.[40] He was already considered responsible for the deaths of 577,000 civilians in the Latvian Soviet Socialist Republic (SSR) and the deportation of 175,000 others as slave labour.[41] Model was also in charge of the German troops that quelled the sixty-three-day (1 August–2 October 1944) Warsaw Uprising. Of the arrested field marshals, nine were detained by the Americans, four by the British and as many by the Soviet military. The German field marshals in US custody during and after the Second World War were Wilhelm Keitel, Albert Kesselring, Robert Ritter von Greim, Wilhelm Ritter von Leeb, Wilhelm List, Erchard Milch, Gerd von Rundstedt, Wolfram von Richthofen and Maximilian von Weichs. While held by the US Army, von Richthofen died because of poor health and von Greim committed suicide. Kesselring was transferred to British custody in 1946. The four field marshals held by the British (five with the addition of Kesselring) were Walther von Brauchitsch, Ernst Busch, Erich von Manstein and Hugo Sperrle. Von Brauchitsch and Busch died while in British custody. The four German field marshals taken prisoner by the Red Army were Georg von Küchler, Paul Ludwig Evald von Kleist, Ferdinand Schörner and Friedrich von Paulus. Von Kleist died in a Soviet prison.

Göring and Keitel did not take any active part in any German campaign during the Second World War. Both were arrested (with Göring actually surrendering to US forces) after Nazi Germany's unconditional capitulation.

Von Paulus was the first German field marshal to become a prisoner of war. He led the German drive to Stalingrad. On 31 January 1943 his Sixth Army was cut off and faced with surrender during a Soviet counteroffensive. To prevent him from surrendering, Adolf Hitler promoted him to field marshal. The Führer expected him to commit suicide as there was no precedent of a German officer holding this rank ever being captured alive, but von Paulus did not comply. After his surrender, he was initially detained in the Voikovo prison camp No. 48, near Ivanovo, some 158 miles (254km) north-east of Moscow.

Field Marsal Paul Ludwig Evald von Kleist was arrested by US troops in Bavaria, in late April 1945. Two field marshals, Erhard Milch and Ernst Busch, were taken prisoner on 4 May 1945 and a further two, Robert Ritter von Greim and Wolfram von Richthofen, four days later. Albert Kesselring, Maximilian von Weichs and Ferdinand Schörner were also arrested in May 1945.

Field Marshal (Luftwaffe) Robert Ritter von Greim commanded Luftflotte 6 during the Russian campaign. In late 1942, his only son Hubert Greim, a JG 2 fighter pilot, was shot down over Tunisia. He bailed out and spent the remainder of the war in a POW camp in the United States. On 26 April 1945 Robert Ritter von Greim, replaced Göring as commander-in-chief of the Luftwaffe. He was arrested by US troops in early May in Austria and committed suicide in his cell, in a US-controlled prison in Salzburg on 24 May 1945, aged 52.[42]

Ernst Busch commanded the Army Group Centre on the Eastern Front (October 1943–June 1944) and the Army Group North-west in Western Germany and the Netherlands (April–May 1945). He surrendered to British troops on 4 May 1945 and was kept in POW Camp Aldershot, 31 miles (50km) south-west of London. Busch died as POW in England, on 17 July 1945, aged 60.[43]

Luftwaffe Field Marshal Albert Kesselring was the overall commander in Italy (1943–45) and commander-in-chief of the German forces in the Western Front (March–April 1945). He surrendered to elements of the US 101st Airborne Division on 9 May 1945, at Saalfelden, near Salzburg, in Austria. Kesselring was kept under guard in a hotel at Berchtesgaden, in Bavaria, some 110 miles (180km) south-east of Munich, until 15 May, when he was taken to Mondorf-les-Baines. In 1946, after being held in various POW camps by the US Army, he was transferred to British custody. On 17 February 1947 Kesselring was brought in front of a British military court in Venice accused of being responsible for the shooting of 335 Italians by German troops in the Ardeatine massacre on 23 March 1944, as a reprisal for a bomb attack by Italian partisans. On 6 May 1947 he was sentenced to death by a firing squad.[44] With the death penalty having been abolished in Italy in 1944, British politicians, including former Prime Minister Winston Churchill, military commanders including Field Marshal Harold Alexander and military historians including Basil Liddell Hart and J.F.C. Fuller, eventually succeeded in having Kesselring's sentence commuted.[45] In May 1947 he was transferred from Maestre Prison, near Venice, to Wolfsberg, in Carinthia, and from there, in October 1947, to Werl Prison, in Westphalia. While in prison, he wrote reports on the Second World War battles and tactics for the US Army Historical Division.[46] In July 1952, Kesselring was diagnosed with a cancerous growth in his throat (being a constant chain-smoker).[47] He was transferred to a hospital under guard. In October 1952, he was released from prison on the grounds of ill health. Kesselring died in a sanatorium at Bad Nauheim, near Frankfurt on 16 July 1960, aged 74, following a heart attack.

Field Marshal Eberhard von Mackensen was also sentenced to death by a court in Rome, on 30 November 1946, for his role in the Ardeatine massacre. His sentence was commuted to twenty-one years' imprisonment. He was released on 2 October 1952, after serving five years. Von Mackensen died on 19 May 1969, in Neumünster, in Schleswig-Holstein, aged 79.

The western Allies normally executed war criminals by hanging. This was due to the fact that the firing squad was viewed as an honourable way to die, which war criminals did not deserve. This is why Hermann Göring's and Alfred Jodl's pleas, after their conviction, to be executed by firing squad and not by hanging were ignored by the Allies. Of the German officers convicted for war crimes, only two were executed by firing squad. They were Major General Anton Dostler and Captain (Hauptmann) Curt Bruns. Thirty-year-old Bruns was sentenced to death while the war was still going on in the Pacific. He was condemned for ordering the execution of two American POWs on 20 December 1944 near Bleialf, in Rhineland-Palatinate, in western Germany, because they were speaking fluent German.[48] At the time, he was serving in the 18th Volksgrenadier Division. The verdict was confirmed on 8 May and his execution was carried out in Denstorf, 128 miles (206km) from Berlin, on 14 June 1945. Under US Military Law Bruns was allowed to wear his uniform, stripped off insignia, before being shot. Dostler was executed by a US Army firing squad on 1 December 1945 in Aversa, near Caserta, in southern Italy, aged 54. He was sentenced to death by a military court in Caserta for the execution of fifteen US commandos, including two officers, after their capture by German troops near La Spezia, in north-western Italy. At the time, Dostler was commanding the LXXII Army Corps.

The arrest of two field marshals, von Richthofen and von Manstein, was made while both were under treatment in German hospitals. Von Richthofen, a Luftwaffe officer, commanded the 8th Air Corps (1939–42) and Luftflotte 2 (1943–44) in operations, mostly on the Eastern Front. He also led his forces during the Balkan and the Italian campaigns. In September 1944, von Richthofen retired on medical grounds and sent to a Luftwaffe hospital at Bad Ischl, in Gmunden, in southern Upper Austria. A month later, he was operated on, suffering from a brain tumour. After Nazi Germany's surrender, the hospital was taken over by elements of the US Third Army with von Richthofen becoming a prisoner of war. He died in captivity two months later, aged 49. His death prevented his subsequent prosecution for war crimes at the High Command trials.

Von Manstein's detention began on 26 August 1945 in a POW camp near Lüneburg.[49] Later, he was transferred to Island Farm, also known as Special Camp XI, in Bridgend, in south Wales. In 1949 he was tried in Hamburg for war crimes and convicted of nine of the seventeen counts including the poor treatment of prisoners of war and failing to protect civilian lives in the sphere of operations. His sentence of eighteen years in prison was reduced to twelve.[50]

IMPRISONING THE ENEMY

Two field marshals, Schörner and von Kleist, were arrested by the Western Allies but were handed over to the Red Army. The Moscow Declaration of October 1943 promised that 'those German officers and men and members of the Nazi Party who have been responsible for or have taken a consenting part in atrocities, massacres and executions will be sent back to the countries in which their abominable deeds were done in order to be judged and punished according to the laws of these liberated countries and of free governments which will be erected therein'. After commanding various army groups in the Eastern Front in late 1944, Schörner became Nazi Germany's last commander-in-chief of the Army. Arrested in Austria by the US Army on 18 May 1945, he was handed over to the Russians. In February 1952, he was tried for war crimes and sentenced to twenty-five years in prison. The sentence was reduced to twelve and a half years two months later. In 1954 he was handed over to the East German authorities. Schörner was released from prison in 1955.[51] Returning to West Germany, he was arrested for the executions of German soldiers accused of desertion. He was tried and sentenced to four-and-a-half years in prison. Schörner was released on 4 August 1960. He died on 2 July 1973 in Munich. At his death, Schörner was the last living German field marshal.

Seven field marshals in Nazi Germany were dismissed from their command during the war and never again occupied any military post. All were arrested by the Allies after the German surrender and tried for war crimes except Fedor von Bock. He lost his life on 4 May 1945, aged 64, while heading to Hamburg with his wife when their car was attacked by a Royal New Zealand Air Force fighter-bomber.[52] Von Block had lost the command of the Army Group South on 17 July 1942 on Hitler's orders, during the German offensive on Stalingrad. Field Marshal Wilhelm Ritter von Leeb was relieved of his command on 15 December 1941. Field Marshal Walther von Brauchitsch was the commander-in-chief of the army on 19 December 1942, when he was dismissed by Hitler. Wilhelm List was relieved of his command on 22 November 1942 and Georg von Küchler on 31 January 1944. Two more field marshals were dismissed later in the year – von Kleist and Sperrle. Gerd von Rundstedt was relieved of his command (for the second time) on 9 March 1945.

A heart attack Walther von Brauchitsch suffered a month earlier and German Army's failure to take Moscow caused his dismissal from his command post.[53] The former commander-in-chief of Nazi Germany ground forces spent the last three years of the war in his estate, near Prague, where he was arrested by British troops in August 1945. He was detained in Camp 198, also known as Island Farm POW camp, in South Wales. Von Brauchitsch died of bronchial pneumonia in a British-controlled military hospital in Hamburg, on 18 October 1948, aged 67, before facing trial for war crimes related to the shooting of captured Red Army commissars by German troops.

Field Marshal Wilhelm Ritter von Leeb was relieved of his command (Army Group North) on 16 December 1941, during the battle of Moscow.[54] Someone who knew him said if he 'ever tried to smile, it would crack his face'.[55] Tried in Nuremberg by a US military tribunal for the murder of Jews by his troops in Lithuania, von Leeb was found guilty and sentenced to three years' imprisonment.[56] He was released after serving his prison term. Von Leeb died on 29 April 1956 in Füssen, Bavaria, close to the Austrian border, aged 79.

Field Marshal Wilhelm List led German troops in Poland, France and the Balkans, as well as Army Group A in southern Russia. List's failure to capture Grozny infuriated

Hitler and caused his dismissal from his command post on 9 September 1942. In 1947 he was charged with the killing of hostages by his troops during the invasion and occupation of Yugoslavia. In February 1952, List was convicted by a US military court in Nuremberg (the Hostage Trial) and sentenced to life imprisonment. He was released from prison in December 1952, officially because of ill health. List died on 17 August 1971 in Garmisch-Partenkirchen, in Bavaria, aged 91.

Field Marshal Georg von Küchler commanded Army Group North on the Eastern Front. On 31 January 1944, after his failure to capture Leningrad, he was replaced by Field Marshal Walter Model and went into retirement. In 1948 von Küchler was sentenced to twenty years' imprisonment for crimes against humanity committed during the German invasion of the Soviet Union. He was charged over the murder of Red Army commissars and of 240 mentally disabled civilians in German-occupied territories in Russia.[57] His sentence was reduced to twelve years, in 1951. He was released two years later on compassionate grounds. Von Küchler died on 25 May 1968 in Garmisch-Partenkirchen, in Bavaria, aged 86.[58]

Field Marshal Paul Ludwig Evald von Kleist commanded Army Group A in southern Russia during Operation Barbarossa. He was dismissed on 30 March 1944 following a successful offensive launched by the Red Army in central Ukraine. Hitler was furious when von Kleist asked permission to pull back his forces to more defensive positions and had him replaced with Ferdinand Schörner.[59] Arrested by US troops in late April 1944 in Bavaria, he was extradited to Yugoslavia in September 1946. He was tried there and sentenced to fifteen years in prison for war crimes committed mostly in Belgrade between April and June 1941. In 1948 von Kleist was extradited to the USSR, where he was sentenced to fifteen years' imprisonment. He died of heart failure in his cell in Vladimir Central Prison, 120 miles (200km) east of Moscow, on 13 November 1954, aged 73.

Field Marshal (Luftwaffe) Hugo Sperrle commanded the German air forces in the West until his dismissal on 23 August 1944 because of the poor performance of Luftflotte 3 during the Allied invasion of Normandy.[60] He was arrested by the British Army on 1 May 1945 and was later charged with war crimes during the High Command Trial. Sperrle was acquitted twice – in 1947 in Nuremberg and six years later, when he was brought to trial in front a West German court in Munich. He died on 2 April 1953, in the Bavarian capital, aged 68.

Field Marshal Gerd von Rundstedt commanded Army Group A in France and in the Soviet Union. He was relieved of his command in December 1941. Nine months later, he was appointed commander-in-chief of the German troops on the Western Front. He was dismissed once again, on 9 March 1945, after the advance of Allied forces to the Rhine and the capture of Ludendorff bridge at Remagen intact. Von Rundstedt was captured by elements of the US 36th Infantry Division in a sanatorium, in Bad Tölz, in southern Bavaria.[61] He was held at the Allied facility for detaining high-ranking German officials, known as ASHCAN, in a hotel at Mondorf-les-Bains in Luxemburg and then at an American detention centre at Wiesbaden, in central-western Germany. In July 1946, von Rundstedt was handed over to British custody. He was transferred to Island Farm (POW Camp 198) in South Wales and was then hospitalised in Norfolk, suffering from cardiac problems and arthritis. Von Rundstedt was not brought to trial for the shooting of surrendered soldiers by his troops in Poland, France and the Soviet Union. British Army doctors reported that due to health problems, he was unfit to face the charges. He was hospitalised in Münster, in Lower Saxony, and in Hanover. Von Rundstedt died of a heart failure on 24 February 1953 in an elderly persons' home, near Celle, in Lower Saxony, aged 77.

Two field marshals, Erwin Rommel and Günther Kluge, never fell into Allied hands. They committed suicide to avoid arrest by the Gestapo, after being implicated in the unsuccessful 20 July 1944 plot to assassinate Hitler. Rommel, who commanded the German forces in North Africa in 1942–43 and in Normandy during the Allied invasion in June 1944, took a cyanide pill at Herlingen, near Ulm, on 14 October 1944[62] aged 52, and Kluge, who commanded the German Army in the West, used potassium cyanide on 19 August 1944 in Metz, northern France.[63] Field Marshal Erwin von Witzleben, a leading conspirator of the plot, was arrested on 7 August 1944 by the Gestapo, sentenced to death and was hanged the same day, aged 62.

Field Marshal Walter von Reichenau died in a plane crash at Lviv, in western Ukraine, on 17 January 1942, aged 57. He was commanding the Army Group South on the Eastern Front at the time. Austrian-born Eduard von Böhm-Ermolli, who died on 9 December 1941, aged 85, received an honorary promotion to the rank of field marshal on 31 October 1940.

Field Marshal Maximilian von Weichs was one of the defendants who were tried before a US military court in Nuremberg for hostage taking and wanton shooting of hostages in German-occupied Yugoslavia, Greece and Albania between 1941 and 1944. The other defendants were: Colonel General (Generaloberst) Lothar Rendulic, Major Generals Walter Künze, Helmuth Felmy, Hubert Lanz, Ernst von Leyser, Hermann Foertsch, Ernst Dehner, Wilhelm Speidel and Kurt Ritter von Geitner, and Brigadier General Franz Böhme. Of the twelve defendants indicted, Böhme committed suicide before being formally charged as a war criminal and von Weichs was severed from the trial for medical reasons. The other defendants received prison sentences ranging from seven years to life imprisonment. Künze was sentenced to life imprisonment, Rendulic and Speidel to twenty years in jail, Felmy to fifteen years, Lanz to twelve years, von Leyser to ten years and Dehner to seven years. Foertsch and von Geitner were acquitted. In 1951 those imprisoned were released with the exception of Künze, who remained in jail until 1953.

Von Weichs commanded Army Group B in southern Russia and later Army Group F in the Balkans. He also had, from his headquarters in Belgrade, the overall command of the German forces in the Balkans between 1943 and 1944. In March 1945, he retired from the German Army following the withdrawal of his forces from the Balkans and Hungary. In May 1945, von Weichs surrendered himself to US troops[64] and was jailed until 1948. He was removed from the Hostages Trial for medical reasons without having been charged or sentenced. Von Weichs died in Burg Rösberg, near Bonn, on 27 September 1954, aged 72.

Austrian-born Böhme, who commanded the XVII Mountain Corps between 1940 and 1943, committed suicide in Nuremberg on 30 May 1947, aged 62. Fellow Austrian Rendulic commanded the Second Panzer Army in Yugoslavia (1943–44). His twenty-year sentence was reduced to ten years. He was released in 1951. Rendulic died on 17 January 1971 in Fraham, in Upper Austria, aged 83.

Künze commanded the First Army. He was sent to prison for life but was released in 1953. He died on 1 April 1960 in Detmold, in North Rhine-Westphalia, aged 77. Felmy commanded the LXVIII Army Corps in Yugoslavia and the XXXIV Army Corps in Greece.[65] In 1948, he was convicted of war crimes committed in Greece by his troops and was given a prison sentence of fifteen years. He was released from prison on 15 January 1951. Felmy died on 14 December 1955, in Darmstadt, near Frankfurt, aged 80.

Lanz commanded the XXII Mountain Corps (1943–45). He was sentenced to twelve years' imprisonment for war crimes and crimes against humanity. He was released from jail in 1951. Lanz died on 15 August 1951 in Munich, aged 86.

Von Leyser was Corps commander under Rendulic and Böhme. He was sentenced to ten years in prison, but was released earlier, in 1951. Von Leyser died on 23 September 1962 in Garstedt, near Hamburg, aged 81.

Foertsch was chief of staff of the Twelfth Army in the Balkans. He died on 27 December 1961 in Munich, aged 66. Dehner served as Corps commander under Rendulic. Imprisoned for eleven years, he was also released earlier (1951). Dehner died on 13 September 1970 at Königstein-im-Taunus, in Hesse, aged 81.

Speidel served as military commander in German-occupied Greece. Von Geitner was the chief of staff of military commanders in German-occupied Yugoslavia and Greece.

Milch was brought in front of a US military court in 1947. He surrendered on 4 May 1945 on a Baltic coast to Lieutenant Colonel Derek Mills-Roberts, who was leading elements of British Army's No. 6 Commando Unit. So infuriated was Mills-Roberts with Milch's views about concentration camps that he took the baton from under the field marshal's arm and broke it over his head. Milch was tried as a war criminal in 1947 in Nuremberg by a US military court and sentenced to life imprisonment. He was taken to Landsberg Prison, 40 miles (65km) west-south-west of Munich. His sentence was commuted to fifteen years. He was released earlier, in June 1954. Milch died in Düsseldorf on 25 January 1972, aged 79.

Wehrmacht commanders

Field Marshals Hugo Sperrle (Luftwaffe), Wilhelm von Leeb and Georg von Küchler, convicted for crimes against humanity during the Hostages Trial, were also brought to justice by the US military authorities, also in court room 600 of the Justizpalast in Nuremberg, for having committed war crimes. In the High Command Trial, held between 28 November 1947 and 28 October 1948, were also tried Admiral Otto Schniewind, Colonel Generals Johannes Blaskowitz, Karl-Adolf Hollidt, Hermann Hoth, Georg-Hans Reinhardt, Hans von Salmouth and Rudolf Lehman, and Lieutenant Generals Hermann Reineque, Karl von Roques, Otto Wöhner and Walter Warlimont. A German military judge, Rudolf Lehmann, was added to the defendants of the High Command Trial.

Of the fourteen defendants indicted, Sperrle and Schniewind were acquitted on all accounts, committed suicide during the trial. The remaining eleven received prison sentences ranging from five years to lifetime imprisonment. Warlimont and Reinecke were sentenced to life imprisonment, von Roques and von Salmouth to twenty years, Küchler, Hoth and Reinhardt to fifteen years, Wöhner to eight years, Lehmann to seven years and Hollidt to five years.

Blaskowitz commanded Army Group H in Holland when he surrendered his forces and himself to the I Canadian Corps in Wageningen, central Netherlands, on 5 May

1945. He was charged with the execution of two German deserters after the end of hostilities, during the High Command Trial. On 5 February 1948 Blaskowitz committed suicide, jumping off a balcony of the palace of Justice.[66] He was posthumously acquitted on all accounts.[67]

Colonel General (Generaloberst) Karl-Adolf Hollidt was assigned the command of the Sixth Army in March 1943 after the humiliating defeat in the Battle of Stalingrad.[68] In late 1944, he was relieved of his command and sent home. In May 1945, Hollidt was arrested by the US Army to be tried for the unlawful use of prisoners of war mostly on the Eastern Front. During the High Command Trial, Hollidt was sentenced to five years' imprisonment. In December 1949, he was released on good time credit.[69] Hollidt died in Siegen, in Northern Rhineland-Westphalia, on 22 May 1985, aged 94. At the time he was the last surviving generaloberst (colonel general) of the Wehrmacht.

Colonel General Hermann Hoth commanded the Fourth Panzer Army and the Twelfth Army on the Eastern Front. He surrendered himself to US troops on 7 May 1945.[70] He was tried for war crimes and crimes against humanity during the High Command Trial in Nuremberg. Found guilty, Hoth was sentenced to fifteen years in prison. He served his time in Landsberg prison, near Augsburg, in Bavaria.[71] He was released on parole in 1954. Hoth died on 25 January 1971 in Goslar, Lower Saxony, aged 85.

Colonel General Georg-Hans Reinhardt commanded the Third Panzer Army and Army Group Centre on the Eastern Front. He retired from active duty in January 1945. Five months later, he was arrested by British SAS troopers as a suspected war criminal. Reinhardt was charged with the mistreatment of Soviet POWs by his troops and for the murder, deportation and hostage taking of civilians, including Jews, in German-occupied countries in Eastern Europe. Found guilty as charged, he was sentenced to fifteen years in prison. Reinhardt served most of his term in Landsberg prison. He was released on compassionate grounds in 1952.[72] He died in Bautzen, in Eastern Saxony, on 22 November 1963, aged 76.

Colonel General Hans von Salmuth commanded the Second and the Fourth Armies during the Soviet campaign and the Fifteenth Army in France until late 1944, when he was relieved of this command. He was arrested after the German surrender and brought in front of the military tribunal in Nuremberg (High Command Trials) for the implementation by troops under his command (XXX Corps) of the Commissar Order in German-occupied territories of the Soviet Union. The Order stipulated that any captured Red Army political commissar was to be executed, contrary to international law.[73] Found guilty, von Salmuth was sentenced to twenty years' imprisonment. In 1951 his sentence was commuted to twelve years. He was released from prison two years later.[74] Von Salmuth died on 1 January 1962 in Heidelberg, Baden-Württemberg, aged 73.

Colonel General Rudolf Schmidt commanded the Second Panzer Army from December 1941 to April 1943. In September 1942, his troops were involved in war crimes while conducting anti-guerrilla operations in the Soviet Union. During these operations at least a thousand people were killed, entire villages were razed and more than 18,000 people were deported. On 10 April 1943 Schmidt was relieved of his command, after the arrest of his brother (Hans-Thilo Schmidt) by the Gestapo for spying for the French, and remained an outcast until the end of war. On 16 December 1947 he was arrested by the Soviets near Weimar and transferred to Moscow. He was detained for four years in the soviet capital's Vladimir Central and the Butyrka Prisons, before he was brought in front of a military tribunal. Found guilty of war crimes, Schmidt was sentenced to twenty-five years in prison. On 30 September 1955 he was among the last German prisoners to be released from Soviet custody and repatriated. Schmidt died aged 70, two years later, on 7 April 1957, in Krefeld, north-west of Düsseldorf, in North Rhine-Westphalia.

Rudolf Lehmann, a jurist and military judge, was in charge of the Judicial Corps (Judge Advocate General) of the Wehrmacht, with the rank of generaloberstabsrichter. He was arrested by US troops in May 1945 and held in a POW camp. Lehmann was charged as war criminal for his contribution in the drafting of the Commissar Order. Found guilty, he was sentenced to seven years' imprisonment. He was released from Landsberg prison on 16 August 1950. Lehmann died in Bonn on 26 July 1955, aged 64.

Lieutenant General Friedrich-Georg Eberhardt commanded various divisions, including the 60th and the 38th Infantry, until December 1944. From then on,he served as a judge at the highest military court (Reichskriegsgericht). On 8 May 1945 he was arrested by Allied troops and was detained until 1947. Eberhardt died on 9 September 1965 in Wiesbaden, aged 72 or 73.

Major General Hermann Reinecke was head of the general office of the High Command of the Armed Forces (Oberkommando der Wehrmacht or OKW) of Nazi Germany. In the High Command Trial in Nuremberg, he was charged with the creation and implementation of the prisoners of war policy towards Russian POWs, known as the 8 September 1941 Regulations.[75] He was sentenced to life imprisonment but by 1955 he walked out of Landsberg prison a free man. Reinecke died on 10 October 1975 in Hamburg, aged 85.

Major General Karl von Roques commanded Army Group South during Operation Barbarossa until his retirement from the military on 31 March 1943. After the German capitulation, he was charged in Nuremberg with war crimes and crimes against humanity, carried out by troops under his command in German-occupied parts of the Soviet Union. These crimes included extermination policies against the Soviet partisans as well as against Slavic and Jewish population. He was sentenced to twenty years in prison. In late 1949, he was transferred with health problems from Landsberg prison to a hospital in Nuremberg. Von Roques died there on 24 December, aged 69.

Major General Otto Wöhner commanded Army Group South III in western Hungary until April 1945. He was tried in Nuremberg for crimes committed in early 1942 by troops of the Eleventh Army in Ukraine and Latvia. He was chief of staff of the particular formation at the time. Wöhner was charged for his cooperation with the paramilitary troops (Einsatzgruppen) that carried out the massacres of Babi Yar and Rumbula.[76] Found guilty as charged, he was sentenced to eight years' imprisonment. He was released from prison in February 1951. Wöhner died on 5 February 1987 in Burgwedel, near Hanover, aged 92.

Committed suicide I

Field Marshals Robert Ritter von Greim (Luftwaffe) and Colonel General Johannes Blaskowitz were not the only high-ranking officers of Nazi Germany who committed suicide while in Allied custody. Admiral Otto von Schrader killed himself while in Norwegian hands, Major General Otto von Stülpnagel in French and Luftwaffe Major General Walter Boenicke in British captivity.

Von Schrader, a submariner until early 1940, participated in the Norwegian campaign as commanding officer of the light cruiser *Königsberg*, which was badly damaged during the invasion and sunk. He was later appointed commander-in-chief of the German-occupied Western Norway. After the surrender of Nazi Germany, he was arrested by British troops. Von Schrader committed suicide on 19 July 1945 during his detention in Bergen, aged 57.

Stülpnagel was military commander in German-occupied France until his resignation from the military in February 1942. After the German surrender, he was arrested in Berlin by Allied forces and handed over to French authorities to be tried for the execution of hostages and the deportation of Jews and communists, carried out in German-occupied France by troops under his command. Stülpnagel hanged himself in his cell in Cherche-Midi prison, in Paris, on 6 February 1948, aged 69, prior to the beginning of his trial.

Boenicke commanded Luftflotte 3 and eventually the defence of Berlin's Air Region III. In May 1945, he surrendered to British troops and on 21 April 1947, while interned at Münster, in Lower Saxony, he committed suicide.

Major General Karl-Gustav Sauberzweig was commanding the IX Corps of Army Group H in northern Germany at the end of the hostilities in Europe. He surrendered to the British Army at Preetz, in Schleswig-Holstein, on 26 September 1945. He was detained in Camp No. 6, formerly Neuengamme concentration camp, near Hamburg. On 20 October Sauberzweig committed suicide, aged 47, by swallowing poison, rather than facing extradition and trial for war crimes in Yugoslavia.[77] Until October 1944, he had commanded in the Balkans the 13th Waffen Mountain Division of the SS Handschar (1st Croatian), the first non-Germanic Waffen-SS division.[78]

Lieutenant General Wolfgang Erdmann commanded the 7th Parachute Division in the fight during the Allied invasion of the Netherlands (Operation Market Garden) in September 1944. He surrendered to Allied forces at Oldenburg, in Lower Saxony, with the end of hostilities and the German capitulation. He committed suicide on 5 September 1946 aged 47 while in British custody at Münster.

Field Marshal Walter Model was not the only high-ranking officer of Nazi Germany who committed suicide in order to avoid falling into enemy hands or to thus accepting full responsibility for a failed mission. Captain (Kapitän zur See) Hans Langsdorf shot himself with a pistol on 20 December 1939, in a hotel room in Buenos Aires, the capital of Argentina.[79] Three days earlier, he had his ship, the pocket battleship *Admiral Graf Spee*, scuttled off the coast of Uruguay and his crew taken off by Argentine barges. The German battleship had been unable to escape a pursuing squadron of British Royal Navy ships following the Battle of the River Plate.

On 18 August 1943, the Chief of the General Staff of the Luftwaffe, 44-year-old Colonel General Hans Jeschonnek, shot himself with a pistol, in his office in Goldap, East Prussia. He had reportedly experienced an emotional breakdown over the failure and inability of Luftwaffe to defend Germany. In the previous forty-eight hours, heavy industry installations in Bavaria and the German secret weapons research centre at Peenemünde had been attacked by hundreds of US Army Air Force and British Royal Air Force bombers. V-1 and V-2 long-range reprisal rockets were tested at the site, on an island off the Pomeranian coast in the Baltic Sea, before being launched from elsewhere against British targets, including urban centres, in 1944 and 1945. Intelligence about Peenemünde was allegedly obtained from the secretly recorded conversations of a

German officer (Major General Wilhelm Ritter von Thoma), who was a prisoner-of-war in Great Britain.

In early 1943, two lieutenant generals, Arno Jahr and Günther Angern, committed suicide near Stalingrad. On 21 January 52-year-old Jahr killed himself near Podgornoye, after the encirclement of his 387th Infantry Division by Soviet forces.[80] Forty-nine-year-old Angern killed himself on 2 February 1943 near Stalingrad, after failing to avoid the encirclement of his 16th Panzer Division by the Red Army.[81] He and his troops even tried unsuccessfully to pass through the front lines wearing captured Soviet uniforms.

Six months later, 49-year-old Lieutenant General Gustav Schmidt committed suicide to avoid capture by the enemy in the course of the Soviet Belgorod-Kharkov offensive operation. Schmidt's 19th Panzer Division suffered heavy casualties while trying to retreat through Ukraine.[82] In April 1945, during the battle of Berlin, 66-year-old Lieutenant General Arthur Kobus committed suicide rather than surrender to the Red Army.[83] Major General Decker and Brigadier General Barde also committed suicide prior to Nazi Germany's capitulation.

Forty-five-year-old Karl Decker killed himself on 21 April 1945, after the defeat of his encircled XXXIX Panzer Corps in the Ruhr area of Germany in North Rhine-Westphalia. Forty-seven-year-old Konrad Barde commanded the 198th Infantry Division until 26 April 1945. The formation, including its commanding officer, were forced to surrender to the US Army in Weilhen, in Oberbayern, in south Bavaria. Barde committed suicide while in US custody on 4 May, in Traunstein, Bavaria.

Four days later, on 8 May, in Berlin, 49-year-old Admiral Hans-Georg von Friedeburg signed the instrument of the German surrender on behalf of his country's naval forces. He was then transferred to northern Germany in British custody. In Plön, the same day, Kriegsmarine's last commander-in-chief, committed suicide by swallowing poison. Kobus and von Friedeburg were both born in the German imperial territory of Elsass-Lothringen (Alsace-Lorraine), a part of France since the end of the First World War.

A day after the German capitulation, 48-year-old Major General Erpo Freiherr von Bodenhausen committed suicide in the Latvian SSR to avoid capture by the Red Army. His 12th Panzer Division was among the German forces that had been isolated in the Courland Peninsula since 31 July 1944. On 12 May 1945 189,112 German soldiers, including forty-two generals, surrendered in Courland and were led away to captivity.[84]

Forty-seven-year-old Major General Eberhard Kinzel committed suicide on 25 June 1945 in Flensburg, near Kiel, with his girlfriend (identified as Erika von Aschoff). He commanded Fremde Heere Ost (FHO), a military intelligence organisation of the Supreme High Command of the German Army (Obercommando des Heeres or OBH), from 1938 until 1942 and the 337th Volksgrenadier Division in 1945. Kinzel was a member of the delegation that participated in the negotiations with British Field Marshal Bernard Montgomery on 4 May 1945, on Lüneburg Heath, near Hamburg, for the unconditional surrender of the German forces in the Netherlands, north-west Germany and Denmark.

Fifty-six-year-old Major General Werner Freiherr (Baron) und zu Gilsa killed himself on 8 May 1945 either in Dresden Castle to avoid capture by the Red Army, or at Litoměřice, north-west of Prague, while in Soviet custody. He commanded the LXXXIX Army Corps until March 1945, when he was appointed military commander of Dresden.

A low-ranking German officer (Lieutenant) of Dutch descent, Josef Terboven, was Reichskommissar during the German occupation. He was responsible for the massacre in Beisfjord, near Narvik, in northern Norway, on 17 July 1942, of 288 Yugoslav political prisoners and for the deportation of 532 Norwegian Jews to the extermination camp in Auschwitz, Germany. On 8 May 1945 46-six-year-old Terboven committed suicide in a bunker at Asker, near Oslo by detonating 50kg of dynamite.[85]

Major General (SS-Obergruppenführer) Matthias Kleinheistercamp and Brigadier General (SS-Brigadeführer) Fritz Freitag were two of the SS officers who killed themselves to avoid being led into captivity by the enemy. Fifty-one-year-old Kleinheistercamp committed suicide on 29 April 1945 in the village of Halbe, near Berlin, while in Soviet custody. According to another account, he was killed on 2 May 1945 in the same area, at the head of the XI SS Army Corps, while fighting against the Red Army. Freitag, also 51 years old, shot himself on 10 May 1945 in the village of St Andrä, near Graz, in Austria, to avoid falling into Soviet hands.

Sixty-three-year-old Major General Hermann Geyer committed suicide on 10 April 1946 in a location near Wildsee, in southern Germany. He had commanded IX Army Corps until 1943.

Luftwaffe Captain Herman Görtz was a German spy. He was active in England in mid-1935 and in Ireland from mid-1940 to early 1941. In February 1936, Görtz was arrested by the British police and tried for espionage. He was convicted and sentenced to four years in prison. In February 1939, he was released from Maidstone Prison and was repatriated. In the summer of 1940, Görtz was parachuted into Ireland on an espionage mission. In November 1941, he was arrested by the Irish police and held in Mountjoy Prison and later in a military installation (Custume Barracks), both in Athlone, some 100km west of Dublin. On 23 May 1947 Görtz was transferred to Dublin Castle, where he was informed that he was to be deported to Germany the next day. Fearing that he would be handed over to the Russians, he committed suicide by taking poison (believed to be prussic acid) from a tiny glass phial.[86] He was 56 years old.

High-ranking officers

The first German general to be captured by Allied forces during the Second World War was Lieutenant General Johann von Ravenstein.[87] He was taken prisoner in North Africa as early in the war as 1941, while commanding the 21st Panzer Division. Heading to the headquarters of the neighbouring 15th Panzer Division in his staff car on a desert road on 28 November and, having taken a wrong turn, von Ravenstein was ambushed near Sidi Rezegh, Libya, by elements of the 21st Battalion, 2nd New Zealand Division. His orderly had been wounded by enemy fire, when von Ravenstein and his driver were forced to raise their hands in surrendering. The captured general was promptly taken to Tobruk and the operational maps he was carrying proved helpful to the Allies in preparing against forthcoming attacks by the 21st Panzer Division.[88] While transported from Tobruk, the ship was sunk by an Italian torpedo boat. After two hours in the sea, von Ravenstein was rescued by a British Royal Navy corvette and taken to Alexandria. The captured general was held in various prisoner of war camps, initially in Egypt, then in South Africa and lastly in Canada (Ontario). After the German capitulation, von Ravenstein was transferred to a POW camp for officers, Bridgend, in Wales. In November 1947, he was repatriated to West Germany, already suffering from heart problems.[89] Von Ravenstein died on 26 March 1962 in Duisburg, in North Rhine-Westphalia, aged 73.

On 8 April 1940, a rear admiral (konteradmiral) and a brigadier general (generalmajor) were taken prisoner for a few hours during the Norwegian campaign. They were among the survivors of the heavy cruiser *Blücher* that was hit by coastal torpedo batteries fired into Oslofjord and sank with major losses estimated at 600 to 1,000 sailors and soldiers.[90] Rear Admiral Oskar Kummetz, who was leading a flotilla of warships, and Major General Erwin Engelbrecht, commander of the 163rd Infantry Division, managed to swim ashore. They were detained by Norwegian guardsmen (Royal Palace troops) at a farm near Drøbak, the winter harbour of Oslo, along with other survivors.[91] They were abandoned by their captors hours later before the arrival of German troops in the area. In March 1944 Kummetz became commander-in-chief of the Naval High Command for the Baltic Sea in Kiel. He died on 17 December 1980 in Neustadt, in Rhineland-Palatinate, aged 89.

Engelbrecht remained on occupation duty in Norway until June 1941. He later led the 163rd Infantry Division in the fight against the Soviet Union alongside the Finnish Army. On 13 September 1943 he was appointed commander of the XXXIII Army Corps. In late April 1945 Engelbrecht surrendered to the US Army. He was released from captivity in 1947. Engelbrecht died on 8 June 1964 in Munich, aged 72.

Kummetz and Engelbrecht were captured by the enemy for hours. Two high-ranking Luftwaffe pilots, Major Wolf-Dietrich Wilcke and Colonel Werner Mölders, who were downed in France in 1940, ended up as POWs for a few days. Wilcke, a captain (hauptmann) at the time, was shot down west of Rethel, near Reims in northern France, on 18 May, while in aerial combat against eight French fighter aircraft. He bailed out and was taken prisoner.[92] Wilcke was liberated on 22 June 1940 upon the armistice with France. He was killed on 23 March 1944, aged 31, near Schöppenstedt, in Lower Saxony, during an engagement against a US Army Air Force formation, consisting of over a thousand bomber and fighter aircraft. Wilcke was credited with 162 kills in 732 combat missions, mostly over the Eastern Front.[93]

On 5 June 1940, Mölders, a major at the time, was shot down while engaged in aerial battle near Compiègne, in northern France.[94] Captured by French troops, he was liberated seventeen days later, upon the armistice with France. Mölders died, aged 28, on 22 November 1941, when the plane he was travelling in as a passenger from Crimea crashed on landing at Breslau (present-day Wrocław) in south-west Poland.[95] He was credited with 102 aerial victories in 642 combat missions, claimed mostly over the Western Front.[96]

Two German submarine commanders, Captains Günther Lorentz and Gerhard Glattes, were to serve the longest terms as prisoners of war in Western Allied hands: both seven and a half years. Glattes, in fact, was released one day earlier. Lorentz was taken prisoner on 25 February 1940, when his *U-63*, a type IIC U-boat, was sunk south of Shetland in the North Atlantic by a mix of depth charges and torpedoes from three British warships (HMS *Escort*, *Inglefield* and *Imogen*) and one submarine (HMS *Narwhal* or HMS *Rorqual*).[97] Of the crew, one man died and twenty-four were rescued by the British and sent to POW camps, initially in Great Britain and later in North

America. Lorenz was released and repatriated in 1946. He died on 17 January 1989, aged 75 or 76.

Glattes was taken prisoner when his *U-39*, a type IXA U-boat, was hunted down on 14 September 1939 north-east of Ireland by three British Royal Navy destroyers (HMS *Faulknor*, *Firedrake* and *Foxhound*). Disabled by depth charges, the submarine sunk. *U-39* was the first of many U-boat losses in the war.[98] The forty-four crewmen, including Glattes, were rescued.[99] They were detained briefly on Orkney Island and in the Tower of London before their transfer to a POW camp in Oldham. They were eventually shipped to Canada for detention, at the Lethbridge POW camp. Glattes was released for repatriation on 8 April 1947. He died on 25 October 1986, aged 77.

Major General Heinrich Kreipe was the only general to be abducted by the Allies and evacuated to Allied-occupied territory. He had participated in the Siege of Stalingrad until May 1942 before being appointed commander of the 22nd Air Landing Division, deployed on Crete since late 1942. Kreipe was military commander in eastern Crete on 26 April 1944 when his staff car was ambushed at night, near Heraklion, by two members of the British Special Operations Executive (SOE), Major Patrick Leigh Fermor and Captain William Stanley Moss. Kreipe was taken cross-country over the mountains to the southern coast of the island, where he and his captors were picked up by a British vessel on 14 May and ferried to Egypt. From there, he was sent to a POW camp in Canada and eventually to Great Britain (Special Camp XI in Bridgend, in South Wales). He was released from captivity in 1947. Kreipe died at Northeim, Lower Saxony, on 14 June 1976, aged 81.

Lieutenant General (Generalleutnant) Arthur Schmitt was the first German general to surrender to Allied forces. This occurred on 2 January 1942 during the North African campaign, when General Isaac Pier de Villiers, commander of the 2nd South African Division, accepted his surrender, as well as that of his 555th Infantry Division, near Bardia, a Libyan seaport located close to the border with Egypt.[100] He was held in Canada until 1946, when he was transferred to Great Britain. Schmitt had also been captured by the British Army in South-West Africa during the First World War. In 1948, after his (second) release from British custody, Schmitt settled in Munich, where he died, on 15 January 1972, aged 83.

Oscar Dirlewanger was allegedly beaten to death by his Polish guards at Altshausen POW camp on 7 June 1945.[101] He was an SS-oberführer (senior colonel) who led the 36th Waffen Grenadier Brigade to a spree of crimes against humanity in Poland, the Byelorussian SSR, Slovakia and Hungary between 1940 and 1944. Most of his troopers were convicted criminals picked up from various German and Austrian prisons. Back in 1934, he had been convicted and jailed for two years for the rape of a 14-year-old girl.[102] Dirlewanger was arrested by French troops on 1 June 1945, near Altshausen, a small Swabian municipality in southern Germany. He was hiding in a remote hunting lodge, wearing civilian clothes and was using a false name. He died between 5 and 7 June 1945, aged 49, as a result of ill treatment. The French said he died of a heart attack and was buried in an unmarked grave. According to another source, Dirlewanger escaped and eventually joined the French Foreign Legion.[103]

On 8 June 1945, a day after Dirlewanger's lynching, another SS officer, Karle August Hanke, died in the hands of his captors. Hanke was the Gauleiter (Regional

Leader) of Lower Silesia on 29 April 1945, when he was promoted to SS-Reichsführer and took the place of the ousted Heinrich Himmler as supreme commander of the Schutzstaffel (SS).[104] More than a thousand civilians were executed on Hanke's order in Breslau (present-day Wrocław, in south-western Poland). On 5 May 1945, one day before the surrender of Breslau to the Red Army, Hanke managed to fly out of the besieged capital of Silesia and reach Prague. On 8 June he was captured by Czech partisans near Neudorf, in north-west Czechoslovakia, wearing the uniform of an SS private. When he tried to escape, 41-year-old Franke was shot and wounded by his captors. He was then beaten to death by the partisans with rifle butts.[105]

Captain (Kapitän zur See) Karl-August Nerger had nothing to do with the Kriegsmarine, having retired from the Imperial Navy as early as 1919. However, he was arrested by the Red Army in his house in Dresden in mid-1945 and incarcerated at the former Sachsenhausen concentration camp, 35km north of Berlin, which had become the NKVD special camp No. 7. Nerger was held there until his death, on 12 January 1947, aged 71. He was allegedly beaten to death by another inmate, identified as Wilhelm Wagner.[106] The official cause of death was reported as cachexia.

The two high-ranking prisoners that were 'victimised' by the Allies more than anybody else were Major Generals Hans Cramer and Wilhelm Ritter von Thoma. Cramer was used by British Intelligence to deceive the German high command about the destination of the Allied forces in their forthcoming invasion of north-western Europe, and Thoma was made to provide information of strategic significance. Cramer, commander of the XI Army Corps, was captured by the British on 12 March 1943 with the capitulation of the Axis forces in Tunisia.[107] He was detained in Trent Park, a special camp for German generals and staff officers, in north London. About a month before the Normandy landings, the last commander of the XI Army Corps was released for health reasons related to asthma. During his repatriation journey, he was 'allowed' to see British troops preparing for the invasion and not American troops, whose area of concentration was – in terms of distance – closer to Normandy. Even the Allied bombing prior to the invasion was part of an elaborate scheme to give the impression to the enemy that the attack should be expected not in Normandy but further north.[108] It was no wonder that on D-Day the larger proportion of the German forces was kept by their high command between Pas-de-Calais and the River Seine.[109] Back home, Cramer was treated with suspicion by the SS. On 26 July 1944, weeks after the Allied invasion in Normandy, he was arrested and detained, initially in Prinz Albrecht Strasse prison, in Berlin and later in the Ravensbrück concentration camp, 56 miles (90km) north of the German capital, until 5 August. One month later, Cramer was dismissed from the military. In May 1945, after the German capitulation, he was arrested by the British and remained in their custody until early 1946. Cramer died on 28 October 1968 in Hausberge in North Rhine-Westphalia, aged 72.

Von Thoma had commanded the 20th Panzer Division in the Battle of Moscow in late 1941 and briefly Rommel's Panzer Army in Tunisia in October 1942. On 4 November he was captured by the British, 66 miles (106km) west of Alexandria, in northern Egypt, after the second battle of El Alamein. In Trent Park, where he was detained, von Thoma was recorded by a bagging spy system in the camp to reveal the existence of the Nazi V-1 flying bomb programme in his discussion with another

POW (Major General Ludwig Grüwell).[110] His leg was amputated in 1946 while still in British custody. After his release, von Thoma settled at Dachau, some 20km north-west of Munich, where he died of a heart attack, on 30 April 1948, aged 56.

Surrendered I

At the time of his arrest near Stalingrad in early 1943, Colonel General (Generaloberst) Walter Heinz was the second-highest-ranking German officer taken prisoner by the Allies, behind Field Marshal Friedrich von Paulus. Heinze commanded the VIII Army Corps, one of the Wehrmacht formations that took part in the siege of the USSR's most emblematic city during the Patriotic War. He died, aged 65, on 9 February 1944, while in Soviet captivity. Major General Reiner Stahel and Brigadier General Louis Tronnier also surrendered to the Red Army during the war. Lieutenant Generals Erick-Oskar Hansen, Stahel, and Tronnier became prisoners during the retreat of German forces from Romania and Boege during the encirclement of his troops in the Latvian SSR. Tronnier and Stahel, as happened to Colonel General Walter Heinz as early as 1944, were among the German high-ranking officers who died in Voikovo or Camp 48, the first in 1952 and the second three years later. In the same camp also died Lieutenant General Walter von Boltenstern (1952), Lieutenant General Friedrich Bayer (1953), Major General Karl-Wilhelm Specht (1953), Brigadier General Gerd-Paul von Below (1953), Lieutenant General Heinrich-Anton Deboi (1955), Major General Friedrich Hochbaum (1955), Lieutenant General Hans Boeckh-Behrens (1955) and Major General Max Pfeffer (1955).

Pfeffer and Deboi surrendered to the Red Army on the conclusion of the battle of Stalingrad, in February 1943. Colonel General Max Pfeffer was commanding the IV Army Corps and Lieutenant General Heinrich-Anton Deboi the 44th Infantry Division. Both were convicted as war criminals and died in captivity – Pfeffer on 31 December 1955, aged 72, and Deboi on 20 January 1955, aged 61.

Hochbaum commanded the XVIII Army Corps from June 1944 until May 1945. He surrendered to the Red Army in East Prussia. Hochbaum died in Voikovo, on 28 January 1955, aged 60. Specht was a member of the impromptu court martial that tried the German officers involved in the 20 July 1944 plot to assassinate Hitler before handing them over to the People's Court. He surrendered to the Red Army in May 1945 and died in Russian captivity on 3 December 1953, aged 59. Bayer commanded the 153rd Division. He surrendered to Bulgarian troops while trying to flee Romania. Bayer was handed over to the Red Army and was eventually detained in Voikovo prison camp, where he died on 5 August 1953, aged 65. Boeckh-Behrens commanded the L Army Corps, one of the German formations that were encircled by the Red Army on the Courland peninsula, in the Latvian SSR, from 31 July 1944 until 10 May 1945. After his surrender, Boeckh-Behrens was detained in Voikovo, where he died on 13 February 1953, aged 56. Herzog, the last commander of the XXXVIII Army Corps, also surrendered in the Courland pocket. He died on 8 May 1948 in a POW camp, near Vorkuta, aged 59. Vorkuta is located in the extreme north of European Russia, 99 miles (160km) above the Arctic Circle.

Von Boltenstern commanded the 196th Reserve Panzer Division in France. In May 1944, the unit was disbanded and its commander was discharged from active service.

GERMANS

After the German capitulation, von Bolenstern was arrested by the Red Army and ended up a detainee in Voikovo. He died there on 19 January 1952, aged 62. Von Below commanded an augmented unit (374th Grenadier Regiment) and eventually various reserve forces. In early May 1945, he surrendered to the Russians. Von Below died in Voikovo on 8 December 1953, aged 61.

Stahel and Tronnier surrendered to the Red Army in September 1944. Stahel commanded the German occupation forces in Warsaw during the uprising in the Polish capital (1 August–3 October 1944). On 3 August he was transferred to Bucharest with Romania being already under siege by the Red Army. Seventeen days later, Stahel was arrested by the NKVD together with the country's former strongman, the pro-Axis Field Marshal Ion Antonescu. He was charged with war crimes committed by his troops in Warsaw against the revolting Poles. Stahel died in his prison cell, with exact date of his death subject to controversy. According to Soviet sources, he died in Vladimir prison on 30 November 1952, aged 63. The prison is 120 miles (200km) east of Moscow. According to another source, Stahel died of a heart attack three years later, on 30 November 1955, in a prison camp for officers in Ivanovo, 162 miles (254km) north-east of Moscow.

Tronnier commanded the 62nd Infantry Division in eastern Romania, where he was forced to surrender to the Red Army on 25 August 1944. He died on 27 January 1952, at Voikovo prison camp, aged 54.

Major General Arthur Kullmer died in Soviet captivity on 28 March 1953, aged 56. He had commanded the XLIII Army Corps. Brigadier Generals Fritz-Georg Rappard and Johann-Georg Richert were executed by the Russians as war criminals after their surrender. Rappard was commanding the 7th Infantry Division and Richert the 35th Infantry Division, when they became prisoners of war. Fifty-three-year-old Rappard was executed at Velikiye Luki, in western Russia, on 29 January 1946 and 55-year-old Richert in Minsk, in Byelorussian SSR, one day later.[111]

Colonel Walter Nikolai had led the German secret services (Abteilung IIIb) during the First World War. Mata Hari and Elsbeth Schragmüller (also known as 'Fräulein Doktor') were among the spies he employed. In 1945, after the German capitulation, Nikolai was arrested by Soviet troops and brought to Moscow. He died in the hospital at the Butyrka prison on 4 May 1947, aged 73.

Among the high-ranking Wehrmacht and Waffen-SS officers who surrendered to the Red Army and survived Soviet captivity were Major Generals Hans Mikosch, Karl Stecker and Helmuth Weidling, Lieutenant Generals Hansen and Schmidt, and Brigadier General Wilhelm Mohnke. Mikosch commanded the 13th Panzer Division on the Eastern Front. In May 1944, he was appointed commandant of Boulogne, in northern France. Less than a year later, he surrendered to Soviet forces in East Prussia. He was held in the Soviet Union for ten years. After his repatriation, he settled in Reichhof, near Cologne, where he died on 18 January 1993, aged 95.

Stecker commanded the XI Army Corps. He was the last general to surrender to the Red Army in Stalingrad and remained in Soviet captivity until 1955. Stecker died on 10 April 1973 in Riezlern, in Austria's westernmost state of Vorarlberg, aged 88.

Weidling was the last commander of Berlin. Before that, until 22 April 1945, he commanded the LVI Panzer Corps. Weidling surrendered to the Red Army on 2 May and later was held at Butyrka and Lefortovo prisons, in Moscow.[112] On 27 February 1952, he was sentenced to twenty-five years' imprisonment by USSR's Supreme Tribunal.

Weidling died of a heart attack in his cell, in Wladimirowka prison, in Wladimir, on 17 November 1955, aged 64.

Hansen surrendered to the Red Army on 30 August 1944, following a Soviet offensive that triggered King Michael's coup d'état and Romania's switch from the Axis to the Allies. At the time, Hansen was commandant of Bucharest, having previously commanded the LIV Army Corps on the Eastern Front. He was held in the Soviet Union until 1955.[113] Hansen died in Hamburg on 18 March 1967, aged 77.

SS-Brigadeführer (Brigadier General) Wilhelm Mohnke commanded the 1st Panzer Division Leibstandarte SS *Adolf Hitler* during the Battle of the Bulge. In March 1945 he took the command of the centre government district of Berlin, which included the Reich Chancellery and the Führerbunker.[114] On 2 May Mohnke was forced to surrender to the Red Army and seven days later, he was flown to Moscow.[115] He was jailed in Lubyanka prison and then was transferred to the Voikovo prison camp. On 10 October 1955 Mohnke was released and repatriated. He was never tried for the shooting of British, Canadian and American prisoners of war by troops under his command in France (in mid-1940) and Belgium (in late 1944). Mohnke died on 6 August 2001 in Barsbüttel, near Hamburg, aged 90.

Major Generals Friedrich-Jobst Vockamer von Kirchensitytenbach and Rolf Wuthmann, Lieutenant General Siegmund Freiherr von Schleinitz and Brigadier Generals Gustav Gihr and Harald Schultz were also released from Soviet captivity in 1955.

Gihr surrendered to the Red Army on 27 June 1944 near Bubruysk, in eastern Belarus, with most of his troops (4th Infantry Division). He died four years after his repatriation, aged 65. Wuthmann surrendered with his troops (IX Army Corps) in Sambia, present-day Kaliningrad, in April 1945. He died on 27 October 1977, aged 84.

Von Schleinitz and his troops (361st Infantry Division) surrendered to the Red Army in Pomerania, on the southern shores of the Baltic Sea, in April 1945. He died on 30 November 1966, aged 78.

Major General von Kirchensitytenbach and Brigadier Generals Ehrefried-Oskar Boege and Harald Schultz surrendered to the Red Army on 10 May 1945, after a long-lasting encirclement of their troops in the Courland peninsula, then part of the Latvian SSR.

Von Kirchensitytenbach was commanding the remnant of the Sixteenth Army. He died on 3 April 1989, in Munich, aged 94. Brigadier General Boege was commanding the Eighteenth Army. He died on 31 December 1965, in Hildesheim, near Hanover, aged 76.

Schultz, the last commander of the 24th Infantry Division, died on 15 March 1957, aged 61, less than two years after his repatriation.

Surrendered II

Several high-ranking officers of the Wehrmacht surrendered to western Allied forces during and immediately after the Second World War, including Colonel Generals Hans-Jürgen von Arnim and Georg Lindemann, Major Generals Hermann Balck, Theodore Busse, Ernst August Köstring and Kurt von Tippelskirch, and Lieutenant Generals Fritz Bayerlein, Ferdinand Heim and Karl Wilhelm von Schlieben.

Colonel General (Generaloberst) von Arnim became a prisoner of war as early as March 1943. Days after replacing Erwin Rommel as commander of the German and

Italian forces of the Army Group Africa in Tunisia he was forced to surrender to British troops. Von Arnim was initially interned in Trent Park in north London. He was later transferred to Camp Clinton, Mississippi in the United States, until his release and repatriation via England on 1 July 1947. Von Arnim died on 1 September 1962 in Bad Wildungen, in Hesse, aged 73.

Von Schlieben surrendered to US troops in June 1944. He had commanded the 709th Infantry Division during occupational duties in France until 23 June 1944, when he was appointed commandant of the port of Cherbourg, in the north of the country. Only three days later, he was forced to surrender with 800 of his troops to the US 9th Infantry Division. He was held in prisoner of war camps in Great Britain, including Trent Park, north London, and Island Farm or Camp 198 in South Wales. He was released on 7 October 1947. Von Schlieben died on 18 June 1964 in Giessen, in the federated state of Hesse, aged 69.

Heim had been dismissed (unfairly) from the army in January 1943, blamed for the performance of his 48th Panzer Corps during the siege of Stalingrad.[116] In August 1944, he returned to active service and was appointed commandant of the port of Boulogne, in northern France. Less than a month later, on 23 September, he surrendered to the 3rd Canadian Infantry Division.[117] He was detained in England, mostly in Island Farm, South Wales, and Camp 18 Featherstone Park, in Northumberland, until his release and repatriation, on 12 May 1948.[118] Heim died on 14 November 1977 in Ulm, in the state of Baden-Württemberg, aged 82.

Bayerlein commanded the LIII Army Corps for two months, from February to April 1945. He surrendered to the US Army on 19 April while his troops were encircled in the Ruhr Pocket. He remained in British custody until April 1947. Bayerlein died in Würzburg, in Bavaria, on 30 January 1970, aged 71.

Colonel General Lindemann and Major Generals Balck, Busse, Köstring and von Tippelskirch surrendered to Allied forces in May 1945. Von Tippelskirch commanded Army Group Vistula for twenty-four hours, on 28 April 1945, and was replaced by Colonel General Kurt Student. He surrendered to elements of the British–Canadian 21st Army on 2 May in Ludwigslust, a castle town near Schwerin, in north-east Germany. He remained in British custody (mostly in Island Farm or Camp 11 in England) until 4 December 1946, when he was transferred to US custody (Allendorf POW camp, in Germany) until his release, three years after becoming a POW. Tippelskirch died on 10 May 1957 in Lüneburg, in Lower Saxony, aged 65.

Köstring, who was Russian-born and fluent in the language, surrendered to the US Army on 4 May 1945. Until then he had helped in the creation of pro-Nazi national legions among the Russian people. He also helped in raising Andrey Vlasov's National Liberation Army. He was detained in prisoner of war camps until 1947. Köstring died on 20 November 1953 in Unterwössen in Bavaria, aged 77.

Busse surrendered between 4 and 7 May 1945. He had taken the command of the Ninth Army on 21 January. Three months later, during the Battle of Berlin, his troops were annihilated west of Frankfurt. He led the remnant of the Ninth Army west of the Elbe River, where he surrendered. He remained a prisoner of war until 1948. Busse died in Wallerstein, in Bavaria, on 21 October 1986, aged 88.

Lindemann was arrested by Allied troops in his Headquarters in Silkeborg, in eastern Denmark, on 6 May 1945. At the time, Lindemann was commanding all

German forces in Denmark, having previously led the Eighteenth Army in campaigns around Leningrad. He was held in US custody until late 1948. Lindemann died on 25 September 1963, in Freudenstadt, near Tübingen, in southern Germany, aged 79.

Balck surrendered to the US XX Corps in Austria, on 8 May 1945. He commanded the reconstituted Sixth Army when it received the final blow in Hungary.[119] Balck remained in captivity until 1947. He was also sentenced in absentia by a French military court to twenty years of hard labour for war crimes committed by his troops in the Vosges mountains, in the fall of 1944, but was never extradited. Balck died on 29 November 1982 in Asperg, in Baden-Württemberg, aged 88.

Brigadier General Bernhard von Lossberg was captured by British troops on 5 May 1945 in Neustadt, in Holstein. Until February 1945 he was chief of staff of the command of the VIII Army Corps, then deployed in Breslau. He remained in British captivity until 26 July 1946, when he was released for repatriation from the London District Cage (LFC).[120] Von Lossberg died on 15 March 1965, aged 66.

Lieutenant General August Krakau commanded the 7th Mountain Division from 10 September 1942 until 8 May 1945. He remained in captivity until late 1947. Krakau died on 7 January 1975, aged 80. Lieutenant General Willibald Utz, commander of the 2nd Mountain Division since 9 February 1945, surrendered to Allied troops in Württemberg, near Stuttgart, three months later.[121] He remained in captivity until 1948. Utz died on 20 April 1954 in Bad Reichenhall, Upper Bavaria, aged 61.

Lieutenant General Edgar Feuchtinger, who surrendered to the British Army in Hamburg, was a deserter at the time. On 25 January 1945, instead of taking up his new assignment, the command of the 20th Panzer Grenadier Division, Feuchtinger disappeared until 29 May, when he surrendered himself to the Allies, wearing his uniform. He was detained in various POW camps in Great Britain, including Trent Park, north London. He was released as early as 1946 from an internment camp ran by the US Army in Allendorf, north-west of Hesse. Feuchtinger died from a stroke in Berlin, on 21 January 1960, aged 65.[122]

Major General Horst von Mellenthin, commanding the VIII Army Corps, was held by the British after his surrender on 8 May 1945, whereas Brigadier General Friedrich von Mellenthin, his younger brother, was detained by the US Army. Friedrich was commanding the 9th Panzer Division when he surrendered on 3 May 1945. The two brothers spent two and a half years in internment. After his release, Friedrich emigrated to Johannesburg in South Africa, where he died on 28 June 1997. Horst died on 8 January 1977 in Wiesbaden, a spa town in the state of Hesse, aged 79.

War criminals

Austrian-born Luftwaffe Colonel General Alexander Löhr had led German air forces in the bombing of Belgrade and the battle of Crete. On 9 May 1945 he was commanding the German forces in the Balkans when he surrendered in Zagreb (the present-day capital of Croatia) to Josip Broz Tito's communist partisans. Brought to trial in Belgrade, Yugoslavia's capital, 61-year-old Löhr was found guilty of war crimes as the indiscriminate bombing of civilian targets by the Luftwaffe, during the German invasion of the country in April 1941, had resulted the death of about

17,000 civilians. He was held in a small cell with ten more German POWs – all in chains and wearing only their underwear.[123] Löhr was executed by firing squad on 26 or 27 February 1947.

Fifty-three-year-old Major General Gustav Fehn surrendered to the communist partisans in Yugoslavia in early June 1945, following the defeat of his formation, the XV Mountain Corps, by Tito's forces during the Lika-Primorje operations in western Bosnia between 20 March and 15 April 1944. Fehn was executed without trial in Ljubljana (the present-day capital of Slovenia) by communist partisans on 5 June 1945.

Lieutenant General Hans von Graevenitz was also taken prisoner in Yugoslavia. Until 1 April 1943 he was Nazi Germany's inspector of Prisoner of War affairs. Six days later he was appointed commander of 237th Infantry Division. The German capitulation found von Graevenitz and his division isolated in Yugoslavia. He and his men surrendered to Tito's forces north of Fiume (present-day Rijeka, in Croatia), on 7 May 1945. He remained in Yugoslav custody until his release on 20 October 1950. Von Graevenitz died in Stuttgart on 9 December 1963, aged 69.

Major Generals Maximilian de Angelis and Martin Fiebig were extradited by the Western Allies to Yugoslavia after the war. Fifty-six-year-old Fiebig was the last commander of the Luftwaffe's Command South-East (Luftwaffenkommando Südost), headquartered in Thessaloniki in northern Greece. He was in British captivity on 6 February 1946, when he was extradited to Yugoslavia. He was tried for his role in the bombing of Belgrade in April 1946. On 10 September 1946 Fiebig was sentenced to death. He was executed by firing squad on 23 October 1947.

Luftwaffe's Captain (Hauptmann) Joachim Kirschner was shot down on 17 December 1943 near Metković, in present-day Croatia, by Italy-based US Army Air Force P-47 fighters.[124] At the time, he was credited with shooting down 188 Allied planes in aerial combat. Kirschner bailed out and landed between the villages of Bjeloevići and Donje Hrasna. He was captured by communist partisans. Twenty-three-year-old Kirschner was later executed by elements of Josip Broz Tito's 29th Hercegovina Division.

Hungarian-born de Angelis, who commanded the Sixth Army from April to July 1944, was extradited to Yugoslavia by the US Army on 4 April 1946. He had been captured in Austria on 9 May 1945. In Yugoslavia in October 1948 he was convicted for war crimes committed earlier by his retreating troops and sentenced to twenty years in prison. Five months later he was extradited to the Soviet Union, where he was convicted mostly of war crimes committed by his troops when he commanded the XXXXIV Army Corps. De Angelis was sentenced two times twenty-five years in prison but was released in autumn 1955. He settled in Hanover and eventually Granz, in Austria, where he died on 6 December 1974, aged 85.

After the war, thirty-eight German officers held by the British in Neuengamme internment camp (No. 6), near Hamburg, were extradited to Yugoslavia.[125] They were tried for war crimes in Sarajevo, the capital of present-day Bosnia, from 20 to 30 August 1947. Ten of the convicted were executed and the remnant received various prison sentences.

Several German generals were captured before being led to captivity by Allied troops. Lieutenant General Hans Tröger was commanding the 13th Panzer Division in late August 1944 when his troops were encircled by Soviet and Romanian forces, following Romania's switch allegiance from the Axis powers to the Allies. He led an element of the division into Bulgaria, another country of the region that had been aligned in the meantime to the Allies. He was captured by Bulgarian forces and handed over to the Red Army.[126] He remained in Soviet custody until his release and repatriation in 1955. Tröger died on 21 January 1982 in Schwangau, in Bavaria, aged 85.

Detained I

Major General Heinz Eberbach was surprised in his bed in Amiens by British troops on 31 August 1944. Ten days earlier, most units of his Fifth Panzer Army had been destroyed in the Falaise Pocket in north-western France. He was detained in Trent Park, north London, until his release in 1948. Eberbach died on 13 July 1992 in Notzingen, in southern Germany, aged 96. In Trent Park was also held Eberbach's son, Heinz-Eugen, a U-boat commander. He and his crew were captured by Allied troops off the military port of Toulon, in southern France, on 27 August 1944, after scuttling their submarine, *U-230*, to avoid capture.[127] Heinz-Eugen was also set free and repatriated on 28 February 1946 – almost two years ahead of his father's release from Trent Park.

Major General Erwin Vierow was chief of staff of the Wehrmacht forces deployed in the Somme area of northern France on 1 September 1944 when he was captured by British troops. He was released and repatriated in late 1947. Vierow died on 1 February 1982, aged 91.

Major General Edwin Graf von Röthkirch und Truch was captured by elements of the US 37th Tank Battalion west of Koblenz, in the state of Rhineland-Palatinate, on 6 March 1945, while wandering into the enemy lines.[128] At the time, he had completed about four months as commanding officer of the LIII Army Corps. He was interned in prisoner of war camps for high-ranking officers in England, including Trent Park and Island Farm, until late 1947. Polish-born von Röthkirch died on 29 July 1980 in Rettershof, in Kelkheim, aged 91.

Brigadier General Walther Bruns was assigned to the Army High Command from January 1945. He was captured by British troops in a military hospital on 8 April 1945 and was detained in the Island Farm (Special Camp 11). He was released from the London District Cage (LDC) on 21 February 1948. Bruns died on 15 April 1957 in Göttingen, Lower Saxony, aged 66.

Major General Edgar Röthricht commanded the LIX Army Corps. He surrendered to western Allied forces on 8 May 1945 and remained in captivity until late 1947. Röthricht died on 11 February 1967, aged 74. Major General Hans von Tettau was the last commander of the 24th Infantry Division when he surrendered on 8 May 1945. He was released after two years in western Allied captivity. Von Tettau died on 30 January 1956, aged 67.

Major General Curt Liebmann was arrested by the British Army in May 1945 although he had retired from the military on 30 October 1939. Until then he had commanded the Fifth Army. He remained in British custody until 1947. Liebmann died on 2 July 1960 in Holzminden, in Lower Saxony, aged 70.

Brigadier General Maximilian Jais was arrested by Allied troops in May 1945, although he had retired from the military in September 1944. Until then he was the commanding officer of the German occupation forces in Luxemburg. He was held by the Allies until 12 May 1947. Jais died ten years later, on 24 January 1957, aged 65.

Major General Walther Fischer von Weikersthal was commanding the LXVII Army Corps headquartered in Brussels until the summer of 1944. He surrendered to the US 35th Infantry Division on 8 May 1945. He was released in late 1947 and died six years later, on 11 February 1953, aged 62.

Brigadier General Bernhard Klosterkember and his 180th Infantry Division surrendered to the Allies in late April 1945 in the Ruhr Pocket in North Rhine-Westphalia. He remained in captivity until 1947. Kosterkember died on 19 July 1962 in Bremen, aged 65. Lieutenant Colonel (Oberstleutnant) Theodor von Hippel commanded the Bradenburgers' Commando Unit (Bau-Lehr-Bataillon z.b.v. 800) in May 1943 when he surrendered to Allied troops in Tunisia.[129] He was released from captivity in late 1945. Von Hippel died on 1 January 1977 in Kiel, aged 86.

The German 133rd Fortress Division (133 Festungs-Division) in Crete remained fully armed under British authority from January to late June 1945.[130] Only then the divisional commander, Brigadier (Generalmajor) Hans-Georg Benthack was sent for detention to POW Camp No. 1 in Grizedale Hall, Cumbria. On 9 January 1946 he was transferred to the Island Farm Special Camp No. 11, near Bridgend, in South Wales. He was repatriated from POW camp No. 186 (Berechurch Hall Camp in Essex) on 12 May 1948. Benthack died on 17 August 1973, in Hamburg, aged 79.

Committed suicide II

Several Waffen-SS commanders and SS officials committed suicide before being captured by Allied troops or during their detention after Nazi Germany's capitulation. Between mid-1943 and late 1944 SS Lieutenant General (Gruppenführer) Karl-Gustav Sauberzeig commanded the IX Mountain Corps of the SS Handschar (1st Croatian) in Bosnia-Herzegovina, then part of German-occupied Yugoslavia. When he surrendered to Allied forces in northern Germany in May 1945 he was a Corps commander within Army Group H. He was detained by his captors in Camp No. 6, formerly Neungamme concentration camp. Forty-seven-year-old Sauberzeig committed suicide within the camp by swallowing poison on 20 October 1946.

Two major generals of the SS who had the same surname but were not relatives, also killed themselves to avoid falling in enemy hands. Fifty-one-year-old SS Major General (Obergruppenführer) Friedrich-Wilhelm Krüger committed suicide in Eggelsberg, Upper Austria, on 10 May 1945.[131] Until February 1945, he commanded V SS Mountain Corps. Then he was transferred to Army Group Ostmark as Corps commander. Krüger was accused of war crimes committed by his troops in German-occupied Poland.

SS Major General Walther Krüger was commanding the VI SS Army Corps (Latvian). He committed suicide in the Courland Pocket (Liepāja in the Latvian SSR) on 22 May 1945, fourteen days after the surrender of Nazi Germany, aged 55.

Austrian-born SS Lieutenant General Odilo Globočnik was suspected of war crimes committed in Poland in mid-1943 and in the German-occupied part of Italy in late 1943. He was captured by British troops on 31 May 1945 in Carinthia, southern Austria, and sent to Paternion interrogation centre in the Villach Land district. While in detention, 41-year-old Globočnik committed suicide by biting on a cyanide capsule. Austrian-born SS Major (Sturmbannführer) Hermann Höffle was captured in May 1945 and was held at the Wolfsberg detention centre in Carinthia. In 1961 he was arrested for war crimes and imprisoned in Vienna. Höffle hanged himself in his cell on 22 August 1962 before the trial could begin. He was 51 years old.

Danish-born SS Colonel (Standartenführer) Heinrich Petersen commanded the 18th SS Volunteer Panzer Grenadier Division *Horst Wessel* from March 1945. On 9 May 41-year-old Petersen committed suicide, near Pilsen, in Bohemia.

POW massacres

In June 1940, near Bois d'Erain in France, elements of the German Grossdeutscheland Division massacred captured African soldiers and their white officers. They belonged to (Free) French Army's 4th Colonial Division.[132] The German commander, Gerhard von Schwerin, who later rose to the rank of major general (general of the Panzertruppe), was never convicted for war crimes. No one was punished either for the torture and murder of eleven Afro-American POWs on 17 December 1944 in Wereth, near Liège, Belgium, during the Battle of the Bulge, by elements of the 1st SS Panzer Division.[133] The victims belonged to US Army's 333rd Artillery Battalion.

On 27 May 1940, ninety-seven British POWs, all members of the Royal Norfolk Regiment, were lined across a wall in Le Paradis, northern France, and machine-gunned by elements of the SS Division *Totenkopf*. After the war, a company commander, SS-Captain (SS-Hauptsturmführer) Fritz Knöchlein, was brought to trial for the massacre and sentenced to death by a military court in Rotherbaum, near Hamburg. He was hanged in Hamelin prison, Lower Saxony, on 21 January 1949, aged 37.

Colonel General (Generaloberst) of the Waffen-SS Josef Sepp Dietrich surrendered to the US 36th Infantry Division in Austria on 9 May, accompanied by his wife. On 16 May 1946 he was sentenced to life imprisonment by a US military tribunal in Dachau, for his responsibility in the murder of eighty-four American prisoners of war in Malmedy, Belgium, by elements of his Sixth Panzer Army, in December 1944, during the Battle of the Bulge.[134] His sentence was eventually reduced to twenty-five years. Dietrich was released on parole from Landsberg prison ten years later, on 22 October 1955. In August 1956, he was arrested again and brought to trial before a West German court in Munich for his participation in the killing of SA leaders in the night of the long knives between 30 June and 2 July 1934. Following his conviction, he returned to Landsberg Prison for a nineteen-month prison term.[135] He was released due to a heart problem on 2 February 1958 – having served almost his entire sentence. Dietrich died of a heart attack on 21 April 1966 in Ludwigsburg, near Stuttgart, aged 73.

Heinrich Himmler's former adjutant, SS Full Colonel (Standarteführer) Joachim Peiper, was sentenced to death by hanging for his part in the Malmedy massacre. His troops were also responsible for the massacre earlier, on 19 September 1943, of twenty-four Italian civilians, including one woman, in Boves near Turin, north-western Italy, as a reprisal for the killing of one German soldier by Italian communist guerillas. The massacre was carried out two weeks after fascist Italy ceased being a belligerent power of the Rome–Berlin Axis with the signing of the armistice of Cassibile between the Kingdom of Italy and the Allies. Peiper fought as regimental commander of the 1st SS Panzer Division Leibstandarte SS *Adolf Hitler* (LSSAH) on the Eastern Front, in Belgium and in Hungary. On 8 May 1945 he did not surrender with his troops in Austria but trekked home to Germany instead. He was arrested by US troops there on 22 May.[136] For the execution of the eighty-four US POWs by his troops, Peiper was sentenced to death, on 16 July 1946. In 1951 his sentence was commuted to thirty-five years.[137] In 1954, he was released from prison. In 1972 Himmler's former adjutant settled in Traves, eastern France, and started translating military history books for a German publisher. In 1968 two courts, one in Italy and one in West Germany (Stuttgart) concluded with regard to the Boves massacre that there was insufficient suspicion of criminal activity on the part of Peiper to warrant prosecution. On 14 July 1976 61-year-old Peiper died from smoke inhalation when his house in Traves was burned down, reportedly by French anti-Nazis.

SS Brigadier General (Brigadeführer) Kurt Meyer was convicted of the murder of eleven unarmed Canadian POWs by elements of his 12th SS Panzer Division *Hitlerjugend* in the Ardenne Abbey, near Caen, after the Allied landings in Normandy, in June 1944. He was captured by Belgian partisans on 6 September 1944 in a village close to the River Meus during the retreat of the German forces and was handed over to the US Army. Meyer was held in a POW camp near Compiègne, in northern France, and later in Trent Park, north London. He was transferred to Germany on December 1945 to face trial for the Ardenne Abbey Massacre. Meyer was sentenced to death by a military court in Aurich, Lower Saxony. On 14 January 1946 his sentence was commuted to life imprisonment. In April 1947, Meyer was transferred to Canada. He served five years of his term at the Dorchester Penitentiary, New Brunswick, before being released and repatriated. Back home, he became active in HIAG, an organisation made up of Waffen-SS apologists. He died on his 51st birthday, on 23 December 1961, in Hagen, near Dortmund, aged 51.

SS-Colonel (SS-Standartenführer) Helmut Knochen (a schoolteacher before joining the SS in 1936) commanded the Security Police (Sicherheitspolizei) in German-occupied France. In March 1947, he was sentenced to death by a British military court, convicted of the execution of captured British paratroopers south of Paris in August 1944 and for the murder of captured British Special Executive Agents (SOE) in Paris.[138] In September 1948, his sentence was commuted to life imprisonment and later to twenty-one years in prison. In 1954 Knochen was sentenced to death by a French military court, convicted of the murder of captured Resistance fighters and the deportation of French Jews to concentration and death camps. His sentence was commuted to life imprisonment. In November 1962, Knochen obtained a presidential pardon from Charles de Gaulle and was released from prison. According to French Premier Pierre Mendes France, the pardon was a demand of German Chancellor Konrad Adenauer. Kochen died on 4 April 2003 in Baden-Baden, in Baden Württemberg, aged 93.

SS-Major (SS-Sturmbannführer) Hans Kieffer (a policeman before joining the SS in 1933) was head of the Intelligence Agency of the SS (Sicherheitsdienst or SD) in German-occupied France, headquartered in Paris. After the war, he was arrested by British troops in Garmisch-Partenkirchen, an Alpine town in Bavaria, where he was working as a cleaner in a hotel.[139] He was brought to justice for ordering the execution of five British Special Air Service (SAS) troopers who were captured after landing by parachute south of Paris on 4 July 1944.[140] Kieffer was sentenced to death by a British military court. On 26 June 1947 he was hanged at Hamelin Prison by British Executioner Albert Pierrepoint.

Colonel (SS-Obersturmbannführer) Fritz Emil Dietrich was involved in the mass murder of Jews in the port city of Liepāja, in present-day western Latvia, from 15 to 17 December 1941.[141] After the war, he was convicted in Dachau and sentenced to death, not for the civilian massacre in Latvia but for the murder of seven US airmen, who were captured after parachuting from disabled aircraft. Dietrich was executed by hanging on 22 October 1948 in Landsberg Prison, aged 50.

SS-Captain (SS-Hauptsturmführer) Friedrich (Fritz) Hartjenstein was sentenced to death for the execution of a RAF pilot and four female agents of the British SOE (Special Operations Executive). Diana Rowden, Vera Leigh, Andrée Borrel and Sonya Olschanezky,[142] were executed on 6 September 1944 in Natzweiler-Struthof, a Nazi concentration camp in the Vosges Mountains in eastern France. They were inserted (unconscious after injection) into the camp's crematorium oven.[143] A camp doctor, Werner Rohd, was also convicted of their murder after the war. He was tried, sentenced to death and executed by hanging. Hartjenstein served as an official in various concentration camps (Sachsenhausen, Niederhagen, Natzweiler-Struthof and Flossenbürg) and in Birkenau, the main camp of Auschwitz, as commandant. In June and July 1946, he was tried in Wuppertal for the execution of the RAF pilot and the SOE agents. On 30 July Hartjenstein was sentenced to death. He was then extradited to France, where he was tried for other war crimes, eventually receiving a third death sentence. Hartjenstein died of a heart attack on 20 October 1954 in Paris, aged 49, while awaiting execution.

Friedrich Hildebrandt was a Nazi Party politician and a major general (SS-obergruppenführer) of the SS. He was arrested and tried in Dachau (Airmen's Trial) in December 1945 for ordering the shooting of a US aircrewman in his capacity as Reich governor (Reichsstathalter) of the state of Mecklenburg and of the city of Lübeck.[144] Hildebrandt was condemned and put to death by hanging on 5 November 1948 in Landsberg Prison, aged 50.[145]

Richard Drauz was involved in the execution of a downed US airman in his capacity as regional party leader (gauleiter) in Heilbronn County, between Stuttgart and Heidelberg. On 6 April 1945 he accused fourteen civilians of treason after they raised white flags on their homes while Allied forces were approaching and ordered their summary execution by paramilitary troops.[146] In July 1945, Drauz was arrested by US troops while hiding under the false name Richard Binder in a monastery at Montabaur, in Rhineland-Palatinate. On 11 December 1945 he was sentenced to death by a US military tribunal in Dachau. Drauz was executed by hanging on 4 December 1946 in Landsberg Prison, aged 52.

Two NCOs were executed after the war for killing without a trial a captured RAF pilot and a Dutch civilian in the Netherlands. After bailing out from a disabled Lancaster bomber, Gerald Hood was hiding with Bote van der Wal, a local resistance fighter, in his family house at Almelo in eastern Holland. On 13–14 June 1945 they were arrested by an SS party and executed on the spot. On 12 December 1945 two members of the arresting party (Ludwig Schweinberger and Georg Sandrock) were indicted for the crime, in the Almelo court house, by a British military tribunal and sentenced to death. They were hanged in Hamelin Prison, Germany. A third member of the SS party, Franz Joseph Hegemann, was sentenced to life imprisonment.

At least 129 Wehrmacht, SS and police officers and NCOs were sentenced to death after the war for their involvement in the murder of Allied POWs, mostly US airmen. They were hanged in four prisons: Landsberg (109 prisoners); Bruchsal, near Karlsruhe, in south-west Germany (thirteen); in Salzburg (four); and in Rheinbach, near Bonn, in North Rhine-Westphalia (three).[147]

SS Major General (Obergruppenführer) Herbert Gille commanded a division, the 5th SS Panzer Viking, made up of volunteers from Denmark, Norway, Finland, Estonia, the Netherlands and Belgium. The division, after fighting on the Eastern Front, surrendered to the US Army on 9 May 1945 near Füstenfeld, southern Austria. He was detained until 1948. Gille died on 26 December 1966 in Stemmen, in Lower Saxony, aged 69.

SS Lieutenant Colonel (Obersturmbannführer) Max Wünsche was briefly assigned as an orderly officer for Hitler back in 1938. His last command was the 12th SS Panzer Division, one of the German formations trapped by Western Allied forces in the Falaise Pocket in Normandy in August 1944. On the night of 20 August Wünsche escaped on foot, but later was wounded and taken prisoner by British troops. He spent the rest of the war detained in a POW camp (No. 165) in Caithness, in Scotland. He was released and repatriated in 1948. Wünsche died on 17 April 1995 in Munich, aged 80.

SS-Brigadier (Brigadeführer and Generalmajor der Polizei) Walter Schellenberg was Heindrich Himmler's intelligence chief. He was arrested by the British after the German surrender and tried for war crimes. On 4 November 1949 he was sentenced to six years' imprisonment for his role in the murder of Soviet POWs. He was released from prison after two years on the grounds of ill health. Schellenberg died on 31 March 1952 in Turin, Italy, aged 52.[148]

SS Captain (Hauptsturmführer) Karl Wilhelm Krause, of the 12th SS Panzer Division *Hitlerjugend*, fled westward in early May 1945 to avoid the advancing Red Army. He eventually surrendered to US troops. He was interrogated and interned until June 1946.[149] Despite being an SS officer, he was not considered to have been a war criminal and was eventually released.[150]

Naval commanders

Several admirals of the Kriegsmarine, the Navy of the Third Reich, were (also) arrested by the Allied forces after the German capitulation and imprisoned. Three of them, Vice Admirals (Vizeadmiral) Heino von Heimburg and Theodore Arps, and Rear Admiral (Konteradmiral) Adalbert Zuckschwerdt, died in captivity.

Arps was in charge of the Naval Intelligence Service (Marinen Achrichtendiest) in 1939. He was captured by US troops in Torgau on 8 May 1945. He died on 28 April 1947 in a POW camp near Garmisch-Partenkirchen, aged 63.

Von Heimburg was a member of the People's Court, a Nazi special court. He was arrested by the Red Army in March 1945. Months later, he died in a POW camp near Stalingrad, aged 55 or 56.

Zuckschwerdt was arrested by the US Army on 14 May 1945, although he had retired from the Kriegsmarine on 31 May 1944. He died on 1 July 1945 in a British POW camp (Internierungslager Staumühle), near Hövelhof, North Rhineland-Westphalia, aged 71.

Two admirals of the fleet (generaladmiral), Walter Warzecha and Wilhelm Marschall, were both arrested by western Allied troops after the German capitulation and held in captivity until late 1947. Warzecha was the last chief of the High Command (Uberbefehlshaber) of the Kriegsmarine. By 22 July 1945, he had supervised the dissolution of the German naval forces. Warzecha died of a heart attack on 30 August 1956 in Hamburg, aged 65. Marschall had briefly been the commander of German-occupied France. He died on 20 March 1976 in Mölln, in Schleswig-Holstein, aged 89.

Vice admirals (vizeadmiral) taken prisoner after the termination of hostilities in Europe included Friedrich Hüffmeier, Friedrich Frisius, Friedrich Lützow, Karl Topp and Gustav Kleikamp.

Hüffmeier was the last commander of the Channel Islands (Guernsey and Jersey). On 9 May 1945 following the surrender of his occupational forces, he was taken prisoner and remained in captivity until 2 April 1948. Hüffmeier died on 13 January 1942 in Münster, in North Rhine-Westphalia, aged 74.

Frisius signed the unconditional surrender of Dunkirk on 4 May 1945. He was held as prisoner of war at Island Farm (Special Camp 11, at Bridgend, South Wales) until 6 October 1947. Frisius died on 30 August 1970 in Lingen, in Lower Saxony, aged 75.

Kleikamp and Lützow were also released and repatriated in 1947. Lützow was the official spokesman of the Naval Command until the spring of 1945. He was taken prisoner in May and remained in British custody for about two years. Lützow died on 1 November 1964 in Celle, in Lower Saxony, aged 83.

Kleikamp was captured by British troops on 7 May 1945 and held as prisoner of war until his repatriation on 18 April 1947. He died in poor health on 13 September 1952 in Mülheim-an-der-Ruhr, near Essen, aged 56.

Topp was the first commander of the battleship *Tirpitz*. He was captured by the western Allies and held as POW until late 1946. Topp died on 24 April 1981 in Voerde, near Wesel, in North Rhine-Westphalia, aged 86.

Rear Admirals (Konteradmiral) Otto Kähler and Walter Hennecke were taken prisoner by the Allies in the summer of 1944. Kähler was commanding Nazi Germany's Brittany-based naval forces. He remained in captivity until February 1947. Kähler died on 2 November 1967 in Kiel, aged 73. Hennecke surrendered to elements of the US 9th Infantry Division at Cherbourg on 29 June 1944. On 1 July he was transferred to the British POW camp at Trent Park, north London. He was released and repatriated on 17 April 1947. Hennecke died on 1 January 1984 in Bad Lippspringe, in North Rhineland-Westphalia, aged 85.

Luftwaffe commanders

Luftwaffe's top brass, including Field Marshals Wolfram von Richthofen, Hugo Sperrle and Robert Ritter von Greim, and Colonel Generals (Generaloberst) Walther Boenicke and Alexander Löhr were led to captivity, during or immediately after the Second World War, as has been mentioned already. Colonel General Hans-Jürgen Stumpf, Luftwaffe's chief of the general staff, was also taken prisoner by the Allies. He was one of the signatories to Nazi Germany's formal surrender instrument, on 8 May 1945.[151] Stumpf was released from British captivity in 1947. He died on 9 March 1968 in Frankfurt, aged 78.

Major General (General of the Flieger) Karl Koller, a former chief of staff of the Luftwaffe, was arrested by British troops on 7 May 1945 at Castle Fischorn, in Zell-am-See, near Innsbruck, in northern Austria.[152] He was held in a POW camp in Oxfordshire, England, until December 1947. He had also been in British captivity during the First World War as a pilot of the Imperial Air Force. Koller died four years later, on 22 December 1951, in his hometown of Glonn, near Munich, aged 53.

Major General Ludwig Wolff commanded Luftwaffe's 5th Air Division.[153] He was also operationally responsible for Nazi Germany's XVII District (XVII Air Luftgave). He was captured by British troops near Hanover in May 1945 and remained in detention until February 1948. Wolff died two years later, on 17 May 1950, in Neustadt, in Holstein, aged 63.

Brigadier General (Generalmajor) Oskar Dinort was the last commander of the Luftwaffe's 3rd Air Division. After his surrender in May 1945 he remained in British custody until 1947. Dinort died on 27 May 1965 in Cologne, aged 63.

Dietrich Peltz, a Luftwaffe bomber pilot, was 29 years old on 1 November 1943 when he was promoted to brigadier general, becoming the youngest general of Nazi Germany's armed forces. His last command was the I Air Corps (I Fliegerkorps). On 8 May 1945 he was arrested and briefly held by the British forces. Peltz died on 10 August 2001 in Munich, aged 87.

Three Luftwaffe pilots and a major general were led to captivity without having been captured or surrendering. First Lieutenant (Oberleutnant) Armin Faber was taken prisoner by the British on 23 June 1942 when he landed by mistake at RAF Pembrey, near Burry Port in South Wales. Disoriented during a dogfight with RAF fighters, the German pilot had reportedly mistaken Bristol Channel for the English Channel.[154] His plane was the first Focke-Wulf Fw 190 to be captured intact by the Allies during the Second World War. Faber was led to RAF Fairwood Common for interrogation and then shipped to Canada for detention. He was released and repatriated before the end of the war due to ill health (suffering from epilepsy).

On 29 May 1942, a Luftwaffe pilot mistook British troops for Italians and landed his plane on an enemy airfield in Libya.[155] On board was Major General Ludwig Grüwell, commander of the Panzer Army Africa (Panzer Armee Afrika), who thus became a prisoner of war along with the crew. He was detained in Trent Park, north London.[156] In the summer of 1944, Grüwell was transferred a detention facility in Canada. After his repatriation, he settled in Essen, North Rhine Westphalia. Grüwell died there on 25 September 1958, aged 66.

Hans Guido Multke, a cadet (fähnrich) flying for the Luftwaffe's Jagdgeschwader 7 fighter wing, was arrested on 25 April 1945 after landing a Messerschmitt Me 262 by mistake, as he claimed later, at a Swiss air base. He was held in the neutral country until the end of the war. The aircraft was returned by the Swiss to West Germany twelve years later, on 30 August 1957. Multke died on 8 April 2004 in Munich, aged 83.

A few thousand airmen, including most of their senior commanders, also became POWs during the 1939–45 war. They were either captured during a combat mission or surrendered to Allied troops after Nazi Germany's capitulation. Colonel General (Generaloberst) Bruno Loerzer and Lieutenant General (Generalleutnant) Joseph Schmidt were both captured by Allied troops. Colonel General Otto Dessloch and Lieutenant General Alexander Holle surrendered to Allied troops in May 1945 after the German capitulation. Loerzer, a pilot credited with shooting down forty-four enemy aircraft in aerial combat (aerial victories) during the 1914–18 War, retired from the Luftwaffe in April 1945. He had commanded II Air Corps from 1942 until 1943. Loerzer was removed from his command because of the heavy losses his force suffered in Sicily. He was then assigned to the Führerreserve, a pool of temporarily unoccupied high-ranking officers awaiting new assignments. Loerzer was captured by US troops in May 1945 and held until 1948. He died twelve years later, on 23 August 1960, in Hamburg, aged 69.

Schmidt commanded Luftwaffe's 3rd Air Fleet (Luftflotte 3) and later air units during the Defence of the Reich. Between 1938 and 1942, he was head of the Luftwaffe's military intelligence (Abteilung 5). He was captured on 27 April 1945 and remained in captivity until his release on 1 April 1948. Schmidt died on 30 August 1956, in Augsburg, in Bavaria, aged 54.

Dessloch was the last commander of the 6th Air Fleet (Luftlotte 6).[157] Earlier, in September 1944, as head of the Luftwaffe's newly redesignated 3rd Air Fleet (which was named Air Command West), he carried out Hitler's order to bomb Paris. Some 200 civilians were killed in the bombing of the newly liberated French capital. Dessloch was interned by the Allies from May 1945 until his discharge in late 1947. He died on 13 May 1977 in Munich, aged 87.

Holle commanded the 3rd Air Fleet (Luftflotte 3) until September 1944, when he was sent to Denmark to command the 6th Air Korps (VI Fliegerkorps). On 8 May 1945 he surrendered to British troops and remained in captivity until February 1948. Holle died on 16 July 1978, in Munich, aged 80.

One of the first pilots to be captured by the Allies during the 1939–45 war was Colonel (Oberst) Artur von Casimir, a bomber pilot. He was a wing commander of the Luftwaffe's Kampgruppe 100. His Heinkel He IIIH-2 bomber was hit on 29 May 1940, over Troms County, northern Norway, during an attack by two RAF Hawker Hurricane fighters. He was captured and taken prisoner after making an emergency landing at Nortland. Von Casimir was handed over to the British Army by his Norwegian captors. He was detained in POW camps until 1948, when he was released and repatriated. Von Casimir died on 15 December 2005, aged 97.

Colonels Wolf-Dietrich Wilke and Werner Mölders were captured by the French Army on 5 June 1940 when their Messerschmitt Bf 109 E-4 fighters were shot down during aerial combat over northern France. As has already been mentioned, both pilots were liberated three weeks later upon the armistice with France.[158]

Second Lieutenant (Leutnant) Hans Strelow was one of the Luftwaffe pilots who committed suicide to avoid being captured by the enemy. He was credited with sixty-four aerial victories. Twenty-two-year-old Strelow was killed on 22 March 1942 after force-landing in his Bf 109 east of Mtsenk, western Russia.[159] The 51st Fighter Wing (Jagdgeschwader-51 or JG-51) was his last unit.

Second Lieutenant Herbert Bareuther was shot down over Warsaw in mid-August 1944 during combat against Soviet fighter aircraft. He bailed out injured and was captured after landing by Russian partisans.[160] He was later freed by German troops. On 30 April 1945, having resumed combat missions, 30-year-old Bareuther was killed when his aircraft was hit by Soviet flak over Pasewalk, in western Pomerania, northeastern Germany. He had accumulated fifty-five aerial victories. Bareuther was one of the squadron leaders of the Luftwaffe's 3rd Fighter Wing (Jagdgeschwader-3 or JG-3).

Captain (Hauptmann) Wolf-Dietrich Huy (forty aerial victories) was shot down in his Messerschmitt Bf 109 G-2 fighter on 29 October 1942 over El Alamein in North Africa.[161] He spent the rest of the war in British custody, detained in the Great Bitter Lake POW camp, Egypt, until his release and repatriation in March 1947. Huy died on 13 July 2003 in Gernschbach, in Baden-Württemberg, aged 85.[162]

Second Lieutenant Wilhelm Crinius was shot down on 13 January 1943 near El Kala, a seaport of Algeria close to the Tunisian border, with his Bf 109 falling into the sea. He spent twenty-four hours in the sea before being rescued by French sailors. He could claim 114 aerial victories.[163] He was detained in British POW camps for four years. Crinius died on 26 April 1997 in Sturch, Lower Saxony, aged 76.

Surrendered III

Captain (Hauptmann) Kurt Velter (sixty-three aerial victories) was the last commander of the 10th squadron of Luftwaffe's 11th Night Fighter Wing (Nachtjagdgeschwader-11). He surrendered to British forces at Schleswig air base, northern Germany, before Nazi Germany's formal capitulation. The particular air base was later used by the Royal Air Force (RAF) until 1958. Velter remained in captivity for only three months. It became known that while in captivity he wrote two reports on the role and capabilities of the Me 262 jet fighter. He was killed in a road accident four years later, on 7 March 1949, at Leck, near Flensburg, in Schleswig-Holstein, aged 33.

Two days before the German capitulation on 6 May 1945, the Flensburg-Schäferhans air base, near Kiel, in Schleswig-Holstein, was surrendered to Allied forces by Major Karl Borris. He and his men were taken to a makeshift POW camp nearby.[164] Borris, whose last command was the 26th Fighter Wing (Jagdgeschwader-26 or JG-26), accumulated forty-three aerial victories during the 1939–45 war. He was also the first pilot to fly – in August 1941 – the Focke-Wulf Fw 190. Borris died on 18 August 1981 in Bornum, a village in Saxony-Anhalt, aged 65.

Major Werner Shröer was credited with shooting down 114 Allied aircraft in combat missions. When he surrendered to British troops in Schleswig-Holstein in May 1945, he was commanding the 3rd Fighter Wing (Jagdgeschwader-3 or JG-3). Shröer remained in British custody until 7 February 1946. The first years after the war he worked as a taxi driver to support his family. Shröer died on 10 February 1985 in Ottobrunn, near Munich, aged 66.

Captain Hans Dortenmann (eighteen aerial victories) surrendered to the British on 6 May 1945. After his release he studied civil engineering and architecture and worked in construction. On 1 April 1973 Dortenmann committed suicide in Heidelberg, aged 51.

Captain Dietrich Schmidt (forty-three victories) was staffelkapitän of Luftwaffe's 11th Night Fighter Wing (Nachtjagdgeschwader-11 or NJG-11). He was arrested by the British in May 1945 in Achlesvig-Holstein, in northern Germany and was held in captivity for only three months (until August 1945). After the war, he attended Heidelberg University and eventually obtained a doctorate in chemistry. Schmidt died on 6 March 2002 in Hofheim, Hesse, aged 82.

Major Werner Hoffmann (fifty-one aerial victories) was detained by the British for three or six months in Wiedelah, near Hanover, in Lower Saxony, after his surrender in early May 1945.[165] He was the last commander of I/5th Night Fighter Wing (I/Nachtjagdgeschwader-5 or I/NJG-5). Hoffmann died on 8 July 2011 in Bremen, aged 93.

Major Heinz-Wolfgang Schnaufer was a night fighter pilot credited with 121 aerial victories. In May 1945, he surrendered to the British with his unit, the 4th Night Fighter Wing (Nachtjagdgeschwader-4 or NKG-4). He was taken to England for interrogation as the British wanted to know more about the stimulating psychoactive drugs said to be taken by Luftwaffe pilots before combat missions. Schnaufer remained in British captivity until November 1946, when he was repatriated for health reasons as he was suffering from diphtheria and scarlet fever.[166] Schnaufer was killed on 15 July 1950 in a road accident in Bordeaux, France, during a business trip, aged 28.

Major Theodor Weissenberger (208 victories) was killed aged 35 on 11 June 1950 driving a circuit at the Nürburgring in Rhineland-Palatinate, having become a racing driver after the war. He was in British captivity from May 1945 until early 1946.[167] His last unit was a squadron of the Luftwaffe's 7th Fighter Wing (Jagdgeschwader-7 or JG-7G 7).

Colonel (Oberst) Viktor Bauer (106 aerial victories) was a wing commander on EJG-1 Fighter Wing.[168] He was detained for two months after his surrender to the British Army – from May until July 1945. Bauer died on 13 December 1969 in Bad Homburg, in Hesse, aged 54.

Lieutenant Colonel (Oberstleutnant) Hans-Joachim Jabs was a night fighter pilot credited with fifty aerial victories during the 1939–45 war. After surrendering to British troops in May 1945, he was detained until 1946. He died on 26 October 2003 at Lüdenscheid, North Rhine-Westphalia, aged 85.

Captain Emil Clade (twenty-six or twenty-seven aerial victories) commanded a mission on 7 August 1942 that shot down near Alexandria, Egypt, the transport of Lieutenant General William Gott, the newly appointed commander of the British Eighth Army in North Africa. He surrendered to British troops on 8 May 1945 near Salzburg and then was handed over to the US Army for detention. Clade died on 31 May 2010, in Hambach, in Rhineland-Palatinate, aged 94.

First Lieutenant (Oberleutnant) Bernhard Vechtel was credited with 108 aerial victories and the 51st Fighter Wing (Jagdgeschwader-51 or JG-51) was his last unit. On 1 May 1945 he deserted and went to his hometown, Warendorf, near Münster, in North Rhine-Westphalia, where he was arrested by British troops a day later. Vechtel died on 21 August 1975 in Speyer, near Heidelberg, in south-west Germany, aged 55.

Second Lieutenant (Leutnant) Willy Unger (twenty-four aerial victories) was captured by US troops in April 1945. Jagdgeschwader-7 or JG-7, equipped with Me 262 jet fighters, was his last unit. He was released by the end of the month. Unger died on 25 June 2005 in Warstein, North Rhine-Westphalia, aged 85.

Major Martin Drewes (fifty-two aerial victories) was the last commander of the 1st Night Fighter Wing (Nachtjageschwader-1 or NJG -1). He was captured by US troops in May 1945 and remained in captivity until 1947. He died on 13 October 2013 in Blumenau, southern Brazil, aged 94.

Colonel (Oberst) Joachin Helbig was a bomber pilot. He surrendered to US forces in May 1945 and was released in 1946. Helbig died on 5 October 1985 in Malente, near Lübeck, aged 70, following an automobile accident while on vacation in Spain.

Austrian-born Colonel Peter Werfft (twenty-six aerial victories) surrendered to the US Army on 3 May 1945 near Saalach, in the state of Salzburg, having previously disbanded his II/27th Fighter Wing (II/Jagdgeschwader-27 or JG-27). He remained in US custody until early 1946. Werfft died on 23 July 1970 in Wien, aged 65.

Captain (Hauptmann) Alfred Grislawski (133 aerial victories) surrendered to the US Army in May 1945 and was detained in a POW camp near Salzburg. He was released in 1947. Grislawski died on 23 June 2003 in Herne, North Rhine-Westphalia, aged 83.

Major Günther Schack (174 aerial victories) commanded a squadron (IV) of the 3rd Fighter Wing (IV/Jagdgeschwader-3 or JG-3). He was shot down fifteen times, taking to his parachute four times. He surrendered to the US Army on 4 May 1945 and was detained in a POW camp at Hennsted, Schleswig-Holstein. He was released in 1946. After his release, he lived a secluded life in the Eifel Mountains, close to the German–Belgian frontier and devoted himself to philosophical research. Schack died on 14 June 2003, in Nideggon, North Rhine-Westphalia, aged 85.

Colonel Wolfgang Falck surrendered to the US Army on 3 May 1945 in Bavaria. He was released from captivity as early as June 1945. Falck died on 13 March 2007 in St Ulrich, in Tyrol, Austria, aged 96.

Colonel Werner Baumbach commanded the Luftwaffe's secret bomber wing (Kampfgeschwader-200 or KG-200). He was arrested by Allied troops in May 1948 and remained in captivity for three years. He then emigrated to Argentina, where he was employed as a test pilot. Baumbach was killed in a crash while evaluating a Lancaster bomber for the Argentinian Air Force on 20 October 1953 in Berazategui, near Buenos Aires, aged 36.

Lieutenant Colonel (Oberstleutnant) Hansgeorg Bätcher was a top bomber pilot. He commanded Kampfgerschwader-54 or KG-54, equipped with jet-powered Me 262 fighters when he surrendered to US troops in May 1945. Bätcher died on 23 April 2003 in Uelzen, Lower Saxony, aged 89.

Major Wilhelm Batz (237 aerial victories) commanded II Gruppe, based at Zeltweg air base in Austria. He surrendered to US troops and was sent to Bad Aibling, 35 miles (56km) south-west of Munich. Batz died on 11 September 1988, aged 72.

First Lieutenant (Oberleutnant) Walter Wolfrum (137 victories) surrendered to elements of US 90th Infantry Division in early May 1945.[169] After the war he became a successful aerobatics pilot. Wolfrum died on 26 August 2010 in Schwabach, near Nuremberg, aged 87.

Handed over

Several German pilots, after being captured by or being surrendered to the US Army, were handed over to the Russians because of their previous combat activities on the Eastern Front. Colonel (Oberst) Hermann Graf (200 aerial victories) surrendered to US troops on 8 May 1945. He was eventually handed over to the Russians. He remained in Soviet captivity until 1949. Graf was among the first German military officers to be repatriated from the USSR. He died on 4 November 1988 in Engen, Baden-Württemberg, aged 76.

Major Adolf Borchers (132 aerial victories) was almost captured by the British on 31 August 1940 when he ditched his Bf 109 E-1 in the Thames Estuary, in south-east England, during the Battle of Britain. He was rescued by the Germans and continued to fly combat missions, mostly on the Russian front. In early May 1945, when he surrendered to US troops at Pisek/Brün (in the present-day Czech Republic), he was commanding a squadron (III) of the 52nd Fighter Wing (III/Jagdgeschwader-52 or JG-52). On 24 May he was handed over to Russian forces and remained in Soviet custody until 1955. Borchers died on 8 February 1996 in Oberstaufen-Steibis, a municipality of Bavarian Swabia, aged 82.

Captain (Hauptmann) Rudolf Trenkel was credited 138 aerial victories.[170] On 16 October 1944, while commanding a squadron (II of the 52nd Fighter Wing II/Jagdgeschwader-52 or JG-52), based at the time in Krakow, in German-occupied Poland, he was shot down. He survived by bailing out.[171] He surrendered to elements of the US 90th Infantry Division, near Pisek, and was held at Strakonice POW camp (in present-day Czech Republic). There, he married his fiancée, Ida Sehnal, who was among the civilian refugees. On 15 May 1945 he was handed over by the Americans to the Red Army. After four weeks, he was repatriated from the USSR due to the wounds received in his last combat (15 March 1945) when he bailed out from his stricken Bf 109 G-14. Trenkel died on 26 April 2001 in Vienna, aged 83.

Captain Eberhard von Boremski (100 aerial victories) surrendered to US troops in May 1945. He was extradited to Czechoslovakia and from there to the USSR. He remained in Soviet captivity until 1955. Boremski was killed in a flying accident on 16 December 1963 in Hamburg, aged 49.

Lieutenant Colonel (Oberstleutnant) Kurt Bühligen, Major (Major) Hans Hahn, First Lieutenant (Oberleutnant) Edmund Rossmann and Second Lieutenant (Leutnant) Otto Würfel were four Luftwaffe pilots who were captured by the Red Army during combat missions. Bühligen (122 aerial victories) was commanding a squadron (IV) of the 2nd Fighter Wing (IV/Jagdgeschwader-2 or JG-2) when he was taken prisoner by Soviet troops. He was released and repatriated in 1950. Bühligen died on 11 August 1985 in Nidda, near Frankfurt am Main, aged 67.

Hahn (108 aerial victories) was captured on 21 February 1943 near Staraya Russa, south of Veliky Novgorod, in western Russia, after making a forced landing during combat against Soviet fighters. He remained in Russian custody until late 1950. At home following his repatriation he was welcomed by his son. His wife had left him for another man. Hahn died of cancer on 18 December 1982 in Munich, aged 68.

Rossmann (ninety-three aerial victories) was captured by Soviet troops on 9 July 1943 when he landed at Obeyan, near Kursk, to rescue a fellow pilot, who had force-landed behind enemy lines.[172] Rossmann died on 4 April 2005 in Krefeld, near Düsseldorf, aged 87.

Würfel (seventy-nine aerial victories) was taken prisoner on 23 February 1944, after landing with his parachute near Rohachow in present-day Byelorussia. A while earlier his Fw 190 fighter had collided in mid-air with another Luftwaffe aircraft. He died from typhus in POW camp 280/5, located near Stalino, in eastern Ukraine, on 22 December 1944, aged 24.[173]

First Lieutenant Franz-Josef Beerbroke, whose mother was Russian, was credited with 117 aerial victories as a Luftwaffe fighter pilot. He was captured by the Red Army in November 1941 when his Bf 109 F-2 aircraft suffered engine failure, after being hit by enemy fire, near Smolensk, 220 miles (360km) south-south-west of Moscow, and force-landed. He was released and repatriated in May 1945. Beerbroke died on 13 December 2004, in Olfen, in North Rhine-Westphalia, aged 84.

Brigadier General (Generalmajor) Ernst Bormann, a bomber pilot, was the last commander of Luftwaffe's Kampfgeschwader-76 or KG-76. He surrendered to the Red Army in May 1945 and discharged on 9 October 1955. Bormann died on 1 August 1960 in Düsseldorf, aged 62 – weeks after earning a doctorate from a university.

Women pilots

Beate Köstlin, Luftwaffe's only female pilot, was arrested and held briefly for interrogation by the British Army in late April 1945 after landing in Leck, north Friesland, in Schleswig-Holstein. She had just escaped from an embattled Berlin, flying a Siebel Fh 104 aircraft and had on board her wounded son and his nanny. Her (first) husband, Hans-Jürgen Uhse, a stunt pilot instructor, had been killed in an air crash in Berlin days earlier. Köstlin was trained as an aviator in 1937. During the war, she served in a Luftwaffe aircraft ferrying unit (Überführungsgeschwader-1), delivering military planes from war factories to various, even front-line, squadrons. In 1944 she was promoted to captain (hauptmann). In the post-war period, Köstlin was involved in business. In 1962 she opened what was considered to be the first sex shop in the world.[174] Köstlin died of pneumonia in a clinic in St Gallen, north-eastern Switzerland, on 18 July 2001, aged 81.

Hanna Reitsch was arrested after the German capitulation and remained in US custody for eighteen months. She was a prominent aviator and a Luftwaffe test pilot. She was also the first female to fly helicopters and jet-powered planes.[175] Reitsch, who was never married, died of a heart attack on 24 August 1979 in Frankfurt-am-Main, Hesse, aged 67. There have been claims that she committed suicide by swallowing a pill that had been given to her by Hitler in the Führerbunker in late April 1945.

Paratrooper commanders

Of the senior commanders of Nazi Germany's paratrooper (fallschirmjäger) forces, an elite branch of the Luftwaffe, Lieutenant General (Generalleutnant) Wilhelm Süssmann, was killed in action on 20 May 1941 during the Battle of Crete, and Major General (General der Fallschirmtruppe) Bruno Bräuer was executed after the war, having been convicted of crimes against humanity. Furthermore, Lieutenant General Alfred Sturm became a POW twice during the 1939–45 war; Major General Hermann-Bernhard Ramcke was captured by US troops while trying to evade capture in northern France and Lieutenant General Wolfgang Erdmann committed suicide while in British captivity; the rest were forced to surrender, mostly to US and British troops.

Süssmann was the commanding officer of the 7th Air Division (7. Flieger-Division), as the 1st Parachute Regiment was named from 1938 until 1943.[176]

On 21 May 1941 Sturm, then a colonel (oberst) commanding the 2nd Parachute Regiment, was captured by Allied forces in the village of Pigi, near Rethymno, for ten days, during the battle of Crete. He later led an elite force in the war in North Africa. On 23 April 1945 Sturm, now a lieutenant general (generalleutnant) commanding a force in the mountain village of Thale in Saxony-Anhalt, in Central Germany, surrendered to British troops. He remained in captivity, mostly detained in Trent Park, north London, until 5 June 1947. Sturm died on 8 March 1962 in Detmold, North Rhine-Westphalia, aged 74.

Erdmann, who commanded the 7th Parachute Division, surrendered to British troops in May 1945. He committed suicide on 5 September 1947 in Münster, North Rhine-Westphalia, while in British custody, aged 47.

Colonel General (Generaloberst) Kurt Arthur Student was the founder of the German paratrooper forces and their most senior commander throughout the war.[177] He was involved in battles in the Netherlands (1940), Crete (1941) and Russia (1942), as well as in Italy and in Holland in 1944. On 13 July 1943 Student was put in charge of the First Parachute Army. On 28 May 1945 he was captured by British troops in Schleswig-Holstein (according to other sources, he surrendered). Student was transferred to Island Farm or Special Camp 11, in Bridgend, South Wales. On 31 March 1946 he was transferred to the London Detention Cage for interrogation. He was accused of mistreatment and murder of British and Commonwealth POWs as well as of crimes committed by German paratroopers in Crete in May 1941.[178] Student was brought to trial and sentenced to five years' imprisonment, but was given an early discharge in 1948 for medical reasons.[179] He died on 1 July 1978 in Lemgo, a town near Bielefeld, in North Rhine-Westphalia, aged 88.

On 10 March 1945, Major General Alfred Schlemann, who succeeded Student in command of the First Parachute Army, ordered his forces to retreat after the Battle of the Reichswald in North Rhine-Westphalia. Eleven days later, he was wounded in an Allied air attack at Haltern-am-See and transferred to a hospital. From 8 May 1945, when he was arrested by British troops, until his release from Island Farm or Special Camp, in England, and repatriation, on 22 March 1952, he was a prisoner of war. Schlemann died on 24 January 1986, aged 91 in Ahlten, a village in the Hanover region of northern Germany.

Lieutenant General Hellmuth Böhlke commanded the First Parachute Army until 16 April 1945, when he was transferred to the Führerreserve, a pool of temporarily unoccupied high-ranking officers awaiting new assignments. He was detained by the Allies for two years after the German capitulation. Böhlke died on 8 April 1956 in Bad Mergentheim, in Baden-Württemberg, aged 63.[180]

Major General Erich Straube was the next and last commander of the First Parachute Army. The force under his command, which lasted only ten days (from 28 April to 8 May 1945), had suffered heavy casualties between 31 August and 5 September 1944 in the vicinity of Mons, Belgium. Some 3,500 Germans were killed in that battle and a further 25,000 were taken prisoner. Strauber managed to escape. He was later captured and held in British custody. Straube died on 31 March 1971, in Osterode/Harz, in Lower Saxony, aged 84.

Major General Richard Heidrich was the last commander of the I Parachute Corps (I Fallschirmkorps). He assumed command on 7 February 1945 and led his troops in the battle of Bologna, northern Italy, between 9 and 21 April 1945. On 3 May he and the remnant of his troops surrendered to Allied (mostly British) forces in the Trento–Bolzano–Beluno area. He remained in captivity until July 1947. Heindrich died five months later, on 22 December 1947, in Bergedorf, a district of Hamburg, aged 51.

Major General Eugen Meindl assumed command of the II Parachute Corps (II Fallschirmkorps) on 5 November 1943. His troops had been annihilated in the Falaise Pocket by 21 August 1944, after the Normandy landings. Meindl was captured by US forces at Grossbrokendorf, near Schleswig, on 5 May 1945. He was then detained by the British Army until September 1947. Meindl died on 24 January 1951, either in Donaueschingen, in Baden-Württemberg, or in Munich, aged 58.

Of the divisional commanders, Lieutenant General von Heyking surrendered to Allied troops as early as September 1944. Brigadier General Heilmann did the same in March 1945. Lieutenant General Wolfgang Erdmann committed suicide as a POW some sixteen months after his surrender to British troops.

The rest of Hitler's senior paratrooper commanders surrendered at the end of the hostilities in May 1945, with the exception of Ramcke, who was caught by Allied troops in September 1944 while trying to evade capture. Ramcke commanded the 2nd Parachute Division until early August 1944, when he assumed command of the garrison of Brest (Fortress Brest), in northern France's Brittany region. A fanatical Nazi, Ramcke refused to surrender the port city and the local naval base to the Allied forces as he was determined to carry out Hitler's order to fight to the last man. On 18 September 1944 most of the surviving German troops were forced to surrender. Ramcke attempted to escape from Brest but was captured a day later. He was detained in Trent Park, north London, initially and later in the United States (Camp Clinton and Camp Shelby, both in the state of Mississippi).[181] In March 1946, Ramcke was transferred as a prisoner to Europe – initially to Belgium, then to England (London Cage) and finally to France, where he was brought to trial for the execution of French civilians, the looting of civilian property and the intentional destruction of houses and infrastructure in Brest. Also, in Crete in 1941 he had ordered his men to attack civilians once the mutilated bodies of German paratroopers were found in their area.[182] On 21 March 1951, Ramcke was sentenced to five years and six months' imprisonment. He was released after three months either on account of his age or due to having already been held in French captivity for five years before the verdict.[183] Ramcke died on 4 July 1978 in Kappeln, in Schleswig-Holstein, aged 79.

Brigadier General (Generalmajor) Hans Kroh, the commanding officer of the 2nd Parachute Division, was appointed as Ramske's second-in-command on 11 August 1944. He was taken prisoner a month later, on 18 September, when Brest fell into Allied hands. He remained in US captivity until the summer of 1948, when he was released and repatriated.[184] Kroh died on 18 July 1967 in Braunsweig, Lower Saxony, aged 60.

Brigadier General (Generalmajor) Hans Korte commanded the 1st Parachute Division until February 1944.[185] When he surrendered to the British Army, in May 1945, he was commanding the 2nd Air Division (2. Flieger-Division). He remained in British captivity until October 1947. Korte died on 8 April 1990, aged 90. Brigadier General Karl-Lothar Schulz replaced Korte as commander of the 1st Parachute Division. He led his troops in the fight against Allied forces on the Eastern Front, as well as in the Battle of Anzio in Italy in April 1944. On 2 May 1945 he surrendered to the US Army in northern Italy.[186] He had just crossed the Po River and was withdrawing towards the Alpine mountains. He was released two years later, on 17 October 1947. Schulz died on 20 September 1972 in Wiesbaden, in the state of Hesse, aged 65.

Brigadier General Sebastian-Ludwig Heilmann led the 5th Parachute Division in combat in north Italy and in the Ardennes, Belgium. He was captured by the US Army in March 1945 on the Eifel Plateau, on the German–Belgian border. His division surrendered in mid-March 1945 near Nürburgring, in Rhineland-Palatinate. The rest of the division surrendered in the Ruhr Pocket one month later. He was released in 1947. Heilmann died on 26 October 1959 in Kempten, Bavaria, aged 56.

Lieutenant General (Generalleutnant) Rüdiger von Heyking commanded the 6th Parachute Division from May 1944.[187] He was captured in Mons four months later, on 4 September 1944, during the German retreat from Belgium. He spent part of his captivity in Trent Park, north London. On 1 March 1945 von Heyking was transferred to the Soviet authorities, accused over crimes committed by his troops on the Eastern Front between September 1942 and November 1943 when he was commanding the 6th Luftwaffe Field Division (Luftwaffen Feld-Division.6). He was detained in Russia until his release and repatriation in 1955. Von Heyking died on 18 February 1956 in Bad Godesberg, in southern North Rhine-Westphalia, aged 52.

Forty-seven-year-old Lieutenant General Wolfgang Erdmann, the last commander of the 7th Parachute Division, committed suicide on 5 September 1946, while in British captivity in Münster, North Rhine-Westphalia. He had surrendered his troops in Oldenburg, Lower Saxony, on 8 May 1945.[188] The 10th Parachute Division was raised in March 1945 and fought in Austria and Moravia. Lieutenant General Gustav Wilke, the divisional commander, surrendered to the Red Army in May 1945. He remained in Soviet captivity until mid-1955. Wilke died on 14 March 1977, in Oberstdorf, North Rhine-Westphalia, aged 79.

All the officers who commanded Luftwaffe's 1st Parachute-Panzer Division *Hermann Göring* were detained after their surrender to Allied troops in early May 1945, including Major General Walther von Axtheln, who was replaced as divisional commander as early as May 1940. After the German surrender, he was detained by the British until 1947. Axtheln died on 6 January 1972 in Traunstein, in Bavaria, aged 78.

The division's next commander, Major General Paul Conrath, left on 15 April 1944 to become inspector of the parachute forces. After the war, he was arrested by the US Army and briefly remained in captivity. Conrath died on 15 January 1979, in Hamburg, aged 82.

The division's next commander was Brigadier General (Generalmajor) Hanns Horst von Necker, who held the post until 8 February 1945.[189] He was interned by the British from 1945 until 1947. Von Necker died on 27 February 1979 in Bad Münstereifel, North Rhine-Westphalia, aged 77.

Brigadier General Max Lemke then headed the division for eighty-eight days (9 February–9 May 1945) and was the last commander of Hermann Göring's favourite unit. After the German surrender, he remained in Allied custody from 12 May until 18 June 1945. Lemke died on 29 May 1985, aged 90.

Civilian massacres I

After Nazi Germany's capitulation, Colonel General (Generaloberst) Kurt Student was captured by the British to answer charges that he ordered the murder of Allied POWs by elements of his XI Air Corps and reprisals against civilians during the German invasion of Crete. In May 1947, he was found guilty of the execution of British and Commonwealth prisoners by his forces and was sentenced to five years' imprisonment. One year later, he was given a medical discharge and was released from prison. He was never tried for crimes against Greek civilians committed in Crete. Greece's demand, in September 1947, to have Student extradited for the murder of 3,000 Cretans in 1941 was declined.

Major General (General der Flieger) Alexander Andrae, who took over as commander-in-chief of the German forces in occupied Crete, was extradited to Greece after the war. He was tried in Athens and sentenced to four life terms. In 1951 his sentence was commuted by King Paul of the Hellenes to four years' imprisonment. Andrae was released from prison one year later.

Two major generals, Bruno Bräuer and F.-W. Müller were convicted as war criminals after the German capitulation and executed. General der Fallschirmtruppe Bräuer was the first German officer to be trained in parachute drops. He commanded Nazi Germany's first parachute battalion, the Fallschirmjäger Battalion (the Parachute Soldiers Battalion) when it was formally raised in 29 January 1936. Bräuer led parachute units into battle in Norway, the Netherlands, Crete and on the Eastern Front. In January 1945, he suffered a nervous collapse near Breslau, the present-day Wrocław, in south-western Poland, when his 9th Parachute Division suffered heavy losses. As a result, Bräuer was relieved of his command and hospitalised. Four months later, he was captured by British troops and remained in custody until his extradition to Greece to be put on trial for ordering, as commander of Crete, the deportation of about 100 Greek Jews.[190] He was sentenced to death unfairly, according to the author and historian Anthony Beevor.[191] Fifty-four-year-old Bräuer was executed in Athens by firing squad on 20 May 1947, the sixth anniversary of the German invasion of Crete.

He died along with Major General F.-W. Müller, an Army officer who had replaced Bräuer as commander of Fortress Crete (Festung Kreta) on 1 July 1944. At the time, he was commanding the 22nd Air Landing Division (22. Luftlande-Division). Müller was the last commander of the Fourth Army when he surrendered to Russian troops in East Prussia in May 1945.[192] After the war he was extradited to Greece to be tried for the massacres of hostages as reprisals. Müller was also accused of the murder of a hundred Italian Army officers who were captured by or surrendered to his troops during the Dodecanese Campaign (8 September–22 November 1943) following their country's decision to sign an armistice with Allies on 3 September 1943. Müller was sentenced to death and executed by firing squad in Athens on 20 May 1947, aged 49.[193] He was also accused of the Viannos massacre. Between 14 and 16 September 1941, more than 500 civilians were massacred by German troops in this small township near Heraklion, in central Crete. Almost two weeks later, on 8 October 1941, thirty (mostly male) civilians of the village of Kallikratis in south-western Crete were murdered by a force led by Friedrich Schubert, a Greek-speaking sergeant (oberfeldwebel) of the Wehrmacht. This force, answerable to no one, was raised to suppress local resistance activity. The force committed numerous atrocities in Crete until early 1944 and in northern Greece later on. After the German capitulation, Schubert was arrested in Greece and on 5 August 1947 was brought to trial for war crimes and crimes against humanity. He was found guilty of 271 murders and several other crimes including arsons, rapes, lootings, etc. He was sentenced to death twenty-seven times and several years of imprisonment. Schubert was executed by firing squad on 22 October 1947, aged 50, in Eptapyrgio, a medieval fortress in Thessaloniki used as a penitentiary facility since the 1890s.

Major General (General der Gebirgstruppe) Karl von Le Suire was responsible for the massacre of civilians at Kalavryta in Greece. On 13 December 1943 firing squads of his 117th Jäger Division (117. Jäger-Division) murdered 693 male inhabitants of this small town in the northern Peloponnese in reprisal for the execution of seventy-seven captured German soldiers by Greek (leftist) resistance fighters. On July 1944 von Le Suire assumed the command of the XXXXIX Mountain Corps that was deployed on the Eastern Front. He surrendered to the Red Army on 8 May 1945. Von Le Suire was never tried for the Kalavryta massacre as the Russians refused to have him extradited. He died of heart failure in a POW camp near Stalingrad on 18 June 1954, aged 55.[194]

On 10 June 1944, elements of the 4th SS Polizei Panzergrenadier Division murdered 228 men, women and children in Distomo, a small village near Delphi on the Greek mainland, during anti-partisan operations.[195] No one was punished for this massacre after the war as the man who ordered it, SS-Brigadier (SS-Brigadeführer) Karl Schümers, the divisional commander, was killed two months later (on 10 June), when his car drove over a landmine near Arta in north-western Greece.

Civilian massacres II

SS-Lieutenant General (SS-Obergruppenführer) Jürgen Stroop served as the SS and police commander in German-occupied Poland and Greece. On 10 May 1945 he surrendered to US troops in the of village Rottau, near Stendal in north-eastern Germany. He was convicted of the murder of nine US prisoners of war near Wiesbaden, in central-eastern Germany, between October 1944 and March 1945. He was the regional commander of the local SS forces from the autumn of 1943. Stroop was handed over by the US Army to the Polish post-war authorities to be tried for his role in the suppression of the Ghetto Uprising in Warsaw, in April–May 1943 and for the mass murder of Polish civilians. On 23 July 1951 he was convicted of war crimes and crimes against humanity and sentenced to death by hanging. He was executed at Mokotów prison, in Warsaw, on 6 March 1942, aged 56.

Forty-six-year-old Franz Konrad, an Austrian-born SS-senior lieutenant (SS-obersturmführer) was also executed that day. He had been convicted for his part, as SS and police chief (Polizeiführer) in Warsaw, in the liquidation of the Warsaw ghetto that led to the murder of more than 50,000 Jews and the deportation of hundreds of thousands more to death camps. Civilian massacres were also carried out by Waffen-SS and Wehrmacht troops in Wola, near Warsaw (40,000–50,000 dead), Ochota (Rzézz Ochoty), a Warsaw district (10,000 dead), Bydgoszcz, in northern Poland (1,200–1,400 dead) and in other parts of the country during the German occupation.

GERMANS

Several high-ranking commanders of the German Army and the SS were involved in the mass murder of 13,000 Polish Home Army fighters and up to 20,000 civilians in the sixty-three-day Warsaw Uprising (1 August–2 October 1944).[196] None of them were convicted for these atrocities. Field Marshals Walter Model and Ritter von Greim committed suicide before being brought to trial. Lieutenant General (Generalleutnant) Rainer Stahel died of a heart attack on 30 September 1945 at the Voikovo prison camp in the Soviet Union, aged 63.

Lieutenant General of the Waffen-SS (SS-Obergruppenführer) Heinz Rainefarth, who commanded the XVIII SS Corps, was arrested by the British in May 1945 for war crimes committed by his troops in Warsaw. He was eventually acquitted by a Hamburg court because of a lack of evidence. Having testified as a witness at the Nuremberg Trial, Rainefarth seems to represent another case of selective prosecution by the Allies. He was not extradited to Poland and died on 7 May 1979, aged 75.

SS-Lieutenant General (SS-Obergruppenführer) Erich von dem bach Zelewski was never tried for his role in the brutal suppression of the Warsaw Uprising, probably in exchange for his testimony against his former superiors at the Nuremberg Trials. Between February and May 1945, he commanded a corps of Army Group Vistula. He was released from prison in 1947. Zelewski was convicted later by a West German court for the murder of a political opponent back in the 1930s. He died in his cell in a Munich prison on 8 March 1972 weeks after his 73rd birthday. His son, Eberhard, emigrated to the United States and eventually joined the US Army.[197]

According to German historian Jochen Böhler, the Wehrmacht also mass murdered at least 3,000 Polish prisoners of war during the 1939 campaign.[198] In his words, the campaign was for Nazi Germany a prelude to a war of extermination. On 3–4 November 1943 up to 43,000 Jews were massacred by SS troops in the Lublin region of German-occupied Poland. They were taken from the Majdanek, the Poniatowa and the Trawniki concentration camps and executed. SS-Lieutenant General Jakob Sporrenberg, who was SS and Police commander in Lublin at the time, organised and carried out the operation that is also known as the Aktion Erntferst massacre.[199] In May 1945 he was captured by British troops in Oslo and transferred to the MI19 Interrogation Centre in Kensington Palace Gardens, also known as the London Cage. In October 1946 Sporrenberg was extradited to Poland to be tried for crimes against humanity. He was found guilty by a Polish court in Warsaw and sentenced to death. Sporrenberg was hanged on 6 December 1952 in Mokotow prison in the Polish capital, aged 50.

SS-Lieutenant General Friedrich Jeckeln was taken prisoner by the Red Army in Halbe, near Brandenburg, in Lower Saxony, on 28 April 1945. He was tried as a war criminal in Riga, the capital of the Latvian SSR, by a Soviet military tribunal. Jeckeln was charged with ordering and organising the death of at least 100,000 Jews, Romani and other civilians in the German-occupied former Baltic States. He was in charge of the SS-Mobile Killing Squads 'C' (SS-Einsatzgruppen 'C'), which were involved in the Babi Yar (33,771 dead) and Rumbula (25,000 dead) and Kamianets-Podilskyi (23,000 dead) massacres in the summer of 1941.[200] Babi Yar is on the northern edge of Kiev in Ukraine. Rumbula is a forested area close to Riga and the Kamianets-Podilsky is in western Ukraine. Jeckelen was convicted for these massacres and sentenced to death. He was hanged in front of 4,000 spectators, at Uzvaras Laukums (Victory Square) in Riga on 3 February 1946, aged 51.

Also tried over these massacres were SS-Brigadier (SS-Brigadeführer) Otto Rasch, SS-Brigadier Kurt Eberhard and SS-Colonel (SS-Standartenführer) Paul Blobel. They were indicted of war crimes and crimes against humanity. Blobel was sentenced to death and hanged on 7 June 1951 at Landsberg prison in south-western Bavaria, aged 56. Eberhard committed suicide in his cell in Stuttgart prison on 8 September 1947, aged 72.[201] Rasch, who commanded the SS-Mobile Killing Units, was indicted of war crimes in September 1947. Five months later, on 5 February 1948, he was released from prison on health grounds. He was suffering from Parkinson's disease and dementia. Rasch died nine months later, on 1 November 1948, in Wehrstedt, Lower Saxony, aged 56.

Odessa, with at least 50,000 dead, was the largest single massacre committed by Axis troops during the 1939–45 war. It was carried out between 22 and 24 October 1941 in this region of south-western Ukraine by Romanian troops.[202] Erich Koch was the chief Nazi civil official in eastern Poland and after the German invasion of the Soviet Union he was named Reich Commissioner (Reichskommissar) for Ukraine and the Baltic States.[203] After the German capitulation he lived incognito for four years in the British occupation zone of Germany.[204] In May 1949, Koch was arrested by British troops and eight months later he was extradited to Poland. He was held in Warsaw's Mokotów Prison for eight years. On 19 October 1958 Koch was charged for taking part in the killing or deportation of more than 300,000 Poles and Polish Jews from 1939 to 1944.[205] On 9 March 1959, he was sentenced to death by the district court of Warsaw. Koch was never tried for the crimes committed in Ukraine, where 4 million civilians died through starvation or execution during the Nazi occupation and another 2½ million were deported to Germany to work as slave labourers.[206] The death sentence was commuted to life imprisonment. Koch escaped the death penalty because of a Polish law barring the execution of a prisoner in ill health. Despite his health issues, he lived until he was 90. He died in his cell in Barcewo Prison, on 12 November 1986.[207]

Mobile Killing Squads

Twenty-four commanders of Mobile Killing Squads (Einsatzgruppen) of the SS were tried by a US military tribunal (II-A) in the Palace of Justice (Justizpalast) in Nuremberg for war crimes committed from 1941 to 1945 in Nazi-occupied territories of Eastern Europe. They were convicted of the murder of about 2½ million people, including Jews, Romani, partisans and commissars of the Red Army.[208] On 10 April 1948 they received fourteen death sentences among other judgments. Two defendants were sentenced to life imprisonment, five received lesser sentences, one committed suicide, one died in prison and another was released on health grounds. Only four executions were carried out.[209] The rest were reduced to lesser sentences. Of those sentenced to death, five were executed by hanging on 7 June 1951 in the courtyard of the Landsberg Prison.[210] They were SS-Lieutenant General (SS-Generalleutnant) Otto Ohlendorf, SS-Brigadier General (SS-Generalmajor) Erich Naumann, SS-Colonel (SS-Standartenführer) Paul Blobel and SS-Lieutenants (SS-Obersturmbannführer) Werner Braune and Eduard Strauch.

Ohlendorf was an economist by education and a Leipzig and Göttingen Universities graduate. He had been a member of the Nazi Party since 1925. Ohlendorf had commanded Mobile Killing Squad D (Einsatzgruppe D) since June 1941.[211] His men perpetrated mass murder in Moldova, south Ukraine and north Caucasus, primarily by shooting, and had an integral role in the implementation of the 'Final Solution to the Jewish Question' (Die Endlösung der Judenfrage) in the Nazi-occupied Eastern Europe.[212] Ohlendorf was arrested by British troops on 23 May 1945 in Lüneburg, 30 miles (50km) east of Hamburg, in Lower Saxony.[213] Justifying the murder of children by his troopers, he stated: 'The children were people who would grow up and surely being the children of parents who had been killed, they would constitute a danger no smaller than their parents ...'[214] He spent three years in detention before the execution of his death sentence, aged 44.[215]

Naumann commanded the Mobile Killing Squad D (Einsatzgruppe D) from November 1941 until February or March 1943. In a report dated 15 December 1942 it was recorded that Naumann's troopers had shot a total of 134,000 people in western Russia. From September 1943 to July 1944 he commanded the security police in the Netherlands. He was executed as war criminal, aged 46.

Blobel studied architecture and worked as an architect from 1924 until 1931. In December 1931 he became a member of the Nazi Party and joined the SS (Schutzstaffel). As a commanding officer of the Mobile Killing Squad C (Einsatztruppen C) Blobel was involved in war crimes in Ukraine, including the Zhytomyr, Bila Tserkva and Babi Yar massacres carried out in August and September 1941. On 13 January 1942 he was relieved of his command for health reasons due to alcoholism. In October 1944 he led an anti-partisan unit in Yugoslavia. More than 59,018 killings were attributed to Blobel during the Einsatzgruppe Trial, although he claimed he had personally killed 10,000 to 15,000 people. He was hanged, aged 56.

Braune was sentence to death in Nuremberg for his involvement as the commanding officer of the Special Detachment 11a (Einsatzkommando 11a) of Einsatztruppen D in the murder of 14,000 people, mostly Jews, in southern Ukraine and in Crimea from 11 to 13 December 1941. He was hanged, aged 42.

Belgian-born Strauch was sentenced to death during the Einsatzgruppen Trial in Nuremberg and then handed over to the Belgian authorities to be tried for crimes committed in Belgium. He was convicted again as charged and sentenced to death but was not executed after being diagnosed as mentally ill. Strauch died in Belgian custody in a hospital in Uccle, in central Belgium, on 15 September 1955.

SS-Colonels (SS-Standartenführer) Walter Blume, Martin Sandberger, Willi Seibert and Eugen Steimle, SS-Lieutenant Colonels (SS-Obersturmbannführer) Ernst Biberstein, Walter Haensch and Adolf Ott, SS-Major (SS-Sturmbannführer) Waldemar Klingelhöffer and SS-Senior Lieutenant (SS-Obersturmführer) Hans Schubert also received the death penalty during the Einsatztruppen Trial but their sentences were commuted to prison terms. Life imprisonment became the sentence for Sandberger, Biberstein, Ott and Klingelhöffer. Blume received a commuted sentence of twenty-five years, twenty for Steimle, fifteen for Seibert and Schubert ten years.

Blume commanded Sonderkommando 7a of Einsatzgruppen B during the German invasion of the Soviet Union. He was captured by US troops in Salzburg in 1945 and tried in Nuremberg for the murder of 996 Jews by his troops in Belarus and Russia in 1941. Blume was released earlier as a result of a 1951 amnesty. He was released from Landsberg Prison in 1955 after serving only ten years of his sentence. In 1968 Blume was arrested again and tried before a state court in Bremen for the deportation of Greek

Jews to Auschwitz. The charges were dropped on 29 January 1971. Blume died on 13 November 1974 in Dortmund, aged 68.

Sandberger obtained a doctorate in 1935 after studying at the universities of Munich, Cologne, Freiburg and Tübingen. A year later he joined the SS. In 1941 he led Sonderkommando 1a of Einsatztruppen B that committed the mass murder of Jews in Latvia and Estonia. Sandberger admitted during the Einsatztruppen Trial to the killing of 300 to 350 people. He was also accused of the deportation of Italian Jews from Verona, in northern Italy, to Auschwitz. In early 1958, his sentence of life imprisonment was converted into a ten-year prison term. He was released from Landsberg Prison on 9 May 1958. Sandberger died on 30 March 2010 in Stuttgart, in Baden Württemberg, aged 98.

Seibert was the deputy commander of the Mobile Death Squad D (Einsatztruppen D). His death sentence for war crimes was commuted to fifteen years in prison. Seibert was released on 9 May 1958 and died in 2010.

Haensch had obtained a doctorate in Law when he joined the SS in 1935. He led Sonderkommando 4 of the Mobile Death Squad C (Einsatztruppen C) that carried out mass killings in the Ukrainian SSR. In Nuremberg on 10 April 1948 Haensch was found guilty of war crimes and sentenced to death by hanging. His sentence was commuted to life imprisonment and three years later, in January 1951, to fifteen years.[216] Haensch was released in 1955. He died on 21 April 1994 in Engelskirchen, 40km east of Cologne, aged 80.

Ott was involved in war crimes in German-occupied Russia and Belarus in 1941 as commander of Sonderkommando 7a of the Mobile Death Squad B (Einsatztruppen B). He was sentenced to death in 1948. His sentence was commuted to life imprisonment in January 1951. Ott was released from Landsberg Prison seven years later. He died on 10 October 1973 in Inzel, aged 80.

Schubert was an adjutant of Ohlendorf on the staff of Einsatzgruppen D. In December 1941 he organised the killing of approximately 700 to 800 people (mostly Jews and Gypsies) in Simferopol in the Crimean Peninsula. He was the youngest of the twenty-four defendants in the Einsatzgruppen Trial, during which he was accused as an accomplice to the murder of 90,000 people. His death sentence was commuted to ten years' imprisonment but he was released from Landsberg Prison in December 1951. Schubert died on 17 August 1987 in Bad Oldesloe, in Schleswig-Holstein in northern Germany, aged 73.

In 1935 Russian-born Klingelhöffer was an opera singer. In 1941 he was assigned to Mobile Death Squad B (Einsatzgruppen B) as an interpreter and months later he was in charge of a sub-unit, Vorkommando Moscow. At Nuremberg he was convicted of being responsible for the killing of fifty to sixty people between 28 September and 26 October 1941 in German-occupied parts of the Soviet Union including Smolensk and Tatarsk in Russia and Mstislavl in Belarus. On 10 April 1948 Klingelhöffer was sentenced to death by hanging but his sentence was commuted to life imprisonment. On 12 December 1956 he was released from Landsberg Prison on parole. Klingelhöffer died on 18 January 1977 in Villingen-Schwennin, Baden-Württemberg, aged 76.

SS-Brigadier (SS-Brigadeführer) Heinz Jost and SS-Senior Lieutenant (SS-Obersturmbannführer) Gustav Adolf Nosske were sentenced to life imprisonment during the Einsatztruppen Trial.

Jost studied Law and Economics at the universities of Giessen, in the state of Hesse, and Munich. In 1928 he became a member of the Nazi Party and, after working as a lawyer for four years, he joined the SS. He saw combat as a low-ranking officer during the German invasion of Poland in 1939 and then commanded Mobile Killing Squad A (Einsatzgruppe A) until May 1944. In January 1945, Jost retired from the SS with a pension and three months later he was arrested by Allied troops in Gardelegen, Saxony-Anhalt, and brought to trial in Nuremberg for crimes committed by Einsatztruppen A under his command in the Baltic States and in Belarus. Found guilty as charged, Jost was sentenced to life imprisonment. The sentence, reviewed by the Peck Panel, was commuted to ten years' imprisonment. He was discharged from Landsberg Prison earlier, in 1951. Jost died on 12 November 1964 in Bensheim, in the state of Hesse, aged 60.

Nosske was an SS-Lieutenant Colonel (Obersturmbannführer). He commanded death squads of Einsatzgruppe D of the SS that committed many atrocities against the civilian population, including Jews and Roma, in German-occupied parts of Russia and Ukraine. He was tried in 1948 in Nuremberg for crimes against humanity and sentenced to life imprisonment. He was released from Landsberg Prison early, on 12 December 1951. He died on 9 August 1986 in Dusseldorf aged 83.

SS-Brigadier (SS-Brigadeführer) Erwin Schulz was convicted during the Einsatztruppen Trial of presiding over the execution of ninety to 100 people in Lviv, in the Ukrainian SSR, in July 1941 in his capacity as commander of Einsatzcommando 5a of the Mobile Death Squad C (Einsatztruppen C).[217] He was sentenced to twenty years in prison but this was commuted to fifteen years in January 1951. On 9 January 1954 Schulz was released on parole from Landsberg Prison. He died on 11 November 1981 in Bremen, northern Germany, aged 80.

SS-Major Waldemar von Radetzky (sentenced to twenty years), SS-Major Lothar Fendler (ten years) and SS Captain Felix Rühl (ten years) were also convicted in 1948 at the Einsatzgruppen Trial. They were released from prison in 1951. Radetzky died on 21 February 1990 in Lindlar, a municipality 30km east of Cologne, aged 79. Fedler died on 7 March 1983 in Stuttgart, Baden-Württemberg, at the age of 69. Rühl died in 1982 (precise date and location unknown), aged 72.

SS-Senior Colonel (SS-Oberführer) Erich Ehrlinger commanded Einsatzkommando 1b of Mobile Death Squad A (Einsatzgruppen A) that was involved in the mass murder of Jews in Latvia (Daugavpils and Rēzekne), Lithuania (Kovno, near Kaunas) and in the area south of Leningrad. At the end of the war he disguised himself as an NCO and surrendered to British troops using a false name. After his release from a POW camp, Ehrlinger went on with his life, sticking to his false name. In 1958 he was tracked down by the West German authorities and placed under police custody.[218] In 1961, he was convicted of 1,045 cases of murder of Jews and sentenced to twelve years' imprisonment.[219] Ehrlinger was released from prison three years later as his sentence was remitted. He died on 31 July 2004 in Karlsruhe, in Baden-Württemberg, aged 93.

Otto Rasch obtained the academic titles of Dr in Law and Dr in Political Economy before joining the SS in March 1933. He rose to the rank of brigadier (SS-Brigadeführer). Rasch co-organised and took part in the Babi Yar massacre, which saw the murder of 300,000 Jews in central Ukraine in August 1941, carried out mostly by SS troops. Two months later he was discharged from his position as commanding officer of the Mobile Killing Squad C (Einsatzgruppe C). In Nuremberg, at the end of September 1947, Rasch was indicted of crimes against humanity, but the case against him was discontinued five months later because of health issues. The defendant was diagnosed with Parkinson's disease and associated dementia.[220] Rasch died on 1 November 1948 in Wehrstedt, Lower Saxony, aged 56. He and Emil Haussmann, who were declared unfit for stand to trial by medical reasons, were the only defendants at the Einsatzgruppe Trial who escaped sentencing. Haussman committed suicide in his cell in Nuremberg Prison on 31 July 1947, two days before his arraignment (the formal reading of the charging document in the presence of the defendant to inform him of the charges against him), aged 36. He was the commanding officer of Einsatzkommando 12 of the Mobile Killing Squad D (Einsatzgruppe D) that carried out massacres in Ukraine.

Civilian Massacres III

A Bohemian–German SS-lieutenant General (SS-obergruppenführer), Karl-Hermann Frank, was tried, convicted and executed by hanging after the war for his role in organising the massacres of civilians in the villages of Lidice (340 dead) and Ležaky (thirty-three dead) in German-occupied Czechoslovakia in June 1942. The killings were a reprisal for the assassination in Prague by two British-trained Czechoslovak commandos days earlier, on 27 May, of Reinhard Heydrich, the Protector of the Reich (Reichsprotector) in Bohemia and Moravia. Heydrich had died of his wounds on 4 June, when the reprisals were ordered. On 9 May 1945, one day after the German surrender, Frank was arrested by US troops in Rokycany, in the Plzeň region of the present-day Czech Republic, and handed over to the country's newly assigned authorities. On 21 May 1946 in Prague he was convicted of crimes against humanity by a people's court and sentenced to death. Frank was hanged one day later before 5,000 onlookers[221] in the courtyard of Pankrác prison, aged 48.

On 10 June 1944 643 civilians, including women and children, all inhabitants of Oradour-sur-Glane, a town in west-central France, were massacred by elements of the 1st Battalion of the Waffen-SS Division *Das Reich* (SS-Panzerdivision *Das Reich*) as a reprisal for the abduction and murder, one day earlier, in a nearby village, of a divisional officer (Sturmbannführer Helmut Kämpfe) by French resistance fighters. In January 1953, twenty junior officers and non-commissioned officers (NCOs) of the battalion were convicted for the massacre by a military court in Bordeaux and condemned to various prison sentences. The battalion commander, SS-Major (SS-Standartenführer) Otto Weidinger Diekmann, was not brought to justice as he was killed in Normandy a few days after the massacre. Extradition of the divisional commander, SS-Lieutenant General Heinz Lammerding, who had given the order for the killings, to France was not permitted by the West German authorities as he had already been convicted as a war criminal and imprisoned in his country. Lammerding died from cancer on 13 January 1971 in Bad Tölz, in Bavaria, aged 65.

Major-General (Obergruppenführer) of the Waffen-SS Wilhelm Bittrich commanded the II SS Panzer Corps in Normandy, in the Netherlands and finally in Hungary. In March 1945 he was assigned the defence of Vienna. He avoided confrontation with the Red Army and withdrew his divisions to the west, surrendering to the Americans in western Austria on 8 May 1945. Bittrich was extradited to France on charges of ordering the execution of seventeen members of the Resistance in

Nîmes. During his trial his decision on 24 September 1944, during the Battle of Arnhem, to authorise a three-hour ceasefire for the evacuation of more than 2,000 encircled British paratroopers and their treatment by his divisions' infirmary worked in his favour. It is not surprising therefore that he was characterised as the 'chivalrous SS general' by western Allied commentators.[222] Bittrich was sentenced to five years in prison, but having already spent five years in custody he was set free. In 1953 Bittrich was arrested again and put on trial in Bordeaux in relation to other war crimes.[223] A year later, he was acquitted.[224] Bittrich died on 19 April 1973, in Wolfratshausen, in Bavaria, aged 85.

Major General (SS-Obergruppenführer) Carl Oberg served as a senior SS and Police chief in occupied France from May 1942 to November 1944.[225] He became known as the 'Butcher of Paris' for ordering the execution of hundreds of French hostages,[226] as well as the deportation of at least 40,000 Jews to concentration and extermination camps.[227] After the German capitulation, he tried to evade arrest disguised as a Wehrmacht private and using a false name, but weeks later, in June 1945, he was arrested by British troops near Kitzbuhel in southern Austria. Ober was sentenced to death by a British military tribunal, but was not executed. On 1 October 1954, he received another death sentence, this time by a French military court. On 10 April 1958, his sentence was commuted to life imprisonment by decree of France's president Vincent Auriol. One year later, Oberg's sentence was commuted to twenty years' imprisonment with hard labour by decree of Auriol's successor as the country's president, René Coty.[228] The 'Butcher of Paris' was pardoned on 20 November 1962 by France's next President, General Charles de Gaulle.[229] Eight days later, he walked out of prison a free man. According to France's Premier Pierre Mendes France, the pardon of Oberg was a demand of West German Chancellor Konrad Adenauer. Oberg died on 3 July 1965 in Flensburg, in Schleswig-Holstein, aged 68.

Three officers were punished after the war with prison terms for a series of massacres carried out by troops under their command against civilians in north-western Italy in mid-1944. They were Major General (General der Artillerie) Eduard Crasemann, SS-Lieutenant General Max Simon and SS-Major Walter Reder. Elements of the 16th SS Panzer Grenadier Division *Reichsführer* (16.Panzergrenadier-Division *Reichsführer-SS*) murdered: 560 civilians (including children) in Sant'Anna di Stazzema, on 12 August; 159 civilians in Terenzo Monti, between 17 and 19 August; 173 civilians in Vinca, on 24 August, and 770 civilians at Marzabotto, near Bologna, on 29 September. Elements of the 26th Panzer Division (26.Panzer-Division) of the Wehrmacht massacred 174 civilians in Padule di Fucecchio, near Florence, on 23 August 1944. The killings were carried out as reprisals for the activity of Italian partisans in the regions.

Crasemann, who ordered the executions in Padule di Fucecchio, surrendered at the head of his forces (XII SS Army Corps) to the US Army in April 1945. He was detained in POW Island Farm (Camp 198), in Bridgend, south Wales, until 1948, when he was extradited to Italy. Crasemann was tried in Padua for the Padule massacre by a British military court and sentenced to ten years' imprisonment. Crasemann died in Wehl prison in North Rhine-Westphalia, aged 59.

Simon was punished after the war for the Marzabotto and the Sant'Anna di Stazzema massacres. He was sentenced to death by a British military court, but his sentence was later commuted to life imprisonment. In 1954 he was released from prison. Simon was later tried three times by West German courts for the killing of three German civilians near Brettheim, in Baden-Württemberg on 10 April 1945, but was found not guilty. He had ordered their execution by hanging for 'undermining military morale'.[230] Simon died on 1 February 1961 in Lünen, in North Rhine-Westphalia, aged 62.

Austrian-born Reder was arrested by the US Army in Salzburg in May 1945 and remained in British custody until 1948. He was then extradited to Italy to be tried for his role in the Terenzo Monti massacre, as commanding officer of the 16th Reconnaissance (Aufklärungsabteilung) Battalion of the 16th SS Panzer Grenadier Division. Reder was sentenced to life imprisonment and detained in the fortress prison Gaeta, on the coastal road between Naples and Rome. In January 1985 he was paroled and set free. Reder died on 26 April 1991 in Vienna, aged 76.

Lieutenant General Wilhelm Schmalz was commanding the 1st Parachute-Panzer Division *Hermann Göring* (Fallschirm-Panzer Division 1 *Hermann Göring*) when he surrendered to Allied forces on April 1945 near the hill-top town of Bautzen, in eastern Saxony. On 12 July 1950, he was tried in Rome for the massacre of 146 civilians by his troops at Civitella, in Val di Chiana, near Arezzo in central Italy, on 29 June 1944. He was acquitted of all charges. Schmalz died on 14 March 1983 in Braunfels, in Hesse, aged 82.

Hitler's inner circle

Major Generals Wilhelm Burgdorf and Hans Krebs killed themselves inside the Führer Bunker in Berlin on 2 May 1945 following the earlier suicides of Hitler and Goebbels. The bunker was located beneath the Reich Chancellery's garden area, in central Berlin. Hitler's and Eva Braun's bodies were found by Russian soldiers inside the bunker complex.[231] Both had shot themselves with a gun.[232] Fifty-year-old Burgdorf was chief adjutant to the Führer. Forty-seven-year-old Krebs had been sent earlier by Goebbels to deliver a letter to Soviet marshal Basily Chuikov containing surrender terms acceptable by the Germans. The terms were not accepted by Chuikov, who demanded Nazi Germany's unconditional surrender.[233]

SS-Brigadier General (Brigadeführer) Alwin Broder Albrecht and SS-Lieutenant Colonel (SS-Führerbegleitkommando) Franz Schädle also committed suicide inside the bunker. Albrecht was a naval officer (corvettecapitän) until 1 July 1939, when he became one of Hitler's adjutants. At the time, he was persona non grata in the German Navy after marrying a socially inappropriate lady. He rose to the rank of SS-brigadier general (SS-brigadeführer). Albrecht was last seen defending Hitler's Reich Chancellery with a machine gun. His body was never found. It is believed that Albrecht committed suicide on 1 May 1945. He was 41 years old.

Schädle was Hitler's personal bodyguard from 5 January 1945. He replaced SS-Lieutenant General (Obersturmbannführer) Bruno Gesche, Hitler's long-time personal bodyguard. Gesche was demoted to sergeant (SS-unterscharführer) by SS commander (SS-Reichsführer) Heinrich Himmler for disciplinary reasons and transferred to the 16th SS Panzer Division *Reichsführer*. He surrendered to the Allies in north Italy and became a prisoner of war from mid-1945 until 22 March 1947. Gesche died in 1980, aged 76. On 2 May 1945 Schädler, his successor, shot himself in the mouth with a pistol rather than attempt to break out from the Chancellery to escape the Red Army.[234] He was 38 years old.

SS-Lieutenant General (SS-Obergruppenführer) Philipp Bouhler was the chief of the Chancellery of the Third Reich. He was also responsible for the Aktion T4 Euthanasia programme that killed 250,000 disabled adults and children in Nazi Germany. He was arrested with his wife, Helene Majer, by US troops on 10 May 1945 at Schloss Fischorn, in Bruck an der Mur, in the Austrian state of Styria, southern Austria. They were both held in a POW camp at Zell am See, near Innsbruck, in eastern Austria, where his wife killed herself by jumping from a window. Forty-five-year-old Bouhler committed suicide nine days after his arrest by using a cyanide capsule.[235]

Dr Karl Brandt was a physician and a brigadier general (generalmajor) of the Waffen-SS. He and his wife Anni were members of Hitler's inner circle in Berchtesgaden.[236]

Major General Nikolaus von Below was Hitler's Luftwaffe adjutant. On 29 April 1945 he was a witness inside the bunker in Berlin to the last will and testament of the Führer.[237] One day later he was permitted by Hitler to leave the embattled capital of the Third Reich. He was caught by British troops in 1946 and remained in captivity until 1948. Von Below died on 24 July 1983 in Detmold, North Rhine-Westphalia, aged 75.

Luftwaffe Major General Karl Bodenschatz was the liaison officer between Hermann Göring and Hitler. He was seriously injured on 20 July 1944 in a bomb plot explosion at the Wolf's Lair (Volfsschchanze) Eastern Front Headquarters in Rastenburg, East Prussia. He was captured on 5 May 1946 in Reichenhall, Upper Bavaria, and called as a witness at the Nuremberg trials of major Nazi war criminals. He served a two-year term in prison. Bodenschatz died on 25 August 1979 in Erlangen, near Nuremberg aged 88.

Theodore Morell was Hitler's personal physician from 1937 until a few days before his suicide. He was a specialist in venereal and skin diseases – no wonder, as the Führer was diagnosed in 1942 as suffering with progressive paralysis probably caused by a recurrence of syphilis.[238] Morell was captured by American troops on 18 May 1945 and kept in Internment Camp No. 29 (Nazi Germany's Dachau concentration camp). Suffering from aphasic speech disorders, he had to be transferred to Tegernsee hospital, at Trais-Münzenberg, in Hesse. Morell died there on 26 May 1948, aged 61.

Hanscarl von Hasselbach was Hitler's physician in the Wolf's Lair headquarters and also an SS-Major (SS-Sturmbannführer). He was kept in US custody until 1949 and never charged for war crimes. Von Hasselbach died on 21 December 1981 in Pullach im Isartal, a municipality in the district of Munich, aged 78.

Dr Werner Haase was a Hitler's physician and a medical professor. He died of tuberculosis on 30 November 1950 while in Soviet captivity at Butyrka prison, in central Moscow, aged 50.

SS-Major General (SS-Obergruppenführer) Ernst-Robert Grawitz served as a physician at Hitler's Führer Bunker in Berlin during the final stages of the war. Earlier he had performed medical experiments on prisoners, including children. As the Red Army advanced on the German capital, 43-year-old Grawitz killed himself and his family with grenades on 24 April 1945 at their home in Babelsberg, a neighbourhood of Potsdam, south-east of Berlin.[239]

SS-Lieutenant Colonel (SS-Obersturmbannführer) Ernst-Günther Schenck was a military doctor who volunteered to work at the Reichstag during the Battle of Berlin. He was captured by the Red Army on 3 May 1945 and remained in captivity for eight years. Schenck died on 21 December 1998 in Aachen, North-Rhine Westphalia, aged 94.

Vice Admiral (Vizeadmiral) Hans-Erich Voss was the naval liaison officer to Hitler's headquarters and one of the occupants of the Führer Bunker in Berlin. Until March 1943 he commanded the heavy cruiser *Prinz Eugen*. He was among the last people to see both Hitler and Goebbels alive before they committed suicide. On 30 April 1945 he was captured by the Red Army while trying to escape from Berlin. In February 1952 he was sentenced by a court martial in Moscow to twenty-five years in prison. He was released either in December 1954 or January 1955 and was then handed over to the communist East German authorities. Voss died on 18 November 1969 at Berchtesgaden, south-east of Munich, aged 72.

Until May 1938, Helmuth Bringmann, then a frigate captain (fregattenkapitän), commanded *Grille*, Hitler's state yacht, before captaining *Prinz Eugen*. When he surrendered to British troops on 26 May Bringmann, a vice admiral by now, was deputy commanding admiral, North and Baltic Seas. He was detained in Great Britain (Camp No. 1, Island Farm Special Camp 11 and Camp No. 99) from 31 May 1945 until his repatriation on 25 November 1947.[240] Bringmann died on 26 September 1983 in Diessen, a municipality of Landsberg in Bavaria, aged 88.

In 1939 Rear Admiral (Konteradmiral) Karl-Jesko von Puttkamer was the commander of a destroyer. When the war started, he was appointed naval adjutant to Hitler.[241] He was injured on 20 April 1944 when a bomb exploded during the plot attempt to kill Hitler.[242] On 21 April 1945 he was able to fly out of Berlin, already under siege by the Soviet forces. He went to Berghof, in the Bavarian Alps, near Berchtesgaden, by way of Salzburg. On 10 May, he was arrested by US troops and held in captivity until May 1947.[243] Puttkamer died on 4 March 1981 in Munich, aged 80.

Walther Hewel was the Führer's advisor on foreign matters, although he was not a career diplomat and, furthermore, lacked the necessary qualifications. He had been a member of Hitler's inner circle since 1923, when he graduated from the Technical University of Munich. On 2 March 1945, while trying to escape from the embattled Berlin, he committed suicide by biting down on a cyanide capsule and shooting himself in the head at the same time.[244] He was 41 years old.

SS-Lieutenant General (SS-Gruppenführer) Albert Bormann, formerly a bank clerk, was an adjutant to Hitler. He was the younger brother of Martin Bormann, Hitler's personal secretary and head of Hitler's Chancellery, dealing with state, Nazi party and the Führer's personal affairs. On 20 April 1945, Albert Bormann took a flight out of the embattled Berlin and went into hiding until his arrest at a farm in April 1947. He was tried by a Munich court, convicted and sentenced to six months in prison. In October 1949 he was released. Albert Bormann died on 8 April 1989 in Munich, aged 86.

SS-Major (SS-Sturmbannführer) Otto Günsche became Hitler's personal adjutant. He was taken prisoner by the Red Army in Berlin on 2 May 1945. After being held in various prisons and labour camps in the USSR, he was released from Bautzen penitentiary, in East Germany, on 2 May 1956. Günsche died on 2 October 2003, in Lohmar, in North Rhine-Westphalia, aged 86.

SS-Brigadier General (SS-Brigadeführer) Johannes 'Hansl' Baur was Hitler's personal pilot from 1932. The Führer was his best man when Baur married his second wife, Maria. In the First World War, as a pilot he was credited with shooting down six enemy planes in aerial combat. Baur stayed in the bunker complex until Hitler killed himself on the afternoon of 30 April 1945. While trying to flee towards the western

Allied lines on the western side of the Elbe River, he was shot by Soviet troops and taken prisoner.[245] His wound was so serious that on 10 June 1945 his right lower leg had to be amputated. He remained in prison for ten years. On 10 October 1955 he was extradited to France, where he was imprisoned for two years. Maria Baur died while her husband was a POW in the Soviet Union. Johannes Baur died on 17 February 1993 in Herrsching, a municipality of Upper Bavaria, near Munich, aged 95.

US-educated SS-Brigadier (SS-Brigadeführer) Hugo Blaschke was Hitler's personal dental surgeon in Berlin from 1933. On 20 April 1945 he flew out of the embattled Berlin and moved to Austria. He was arrested there by American troops on 20 May 1945.[246] Blaschke remained in US captivity for three years. He died on 6 December 1959 in Nuremberg, aged 78.

SS-Major Helmut Kunz was Hitler's dentist. He also injected morphine into Goebbels' six children to render them unconscious before they were killed by their parents using cyanide capsules.[247] After the German capitulation, he remained in Soviet captivity for ten years.[248] West German courts later refused to convict Kunz for war crimes. He died on 23 September 1976 in Freudenstadt, in Baden Württemberg, aged 55.

Three of Hitler's nurses, Erna Flegel, Elisabeth Lindhurst and Liselotte Chervinska, became Soviet POWs on 2 May 1945. Flegel, Hitler's personal nurse, was one of the last occupants of the Führer Bunker before she was captured by Soviet troops. She was released soon enough and, in her words, the Russians treated her well.[249] Her captors were selected personnel, as she said, and they behaved quite decently. In November 1945 she was interrogated in Berlin by an US Office of Strategic Services (OSS) operative. The interview was released by the CIA in 1981.[250] She never married.[251] Flegel died on 16 February 2006 in a nursing home in Mölln, a town in Schleswig-Holstein, northern Germany, aged 94.

On Lindhurst her captors found Hitler's gold pocket watch and his Party budge. Her whereabouts after that have been unknown ever since. Chervinska was also arrested by the Red Army and her fate is also unknown.

Walter Frentz, a Luftwaffe lieutenant from 1942, was a cameraman and film reporter at Hitler's headquarters. He accompanied the Führer on all his journeys and recorded some of the Nazi era's pivotal events on film. He was also an observer of extraordinary historical events. Frentz stayed with Hitler's inner circle until shortly before the end of the war. He fled Berlin on 24 April 1945 on one of the last planes out. He was arrested by US troops in May in Obersaltzberg, 75 miles (120km) south-east of Munich, and was detained until 1946 in a POW camp at Hammelburg am Main, a town in Bavaria's Lower Franconia.[252] Known as 'Hitler's photographer', he could not find employment until 1952.[253] Frentz died on 6 July 2004 in Überlingen, close to the German–Swiss border, aged 96.[254]

SS-Lieutenant Colonel (SS-Obersturmbannführer) Heinz Linge, a former mason, was Hitler's personal valet and also head of the service staff in the Reich Chancellery. On 2 May 1945 he was one of the last to leave the Führer Bunker.[255] Linge was captured by Soviet troops near See-Strasse, in the embattled Berlin. When his identity was revealed, he was transferred to Moscow and detained in Lubyanka prison. In 1950 Linge was condemned by a Soviet military court to twenty-five years' imprisonment and remained in captivity for ten years, until 1955.[256] He died on 9 March 1980, in Hamburg, aged 66.

Wehrmacht sergeant (Feldwebel) Fritz Tornow was the Führer's dog handler and veterinarian. On 30 April 1945, he was ordered to kill Blondi, Hitler's beloved German shepherd, and her five puppies.[257] When the Red Army took over the bunker complex on 2 May, Tornow was arrested and transferred to Moscow. He ended up in the Lubyanka prison, where he was reportedly tortured by guards. He was repatriated in the mid-1950s. Tornow died in the mid-1990s in Gelsenkirchen.

SS-Senior Colonel (SS-Oberführer) Emil Maurice was Hitler's driver from 1921 until the mid-1930s and one of his first bodyguards.[258] In August 1935, when it turned out that he had Jewish ancestry,[259] Maurice was informally declared 'honorary Aryan',[260] but he had to be transferred from the SS to the Luftwaffe. In 1948 he was arrested and convicted over political activities committed in the 1920s and 1930s. Maurice was sentenced to four years in a labour camp and had 30 per cent of his assets confiscated. He died on 6 February 1972 in Munich, aged 75.

SS-Lieutenant Colonel Erich Kempka was Hitler's primary chauffeur from 1936 to April 1945. He was a member of the Nazi party since 1930 and part of the eight-man squad assigned to protect Hitler in 1931.[261] He was present on 30 April 1945 when the Führer shot himself inside the bunker. He also delivered the petrol that was used for burning Hitler's and Braun's bodies in a garden behind the Reich Chancellery after their suicide.[262] Kempka left the bunker complex on 1 May and managed to reach Berchtesgaden, near Munich, where he was captured by American troops on 20 June. He was released from US captivity on 9 October 1947. Kempka died on 24 January 1975 in Freiberg am Neckar, a town north of Stuttgart, in Baden Wurttemberg, aged 64. Kempka at one time had been engaged to Gerda Daranowski, a private secretary of Hitler's. She later married Luftwaffe Colonel (Oberst) Eckhard Christian.

Christian was attached to Hitler's headquarters. On 1 September 1944 he was promoted to brigadier general and appointed chief of the Luftwaffe Command Staff. On 22 April 1944 he was transferred to the High Command of the Armed Forces (Oberkommando der Wehrmacht or OKW). His wife was one of the two secretaries who volunteered to remain with Hitler in the Führer Bunker.[263] On 8 May 1945 Christian surrendered to British troops in Mürwik, Schleswig-Holstein. He remained in captivity until 7 May 1947. Christian died on 3 January 1985 in Bad Kreuznach, Rhineland-Palatinate, aged 77.

Three of Hitler's personal secretaries experienced Soviet captivity after the fall of Berlin and Nazi Germany's capitulation while the rest were led into Anglo-American captivity. Of the five secretaries of Hitler and Bormann, none were prosecuted for any crime. It was accepted that they were civilian employees who had a professional relationship with the Führer. It is notable that Hitler would regularly have lunch or dinner with two or more of his secretaries – usually Johanna Wolf and Christa Schroeder.[264]

Wolf was Hitler's senior secretary from January 1933 and a member of the Nazi Party from 1929. Between 1929 and 1933 she was a member of Hitler's personal secretariat. The Führer used to call her Little Wölfin (meaning She-Wolf) because of her fascination with wolves and their way of life.[265] On the night of 21/22 April 1945 Wolf was ordered by Hitler to fly out of Berlin for the sake of her 80-year-old mother. She stayed at Berchtesgaden until 2 May and then travelled to her mother's home in Bad Tölz, a spa town in Bavaria. Wolf was arrested there on 23 May by US troops and interned until 14 January 1948.[266] She died on 5 June 1985 in Munich, aged 85.

Emilie Christine Schroeder, also known as Christa, was the second long-serving member of Hitler's staff after Wolf.[267] In March 1930 she began working as a stenotypist in the high command of the Sturmabteilung, the paramilitary wing of the Nazi Party. In June 1933 Schroeder was transferred to Hitler's private staff and based mainly at the Wolf's Lair (Wolfschanze), which eventually became the Führer's Eastern Front headquarters.[268] On 20 November 1944 she joined the Hitler's staff at the Reich Chancellery in Berlin. On 20 April Schroeder left the embattled capital for Obersalzberg, close to the Austrian border. She was arrested by US troops in Hintersee, a municipality in Bavaria, on 28 May and released almost three years later on 12 May 1948.[269] She was eventually employed as a secretary by a construction company in Munich. Schroeder died on 28 June 1984 in Munich, aged 76.

Gerda Christian, née Daranowski, nicknamed 'Dara', was a clerk in an Elizabeth Arden cosmetics salon in Berlin in 1933 before applying to work in the Reich Chancellery.[270] She became Hitler's personal secretary four years later. On 2 February 1944 she married Luftwaffe Colonel Eckhardt Christian. On 1 May 1945, after Hitler's death, she tried to escape from Berlin along with two of her colleagues, Traudl Junge and Krüger. She was taken prisoner by Soviet troops on the morning of 2 May while hiding in a cellar off the Schönhauser-Alee.[271] Christian was reportedly gang raped by Soviet soldiers in the woods near Berlin.[272] In 1946 she divorced her husband because he had not remained with her in the Führer Bunker. Christian was released from a POW camp near Frankfurt on 14 January 1948.[273] After her release, she moved to Dusseldorf, where she worked at the Hotel Eden.[274] In the post-war years she had an affair with Werner Naumann, a former state secretary in the Third Reich's propaganda ministry. Christian died of cancer on 14 April 1997 in Dusseldorf, aged 83.

Junge was the youngest of Hitler's personal secretaries.[275] She was employed in the Reich Chancellery in December 1942 and is mentioned as the typist of the Führer's will at 4 a.m. on 29 April 1945.[276] She left the Führer Bunker on 1 May 1945, along with her colleagues Christian and Else Mary Margarethe Krüger several hours after Hitler's suicide. After failing to make it to the western Allied lines, she returned to Berlin, where she was arrested by Russian troops. Junge was held in various jails in Berlin's Soviet sector until 31 December 1945, when she was admitted to a hospital in the British sector suffering with diphtheria. On 2 February 1946 she was able to travel to Bavaria, where she was held by the American army until mid-1946. Junge died from cancer on 10 February 2002 in Munich, aged 81, shortly after the publication of the German edition of her book *Hitler's Last Secretary: A Firsthand Account of Life with Hitler*.

Krüger remained voluntarily in the bunker until the end although she had a chance to be flown out of Berlin a week before Hitler's suicide. She was Martin Bormann's personal secretary and allegedly his mistress. On 20 April 1945 she became Hitler's secretary when Wolf and Schroeder were ordered to leave Berlin. Krüger left the bunker on 1 May and one day later she was captured by Soviet troops while hiding in a cellar at the Schultheiss-Panzenhofer Brewery on Prinzenallee.[277] She managed to escape with the assistance of the SS-Brigadier (SS-Brigadeführer) Wilhelm Mohnke and reached the British sector of Berlin on a refugee train. On arrival Krüger was arrested by British troops and later gave evidence on Bormann to the Nuremberg trials. On 23 December 1947, after her release, she married her interrogator, Dr Leslie James, a wartime Intelligence officer, and they settled in Wallasey, near Liverpool. They later moved to Cambridge, when her husband became an English fellow at Magdalene College.[278] After her husband's death on 18 August 1995, she went back to Germany. Krüger died on 24 January 2005 in Staufen im Breisgau, in Baden-Württemberg, aged 89.

Austrian-born Constanze Manziarly was Hitler's personal cook and dietitian from 1943. On 30 April 1945 she prepared the Führer's last meal. On 1 May she left the bunker complex along Gerda Christian and Traudl Junge.[279] Manziarly was wearing a Luftwaffe jacket, Junge recalled later. Trying to evade Soviet troops, the three women made their way north to a German Army hold-out in the cellar of Schultheiss-Pantzenhofer Brewery, on the Prinzenallee. Twenty-five-year-old Manziarly was last seen on 2 May being arrested and taken away towards a U-Bahn tunnel by Russian soldiers.[280] Her fate is unknown.[281] Manziarly's arrest was witnessed by Christian and Junge, both hidden in a nearby water supply facility.

Hitler's beloved nephews Heinrich 'Heinz' and Leo-Rudolf Raubal were taken prisoner by the Red Army during the war. Heinrich was tortured to death by his captors.[282] Austrian-born Heinrich 'Heinz' Hitler, a fanatical national socialist,[283] was the son of the Führer's elder half-brother, Alois. He was captured by the Red Army on 10 January 1942 in the Byazma region, near Moscow, being a non-commissioned officer (unteroffizier) of the 23rd Potsdamer Artillery Regiment. He died almost a month later, on 21 February 1942, in the Butyrka prison in central Moscow, aged 21.

Leo-Rudolf Raubal was the son of Hitler's elder half-sister Angela. A lieutenant in the Luftwaffe Engineering Corps, Raubal was wounded during the battle of Stalingrad.[284] When it was suggested that he should be airlifted home, Hitler refused, stating that, as an officer, his nephew should stay with his men.[285] On 23 January 1943 Raubal was captured by the Red Army and taken prisoner. In 1949 he was convicted as a war criminal and sentenced to twenty-five years in the Gulag for supporting Hitler's aggressive policy and for his involvement in the crimes committed by German troops on Soviet soil. He was released and repatriated on 28 September 1955. He returned to his native Linz, in Austria, where he worked as a teacher. Raubal died in Spain during a holiday on 18 August 1977, aged 70.

Joseph Goebbels' stepson was also taken prisoner during the war. Harald Quandt, son of Goebbels' wife (Magda) from her previous marriage, served in the Luftwaffe parachute forces as a lieutenant. He fought in the Battle of Crete and on the Russian front. In early 1944, he was wounded and taken prisoner by western Allied troops in Italy. He remained in captivity for three years. Quandt was the only member of the Goebbels' family to survive the war.[286] Between 1949 and 1953 he studied mechanical engineering in Hanover and Stuttgart. He took over his father's companies when Günther Quandt, who was a successful industrialist, died in 1954. Harald was killed in an aircraft accident on 22 September 1967 in Cuneo, near Piedmont, in north-western Italy, aged 45.

Emmy Sonnemann Göring was a stage actress and second wife of Reich Marshal (Reichsmarschall) Hermann Göring, the supreme commander of the Luftwaffe. She served as Hitler's hostess at many state functions between 1935 and 1942. After the war she was convicted for her activities as a Nazi and sentenced to one year in prison by a West German denazification court. When she was released, she found that 30 per cent of her property had been confiscated.[287] She was also banned from stage acting for five years. Sonnemann died on 8 June 1973 in Munich, aged 80.

Heinrich Himmler's wife, Margrete, and daughter, Gudrun, were arrested after the German capitulation by US troops and held in various camps abroad (Italy and France) and in Germany. They were released in November 1946. Margrete died on 25 August 1967 in Munich, aged 73. Gudrun died on 24 May 2018 at her home near Munich, aged 88.[288] She never renounced the Nazi ideology and repeatedly sought to justify the actions of her father.[289]

She also supported the 'Hangman of Buchenwald', SS-Master Sergeant (Hauptscharführer) Martin Sommer. While serving as a guard in Buchenwald concentration camp, his favourite torture was tying prisoners' wrists together behind their backs and then hanging them a few inches off the ground from cell bars or trees until their arms were dislocated.[290] He also had two Austrian Roman Catholic priests crucified upside down until they were dead – Otto Neururer on 30 May 1940 and Mathias Spannlang on 5 June 1940. In 1943 Sommer was indicted for his brutality by his superiors, received a reduction in rank and was transferred to a combat unit on the Eastern Front. He was captured by the Red Army, having lost his left hand and right leg in a tank explosion. He was released from Soviet captivity and repatriated in 1955. Two years later Sommer was indicted for his complicity in the death of 101 concentration camp inmates. In July 1958 he was convicted over twenty-five deaths and received a life sentence. In 1971 Sommer was sent to a hospital for better treatment of his war wounds. Two years later he was transferred to a nursing home in Schwartzenbruck, a municipality of Nürnberger in Bavaria. Sommer died there on 7 June 1988, aged 73.

Concentration camp officials

The commandants of Mauthausen and nearby Gusen II tried to evade capture when their camps were about to be liberated by Allied forces. Mauthausen and its three satellite camps (Gusen I, II and III) were located 12 miles (20km) east of Linz, in Upper Austria. SS-Captain (SS-Hauptsturmführer) Fritz Seidler, who took over at Gusen II as commandant in 1942, ordered the massacre of inmates in late April 1945 as well as the gassing of those who were sick. On 6 May he was killed in an exchange of fire with US troops. Seidler was 38 years old.

SS-Colonel (SS-Standartenführer) Franz Ziereis was commandant at Mauthausen from 1939. On 3 May 1945 he fled with his family when the camp was about to be liberated by US troops and attempted to hide in the Pyhrn area of Upper Austria. On 23 May he was tracked down by American soldiers. Ziereis was shot three times while trying to evade capture. He died of his wounds the stomach later, at Gusen I, where the US Army had set up a hospital, 131st Evac.[291] He was 39 years old. Ziereis' corpse was hung on the fence of the concentration camp by liberated inmates[292] and was reportedly left there for two weeks.

Hundreds of Nazi concentration camp personnel, including most of their commandants, were arrested, imprisoned and brought to trial by the Allied military authorities after the German capitulation. Trials were held in West German cities, including Dachau, near Munich (Dachau/Mauthausen-Gusen Trials), in Hamburg (Ravensbrück Trials), in Lüneburg, near Hamburg (Bergen-Belsen Trials), in Neuengamme, near Hamburg (Neuengamme Trials), in Munich (Bełzec Trials), in Düsseldorf (Treblinka Trials) and in Hagen, near Dortmund (Sobibór Trials). Several concentration camp officials were also brought to justice in post-war Poland during the Majdanek Trials in Łublin, the Stutthof Trials in Gdańsk and Toruń, the Chełmno Trials in Łodge and the Auschwitz Trials in Kraków. In all these trials, which were held between 1945 and 1964, several concentration camp commandants were convicted of crimes against humanity, sentenced to death and executed.

The war was still on when twelve SS officers, NCOs and kapos (former prisoners who were assigned by the SS to supervise prisoners) were brought to justice in Poland, accused of war crimes committed in the Majdanek concentration camp. On 2 December 1944 in Łublin, five of the defendants in the first Majdanek Trial were sentenced to death by a Soviet–Polish tribunal. SS-Lieutenant Colonel (SS-Obersturmführer) Anton Thernes, SS-Captain (SS-Hauptsturmführer) Wilhelm Gerstenmeier, SS-Oberscharführer Hermann Vögel, SS-Rottenführer Theodor Schollen and kapo Heinrich Stalm were hanged a day later. Kapo Edmund Pohlmann was sentenced to death although he had committed suicide in his cell on 28 November, a day after the beginning of the trial.

The multiple proceedings of the second Majdanek Trial were held between 1946 and 1948 in various Polish cities, including Łublin, Radom Świdica, Kraków, Wadowice, Toruń and Warsaw. Seven of the defendants, who were accused of crimes against humanity, received the death sentence. They were SS-Squad Leader (SS-Scharführer) Kurt Möller, SS-Senior Squad Leaders (SS-Stabsscharführer) Michael Pelger and Franz Söss, SS-Junior Lance Corporal (SS-Sturmmann) Peter Reis, and camp guards Friedrich Buschbaum, Friedrich Gebhardt and Jacob Niessner. Buschbaum's sentence was commuted to fifteen years' imprisonment. He was released and repatriated as early as 31 May 1956. Pelger was hanged on 18 June 1948, aged 40, and Reiss five days later, aged 47. Niessner was executed on 14 July, aged 40, Söss on 20 September, aged 36, Möller on 6 October, aged 30, and Gebhardt on 15 November 1948, aged 49.

SS-Lieutenant Colonels (SS-Obersturmbannführer) Alexander Piorkowski, Martin Gottfried Weiss and Otto Förschner were also sentenced to death during the Dachau Trials by a US military tribunal. They were later hanged in Landsberg Prison, 28 miles (45km) west of Munich. Piorkowski, Dachau's first commandant, was discharged on 31 August 1943 due to corruption charges against him. After the war he was convicted of crimes against humanity, including the mass shooting of Soviet prisoners, committed in the camp between late 1941 and late 1942. Piorkowski was executed by hanging on 22 October 1948, aged 44.

Weiss was the last commandant of Dachau, from which he fled on 28–29 April 1945. He was arrested by US troops in Munich and brought to justice. Weiss was sentenced to death by hanging on 13 December 1945, aged 40. The sentence was carried out on 29 May 1946.[293]

Förschner was executed one day earlier, aged 43. He had served as commandant in two concentration camps, at Mittelbau-Dora, near Nordhause, in central Germany and at Caufering, part of the Dachau system.

SS-Senior Lieutenant (SS-Obersturmführer) Hans Mösser was sentenced to death during the Dachau Trials and was also hanged in Landsberg Prison. Of the nineteen defendants in the Dora Trial, part of the Dachau Trials, held in Dachau between 7 August and 30 December 1947, only Mösser received the death penalty. He commanded the protective custody in the Mittelbau-Dora system. On 30 December 1947 he was convicted of the execution of inmates and for ordering a death march for 3,000 of them on 5 April 1945 during the final evacuation of Dora, Mittelbau's sub-camp.[294] Mösser was sentenced to death and was executed on 26 November 1948, aged 42.

SS-Lieutenant Colonel Rudolf Höss was the first commandant of Auschwitz, in Nazi-occupied Poland. He later served as commandant at Ravensbrück, a women-only concentration camp 56 miles (90km) north of Berlin. Höss was recalled from Auschwitz in December 1943 for having an affair with an inmate, identified as Eleonore Mattaliano-Hodys.[295] The woman became pregnant and had an abortion.[296] Höss evaded arrest for nearly a year after Nazi Germany's capitulation disguised as a gardener and working under the false name Franz Lang.[297] He was arrested by British troops in Gottrupel, a hamlet in Schleswig-Holstein, in northern Germany, on 25 May 1946. He was eventually handed over to the Polish authorities. Following a trial in Kraków, southern Poland, Höss was convicted of war crimes. He was hanged on 16 April 1947, aged 45. The sentence was carried out next to the crematorium of the former Auschwitz I concentration camp. In his memoirs, which he wrote in Poland before his execution, Höss admitted the murder of 1,130,000 inmates in the two camps that he served as commandant.[298] He also complained of being mistreated by his British captors.[299]

A number of SS officers and NCOs were tried in the Soviet–Polish Supreme National Tribunal, in Kraków, for crimes against humanity committed in Auschwitz-Birkenau concentration camps. On 22 December 1947 eighteen of the defendants were sentenced to death. They were hanged in Montelupich Prison, in central Kraków, on 24 January 1948. They were SS Lieutenant Colonels (SS-Obersturmführer) Arthur Liebenschel, Karl Ernst Möckel and Joseph Kollmer, SS-Major (SS-Sturmbannführer) Franz Xaver Kraus, SS-Senior Lieutenant (SS-Obersturmführer) Heinrich Josten, SS-Lieutenant (SS-Untersturmführer) Maximilian Grabner and SS-NCOs Wilhelm Gehring, August Bogusch, Herbert Paul Ludwig, Erich Muhsfeldt, Ludwig Plagge, Fritz Buntrock, Otto Lätsch, Hermann Kirschner, Kurt Hugo, Hans Schumacher, Paul Szczurek and Paul Götze. Camp administrators Hans Aumeier and Arthur Breitweiser were also sentenced to death on 22 December 1947 in Kraków, and hanged in Montelupich Prison on 24 January 1948.

SS-Lieutenant Colonel Liebehenschel had been commandant of the Auschwitz and Majdanek concentration camps. He was arrested by US troops in Trieste, northern Italy, and was later extradited to Poland. Convicted of crimes against humanity in Kraków, Liebehenschel was executed by hanging on 24 January 1948 in Montelupich Prison, aged 46.

Möckel, who was a year older than Liebehenschel, served as the commandant's deputy in the Auschwitz main camp until January 1945.

Kollmer and Josten commanded the camp guard at Auschwitz. Kollmer was convicted over his participation in the mass murder of Jews and for carrying out inmate executions against the shooting wall. He was hanged, aged 46.

Kraus was the main camp's information officer. The day of his execution he was 46 years old. Austrian-born Grabner was condemned for the execution and torture of inmates at Auschwitz and for taking part in the shooting of political officers (commissars) of the Red Army. He was hanged, aged 42.

Gehring was a sub-camp commandant. Bogusch, Kirschner and Hans Schumacher were assistant camp administrators. Muhsfeldt was the crematoria manager at Birkenau.

Plagge was noted for his brutality towards inmates. He was also convicted over his participation in the gassing of thousands of Jews, Sinti (a subgroup of Romani people living in central Europe) and Roma. Plagge was hanged, aged 38.

Buntrock, an SS-NCO, supervised the gas chambers in Auschwitz. He was convicted by the Supreme National Tribunal in Krákow and sentenced to death. He was executed by hanging at Montelupich Prison on 24 January 1948, aged 38.

Ludwig, Lätsch, Hugo, Szczurek and Götze were block overseers (blockführer) at Auschwitz.

Aumeier, an SS administration officer (SS-Schutzhaftlagerführer), served as commandant in a concentration camp (Vaivara) in Estonia and as deputy commandant at Auschwitz. On 22 January 1945, he was transferred to German-occupied Norway, where he commanded a concentration camp at Mysen, in the southern part of the country. Four months later, after Nazi Germany's capitulation, Aumeier was arrested by British troops. In 1946 he was extradited to Poland. He was tried in Kraków, found guilty and sentenced to death for having 144 women shot on his order in Auschwitz in March 1942. Aumeier was executed by hanging on 24 January 1948 in Montelupich Prison, aged 41.

SS-Staff Sergeant (SS-Oberscharführer) Johann Pauls was in charge of the guards at Wesslinken, a subcamp of Stutthof, a concentration camp located east of Gdańsk, northern Poland. He was among the defendants of the first Stutthof trial that was held in Gdańsk after the war. On 31 May 1946 Pauls was convicted of crimes against humanity and sentenced to death by a Soviet–Polish military court. On 4 July 1946 he was hanged at a mountain location (Biskupia Górka or Bishop Hill), not far from the city centre, in front of a large crowd estimated at 11,000.[300] Ten more convicts, half of them women, were also executed by hanging that day, in the same location.

SS-Sergeant (SS-Unterscharführer) Kurt Dietrich was in charge at Seerappen, one of Stutthof's five sub-camps, in which mostly Jewish women were detained. The prisoners were put to work on construction projects for ten to twelve hours a day regardless of the weather.[301] The hard labour, as well as the poor state of their clothing and shoes, and the minimal food rations, caused diseases to spread, primarily typhus and dysentery. Sick prisoners were murdered in a forest near the lake during work. Dietrich was among the defendants of the second Stutthov trial. On 31 January 1947 he was found guilty of crimes against humanity and sentenced to death. He was executed by hanging on 28 October 1948.

SS-Lieutenant Colonel Joseph Kramer was commandant at Auschwitz-Birkenau in 1944 and at Bergen-Belsen in 1945. He was detained by the British Army and was later convicted of war crimes on 17 November 1945 during the Bergen-Belsen Trial held at Lüneburg from 17 September to 17 November 1945. Kramer was hanged, aged 39, on 13 December 1945 on the gallows in the Hamelin Prison, in Lower Saxony, by the British public executioner Albert Pierrepoint.[302]

SS-Senior Lieutenant (SS-Obersturmbannführer) Franz Hössler was also executed that day in Hamelin Prison. Hössler served as deputy commander at Bergen-Belsen under Joseph Kramer until 8 April. A week later he was arrested in the camp and held by the British. Hössler was convicted on 17 November 1945 of having directly shot prisoners only hours before the liberation of the Bergen-Belsen camp on 15 April 1945 and of having sent 575 more for euthanasia in June 1941 when he was serving at Auschwitz I (main camp). Hössler was executed, aged 39.

SS-NCOs Franz Stärfl, Wilhelm Dörr, Peter Weingärtner, Karl Franzioh and Ansgar Pichen also received the death penalty at a British military tribunal at Lüneburg during the Belsen Trial. Their sentences were also carried out in Hamelin Prison on 13 December 1945. SS-Master Sergeants (SS-Hauptscharführer) Stärfl and Dörr were condemned over the murder of prisoners during death marches.

Stärfl, alias Franz Stofel, served as an SS detachment commander at Kleinbodungen, a satellite camp of the Mittelbau-Dora system. On 4 April 1945 he led 610 prisoners in a death march toward the Bergen-Belsen concentration camp. He was also indicted for the murder of prisoners during the six-day march. Four or five prisoners were allegedly shot while trying to escape or because they were slowing the pace. Stärfl was executed, aged 30.

Dörr was involved in the particular death march and with the murder of prisoners. He was hanged, aged 24. Yugoslavian-born Weingärtner, a Bergen-Belsen camp guard, and two cooks, Franzioh and Pichen, were sentenced to death for shooting female prisoners, including a pregnant one, and for beating others 'terribly'.[303] Weingärtner was 32 and Franzioh, alias Flrazich, was 33, when they were hanged. A year younger than Franzioh was Danish-born Pichen, who was a Polish citizen in May 1940 when he was conscripted into the German Army. On 25 November 1942 Pichen was wounded in combat and his left hand was crippled. From then on he served in concentration camps in Nazi-occupied Moravia (part of Czechoslovakia) and later in Poland. He was arrested by British troops when Bergen-Belsen was liberated. Pichen was executed on 13 December 1948 in Hamelin Prison, also by Pierrepoint.

Forty-four officers and NCOs of the SS, concentration camp administrators and civilian employees who had committed crimes against humanity in the Mauthausen and Gusen concentration camps were sentenced to death by a US military tribunal on 13 May 1946 in Dachau.[304] They were General of the Waffen-SS (SS-Obergruppenführer) August Eigruber; SS-Major (SS-Sturmbannführer) Waldemar Wolter; SS-Captains (SS-Hauptsturmführer) Wilhelm Henkel, Viktor Zoller and Adolf Zutter; SS-Senior Lieutenants (SS-Obersturmführer) Johann Altfuldisch, August Blei, Johannes Grimm and Heinrich Eisenhöfer; SS Master Sergeants (SS-Hauptscharführer) Willy Eckert, Heinrich Häger, Julius Ludolf, Emil Müller, Wilhelm Müller, Hans Spatzennegen and Otto Striegel; SS Senior Sergeants (SS-Oberscharführer) Franz Kautny, Hermann Pribyll and Andreas Trumm; SS Sergeants (SS-Unterscharführer) Otto Dradek, Werner Grahn, Hans Hegenscheidt, Anton Kaufmann, Kurt Keilwitz, Gustav Kreindl, Josef Leeb, Josef Niedermayer and Josef Riegler; SS Senior Squad Leader (SS-Stabsscharführer) Karl Struller; SS Squad Leader (SS-Scharführer) Hans Diehl; SS Senior Lance Corporals (SS-Rottenführer) Willy Brünning, Franz Huber, Kaspar Klimowitsch, Erich Miessner, Rudolf Mynzak, Theophil Priebel and Thomas Sigmund; SS Lance Corporal (SS-Sturmmann) Stefan Barczay and Heinrich Fitschok. Death sentences also received Capos Rudolf Friegl, Willy Frei and Georg Gössl, and the civilians/employees Vinzenz Nohel and Leopold Trauner.

Austrian-born General of the Waffen-SS Eigruber was gauleiter and Reich defence commissioner for Upper Austria from 14 May 1938.[305] On 5 May 1945 he fled Linz and managed to hide using forged identification papers. On 11 August he was arrested by US troops in Sankt Pankraz, a municipality in the Traunviertel region, in central Austria. Eirguber was sentenced to death for his responsibility for crimes committed at Mauthausen-Gusen, where more than 90,000 inmates died.[306] He was executed, aged 40.

Zoller served as adjutant in various concentration camps. He was executed aged 35.

Zutter served at Mauthausen-Gusen from June 1942 to early May 1945, mostly as an adjutant under commandant Franz Ziereis. After the war he was sentenced to death for ordering the mass execution of prisoners in the gas chambers.[307] Zutter was hanged, aged 58.

Altfuldisch was convicted over his personal participation in many executions carried out at Mauthausen.[308]

Ludolf served as a commandant in a satellite camp of the Mauthausen-Gusen system. On 11 May 1946, he was condemned for having personally murdered Polish and Russian inmates and for ordering the execution of a Russian prisoner who was recaptured after an escape. Ludolf was executed, aged 54.

Austrian-born Riegler was convicted over his participation in the execution of twenty-six Yugoslav prisoners in November 1944. He was hanged, aged 25.

The forty-four defendants who were sentenced to death in the first of the Mauthausen-Gusen Trials were executed by hanging on 27 and 28 May 1946 in Landsberg Prison. Striegel, who won a last-minute stay, was executed on 20 June.

Of the eight defendants in the second of the Mauthausen-Gusen Trials, four were sentenced to death by hanging, on 21 August 1947, for the killing of prisoners by shooting at Wiener Graben (Vienna Ditch), by chasing them into the electric fence or by gassing.[309] They were also condemned for shooting at exhausted prisoners during the evacuation march. Senior Sergeant (SS-Oberscharführer) Franz Kofler, SS-Senior Lance Corporal Gustav Petrat and kapo Quirin Flaucher were executed on 19 November 1948 in Landsberg Prison.[310] The death sentence of SS-Senior Lance Corporal Michael Heller was reduced to life imprisonment.

Ravensbrück, located near Hamburg, was a concentration camp in which mostly female prisoners were detained. SS-Lieutenant Colonel (SS-Obersturmbannführer) Johann Schwarzhuber, the camp's deputy commandant (lagerführer), was tried by a British military tribunal in Hamburg's Rotherbaum Court during the first Ravensbrück Trial for ordering the execution of fifty female inmates daily, as of January 1945, to combat overcrowding. On 3 February 1947 he was sentenced to death. Schwarzhuber was executed by hanging on 3 March 1947, aged 42.

Ludwig Ramdorf, a Gestapo inspector, and Gustav Binder, a camp warden, were also sentenced to death during the same trial and executed by hanging. On 15 July 1948 Arthur Conrad, an SS warden at Ravensbrück, was sentenced to death as a war criminal, during the fifth of the Ravensbrück Trials. He was executed two months later, on 17 September.

SS-Major (SS-Sturmbannführer) Fritz Suhren was Ravensbrück's commandant. When British forces were close to the camp, he ran away. As a result, he was not among the defendants in the Ravensbrück Trials, although he was hiding in Hamburg at the time. He was eventually arrested by British troops, but managed to escape.[311] Suhren settled at Eppenschlag, a municipality in eastern Bavaria, under the name of Hebert Pakush until his arrest on 23 March 1949 by US troops. He was held in a concentration camp at Deggendorf, a town in the Lower Bavaria district, before being handed over to the French military authorities. They put him on trial at Rastatt, in south-western Germany, in February 1950. On 10 March, Suhren was sentenced to death for ordering the overwork of inmates at Ravensbrück and for the death of hundreds of them as a result of exhaustion and starvation. He was also convicted of ordering in May 1942 in Sauschenhausen, in north-eastern Germany, where he was deputy commandant, the hanging of a prisoner by another prisoner.[312] Suhren was executed on 12 June 1950 at Sandweier, in Baden-Baden, by firing squad, aged 42.

Friedrich Opitz was in charge of a clothing factory that was in operation at Ravensbrück. He was arrested and detained after the liberation of Ravensbrück by British forces. He managed to escape along with SS-Sergeant (SS-Oberscharführer) Hans Pflaum, a director of work labour in the camp, prior to their scheduled trial and both went into hiding under false names. They were recaptured four years later and were handed over to the French authorities, who were conducting another Ravensbrück Trial in Rastatt, Baden Württemberg. Opitz and Pflaum were convicted of beating slave labour women with truncheons, belts and fists, of starving them to death for missing their quota and of sending many of them to the gas chambers. Opitz was also condemned for kicking a Czech prisoner, causing her death. Opitz received the death sentence, which was carried out on 26 January 1948.[313] He was executed on 17 September 1948 in Baden-Baden, aged 49. Pflaum had to stand in front of a French firing squad later, on 12 June 1950, aged 40.

Senior Colonel (SS-Standartenführer) Max Pauly was commandant of Neuengamme, a network of Nazi concentration camps located near Hamburg, from September 1942 to May 1945. He was tried by the British in Hamburg for war crimes. On 13 May 1946 he was found guilty and sentenced to death. He was hanged by Albert Pierrepoint on 8 October 1946 in Hamelin prison, aged 39. Pauly was never tried for the crimes committed from 1939 to August 1942, when he was commandant of Stutthof concentration camp, near Danzig (present-day Gdańsk, in northern Poland).

SS-Senior Colonel Anton Kaindl was the commandant at Sachsenhausen, in Oranienburg, near Brandenburg, from 1943 to 1945. He was captured by the Red Army on 22 April 1945 and was tried for war crimes by a Soviet military court in Pankow, in the Soviet zone of Berlin. He was sentenced to life imprisonment with hard labour. Kaidl died in the Vorkuta Gulag, north of the Arctic Circle, some 1,200 miles (1,900km) from Moscow, on 31 August 1948, aged 46.[314]

SS-Senior Lieutenant (SS-Obersturmführer) Anton Thumann served in various Nazi concentration camps, including Majdanek, near Łublin, in eastern Poland, and in Neuengamme. He was arrested by the British Army and was put on trial before a British military tribunal in Hamburg on 8 March 1946. Charged with war crimes, 33-year-old Thumann was found guilty. On 3 May, he was sentenced to death by hanging. The sentence was carried out by Pierrepoint in Hamelin prison on 8 October 1946, the same day of Pauly's execution.

SS-Lieutenant General (SS-Obergruppenführer) Oswald Pohl was the chief administrator of the Nazi concentration camp system. He was responsible for making profits for the Third Reich from the slave labour of prisoners. After the German capitulation he went into hiding disguised as a farmhand. In May 1945 he was tracked down by British troops near Dresden, Lower Saxony. During his trial in Nuremberg, in front of an American military tribunal, Pohl admitted that about 420,000 prisoners were working in factories and private firms in Nazi Germany during the war.[315] On 3 November 1947 he was convicted of crimes against humanity and sentenced to death.[316] Pohl was executed by hanging on 7 June 1951 in Landsberg Prison, aged 58.

SS-Staff Sergeant (SS-Oberscharführer) Kurt Bolender was one of the defendants during the Sobibór Trials held in Hagen, 15km south of Dortmund, from 6 September

1965 to 20 December 1966. He operated the gas chambers at Sobibór concentration camp. After the war, he was recognised in 1961 while working as a doorman in a night club under a false identity. He was arrested and charged four years later for personally killing approximately 360 Jews at Sobibór and for assisting in the murder of further 86,000 in the same concentration camp.[317] Bolender committed suicide in the Justizvollzupsanstalt Celle prison in Hagen by hanging himself in his cell on 10 October 1966, aged 54, prior to the end of the first of the Sobibór Trials.

SS-Staff Sergeant (SS-Oberscharführer) Kurt Küttner served as the commandant of the Lower Camp of Treblinka II. After the war he was arrested and charged for picking inmates for execution or to be whipped publicly in his presence.[318] Küttner died in prison, in Düsseldorf, aged 57, before the Treblinka Trials began on 10 October 1964.

SS-Captain (SS-Hauptsturmführer) Hans Bothmann was commandant at Chełmno, an extermination camp 31 miles (50km) north of Łódź, in west-central Poland. In mid-July 1944 he supervised the murder of some 25,000 inmates in the camp. He also led SS detachments to arrest the remaining Jews of the Łódź Ghetto and have them transferred to Auschwitz-Birkenau.[319] Bothmann then reported for duty in the 7th SS Division *Prinz Eugen*. He fled to Germany in January 1945. Bothmann committed suicide on 4 April 1946 in Heide, Schleswig-Holstein, after his arrest by British troops, aged 34.[320]

SS-Major Richard Baer was the commandant of the Mittelbau-Dora concentration camp. He fled, at the end of the war and settled near Hamburg. On 20 December 1960 he was tracked down and arrested by the West German police. He died of a heart attack on 17 June 1963 in Frankfurt, aged 51, while in pretrial detention and before he could stand trial.

SS-Colonel (SS-Oberführer) Hans Loritz was one of the several SS officers who committed suicide after Nazi Germany's capitulation. He served as commandant in various concentration camps in Nazi Germany (Dachau and Sachsenhausen) and in Nazi-occupied Norway. After the war, he was arrested by British troops and detained in Neumünster, in Schleswig-Holstein, northern Germany.[321] Loritz committed suicide on 31 January 1946, aged 50, while waiting to be handed over to the Russians.

Austrian-born SS-Senior Lieutenant (SS-Obersturmführer) Irmfried Eberl was director of the Euthanasia Institute in Brandenburg, and also the first commandant of the Treblinka extermination camp in German-occupied Poland. After the war, being a qualified psychiatrist, he practised medicine in Blaubeuren, near Ulm. In January 1948 37-year-old Eberl was arrested as a war criminal and imprisoned in Ulm, Baden-Württemberg, in south-western Germany. He hanged himself in his cell one month later, on 16 February, to avoid trial.[322]

SS-Senior Colonel (SS-Oberführer) Hermann Pister was the commandant of the Buchenwald concentration camp near Weimar, some 106 miles (170km) north of Nuremberg, from 1942 to 1945. In August 1947, during the Dachau Trial, he was sentenced to death for crimes against humanity. Pister died of natural causes in his cell in Landsberg Prison on 28 September 1948 before the death sentence could be carried out. He was 63 years old.

SS-Sergeant (SS-Oberscharführer) Rudolf Joachim Seck was in charge of the Jungfernhoff concentration camp in Riga, the capital of present-day Latvia. After the war he was tried in Hamburg for war crimes. Seck was convicted for the murder of 1,600 to 1,700 Jews inmates, at the Bikernieki forest on 26 March 1942. In 1951 he was sentenced to life imprisonment. Seck died in 1974 in Flensburg, in Schleswig-Holstein, in northern Germany, aged 65 or 66.

SS-Lieutenant General (SS-Obergruppenführer) Karl Friedrich Otto Wolf was arrested on 13 May 1945 and released in 1947. In 1966 he was convicted of deporting 300,000 Jews to the Treblinka extermination camp and sentenced to fifteen years in prison. He was released from Staubing prison in Lower Bavaria, in 1971, following a heart attack. Wolf died on 17 July 1984, in Rosenheim, in south-east Bavaria, aged 84. A few weeks before his death, he converted to Islam.

SS-Major (SS-Sturmbannführer) Adolf Winkelmann served as a physician in Sachsenhausen and Ravensbrück concentration camps. During his trial in Hamburg he was charged with war crimes, including the selection of 2,000 inmates for a 'death march' in February 1945. Winkelmann died of a heart attack on 1 February 1947, aged 60.

SS-Captain Reinhold Eggers was a security officer in Oflag IV-C at Colditz Castle, near Dresden, Lower Saxony, from 1940 to 1945. After the war, he worked as a teacher in post-war Germany's Soviet zone, in Halle, Saxony-Alhalt. In September 1946 Eggers was arrested by the Russians. He was charged with war crimes and sentenced to ten years of hard labour. The sentence was spent in the Sachsenhausen concentration camp and then in the Torgau prison (formerly Stalag IV-D), located 31 miles (50km) north-east of Leipzig, in the state of Saxony.[323] Eggers died in 1974 near the Constance Lake, close to the border with Switzerland, aged 83 or 84.

SS-Lieutenant (SS-Obersturmbannführer) Karl-Friedrich Höcker was the commandant of Auschwitz I concentration camp from May to December 1944. He unsuccessfully used false papers to avoid being identified by the British when they tracked him down after the German capitulation. He was held for eighteen months in a detention camp and released. In 1965 he was apprehended and put on trial, after which he was sentenced to seven years in prison for aiding and abetting more than 1,000 murders at Auschwitz. He was released in 1970. In 1989 a German court at Bielefeld, North Rhine-Westphalia, sentenced him to four years' imprisonment for his involvement in gassing to death prisoners. Höcker died on 30 January 2000 in Lübbecke, North Rhine-Westphalia, aged 88.

On 31 May 1945 at the Alpine pasture of Mösslacher Alm near the Weissensee Lake in southern Austria five SS officers were tracked down and arrested by British commandos. They were SS-Major General (SS-Gruppenführer) Friedrich Rainer, SS-Lieutenant General (SS-Obergruppenführer) Odilo Globocnic, SS-Majors (SS-Sturmbannführer) Georg Michalsen and Ernst Lerch, as well as SS-Major General (General der Waffen-SS) Wilhelm Koppe, who commanded SS and uniformed police (Ordungspolizei) units in Nazi-occupied Poland. Globocnic, Michalsen, Lerch and Koppe were involved in the deportation, between October 1941 and November 1943, of about 1½ million Polish Jews[324] to various extermination camps (Bełzec, Soribór, Majdanek and Treblinka, mostly), where they were murdered in purpose-built gas chambers.

Austrian-born Globocnic served in Nazi-occupied Poland, where he was responsible for numerous atrocities against the country's Jewish population.[325] In September 1943 he was transferred to northern Italy. As a higher SS and police chief based in Trieste, Globocnic organised the arrest and deportation to death camps of thousands of Italian Jews. After his arrest on 31 March 1945 in Mösslacher Alm he was transferred to a detention facility in Paternion, southern Austria. No long after his arrival there, 41-year-old Globocnic committed suicide in his cell by biting on a cyanide capsule.

Austrian-born Michalsen was also transferred from Poland to Trieste. He served there under Globocnic and was also involved in various war crimes. Michalsen, who was also arrested in Mösslacher Alm on 31 May 1945, remained in British captivity for two years. After his release he worked as an accountant in Hamburg. On 24 January 1961 he was arrested by the West German police and charged with war crimes. He was convicted and imprisoned for twelve years.[326] Michalsen died on 21 May 1993 in Hamburg, aged 86.

Austrian-born Lerch served in Kraków and in Łublin, Poland, until late 1943. He was then transferred to Fiume (present-day Rijeka, in Croatia), in Italy, as an SS and police chief. He was detained after his arrest in Mösslacher Alm on 31 March 1945, but managed to escape from a detention centre operated by the British Army within the former Stalag XVIII-A, a POW camp that was previously run by the Wehrmacht in Wolfsberg, located some 47 miles (75km) east of Hanover. He lived in hiding until 1950, when he was arrested again and sent back to prison. In 1960 Lerch was sentenced to two years' imprisonment by a de-Nazification court in Wiesbaden, the capital of the state of Hesse. After his release he opened a coffee shop, Tanzcafé Lerch,[327] in his native city, Klagenfurt-am-Wörthersee, the capital of Carinthia, the southernmost Austrian state. In 1971 he was brought in front of a court in Klagenfurt accused of being involved in the Holocaust. His case was finally dropped on 11 May 1976 due to a lack of witnesses. Lerch died on in 1997 in Klagenfurt, aged 83.

Koppe commanded various components of the SS and the German uniformed police (Ordungspolizei). He was responsible for numerous atrocities committed in Kraków, where he organised the execution of 30,000 Poles, mostly Jews, because they were suffering from tuberculosis. After the German capitulation, he went into hiding and eventually found employment in a chocolate factory[328] in Bonn using his wife's surname. In 1960 Koppe was arrested and brought to justice. He was accused in a Bonn court of being an accessory to the mass murder of 145,000 people. The trial was adjourned due to Koppe's purported ill health. Six years later the court decided not to prosecute him and had him released for medical reasons. The West German government later refused a Polish request to have Koppe extradited.[329] He died on 2 July 1975 in Bonn, aged 79.

Austrian-born Rainer was also arrested on 31 March 1945. He was tracked down by British commandos near the Weissensee lake in southern Austria. Rainer had served as regional commander (reichsstatthalter) of the Nazi Party in the Austrian states (Reichsgau) of Salzburg (1940–41) and Carinthia (1941–45). In September 1943 he also became high commissioner of a region in the Adriatic, encompassing the cities of Friuli and Istria. Rainer was held in Nuremberg Prison from October 1945 until 13 March 1947, when he was extradited to Yugoslavia. On 10 July he was brought before a military court in Ljubljana, the capital of present-day Slovenia, accused of war crimes committed by SS forces in and around Istria. Found guilty as charged, he was sentenced to death. Rainer was executed by hanging on 19 July 1950 in Ljubljana, aged 47.

SS-Major General (SS-Gruppenführer) Johann 'Hans' Rattenhuber was the head of Hitler's personal Reich Security Service (Reichssicherheitsdiens or RSD) from 1933 to 1945. Elements of the 200-strong RSD participated in the mass murder of 227 Jews at Vinnytsia in west-central Ukraine on 10 January 1942 prior to Hitler's visit to the region. On 1 May 1945 Rattenhuber tried to escape from the bunker complex in Berlin. He was captured by Soviet troops hours or a day later and taken to Moscow. On 15 February 1952 he was sentenced to twenty-five years' imprisonment for war crimes. On 10 October 1955 he was released and handed over to the East German authorities. Less than a year later he was allowed to cross the border to West Germany. Rattenhuber died on 30 June 1957 in Munich, aged 60.

SS-Lieutenant Colonel (SS-Obersturmbannführer) Otto Adolf Eichmann was involved in the mass deportation of Jews to extermination camps in German-occupied Eastern Europe. After the war he was captured by US troops and held in various camps, having presented false documents. When his identity was discovered, Eichmann managed to escape. He fled to Argentina under the name of Ricardo Clement, using a Red Cross-issued passport. Mossad, Israel's intelligence agency, located Eichmann's residence in 1960. He was captured by Shin Bet (Israeli security) agents and brought to Israel, where he was tried for crimes against humanity. Found guilty as charged, Eichmann was sentenced to death. He was executed by hanging on 1 June 1962 in Ramala (Ayalon) Prison, in the central district of Israel, aged 56.

Austrian-born SS-Lieutenant Colonel (SS-Obersturmbannführer) Siegfried Seidl served as commandant in concentration camps (Theresienstadt and Bergen-Belsen) until 3 July 1944, when he became a staff officer to Eichmann and leader of the 5th Paramilitary Death Squad E (Einsatzgruppe E) of the SS. Two months after Nazi Germany's capitulation, on 30 July 1945, he was arrested by the police and handed over to the occupation authorities. Seidl was held by the US Army until 3 June 1946, when he was handed over to Austria's post-war authorities. Three months later he was tried in Vienna by the country's People's Court (Volksgericht). Found guilty of high treason and crimes against humanity, Seidl was sentenced to death. He was executed by hanging on 4 February 1947, aged 35.

In Bratislava, then a major city of Czechoslovakia, 37-year-old SS-Captain (SS-Hauptsturmführer) Dieter Wisliceny, one of Eichmann's deputies, was hanged on 4 May 1948. He played a principal role in the wide-scale deportation of Jews from Greece, Hungary and Czechoslovakia across German-occupied Europe during the Holocaust.

Austrian-born SS-Major (SS-Sturmbannführer) Karl Rahm was the final commandant of the Theresienstadt ghetto and labour camp, which was established in the fortress town of Terezín, some 43 miles (70km) north of Prague.[330] Roughly 33,000 prisoners, mostly Jews, died there, most of them from disease and starvation, and a further 90,000 were deported to extermination camps and forced labour camps in German-occupied Poland, Belarus and the Baltic states.[331] In May 1945 Rahm was captured by US troops in Austria and held for two years until his extradition to Czechoslovakia. Put on trial in Litoměřice for crimes against humanity, Rahm was sentenced to death. He was hanged on 30 April 1947, aged 40, four hours after his guilty verdict had been handed over by the Czech court.

SS Lieutenant (SS-Untersturmführer) Kurt Franz was the last commandant of the Treblinka concentration camp. He enjoyed shooting at prisoners with his pistol or with a hunting rifle. Having been an amateur boxer, he allegedly used prisoners as punching bags. After the closure of the camp in November 1943 he was transferred to Trieste, in northern Italy, where he participated in the persecution of Jews. In late 1944 he was wounded in an exchange of fire between German troops and Italian partisans. After the war Franz worked as a labourer and as a cook, mostly in Düsseldorf, where he was tracked down and arrested on 2 February 1959. On 3 September 1965 during the Treblinka Trials, he was found guilty of the murder of at least 300,000 people and sentenced to life imprisonment.[332] He was released from prison twenty-eight years later for health reasons. Franz died on 4 July 1998 in Wuppertal, in North Rhine-Westphalia, aged 84.

SS-Captain (SS-Hauptsturmführer) Karl Chmielewski was appointed commandant at Herzogenbusch, a concentration camp in Nazi-occupied Holland, after serving for two years in various Mauthausen-Gusen sub-camps as administration officer. At Herzogenbusch he developed a reputation for cruelty, having ordered during inspection the drowning of inmates in buckets of water.[333] In 1943 Chmielewski was deprived of his command and was eventually sentenced to fifteen years in prison for rape and embezzlement. He spent the rest of the war as an inmate at Dachau.[334] After the German capitulation he disappeared in Austria. In 1953 Chmielewski returned to West Germany and took up farming. Months later, he was arrested and charged for perjury, fraud and bigamy. In 1963, when his identity was established, he was brought to justice. Found guilty of 293 counts of murder[335] committed in concentration camps, Chmielewski was sentenced to life imprisonment with hard labour.[336] Because of health issues he spent most of his sentence in a care institution at Bernau am Chiemsee, in south Bavaria, where he died on 1 December 1991, aged 88.

At least 450 SS officers, NCOs and camp guards were condemned for crimes against humanity during the Auschwitz, Bergen-Belsen, Belzec, Chełmno, Mittelbau-Dora, Frankfurt-Auschwitz, Majdanek, Mauthausen-Gusen, Ravensbrück, Sobibor, Stutthof and Treblinka Trials, and received various prison sentences. Of the defendants a total of forty-three were sentenced to life imprisonment and fifty-seven to lesser prison sentences. A further forty-nine defendants were acquitted and released from prison.

Most of the convicted, including some of those serving life sentences, received an early discharge. They were: SS-Captain (SS-Hauptsturmführer) Theodor Meyer; SS-Lieutenant (SS-Untersturmführer) Kurt Franz; SS-Senior Sergeants (SS-Hauptscharführer) Erhard Brauny, Otto Brinkmann, Rudolf Jacobi, Georg König and Karl Seufert; Sergeant Major of the Waffen-SS (Stabsscharführer) Emil Bühring; SS-Sergeant Major (SS-Sturmscharführer) Detlef Nebbe; SS-Staff Sergeants (SS-Oberscharführer) Ewald Foth, Karl Frenzel, Heinrich Matthes, Albert Paulitz, Hans Rach and Wilhelm Simon; SS-Sergeants (SS-Unterscharführer) Hans Koch, Adolf Medefind, August Miete, Willi Mentz, Fritz Peters and Erich Thun; SS-Senior Lance Corporals (SS-Rottenführer) Stefan Baretzki, Karl Eggert, Anton Lechner, Paul Wellitz and Karl Zurell; Rifleman of the Waffen-SS (SS-Schütze) Johann Vormittag; Kapos Jan Brajt, Josef Kilian, Tadeusz Kopczynsky, Waclaw Kozlowski, Alfred Nikolaysen, Josef Reiter, Francizek Szopinski and Marian Zielkowski.

Zielkowski died of a heart attack in his prison cell in Gdańsk on 25 August 1945, some eight months before being brought to trial.

Nebbe, a guard company leader, was sentenced to life imprisonment during the Auschwitz Trials. He was released from prison on 23 October 1956. He died on 17 April 1972 in Kiel, in northern Germany, aged 59.

Simon was sentenced to life imprisonment on 30 December 1947 during the Mittelbau-Dora Trials. He was released from Landsberg Prison seven years later. Simon died on 27 September 1971, in Bochum, in North Rhine-Palatinate, aged 71.

Koch was responsible for inserting Zyklon B into the gas chambers. He died in prison, in Gdańsk, on 14 July 1955, aged 42. Romanian-born Baretzki was captured and held by Soviet troops after the evacuation of Auschwitz. On 17 August 1945 he was released and settled in Koblenz, in Rhineland-Palatinate. Fourteen years later Baretzki was arrested and brought to justice by the West German authorities. On 3 March 1960 during the Frankfurt-Auschwitz Trials, he was condemned for drowning four prisoners in a camp tank and for participating in the murder of 3,000 Jews of the Theresienstadt Ghetto.[337] He was sentenced to life imprisonment plus eight years. Baretzki committed suicide on 21 June 1988 at a hospital in Bad Nauheim, in the state of Hesse, aged 69, after the rejection of an appeal.

Lechner was sentenced to life imprisonment during the Auschwitz Trials for his cruelty towards camp inmates on multiple occasions. He was released from prison on 19 December 1959. Lechner died on 14 September 1975 in Eppingen, in southern Germany, aged 67.

Matthes was responsible for the extermination area of Camp I at Treblinka where the gas chambers were operated. In autumn 1943 he was transferred to Sobibor camp. Matthes was arrested after the war and indicted of crimes against humanity. He was sentenced to life imprisonment during the Treblinka Trials. Matthes died on 16 December 1979 in Bochum Prison, in North Rhine-Westphalia, aged 76.

Josef Kilian was a capo used as public executioner at Mittelbau-Dora concentration camp. On 24 December 1947, during the Dora trial, he was convicted and sentenced to life imprisonment. He was released from Landsberg Prison early.

Frenzel was arrested by US troops in a POW camp near Munich in mid-1945, but was soon released. On 22 March 1962, while working in Frankfurt as a stage lighting technician, he was arrested by the West German authorities and charged with crimes against humanity. Frenzel was sentenced to life imprisonment on 20 December 1966 in Hagen, for personally killing six inmates at the Sobibor concentration camp and for his participation in the murder of approximately 150,000 more. He was released on a technicality twenty-six years later, but was tried again and received the same term, life imprisonment. On 8 October 1985 Frenzel was released from prison because of poor health. He died on 2 September 1996 at Garbsen, near Hanover, aged 85.

Mentz, nicknamed 'Frankenstein' by the inmates, was arrested by the West German authorities fifteen years after the end of the war. He was convicted during the Treblinka Trials of aiding and abetting the murder of twenty-five Jews in the camp, and of being an accessory to the murder of approximately 300,000 more. Mentz was sentenced to life imprisonment. He was released for health reasons on 31 March 1978. He died less than three months later, on 25 June, in Paderborn, North Rhine-Westphalia, aged 74.

Miete was arrested and held briefly by US troops after the end of the war. On 27 May 1960 he was arrested by the West German authorities and charged in Düsseldorf with participating in the mass murder of at least 300,000 people at Treblinka.[338] On 3 September 1965 Miete was sentenced to life imprisonment. Less than twenty years later, on 27 February 1985, he was conditionally released from prison. He died two years later, on 9 August 1987, in Osnabrück, Lower Saxony, aged 78.

On 13 May 1946 and on 21 August 1947 four SS NCOs were found guilty as charged and sentenced to life imprisonment for crimes against humanity committed at Mauthausen-Gusen. They were Michael Cserny, Paul Gützlaff, Josef Mayer and Emil Thelmann.

The recommendations for the reduction of sentences imposed on convicted war and Nazi criminals were made by a three-member independent expert panel, a sort of grace committee. The Advisory Board on Clemency (ABC), which was established in 1950, became known as the Peck Panel, after the name of its head, American jurist David W. Peck. Frederick A. Moran, chairman of the New York Board of Parole, and Brigadier General Conrad E. Snow, a legal advisor to the US State Department, were the members of the committee. ABC considered the clemency petitions of the convicts and the exculpatory briefs of their defence lawyers before making their proposals. The final decisions, made by John J. McCloy, the US High Commissioner in Germany, were announced 31 January 1951.

In seventy-seven of the ninety-nine cases of convicted criminals considered or reviewed by the Peck Panel, a reduction of penalties was recommended. This included seven of the fifteen death sentences converted into imprisonment. After the outbreak of the Korean War, the rearmament (wiederbewaffnung) of West Germany was discussed from the summer of 1950. This is why McCloy decided to allow changes even to death sentences against Nazi and SS convicts, based on recommendations made by the ABC. Even West German President Theodor Heuss contacted the US ambassador, James B. Conant, with a request for pardons. Numerous pleas for leniency from influential individuals, including Justice Minister Wolfgang Haussmann and Bishop (Landesbischof) Martin Haug, were reportedly made. The vice president of the Bundestag, the West German Parliament, Carlo Schmidt spoke out in favour of a commutation. McCloy received political pressure from William Langer, a US Senator from North Dakota, as many of his constituents were of German descent. Langer felt that trial of anyone other than the highest Nazis was contrary to American legal tradition and helped communism.

Nazi doctors

Several German and Austrian physicians, most of them SS (Schutzstaffel) or Waffen-SS officers, served voluntarily in Nazi concentration camps. Many of them were involved in human experimentation and mass murder under the guise of the Euthanasia (Aktion T4) and Hitler's biological weapons programmes. The victims of the euthanasia programme have been estimated at between 275,000 to 300,000.[339] Medical and other tests were performed by physicians, chemists and other scientists on unwilling inmates (men, women and children), mostly Jews, in various concentration camps. These physicians, with some exceptions, were arrested by the Allied military authorities and brought to justice, after Nazi Germany's capitulation. The capture or the punishment (prison sentence or execution) was evaded by those few who managed to flee to South America or to the Middle East and by those who committed suicide before being taken prisoner or while in Allied custody. Of the physicians who were accused of crimes against humanity, some died of natural causes while in captivity or before the conclusion of their trial.

Austrian-born Max de Crinis was a psychiatrist who had joined the SS. He was a co-participant in the euthanasia programme. On 1 May 1945 44-year-old year old de Crinis, after killing his family with potassium cyanide, committed suicide by taking a cyanide tablet himself. Swiss-born Leonardo Conti was a physician and an SS-major (SS-sturmbannführer).

On 19 May 1945 he was arrested and imprisoned. On 6 October 1945 Conti hanged himself in his cell before the beginning of his trial in Nuremberg. He was 45 years old.

Werner Heyde was a psychiatrist and an SS-colonel (SS-standartenführer). He was one of the main organisers of the Aktion T4 euthanasia programme. Heyde worked in Buchenwald, Dachau and Sachsenhausen concentration camps. At the end of the war, he was interned and imprisoned. In 1947 he escaped. On 11 November 1959 he surrendered to the West German police in Frankfurt, after living for thirteen years as a fugitive. On 13 February 1964, Heyde hanged himself in his cell in Butzbach prison in south-western Germany, five days before his trial was to start.[340]

Edward Wirths was a physician and an SS-major (SS-sturmbannführer). He was the chief of the SS doctors in Auschwitz from 1942 to 1945. Wirths was involved in ordering medical experiments on unwilling prisoners, mostly women. He was captured by the Allies after the German capitulation and held in custody by the British. On 20 September 1945 he committed suicide by hanging. He was 36 years old.

Dr Ernst Holzlöhner was a Baltic–German physiologist and an SS major (SS-sturmbannführer). He was captured in June 1945 and interrogated by the British. After the interrogation he committed suicide. He was 46 years old.

Austrian-born SS-Major (SS-Sturmbannführer) Erwin-Oscar Ding-Schuler was a physician who performed medical experiments in various Nazi concentration camps. On 25 April 1945 he was tracked down by US troops, arrested and held. Ding-Schuler committed suicide while in American custody on 11 August 1945, aged 33.

Heinze Thilo was a gynaecologist and an SS-senior lieutenant (SS-obersturmführer). He was accused of war crimes committed in Auschwitz and Gross-Rosen concentration camps. He also participated in the murder of 3,791 Jews who were gassed in Theresienstadt, in German-occupied Czechoslovakia, on 8 March 1944. After the war, he committed suicide in prison, aged 34.

Austrian-born Hans Eppinger was partly of Jewish descent. He served as a physician in various concentration camps, performing experiments upon unwilling inmates. After the war, he committed suicide, aged 67, reportedly using poison, a month before he was to testify at the Nuremberg Trials.

Belgian-born Hans Delmotte was an SS physician. After the German surrender, he tried to flee to Belgium, but was arrested by the US Army. During his transfer to prison Delmotte somehow managed to shoot himself and died instantly from the gunshot wound. He was 28 years old.

August Hirt was an anatomist and an SS-major (SS-sturmbannführer). He performed experiments with mustard gas on inmates at the Natzweiler-Struthof concentration camp, in north-eastern France, during the German occupation. In September 1944 Hirt fled to France and went hiding in Tubingen, southern Germany. Hirt committed suicide on 2 May 1945 in the Black Forest, in the state of Baden-Württemberg, in south-west Germany, aged 47.

Carl Clauberg was a physician and an SS-lieutenant general (SS-gruppenführer). He was captured by the Russians in 1945. Three years later he was sentenced to twenty-five years in prison. He was released in 1955 and repatriated to West Germany with the final group of about 10,000 German POWs. Clauberg was employed by the clinic he used to work at in the 1930s, but soon was arrested to be tried for crimes against humanity. He died before his trial in Kiel in 1957, aged 58.

IMPRISONING THE ENEMY

Dr Rudolf Werner Hippius was a German–Baltic (born in Pskov, close to the Russian–Estonian border) psychologist and sociologist. He conducted racial studies on people in the Adam Mickiewicz University, in Poznań, occupied Poland.[341] He was arrested by the Red Army at war's end and died on 23 October 1945 in a Soviet prison camp near Prague, in Czechoslovakia, aged 40.

Twenty-three physicians and chief administrators were tried in the Palace of Justice (Justizpalast) in Nuremberg by a US military tribunal between 9 December 1946 and 20 August 1947 for crimes against humanity and for being members of a criminal organisation. In the Doctors' Trial, as it is also known, seven of the defendants were sentenced to death, nine received sentences ranging from ten years to life imprisonment and the remainder (seven) were acquitted. The physicians who were sentenced to death on 20 August 1947 were executed by hanging on 2 June 1948 in Landsberg Prison. They were SS-Brigadier Generals (SS-Gruppenführer) Karl Brandt and Karl Gebhardt, SS-Senior Colonel (SS-Oberführer) Joachim Mrugowsky and SS-Captain (SS-Hauptsturmführer) Waldemar Hoven.

Brandt was personal physicist to Hitler before his assignment to administer the Aktion T4 euthanasia programme. On 16 April 1945 he was arrested by the Gestapo and held in Kiel for sending his wife Anni and their son toward the American lines in the hope of evading capture by the Russians.[342] Brandt was saved from execution at that point when Kiel was seized by US troops. However, four months later he was sentenced to death at Nuremberg. He was hanged, aged 44.[343]

Gebhardt was one of Adolf Hitler's personal physicians. Despite being the president of the German Red Cross, in Ravensbrück and Auschwitz he performed medical and surgical experiments on unwilling prisoners related to the treatment of gangrene and sepsis.[344] Gebhardt was executed, aged 50.

Mrugowsky, a bacteriologist, was convicted of carrying out human experimentation at the Sachsenhausen concentration camp related to biological warfare and the treatment of typhus. He was hanged, aged 43.

In the 1920s Hoven visited the United States and worked as movie extra in Hollywood. As a physician and an SS officer he was accused of murdering at Buchenwald some 100 prisoners per week with a lethal injection of phenol. He also used such an injection against Hauptscharführer Rudolf Köhler. The victim, a non-commissioned officer of the SS, was a potential witness in an investigation against an SS female overseer, the notorious Ilse Koch, with whom Hoven had an affair. Hoven was hanged, aged 45.

In Landsberg Prison were also executed, on 2 June 1948, three non-physicians, who were involved in the extermination of inmates in concentration camps as leading administrators. They were Brigadier General (SS-Generalmajor) of the Waffen-SS Rudolf Hermann Brandt,[345] SS-Senior Colonel (SS-Oberführer) Hermann Victor and SS-Colonel (SS-Standartenführer) Wolfram Sievers. They were also tried at Nuremberg and received the death penalty.

Brandt was a lawyer by profession before joining the SS. He eventually became Heinrich Himmler's personal administrative officer. Brandt was famous for his eighty-six-piece Jewish scull collection, claimed to have been created for scientific (anthropological) reasons.[346] He was arrested by British troops on 21 May 1945 and held in an interrogation camp at Lüneburg. Brandt was hanged on 2 June 1948, his 39th birthday.

Sievers was the director of the Military Scientific Research Institute (Institut für Wehrwissenschaftliche Zweckforschung), which supervised the conduct of experiments on human subjects in concentration camps.[347] He was executed, aged 43.

A year older was Brack, a euthanasia programme participant when he was executed. He was sentenced to death for providing equipment and personnel that was used for the mass murder of concentration camp inmates, mostly Jews.[348]

In Landsberg Prison two physicians who had been sentenced to death in Dachau by another US military tribunal had been executed earlier, in May 1946. They were SS-Senior Lieutenant (SS-Obersturmführer) Fritz Hintermayer and Dr Claus Schilling.

Hintermayer was condemned over the killing by injection of two pregnant women and seven mentally ill prisoners in the Dachau concentration camp and its sub-camps during medical tests. He had also participated in executions to confirm the death of the executed. Hintermayer was hanged on 28 May 1946, aged 35.

Schilling, aged 74, was by far the older of the defendants in the Dachau Trial. A specialist on tropical diseases, Schilling carried out experiments on prisoners, aiming at finding a method to immunise people against malaria. Of the at least 1,000 prisoners used in his experiments at Dachau, between 300 and 400 died as a result. Schilling was sentenced to death on 13 December 1945. He was hanged in Landsberg Prison on 28 May 1946.

Two more physicians, SS Captain (SS-Hauptsturmführer) Friedrich Entress and SS-Senior Lieutenant (Obersturmführer) Eduard Krebsbach, were executed in Landsberg Prison one year later, on 28 May 1947, following their condemnation by other Allied tribunals, including the Mauthausen-Gusen Trial, for having performed medical experiments against prisoners in various concentration camps.

Entress was a senior physician at the Mauthausen-Gusen complex. He injected lethal doses of phenol directly into the heart of prisoners. When he was captured by Allied troops in Austria in April 1945, Entress was serving as a surgeon in a Waffen-SS tank division.[349]

Krebsbach was a physician and an SS-major (SS-obersturmführer). He was charged after the war over crimes committed in the Mauthausen-Gusen camp and in a detention facility (Kaiserwald) in Latvia.[350] On 11 May 1945 he was convicted by a US military court in Dachau of killing inmates by administering lethal injection of the chemical compound Benzene. Krebsbach was executed by hanging in Landsberg Prison on 28 May 1947, aged 52.

SS-Captain (SS-Hauptsturmführer) Helmut Vetter was executed in Landsberg Prison on 2 February 1949, aged 39. He was convicted of conducting medical experiments, mostly on Jewish prisoners, at Auschwitz and Dachau, as well as at Gusen, a sub-camp of Mauthausen.

SS-Captain (SS-Hauptsturmführer) Erich Wasicky was a medical officer at Mauthausen-Gusen from 1941 until early 1945. He oversaw the establishment and operation of the gas chambers in the main camp. On 13 May 1946 he was sentenced to death. Wasicky was executed by hanging on 28 May 1947, in Landsberg Prison, aged 36.

Romanian-born ethnic German (volksdeutscher) Fritz Kline, an SS-major (SS-sturmbannführer), was a Hungarian-educated medical doctor. He was initially posted to German-occupied Yugoslavia and then served in various concentration camps in Germany. After the war, he was arrested by the British Army at Lüneburg, in Lower

Saxony Ernst, and detained. Found guilty of crimes against humanity by a British military tribunal, Klein was sentenced to death by hanging. He was executed by Albert Pierrepoint on 13 December 1945 in Hamelin Prison, aged 57.

Ernst Illing was a neurologist and a senior physician of the Luftwaffe.[351] From 1942 to 1945 he was in charge of the Am Spiegelgrund psychiatric-neurological clinic in Vienna, where 250 children were abused to death.[352] After the war he was tried for crimes against humanity by a non-military court in Vienna and on 18 July 1946 he was sentenced to death.[353] He was executed by hanging on 30 November 1946 in the Austrian capital, aged 42.[354]

US Army Master Sergeant John C. Woods was involved in the hanging of forty Nazi criminals who were convicted to death. He was assisted in the Nuremberg and Landsberg executions by Joseph Malta, a military policeman, who volunteered for the task. Woods left the Army in 1947. He died in 1999 in Revere, in Massachusetts, aged 39.

Some 202 convicted Nazis were hanged by the British public executioner Albert Pierrepoint. Most of these executions were carried out in Hamelin (Hameln) Prison, in Lower Saxony.[355] Pierrepoint prided himself on his skill of calculating the drop required to break the prisoner's neck swiftly. Having carried out several hundred hangings, Pierrepoint had unrivalled expertise in the area. He was appointed by the British Army to carry out the hangings and it directed that he was to be treated as the equivalent of a lieutenant colonel. He was flown over to Germany on each occasion. He was assisted on the gallows by three Army NCOs. One of them was Sergeant Major Richard-Anthony O' Neill.[356] Some 145 men and women were hanged at Hamelin plus one, Teofil Walasek, who had been sentenced to death for the murder of an Allied policeman.

Dr Hermann Paul Nitsche was a psychiatrist and a chief official in Hitler's euthanasia programme. He was arrested on 11 March 1945 for the murder of more than a thousand mentally ill and intellectually challenged people during tests. On 7 July 1947 he was found guilty as charged and sentenced to death. Nitsche was executed by guillotine on 25 March 1948 in Dresden, aged 71.

Erich Zoddel, a German citizen, was imprisoned for theft in 1941. In March 1944 still a convict, he was transferred to Bergen-Belsen. After the war, Zoddel was arrested by British troops and tried for crimes committed in the camp in his new capacity as assistant overseer. He was indicted of murdering Maria Konatkwitz, a female detainee, on 18 April 1945, as well as for his abusive behaviour towards prisoners in general. He was sentenced to death during the Bergen Belsen Trials. Zoddel was executed by guillotine on 30 November 1945 in Wolfenbuttel Prison, 8 miles (13km) south of Brunswick, in Lower Saxony, aged 32.

Walter Böttcher, a German public executioner, was employed by the Allied occupation authorities to carry out death sentences. After the war, he settled in East Germany, where he served as public executioner from 1949 until the mid-1960s.

Johann Reichhart was Nazi Germany's chief executioner. He was credited with 3,165 executions[357] from March 1924, when he was employed by the judicial authorities in Munich. Some 250 of those executed were women. The Nazis have been estimated to have guillotined some 40,000 people in Germany and Austria using twenty guillotines between 1938 and 1945. They beheaded more people than during the French Revolution.[358] After the German capitulation, Reichhart was arrested and held briefly in Stadelheim Prison, in Munich's Giesing District. He was then employed by the US Army to assist Woods in the hanging of convicted Nazi war criminals. In the process, his wife divorced him and his son committed suicide in 1950. Rejected by other Germans and dying as an impoverished citizen living only on his First World War pension, he died in a care home near Munich, in 1972, aged 79.[359]

Three German executioners were arrested by the Red Army. Carl Gröpler was credited with 144 executions, including those of four German communists. He died in Soviet custody on 30 January 1946. Wilhelm Röttger was found in a hospital in Hanover and died shortly after his arrest by Soviet troops. Gustav Völpel was a public executioner from 1945 until 1950. In 1950 he was arrested and convicted of burglary and armed robberies. He remained in jail until 1957, when he was executed by the Soviet military.

Several physicians were given prison sentences for crimes against humanity committed during the war. Most of them were released from prison early, including those serving a life term. At the Nuremberg Doctors' Trial, four high-ranking officers were sentenced to life imprisonment for crimes against humanity. They were Colonel General (Generaloberstabsarzt) and chief of the Medical Services of the Armed Forces (Chef des Wehrmachtsanitätswesen) Siegfried Adolf Handloser, Colonel General of the Medical Services of the Luftwaffe Oskar Schröder, Major General (Generalarzt) of the Medical Services of the Luftwaffe Gerhard Rose and SS-Major General (SS-Gruppenführer) Karl Genzken.

Handloser was captured by British troops on 28 May 1945. He was sentenced to life imprisonment by the American Military Tribunal No. 1 on 20 August 1947 and sent to Landsberg Prison. On 31 January 1951 Handloser's sentence was commuted to twenty years on appeal. He was released earlier, in 1954, because of ill health. Handloser died of cancer in Munich a few months later, on 3 July 1954, aged 69.

Schröder was arrested by US troops on 8 May 1945. He was sentenced to life imprisonment, but his sentence was commuted to fifteen years. He was released from Landsberg Prison in 1954 and died five years later, aged 68.

Rose was a physician and an expert on tropical diseases. He was also a professor at the Robert Koch Institute, in Berlin, and a major general (Generalarzt) of the Medical Service of the Luftwaffe. Rose performed experiments on Jews, Romani and mentally ill people at Dachau and Buchenwald. He was sentenced to life imprisonment, but his sentence was commuted to fifteen years on 31 March 1951. He was discharged from Landsberg Prison two years later, on 3 June 1953. Rose died on 13 January 1992 in Obernkirchen, in Lower Saxony, aged 95.

Genzken was accused of conducting experiments from 1941 to 1945 in concentration camps to test the effectiveness of vaccines against typhus, smallpox, cholera and other diseases. He was sentenced to life imprisonment but this was commuted to twenty years. He was released from prison in April 1954. Genzken died on 10 October 1957 in Hamburg, aged 72.

Dr Johann Kremer was a professor of human genetics and an SS official. He was convicted of participating in experimentation carried out on prisoners at Auschwitz-Birkenau. He was sentenced to death in Kraków, but his sentence was later commuted to life imprisonment. In 1958 he was released from prison and repatriated. On 29 November 1960, Kremer was convicted to ten years in prison by a West German court. The court credited Kremmer for the time he had served in Poland and allowed him to walk free. He died on 8 January 1965 in Münster, North Rhine-Westphalia, aged 81.

Dr Heinz Baumkötter was a physician and an SS-captain (SS-hauptsturmführer). He performed medical experiments on prisoners in various concentration camps, including Mauthausen, Natzweiler-Stutthof and Sachsenhausen. He was captured by the Red Army and charged with war crimes. He was sentenced to life imprisonment by a Soviet military court. In 1956 he was released from the mines of the Vorkuta Gulag and repatriated. Following his arrest by the West German police, Baumkötter was tried for war crimes and sentenced to eight years in prison. The court took into consideration his stint in the Soviet Gulag as sufficient punishment and released him. He died on 21 April 2001 in Münster, North Rhine-Westphalia, aged 89.

Many doctors, most of them SS officers, were convicted after the war of crimes against humanity, receiving lesser prison sentences. Among them were SS-Lieutenant Colonel (SS-Obersturmbannführer) Hermann Becker-Freyseng (twenty years) and SS-Oberführer Helmut Pennendick (ten years).

Becker-Freyseng was a physician and a consultant for aviation medicine with the Luftwaffe. He was convicted of carrying out deadly experiments on forty inmates at Dachau during the Doctors' Trial and sentenced to twenty years' imprisonment. The inmates were forced to drink salt water or had it injected into their veins. Half the subjects were given a drug called berkatit, while all were subjected to an invasive liver biopsy without anaesthetic. All the subjects died.[360] Four years later Becker-Freyseng's sentence was commuted to ten years. He was released earlier, in 1952. Eight years later Becker-Freyseng was diagnosed with cancer. He died on 27 August 1961, aged 51.[361]

Of the defendants in the Doctor's Trial, five were acquitted. They were Georg-August Weltz, Siegfried Ruff, Konrad Schäfer, Hans Wolfgang Romberg and Adolf Pokorny. Weltz was a physician and a lieutenant colonel (Oberfeldarzt) of the Medical Services of the Luftwaffe. He was also in charge of the Institute for Aviation in Munich. Ruff was a physician and a first lieutenant in the Medical Services of the Luftwaffe. He headed the Medical Department of the Institute for Aviation. Schäffer, also a physician, was senior staff member in the Institute for Aviation Medicine in Berlin. It has been commented that, after being acquitted at Nuremberg, all three were hired as scientific advisors by the US Army Air Force. Schäffer died in 1951, Weltz in 1953, Romberg in 1981 and Ruff in 1989.

Austrian-born Pokorny, who was also acquitted[362] in the same trial in August 1947, was married to a Jewish physician, Dr Lilly Weil, and mother of their two children until 1935. She spent most of the war period detained in Ghetto Terezin in Austria and later emigrated to Brazil.[363] Pokorny was a specialist in skin and venereal diseases. In his capacity as medical officer of the SS, he officially suggested the compulsory sterilisation of all Soviet prisoners of war. The project was not implemented though due to technical obstacles.[364] The date and place of Pokorny's death are unknown.

Heinrich Schmidt was a physician and an SS-captain (SS-hauptsturmführer). He served as medical officer in the Dachau, Majdanek, Mittelbau-Dora and Bergen-Belsen camps. He was indicted by a US military tribunal, during the Dora Trial, in August 1947 for allowing inmates to die by withholding medical care. The suspected crimes were committed between March and April 1945 in a sub-camp (Nordhausen) of the Mittelbau-Dora system. In December 1947 he was acquitted due to insufficient evidence. Twenty-eight years later, in November 1975, Schmidt was indicted by a West German court in Düsseldorf of alleged crimes committed in Majdanek concentration camp between 1942 and 1943. He was acquitted due to lack of evidence on 20 March 1979, in what is considered the most expensive criminal trial in German history. He was released from prison on 19 April 1979.[365] Schmidt died on 28 November 2000 in Celle, in Lower Saxony, aged 88.

In Austria no one accused of war crimes was sentenced to death after the war. Even those given prison terms had been released by 1955.[366]

Female guards

Of the 55,000 guards in Nazi concentration camps, about 3,700 were women. Most of them were posted in camps located in Germany, Austria and occupied Poland. Fewer served in camps operating in Czechoslovakia and eastern France. These women belonged to an SS (Schutzstaffel) auxiliary formation named Gefolge that provided uniformed personnel to concentration camps. Chief senior inspector (chef oberaufseherin) was the highest rank received by women in the SS concentration camp system.

Anna Klein, Luise Brunner and Ruth Closius-Neudeck were the only women to become SS chief senior inspectors. Klein was posted at Ravensbrück, Nazi Germany's largest concentration camp for women, 56 miles (90km) north of Berlin. More than 130,000 women and children were detained there. In July 1948, she was tried in Hamburg for crimes against humanity, but was acquitted due to lack of evidence. Klein's whereabouts since her release from prison on 21 July 1948 are unknown.

Brunner was a chief senior inspector at Auschwitz II-Birkenau. In July 1948 she was convicted for her involvement in the maltreatment of prisoners and sentenced to three years in prison. Brunner lived up to the age of 77.

A total of eleven women were convicted, during the Ravensbrück Trial held in Hamburg after the war. They were sentenced to death for crimes committed in various concentration camps and hanged at Hamelin Prison, Lower Saxony, by British public executioner Albert Pierrepoint. He carried out his duties assisted by Sergeant Major Richard-Anthony O'Neill.[367] Irma Grese, Johanna Bormann and Elisabeth Volkenrath were hanged on 13 December 1945. Dorothea Binz, Elisabeth Marschall and Greta Bösel were executed on the gallows on 2 May 1946. Vera Salvequart was hanged on 26 June 1947. Ruth Closius-Neudeck (née Hartmann) was executed on 29 July 1948. Ida Bertha Schreiter and Emma Zimmer were hanged at Hamelin on 20 September 1948.[368] Male hanging was typically carried out in pairs. The ten women were executed singly[369] by long-drop hanging.[370]

Aged 60, Zimmer was the oldest female Nazi to be executed as a war criminal after the German capitulation, together with Marschall and Ilse Koch. Zimmer was posted as a guard-overseer (helferin) in various concentration camps. She was known for being brutal and sadistic in her duties, which included the selection of prisoners to be gassed.[371] Zimmer eventually became assistant camp leader at Auschwitz II-Birkenau.[372]

Grese was expelled from home by her father Albert in 1939 when she decided to join the SS-Gefolge formation, aged 17. She served as guard-overseer (helferin) in the women's section of the Bergen-Bergen concentration camp.[373] In 1942 she became a high-ranked overseer (aufseherin) at Ravensbrück. Two years later she was promoted to rapportführerin, the second-highest rank possible for female concentration camp wardens, and posted to Auschwitz. On 17 April 1945 Grese was captured when Bergen-Belsen was liberated by British troops. During the Belsen Trial at Lüneburg she was accused of participating in prisoner selection for the gas chambers and for accompanying a death march of prisoners from Auschwitz to Ravensbrück. Survivors testified that Grese had a habit of beating prisoners with a whip. The press labelled her 'the beautiful beast' and 'the hyena of Auschwitz'.

In Hamelin Prison the night before their execution and until the early hours of 13 December 1945, 22-year-old Grese and Johanna Bormann, also known as Juana, sang Nazi songs.[374] Bormann served in various Nazi concentration camps. In 1939 at Ravensbrück she was assigned to oversee slave labour crews. In October 1942, after her promotion to guard-overseer (helferin), she was transferred to Auschwitz-Birkenau. Two years later she was posted to an auxiliary concentration camp at Hindenburg, present-day Zabrze, near Katowice, in southern Poland. In early 1945, by now a high-ranked-overseer (aufseherin), Bormann was brought back to Ravensbrück. Short in stature, she soon became known for her cruelty. She used to unleash her 'big bad wolfhound' German shepherd on helpless prisoners. Found guilty as charged in a British military tribunal, Bormann was sentenced to death by hanging. She was executed, aged 52.

Volkenrath (née Mühlau) was a former hairdresser. She served as an SS guard-overseer (SS-helferin) in various concentration camps and eventually became a supervising wardress (SS-blockführer) at Bergen-Belsen. She was married to SS-Senior Lance Corporal (SS-Rottenführer) Heinz Volkerath from 1943. Volkenrath was arrested by the British Army in April 1945 and convicted of war crimes during the Bergen-Belsen Trials.[375] She was executed by hanging, aged 26.

Binz started with kitchen work at Ravensbrück. By July 1943, she had been promoted to deputy chief wardress (stellvertretende oberaufseherin). Binz trained some of the cruellest female guards in the camp. She used to carry a whip in hand along with a leashed German shepherd and at a moment's notice could beat or kick a woman prisoner to death or select her to be killed. On 3 May 1945, having fled from the concentration camp ahead of the advancing Soviet troops, Binz was arrested by the British Army in Hamburg. She was convicted by a British military tribunal of perpetrating war crimes. Hours later she attempted to kill herself by slashing her wrists.[376] However, officials intervened before she could bleed to death. Binz was hanged on 2 May 1947, aged 27.

Marschall was an SS head nurse (SS-oberschwester) at Ravensbrück. She participated in medical experiments carried out upon unwilling prisoners by SS doctors. Her duties included the selection of prisoners for execution. Marschall was hanged as a war criminal, aged 60.

Greta Bösel (née Müller) was a trained nurse who became a work input overseer (SS-arbeitseinsatzführerin) in a small extermination camp at Uckermark, near Ravensbrück.[377] After the death march of prisoners out of Ravensbrück, she left the camp with her husband ahead of the advancing Soviet forces. Bössel was eventually arrested by British troops. She was executed on the gallows at Hamelin Prison, aged 38.

Czechoslovakian-born Salvequart, a Sudeten German, was sent to prison by the Gestapo for having dated Jewish men on two occasions. At Ravensbrück, where she was transferred in early December 1944, Salvequart was assigned by the SS to supervise, as a kapo, forced labour and also carry out administrative tasks. She served in the camp's medical wing and oversaw the gassing of thousands of women detainees.[378] In Hamburg during the Ravensbrück Trials Salvequart was also convicted of poisoning the sickly in the medical wing to avoid the effort of having to transfer them to the gas chambers. She was hanged, aged 27.

Schreiter was a high-ranked overseer (SS-aufseherin) at Ravensbrück. After the war she was convicted by a British military court of taking part in the selections of prisoners who were eventually murdered or died as a result of deliberate overwork or neglect. Schreiter was sentenced to death by hanging. She was executed, aged 35.

Ruth Closius-Neudeck (née Hartmann) was a high-ranked overseer (SS-aufseherin) at Ravensbrück. In January 1945 she was transferred to the nearby satellite camp at Uckermark after being promoted to chief senior inspector (chef oberaufseherin). In early April she fled the camp and tried to evade capture. Closius-Neudeck was eventually tracked down and arrested by British troops. On 26 April 1948 she was convicted of selecting 3,000 female prisoners to die in the gas chambers.[379] Closius-Neudeck was hanged, aged 28.

After their execution by Pierrepoint on the gallows of Hamelin Prison the bodies of the eleven women were buried at Wehl Cemetery of the nearby town (Hameln in German).

Swiss-born Carmen-Castro Mory was a journalist who worked as a spy for Nazi Germany in France in the late 1930s. In 1938 she was also the Paris correspondent of *The Manchester Guardian*, an English newspaper. In 1941, having lost the trust of her superiors in the Gestapo, Mory was arrested and detained in Ravensbrück, where she became a kapo. After the war she was convicted in Hamburg of crimes committed in the camp and sentenced to death. Forty-year-old Mory killed herself in her cell by slashing her wrists before the execution could take place.

Several female guards were brought to justice in Poland after the war accused of crimes committed in various concentration camps. For eight of them the sentence was death by hanging. They were local girls, born in the greater area of Danzig, as Gdańsk was named until 1945 before becoming part of Poland.

Jenny Wanda Barkmann, Elisabeth Becker, Wanda Kalacinski, Ewa Paradies and Gerda Steinhoff were convicted in Gdańsk during the first of the Stutthof Trials held from 25 April to 31 May 1946. They were publicly hanged on 4 July 1946, along with six male convicts, at Biskupia Górka (Bishop's Hill),[380] near Gdańsk. The condemned were executed by short-drop hanging in front of a large crowd, estimated at 11,000.[381] A row of simple gallows had been set up in a large open area, four double ones with a triple gallows in the middle. A fleet of open tracks brought the prisoners to the execution ground, their hands and legs tied with cords. The tracks were backed under the gallows and the condemned were made to stand on the tailboard or on a chair bound hand and foot. He or she was collared with a noose around the neck at the centre of the gallows and no hood was put on his or her head. When the preparations were completed, each track was driven forward, leaving the condemned suspended for a torturously short drop. The weight of the body tightened the noose around the neck, effecting strangulation and death in ten to twenty minutes. It is alleged that one man and two women (unnamed) struggled and fought with their guards prior to being hanged, while others seemed to accept their fate relatively calmly.[382]

Barkmann was an SS high-ranked overseer (SS-aufseherin) at Stutthof's sub-camp (SK-III). She was convicted over her brutality against prisoners that caused several deaths and for selecting women and children for the gas chambers. In May 1945 Barkmann was arrested by Soviet troops at the Gdańsk railway station while trying to flee westward. During the trial she was seen to repeatedly arrange her hair in the courtroom and to flirt with Polish guards. Twenty-four-year-old Barkmann was found guilty as charged and sentenced to death. She was hanged first, during the Biskupia Górka public executions of 4 July 1946.

Becker was a cook and a tramway conductor before becoming a high-ranked overseer (SS-aufseherin) in September 1944. She was mainly posted at SK-III. She fled Stutthof's sub-camp in January 1945. On 13 April Becker was arrested by Polish officials in her birthplace of Neuteich, present-day Nowy Staw, in northern Poland. During her trial, she was indicted of selecting at least thirty female prisoners to be gassed. Becker was sentenced to death and was hanged, aged 22.

Kalacinski (also known as Wanda Klaff after her husband's surname) served in Stutthof's sub-camps as an SS guard-overseer (SS-helferin). She was charged with abusing many prisoners.[383] In early 1945 she fled the camp but on 11 June she was arrested by Polish officials. She admitted during her trial striking at least two prisoners every day. Kalacinski was sentenced to death and hanged, aged 24.

Paradies was posted as a high-ranked overseer (SS-aufseherin) mainly at Stutthof.[384] She was convicted for her brutality against prisoners that caused several deaths. Paradies was executed, aged 25.

Steinhoff was posted as a block leader (blockleiterin) at SK-III, Stutthof's sub-camp, on 1 October 1944. By the end of the month she had been promoted to senior inspector (oberaufseherin). In January 1945 Steinhoff left her current post, a sub-camp south of Danzig, and went missing. On 25 May she was tracked down and arrested by Polish officials. She was sentenced to death for the sadistic abuse of prisoners and for her part in the selection of prisoners to be sent to the gas chambers. She was hanged, aged 24.

In other trials held in Kraków in November 1947 two female guards also received the death penalty for crimes committed in concentration camps. They were Maria Mandl and Therese Brandl. Mandl was an Austrian-born SS guard-overseer (SS-helferin) who eventually became a top-ranking official at Auschwitz-Birkenau. It is believed that she was directly complicit in the deaths of 500,000 female prisoners. In May 1945 Mandl fled through the mountains of southern Bavaria to her birthplace, Münzkirchen, the present-day municipality of Schärding, in north-west Austria. She was eventually arrested by US troops and detained at Dachau prison. In November 1946 Mandl was handed over to Poland. One year later she was brought in front of a Kraków tribunal during the Auschwitz Trials indicted of crimes against humanity.

Brandl served as an overseer in the Auschwitz II extermination camp at Birkenau. She was arrested on 29 August 1945 by the US Army in the Bavarian mountains. She was also indicted of crimes against humanity.

Both convicts were found guilty as charged and sentenced to death by hanging. They were executed on the gallows of a Kraków prison – Mandl on 24 January 1948, aged 36 and Brandl four days later, aged 46.

Elisabeth Lupka was an SS high-ranked overseer (SS-aufseherin) at Ravensbrück in March 1943 when she was transferred to Auschwitz-Birkenau as a block overseer

(SS-blockführerin). Lupka used to beat prisoners with a whip and select others for the gas chambers. In January 1945 she accompanied a death march of prisoners to Loslau (present-day Wodzisław Śląski), in southern Poland. On 6 June Lupka was arrested and eventually tried for crimes against humanity. She was found guilty as charged by a military court in Kraków and sentenced to death. Lupka was executed by hanging in Montelupich Prison, on 8 January 1949, aged 46.

Elsa Ehrich was tried in Lublin, Poland, during the Majdanek Trials. She was No. 3 in rank in the SS female guard-overseers (SS-helferinnen). In 1943 she made an attempt while posted at Majdanek to launch a Nazi brothel, but the project was abandoned when one of her slave sex workers was diagnosed with typhus. Ehrich was found guilty of crimes against humanity and sentenced to death. She was hanged on 26 October 1948 in Lublin prison, aged 34.

Ilse Koch served at Buchenwald and Majdanek, where her husband, SS-Colonel (SS-Standartenführer) Karl-Otto Koch, had been commandant. He was executed by a German firing squad in Majdanek nearly a week before the arrival of Soviet troops in the concentration camp, having been accused of corruption. Ilse, also known as the 'Bitch of Buchenwald', had an active role in atrocities committed in both camps in her capacity as a chief senior inspector (chef oberaufseherin). Her trial before a US military court began in early 1947. On 19 August she was sentenced to life imprisonment for crimes against humanity. The sentence was commuted to four years. Koch was released from prison after serving two years. In 1949, after pressure from public opinion, she was rearrested and tried before a West German court. On 15 January 1951 she was sentenced again to life imprisonment. On 1 September 1967 Koch hanged herself in her cell at Aichach women's prison, near Augsburg, in Bavaria, aged 60.

Alice Orlowski was a female work detail overseer in various concentration camps, including Ravensbrück, Auschwitz II-Birkenau, Loslau (Wodzisław Śląski) and Majdanek.[385] She came to be regarded as one of the most brutal overseers. She would whip prisoners across the eyes, causing permanent or temporary blindness to some of them. In January 1945 Orlowski participated in two death marches of prisoners, from Majdanek to Auschwitz-Birkenau and from Auschwitz to Loslau. In May 1945 she was captured by Soviet forces and stood trial in Kraków for crimes against humanity. In September 1947 Orlowski was sentenced to life imprisonment but was released in 1957 after serving ten years.[386] In 1973 she was arrested in Cologne for anti-Semitic remarks she made publicly. She was sentenced to ten months in prison, serving eight of them. In 1975 Orlowski was brought to justice by the West German authorities in Dusseldorf for crimes committed in the Majdanek concentration camp. She died of natural causes on 21 May 1976 during her trial, aged 72 or 73.

Luise Danz was also sentenced to life imprisonment. In 1947 she was tried by a military court in Kraków for crimes committed in various concentration camps during her posting as an SS guard-overseer (SS-helferin). She was condemned for having severely abused female detainees with a bull whip and for having aided in the hanging of Soviet female prisoners. She was released earlier, in 1956. Danz died on 21 June 2009, in Walldorf, Thuringia, in central Germany, aged 91.[387]

Austrian-born Hermine Braunsteiner was sentenced to life imprisonment as a war criminal as late as 1981. She had served as an SS guard-overseer (SS-helferin) in various concentration camps. On 7 May 1945 she fled to Vienna to avoid the advancing

Soviet troops. She was eventually arrested by the Austrian police and turned over to the British military authorities in Germany. Braunsteiner remained incarcerated until 1947. She was eventually sentenced to three years' imprisonment by a court in Graz, Austria, for torturing and mistreating prisoners.[388] In October 1958 Braunsteiner married an American, Russel Ryan, and emigrated, initially to Halifax, Nova Scotia, in Canada and a year later to the United States. The couple settled in Maspeth, a community in the borough of Queens in New York. In 1963 Braunsteiner became an American citizen.[389] A year later, the Nazi-hunting Simon Wiesenthal Centre in Jerusalem alerted the *New York Times* to Braunstein's past activities. She was denaturalised in 1968 and extradited to the Federal Republic of Germany five years later. She stood trial in June 1981 in Düsseldorf, where a life sentence was imposed to her. The complication of diabetes and other health problems, including a leg amputation, led to her release from prison. Braunsteiner died on 19 April 1999 in Bochum, in North Rhine-Westphalia, aged 79.

Four women, most of them guard-overseers, were sentenced to various prison terms by tribunals in the post-war period for crimes committed during their posting in Nazi concentration camps. Herta Elhert, Gertrud Heise and Hildegard Lächert were sent to prison for fifteen years each. Elfriede Mohneke was sentenced to ten years and Irmgard Fürhner to two. Two women, Elfried Huth and 'Jane' Bernigau, were arrested, interrogated and held, but were never prosecuted for war crimes.

Elhert, an SS guard-overseer (SS-helferin) was sentenced to fifteen years in prison during the Belsen Trial. On 7 May 1953 she was given an early release. Elhert died on 4 April 1997 aged 92. She was living in Berlin under the assumed name Herta Naumann.

Heise, an SS chief senior inspector (SS-chef oberaufseherin) from October 1944, was captured by the British Army in April 1945. She was later condemned by a British military court for leading a death march of female prisoners from the Kraków-Płaszów concentration camp to Auschwitz-Birkenau in January 1944.[390] On 22 May 1946 Heise was sent to prison for fifteen years, but her sentence was eventually commuted to seven. She was released from prison in 1953 and settled in Hamburg, where she was last reported alive in the 1970s.

Lächert was a nurse who became a high-ranked overseer (SS-aufsherin) in various camps (Ravensbrück and Auschwitz II-Birkenau). The mother of two children at the time of the trial in November 1947 in a Kraków courtroom, she was sentenced to fifteen years' imprisonment. Lächert was released from a Kraków prison in 1956 and returned to the then West Germany. Twenty-three years later, in 1979, she was tried as a war criminal by a court in Düsseldorf and sentenced to twelve years in prison. Having served ten years in Polish prisons, she was released. Lächert died in Berlin in 1995, aged 75.

Herta Bothe was an SS high-ranked overseer (SS-aufseherin) from September 1942. She was posted at Ravensbrück, Stutthof and Bergen Belsen, with ruthlessness on prisoners being her main characteristic.[391] Bothe was arrested on 15 April 1945 at Bergen-Belsen, when British troops stormed the camp and liberated the detainees. She was imprisoned in Celle, Lower Saxony, and later brought to justice, accused of beating a Hungarian Jew named Éva to death with a wooden block. During her trial Bothe only admitted striking prisoners with her hands. She was sentenced to ten years in prison, but was released early, on 22 December 1951. Bothe lived as Herta Lange in a modest community (the name is not known) in north-eastern Germany until her death on 16 March 2000 aged 79.

Mohneke was an SS high-ranked overseer (SS-aufseherin) in the Uckermark sub-camp near Ravensbrück. During the third Ravensbrück Trial she was sentenced to ten years in prison.[392] She was released on 14 June 1952 for good conduct, after serving only five years. Mohneke died on 11 December 1994 in Berlin, aged 72.

In January 1945 Erna Beilhardt resigned from her post as a high-ranked overseer (aufseherinnen) at a sub-camp near Heiligenbeil, present-day Mamonovo, in west Russia, after becoming disturbed by watching her fellow overseers torturing and killing prisoners.[393] On 14 July she was arrested by Soviet troops in Swinemünde, present-day Świnoujście, in north-west Poland, and brought to justice as a war criminal. During the Stutthof Trials, Beilhardt admitted being a Nazi supporter since 1933. Due to her voluntary resignation as a guard-overseer and from the SS altogether, she received just a five-year prison sentence. Her lack of personal involvement in the murder or torture of inmates also worked in her favour. Beilhardt was released from prison on 21 December 1951, seven months after the completion of her sentence. She settled in Wetter (Hessen), near Marburg, in central Germany, where she died in 1999, aged 91 or 92.

Johanna Langfeld served as an SS guard-overseer (SS-helferin) in various concentration camps.[394] In late 1944 she was dismissed for showing excessive sympathy to Polish female prisoners at Ravensbrück. On 20 December 1945 she was arrested by the US Army in Munich and nine months later she was extradited to Poland to be tried as a war criminal. On 23 September 1946 Langfeld escaped from a Kraków prison and found sanctuary in a convent. The escape was organised by some of her former victims, Polish inmates at Ravensbrück, who helped her to avoid a possible death penalty. They also hid her from the Polish authorities for ten years before smuggling her back to Germany. Langfeld eventually lived with her sister in Munich. She died on 26 January 1974 in Augsburg, 31 miles (50km) west of Munich, aged 74. Langfeld's is the only known case of an SS guard being saved from a death sentence by her own victims.[395]

Irmgard Führner served in the Stutthof camp from 1943 to 1945. She was the camp commandant's stenographer and typist. As late as 2022, she was convicted by a court in Itzehoe, northern Germany, of complicity in the murder of 10,505 Jewish prisoners, non-Jewish Poles and Soviet prisoners of war. She was accused of being part of the apparatus that helped the camp function. On 19 December 2022 96-year-old Führner was sentenced to a two-year suspended prison term.

'Jane' Bernigau was an SS chief senior inspector (SS oberaufseherin) in various concentration camps, including Mauthausen-Gusen. In February 1945 she left Gross-Rosen, in occupied Poland, for Reichenau, Gross-Rossen's sub-camp.[396] She fled from there and, according to the German historian Isabell Sprenger, was interrogated by the authorities several times (the last time in 1976), but was never prosecuted for war crimes. She died in Husum, Schleswig-Holstein, in March 1992, aged 83.

Huth, better known as Rinkel (after her husband), was a female guard at Ravensbrück. She was never questioned by the Allied authorities after the end of the war for her actions in the camp, in which she was the handler of an SS-trained dog. She managed to hide her secret for more than sixty years, even from her German–Jewish husband, Fred William Rinkel, whose family had been murdered in the Holocaust. She married him in San

Francisco in September 1959, nearly three years after her admission to the United States as an immigrant. In October 2004 the American authorities, alerted by the Simon Wiesenthal Centre, arrested her and almost two years later they had her deported to the Federal Republic of Germany. Although the centre insisted on a trial, Rinkel was never accused of any crime. She confessed to working in the concentration camp as a dog handler because this activity was better paid – as she claimed – than the ordinary work of guard-overseer. Rinkel died, aged 96, in a nursing home in Willich, in the then West Germany.

Austrian-born Maria Stromberger was arrested by French troops in her sister's house at Bregenz, western Austria, in mid-1945, and was held to be tried as a war criminal. She had worked at Auschwitz as a nurse for the camp's SS personnel from October 1942 to February 1945.[397] Stromberger was acquitted after former prisoners testified in court that she secretly provided food and medicine to them.[398] Two years later she testified in court against Rudolf Höss, the notorious commandant of Auschwitz. Stromberger lived in relative obscurity in post-war Austria, although she was a national hero among the Polish resistance.[399] On 18 May 1947 she died of a heart attack in Bregenz, aged 59.

Margot Dreschel, Erika Bergmann and Ulla Jürss were tried and condemned in communist East Germany after the war for crimes against humanity committed while serving in Nazi concentration camps. Dreschel (also referred to as Drexler) was a guard-overseer (SS-helferin) at Ravensbrück. In 1942 she was promoted to rapportführerin, the second highest rank possible for a concentration camp warden, and then became an assistant to Josef Mengele, the notorious physician and SS-captain (SS-hauptsturmführer), selecting prisoners for his deadly experiments. Later, at Auschwitz, Dreschel carried out selections of women and children for the gas chambers. In April 1945 she fled westward and one month later she was arrested near Dresden, in the Soviet zone of occupied Germany. Dreschel was tried by a Soviet military court and condemned as a war criminal. She was hanged in May or June 1945 in Bautzen Prison, located in eastern Saxony, aged 36 or 37.

Bergmann served as a high-ranked overseer at Ravensbrück and later in the Genthin sub-camp near Brandenburg. After the war she remained undetected for ten years. In 1955 she was exposed and brought to justice for crimes against humanity. Bergmann was accused of inciting an attack by a dog on prisoners, killing six of them. On 2 November 1955 she was sentenced to life imprisonment.

Jürss was a block overseer (blockfülherin) at Ravensbrück.[400] She was so brutal that she was relieved of her duties and sent home. Jürss lived quietly in the communist East Germany until 1966, when she was tracked down and brought to justice for crimes against humanity. She was eventually sentenced to life imprisonment. The German unification in 1990 found Bergmann and Jürss still in prison, in the Hoheneck Fortress, near Stollberg, in Saxony.[401] In 1991, they were both released on probation. Bergmann died five years later at Guben, in north-east Germany, aged 81. With regard to Jürss, there is no information about her since her release from prison.

Female POWs

On 17 September 1944 British glider-borne troops who landed around Wolfheze, near Deelen airfield, north of Arnhem, in central-eastern Holland, captured 175 prisoners.

Among them was Irene Reimann, a female telegraphist (Blitzmadschen) serving in the Luftwaffe's 201st Regiment, 3rd Fighter Division (3. Jagd-Division), stationed at Schaarsbergen, east of the airfield. She was to enter history as the only female prisoner of war in the Battle of Arnhem.[402] Reimann, one of the uniformed women in the service of Luftwaffe Signals (Luftnachrichtenhelferinner or HIS), was taken prisoner by elements of the 7th King's Own Scottish Borderers, led by a British glider pilot, Staff Sergeant Joe Price, of the 13th Flight Squadron, Glider Pilot Regiment. She was captured in the woods near Schaarsbergen in civilian clothing on the first day of Operation Market Garden, the invasion of the Netherlands by Allied forces.[403] The prisoners were initially held at a school building near the Wolterbeekweg, in Oosterbeck. They were allocated classrooms, with Reimann in a room by herself.[404] She refused all food until it was tested by British troops, fearing that it was poisoned. The prisoners were then transferred to Oosterbeek's Hartenstein Hotel, but when the area was targeted by German mortar fire they were taken to a safer place, a cellar in Sandersweg. Reimann was set free on 20 September three days after her capture. She travelled to Duisburg, in the Ruhr metropolitan area of North Rhine-Westphalia, and resumed her duties with the Divisional Headquarters. There is no information about Reimann's whereabouts in the post-war period. She possibly ended up in communist East Germany.

During the Second World War more than 500,000 women volunteered as uniformed auxiliaries in the Wehrmacht. They were usually assigned administrative or clerical duties, although a great number helped to operate the anti-aircraft system. About 400,000 German women volunteered as nurses. A number of these, called brown nurses because of the colour of their uniform, were committed Nazis. Brown nurses were fully-fledged SS women. German women also served in the HIS (Luftnachrichtenhelferinnen), mainly in Luftwaffe's Signal units. They served also in auxiliary units of the army (Nachrichtenhelferin) and the navy (Kriegshelferinnen), usually assigned administrative or clerical duties. They were also sent to SS units after undergoing training at Reichsschule SS. Most of them belonged to the Women's SS Division, a formation named Gefolge. In January 1945 around 3,500 of these women were said to have been on guard duty in concentration camps. From mid-1945 German uniformed women captured by or surrendered to Allied forces were detained mostly in 'cages'. These were sections of internment camps in Vilvoorde in Belgium and in Recklinghausen, North Rhine-Westphalia. Vilvoorde was managed by the British Army and Recklinghausen by the US Army.

ITALIANS

Some 19,741 officers of fascist Italy's armed forces were captured by or surrendered to Allied troops during the 1939–45 war and detained in POW camps.[1] Romolo Lastrucci was the first Axis general who fell into enemy hands.[2] A brigadier general of the Italian Royal Army (Regio Esercito) from 1939, he commanded the Tenth Army's XXI Corps in North Africa in mid-1940. On the morning of 16 June, six days after his country entered the war, Lastrucci was captured while inspecting fortifications in Cyrenaica's Bardia area, in eastern Libya, not far from the Egyptian border. His two-car convoy was attacked near Marsa Luch by elements of the British 7th Armoured Division. While the other car managed to escape, Lastrucci's suffered an engine problem and was surrounded. The general surrendered after seeing an escorting officer, Captain Francesco Valvo, killed in a brief firefight. Lastrucci was captured carrying the defence plans of the greater area, which were later used by the British in the planning of the battle of Bardia. Between 10 and 16 June some 220 of Lastrucci's soldiers were captured and taken prisoner when the British Army's 11th Hussars (Prince Albert's Own) and the 7th Hussars (Queen's Own) Tank Regiments stormed in and took the Italian front-line forts at Capuzzo and Magdalena.[3] Lastrucci was initially held in a POW camp in Egypt, Geneifa, near the Great Bitter Lake. In late August he was transferred to a POW camp in Dehradun in northern India.[4] In late 1944 Lastrucci was repatriated on health grounds. He died on 29 September 1976 in Rome, aged 87.

On 10 December 1940 Major General Armando Pescatori, commander of the 2nd Italian-Libyan Division, was captured by Allied troops in the desert and was also sent to Dehradun for internment.[5] After his repatriation at the end of the war Pescatori was promoted to lieutenant general. He died on 23 August 1957 in Rome, aged 73.

Also in December 1940, Lieutenant General Sebastiano Gallina was taken prisoner, aged 67, when his Italian-Libyan Army Corps (also known as Maletti Group) was destroyed by British forces in western Egypt. He was also sent to Dehradun for detention. After suffering a mental breakdown, Gallina was repatriated in March 1943 for medical reasons during a POW exchange carried out in Turkey. He was killed on 9 January 1945, aged 72, when the train he was travelling from Giaveno to Turin, in northern Italy, was strafed by Allied aircraft.

Thirteen Italian generals and one admiral became POWs in 1941: Enrico Pitassi Mannella, Umberto Barberis, Vincenzo della Mura, Adolfo de Leone and Rear Admiral Massimiliano Vietina in January; Valentino Babini, Annibale Bergonzoli and Ferdinando Cona in February; Luigi Frusci in March; Prince Amedeo of Savoia and Pietro Pina Parpaglia in May; Pietro Piacentini and Pietro Gazzera in June; and Guglielmo Ciro Nasi in November.

ITALIANS

Divisional General (Generale di Divisione) Pitassi Mannella, an artillery officer, was the commander of Tobruk on 6 January 1941, when the eastern Libyan fortified township was assaulted by Allied forces that were spearheaded by the Australian 16th Infantry Brigade and the British 7th Royal Tank Regiment. The Italians surrendered on 22 January. More than 20,000 officers and men were taken prisoner, including three generals besides Pitassi Mannella and one admiral. They were Lieutenant General Barberis, commander of the 61st Infantry Division *Sirte* and responsible for the eastern fortifications, Brigadier General della Mura, responsible for the western fortifications in Libya, Brigadier General de Leone, chief-of-staff of the XXII Army Corps, and Rear Admiral Vietina, who commanded a 1,500-strong naval contingent.

On the night of 22–23 January 1941 Italian Savoia-Marchetti SM.79 medium bombers carried out a surprise low-level raid, hitting by mistake some 8,000 Italian POWs who had been held by the Allies inside a fenced enclosure. Hundreds of them were killed or wounded.[6]

Pitassi Mannella was detained in the Yol POW camp in India until his release and repatriation in 1946. He died in Rome in 1966, aged 66. Barberis died in January 1961. Della Mura was detained in India until 1943. There is no information about the whereabouts of Mura, de Leone and Vietina in the post-war period.

Lieutenant General Babini was commanding Italy's armoured forces in North Africa on 7 February 1941, when he was captured by the British during the battle of Beda Fomm, fought between Benghazi and El Agheila, in south-western Cyrenaica. Babini remained in Allied custody until 1946. He died on 29 December 1952 in a car crash, aged 63.

Lieutenant General Bergonzoli commanded the defences of Bardia (El Burdi), a Mediterranean seaport in eastern Libya, close to the border with Egypt.[7] When Bardia fell to Allied forces on 5 January 1941, he managed to evade capture, escaping through the desert. On 22 February, after what was for the Italian Tenth Army the disastrous Battle of Beda Fomm, Bergonzoli surrendered to Australian forces.[8] He was detained in India and the United States until his release and repatriation in March 1946. Bergonzoli died on 31 July 1973, in his birthplace, Connobio, in north-western Italy, aged 62.

Lieutenant General Cona took up command of the Tenth Army on 7 February 1941 during the Battle of Beda Fomm, when its commander, Lieutenant General Giuseppe Tellera, was killed in action. In the same battle about 25,000 Italians, including twenty-two generals, were taken prisoner by the Allies.[9] Cona's command was short-lived. His forces were encircled between Benghazi and El Agheila, in south-western Cyrenaica, by the British 7th (Armour) and Australian 6th Divisions and forced to surrender.[10] Cona was captured and led to captivity.[11] There is no information about his whereabouts in the post-war period. The date and place of Cona's death is also unknown. Between 9 December 1940 and 8 February 1941 133,298 Italians were captured by Allied forces in the North African theatre of operation, most of them in Bardia (42,000), Sidi Barani (38,289) and Tobruk (25,000).[12]

Lieutenant General Frusci commanded the Italian forces during the East African campaign that led to the conquest of Abyssinia (present-day Ethiopia). As a governor of Eritrea, in January 1941 he oversaw the defensive actions following the invasion of British forces. With the fall of Eritrea two months later Frusci was arrested by the British and detained in POW camps until the end of the war. He died on 12 June 1949, aged 70.

IMPRISONING THE ENEMY

In 1941 British-educated Prince Amedeo di Savoia, the 3rd Duke of Aosta, was Viceroy and Governor General of Italian East Africa (Africa Orientale Italiana). He was also the commander-in-chief of Italy's forces in Abyssinia, Eritrea and Somaliland. A First World War artillery officer, the prince oversaw the Italian advances in Anglo-Egyptian Sudan, Kenya and British Somaliland.[13] On 18 May 1941 his forces were encircled by British and Colonial troops in the mountain fortress of Amba Alagi and had to surrender.[14] In Abyssinia the prince lost all but 17,000 of his 100,000 troops, who became POWs.[15] Prince Amedeo was interned in a POW camp near Nyeri, north of Nairobi, in central Kenya. He died there on 3 March 1942, aged 43, as a result of complications from both tuberculosis and malaria.[16] He was buried in front of a chapel's altar at Mathari, near Nyeri.

Air Force General Pietro Pinna Parpaglia and Lieutenant General Claudio Trezzani were also captured after the seizure of Amba Alagi by British and Colonial forces. Parpaglia was commanding the Regia Aeronautica's units in East Africa. He was detained in Prem Nagar POW camp, near Nehradun in India, until 20 September 1942, when he was sent to the Monticello POW camp in Arkansas, USA. He was released and repatriated in late 1943, following the proclamation of the armistice between Italy and the Allies on 8 September 1943. Parpaglia died on 9 October 1966 in his hometown of Pozzomaggiore, a municipality near Cagliari, in Sardinia, aged 75.

Trezzani was commanding the Army Corps of Padua. After his capture, he was detained briefly in England and then in the United States, initially in Camp Grossvile, in Tennessee, and later in Camp Monticello, in Virginia. After the Italian surrender, Trezzani was released and repatriated. He joined the newly raised Italian Co-Belligerent Army in the fighting against the German forces still occupying parts of Italy. Trezzani was eventually promoted to lieutenant general. He remained in active service until 1950. Trezzani died on 13 September 1955 in Rome, aged 74.

In early June 1941, a few days after the fall of Amba Alagi, sea-borne Allied troops, spearheaded by the 3/15th Punjab (Indian) Regiment, landed at Assab, the last Italian harbour on the Red Sea. The Italian garrison was taken by surprise during the night and surrendered. Some 547 soldiers, including thirty-five Germans, were taken prisoner.[17]

A Royal Italian Air Fleet general (later Air Vice Marshal), Pietro Piacentini, was captured in bed. Until then he had commanded Regia Aeronautica units in the northern sector of Italian East Africa and had also led an air raid on an RAF base at Khartoum in Anglo-Egyptian Sudan.[18] Piacentini was detained in Kenya initially and then in India. In December 1943, following the armistice between Italy and the Allies, he was released and repatriated. Piacentini died on 25 November 1963 at Como, in north-western Italy, aged 65.

General Pietro Gazzera, minister of War from 1929 to 1933, succeeded Prince Amedeo di Savoia as the acting governor of Italian East Africa following the defeat at Amba Alagi in mid-May 1941. Gazzera's forces withdrew to the Saio mountain fortress in western Abyssinia (between Addis Ababa and the Sudanese border), where they were encircled by British, Commonwealth and Belgian-Colonial troops. On 3 July, a battalion of a Belgo-Congolese Expeditionary Force attacked the fortress and hours later the Italians sued for peace. Three days later Belgian general Auguste-Édouard Gilliaert accepted the surrender of Gazzera, eight of his generals and more than 6,000 Italian soldiers.[19] Gazzera was detained in India, Kenya and the United States. He was repatriated on 20 December 1943 following the armistice between Italy and the Allies. Gazzera died on 30 June 1953 at Cirié, a town in the metropolitan city of Turin, aged 74.

On 6 July 1941, after Prince Amedeo and Gazzera surrendered to the British, Lieutenant General Nasi became the acting Governor-General of Italian East Africa.[20] Less than a year earlier, in August 1940, he had invaded British Somaliland at the head of Mussolini's forces. Following a British offensive that led to the seizure of Addis Ababa in May 1941, the Italians had to retreat to the stronghold of Gondar, in northern Abyssinia. On 28 November, they were forced to surrender. Some 22,000 Italians were taken prisoner, including Nasi.[21] He was sent to a POW camp in Kenya, where he was responsible for 60,000 Italian prisoners, after the death of Prince Amedeo. Nasi was repatriated in 1946. He died on 21 September 1971, in Modena, in northern Italy, aged 92.

Colonel Augusto Ugolini was captured on 21 November 1941 near Culqualber Pass, in northern Abyssinia, during a hand-to-hand fight with British and Colonial troops. He remained in British captivity until November 1945. Ugolini was promoted to brigadier general in 1950 and to lieutenant general on retirement. He died in March 1977 in Rome, aged 89.

Major General Ruggero Tracchia was taken prisoner by British troops near Bardia, in eastern Libya, on 5 January 1941. Until then he had commanded the 62nd Infantry Division *Marmarica*. Tracchia was detained initially in Egypt and later in India. He remained in British captivity until late 1944. Tracchia died on 29 November 1955, in Rome, aged 71.

On 21 March 1941 Major General Salvatore Castagna was forced to surrender Jaghbub to Allied (mostly Australian) forces. Jaghbub, also known as Giarabub, was an Italian garrison located in western Libya, close to the border with Egypt. Castagna was detained in a POW camp near Bombay, in India.[22] He was released and repatriated in November 1946. Castagna died in a military hospital on 3 February 1977, aged 80.

Major Generals Brunetto Brunetti and Nazzareno Scattaglia were captured by British and Commonwealth forces in western Egypt on 11 November 1942 during the second battle of El Alamein. Brunetti was commanding the 27th Infantry Division *Brescia*. He was held as a POW in England until the end of the war. Brunetti died on 5 April 1947, in Rome, aged 59.

Scattaglia was commanding the 17th Infantry Division *Pavia* that was destroyed at El Alamein. He was detained briefly in England and later in the United States. In late 1943 he was transferred to Ford Hereford POW camp for non-cooperators, in Texas.[23] Scattaglia was released and repatriated in February 1946. He died on 16 January 1975, in Rome, aged 87.

Divisional General Fedele De Giorgis (sometimes listed as Fedele Degiorgis or Federico de Giorgis) was captured on the night of 22/23 November 1942 when his 55th Infantry Division *Savona* was destroyed by the British Eighth Army at Halfaya Pass, in north-western Egypt, close to the border with Libya.[24] During this battle, at least 1,500 of De Giorgis' troops surrendered to the enemy, becoming POWs. He died on 4 February in Rome, aged 57.

Lieutenant Generals Etelvoldo Pascolini, Umberto Ricagno and Emilio Battisti were captured by the Russians between 26 and 27 January 1943 during the Italian participation in the German invasion of the Soviet Union. Their forces were encircled and destroyed by the Red Army near Valuyki, 93 miles (150km) east of Belgorod, in western Russia.

Pascolini, commander of the 156th Infantry Division *Vicenza*, remained in Soviet captivity until his repatriation in May 1950. He died on 2 June 1956 in Turin, aged 71.

Ricagno, commander of the 3rd Alpine Division *Julia*, was initially held in the Lubyanka Prison in Moscow and later in a POW camp. He was repatriated on 16 May 1950. He died on 17 July 1964 in Rome, aged 74.

Battisti, commander of the 4th Alpine Division *Cuneense*, was initially held in a prison, where for a time he shared a same cell with German Field Marshal Friedrich von Paulus. Battisti was then transferred to a POW camp. He was released and repatriated on 15 May 1950. He died on 23 November 1971 in Bologna, aged 81.

Lieutenant Generals Alberto Mannerini and Francesco La Ferla were captured by Allied forces in Tunisia in the spring of 1943. Mannerini was taken prisoner on 29 March near Gabès, in southern Tunisia, and remained in Allied captivity until his repatriation on 14 June 1945. Mannerini held the position of the commander general of the Carabinieri Corps until 4 May 1954. He died on 7 February 1962 in Rome, aged 70.

La Ferla, commander of the 101st Motorised Division *Trieste*, surrendered to British forces in Tunisia on 26 April 1943. He was detained in England. La Ferla was released and repatriated after the proclamation of the Italian armistice with the Allies. He was placed at the disposal of the Italian ministry of war and in 1952 he was promoted to lieutenant general. La Ferla died on 22 March 1962 in Palermo, Sicily, aged 75.

Field Marshal (Maresciallo d'Italia) Giovanni Messe commanded the Italian Army in Russia (Armata Italiana in Russia) until November 1942. Three months later he took command of the First Italian Army in North Africa. On 13 May 1943 (one day after his promotion to field marshal), Messe was forced to surrender with his troops to British and New Zealand forces at Enfidaville, near Tunis. As a loyal supporter of the Royal cause, he was eventually picked by the Allies and made chief-of-staff of the Italian Co-Belligerent Army (Esercito Cobelligerante Italiano). Messe remained in the military until his retirement in 1947. He died on 18 December 1968 in Rome, aged 85.

Lieutenant General Paolo Berardi and Major General Arturo Scattini were also captured by the Allies in Tunisia. Berardi was commanding the XXI Army Corps in Tunisia on 12 May 1943 when he was wounded and captured by British troops. He was detained in England until 1943, when he was released and appointed chief-of-staff of the Royal Italian Army. Berardi retired from active service two years later. He died on 13 December in Turin, aged 68.

Scattini was commanding the 80th Infantry Division *La Spezia*. He was held in England until his release and repatriation in 1944, when he joined the Italian Co-Belligerent Army. Scattini was promoted to lieutenant general and remained in active service until 1952. He died on 16 October 1970 in Rome, aged 80.

Lieutenant General Taddeo Orlando and Major General Pietro Belletti were also captured in Tunisia on 13 May 1943. Orlando was detained in England until November 1943, when he was repatriated. He joined the Italian Co-belligerent Army and on 12 February 1944 was appointed minister of war. He retired on 6 March 1945, following allegations that war crimes were committed in Slovenia in 1941 by troops under his command. Orlando died on 1 September 1950 in Rome, aged 65.

Belletti, a former commander of the 105th Infantry Division *Rovigo*, was detained in Wilton Park POW camp, near London, until his release in late 1943. Belletti died on 3 January 1950 in Rome, aged 65.

ITALIANS

Wilton Park also held Major General Giuseppe Falugi. He commanded the 16th Infantry Division *Pistoia* and became a POW on 13 May 1943, after the final surrender of all Axis forces in Tunisia. He was released and repatriated in June 1945. Falugi died in 1962 in Chianni, near Pisa, aged 76.

Achille d'Havet was the first Italian general to become a POW in Sicily. He was taken prisoner by Canadian troops on 12 July 1943, along with the entire command of his 206th Coastal Division. D'Havet, a major general, remained in British captivity until late 1944. On 1 March 1945 he left active service and on 1 July 1946 he received honorary promotion to lieutenant general. D'Havet died on 21 April 1966 in Rome, aged 78.

One day after d'Havet's capture, Major General Giulio Cesare Gotti-Porcinari surrendered to British troops in Sicily along with the remnant of his 213th Coastal Division. He was taken to Egypt and held there as POW until his release in April 1946. Gotti-Porcinari died a few months after his repatriation, aged 58.[25]

Lieutenant General Giovanni Marciani, commander of the XII Army Corps, was captured on 22 July at his headquarters in the Royal Palace of Palermo by elements of the US 2nd Armoured Division. He was held in a POW camp in Saint-Cloud, near Oran, in Algeria. Marciani was released and repatriated in December 1944. He died in 1964 in Mercato San Severino, in south-western Italy, aged 78.

Brigadier General Gino Ficalbi was captured in Sicily on 24 July 1943, when his 202nd Coastal Division was destroyed by Allied forces. He was held by the British in Wilton Park camp near London. In October 1944, after his release and repatriation, he joined the Italian Co-Belligerent Army. He later became trigonal military commander of Florence. Ficalbi died in 1973, aged 82.

Between 8 and 13 September 1943, immediately after the Italian surrender to the western Allies, King Victor Emmanuel III (Vittorio Emanuele III) and Italy's new government, headed by Field Marshal Pietro Badoglio, fled the incoming Germans. Aged Enrico Caviglia, a First World War general who rose to the rank of field marshal in 1926, was left behind to negotiate with Field Marshal Albert Kesselring the surrender of Rome as an open city. After the surrender, Caviglia was allowed by the Germans to retire to a villa, at Finale Liguria, near Genoa, in north-western Italy. He died there on 22 March 1945, aged 82, almost two months before the end of the war in Europe.

Meanwhile, on 12 September 1943, Benito Mussolini, two months after his dismissal by Victor Emmanuel III, was rescued from his 'prison', the isolated Gran Sasso hotel in a mountainous area of central Italy, by 108 German airborne commandos led by Austrian-born SS-Major (later SS-Lieutenant Colonel) Otto Skorzeny.[26] Then the deposed dictator, with Nazi Germany's support, set up a new regime, the Italian Social Republic (Republica Sociale Italiana or SRI), headquartered at Salò, a town and commune in northern Italy. Hitler could not allow the Allies to take full advantage of Italy's 'treachery'.[27] In his villa at Lake Garda, Mussolini was in fact a prisoner of the SS (as well as the members of his puppet government), held in hatred by his countrymen and in contempt by his gaolers.[28] He was even required to hand over his son-in-law, Galeazzo Ciano, to the Germans, who had Italy's former foreign minister shot by a fascist firing squad.[29]

Ciano, a fascist propagandist since 1922 and a career diplomat, married Mussolini's daughter, Edda, in July 1930. In the mid-1930s he fought as a bomber squadron commander during the Italian invasion of Abyssinia. In 1936 Ciano became Italy's foreign minister. In September 1943, he was arrested by authorities of the newly established Italian Social Republic for having voted against Mussolini in the Fascist Grand Council on 24 July 1943, when the Duce's overthrow was decided by a margin of nineteen votes to eight. Ciano was tried in Verona, sentenced to death for treason and executed, at the age of 40. His wife, with their three children, managed to escape to Switzerland on 9 January disguised as a peasant woman. On 20 December 1945, after her return to Italy, Edda Ciano was arrested, tried and sentenced to two years in prison for aiding fascism. She died on 9 April 1995 in Rome, aged 84.

Galeazzo Ciano was executed in Verona with four officials who had also voted against Mussolini in the Fascist Grand Council.[30] They were Field Marshal Emilio De Bono, Luciano Gottardi, Carlo Pareschi and Giovanni Marinelli.[31] For further humiliation the five men were tied to chairs and shot in the back.[32]

Another defendant in the Verona trial,[33] trade unionist Tullio Ciannetti, who had also voted against Mussolini on 24 July 1943, was sentenced to thirty years in prison.[34] He was spared execution after addressing an apologetic letter to Mussolini. After the war, Ciannetti emigrated to Maputo, the capital of Mozambique, in south-east Africa, where he died on 8 April 1976, aged 77.[35]

Umberto Albini, who had also voted against Mussolini on 24 July 1943, was sentenced to death in absentia during the Verona Trial in January 1944. Undersecretary of the Interior until July 1943, Albini managed to flee and take refuge in Allied-controlled southern Italy. He died on 29 November 1973 in Rome, aged 78.

De Bono was 77 when he was executed by firing squad. In October 1922 he had organised and staged Mussolini's March on Rome that signalled the start of the fascist regime in Italy. A field marshal since November 1935, De Bono served as governor of Eritrea, where Italian troops were involved in war crimes.[36]

Mussolini: The slain

On 25 April 1945, with Allied forces advancing in the greater area, Mussolini and his mistress, Clara Petacci, tried to make it to the Swiss border. Two days later they were stopped by local partisans near the village of Giulino, not far from Lake Garda, in northern Italy.[37] On 28 April both were summarily executed, along with other Italian Social Republic (ISR) officials. All accounts agree that Petacci died bravely attempting to shield her lover.[38] The following day, the bodies of Mussolini, Petacci and other executed fascists were transferred by van to Milan, where they were dumped in Piazzale Loreto, a central square. After being kicked and spat upon, the bodies were hung upside down from the roof of a nearby Esso petrol station.[39]

On 29 April a prominent official of the Fascist Party, Achille Starace, was arrested in Milan during his morning jog and taken to Piazzale Loreto.[40] He was shown the body of Mussolini, which he saluted by raising his hand, before being executed.[41] Starace's body was subsequently strung up alongside Mussolini's. Three days earlier Guido Buffarini Guidi, the minister of the Interior of Mussolini's puppet government, was arrested by partisans after failing to escape to Switzerland. He was sentenced to death by an extraordinary court in Milan and executed on 10 July, aged 50. Buffarini Guidi had failed to commit suicide while in custody.[42]

Alessandro Pavolini was executed by the partisans in Milan. Fascist Party militia inspector Roberto Farinacci was also executed by the partisans. Meanwhile, the Italian military and state had been annihilated, not only in German-controlled parts of the country but also abroad, following the proclamation on 8 September of the armistice between the Kingdom of Italy and the United States and Great Britain, also known as the armistice of Cassibile. Ache was the code name for the German operation to forcibly disarm the Italian armed forces within or outside Italy. In a matter of days, the Germans disarmed well over a million out of the 2 million men serving in the Italian Army. Most of them were captured in German-occupied Italy (518,022), in Greece (about 265,000), in Yugoslavia (about 164,000) and in Albania (about 90,000).

Some Italian troops, with no order from superiors and hampered by many desertions, resisted the Germans. Some 20,000 to 30,000 Italians were killed in the fight against German forces. In this case, they were considered by their former allies as traitors and not as POWs. Between 21 and 26 September 1944 on the island of Cephalonia, 1,315 soldiers belonging to the 33rd Mountain Infantry Division *Acqui* were killed in action against the Germans and a further 5,155 were massacred after running out of ammunition and surrendering. Some 280 officers, including General Antonio Gandin, the 52-year-old divisional commander, were among the executed in one of the Second World War's largest POW massacres. The mass murder was carried out mostly by elements of the 1st Mountain Division and the 98th Jäger Regiment, led by Colonel Harald von Hirschfeld. In December 1944, he became the youngest Wehrmacht officer to reach the rank of brigadier general (generalmajor). Less than a month later, on 18 January 1945, Hirschfeld was fatally wounded during combat at the Dukla Pass (in present-day Slovakia), while commanding the IV Falksgrenadier Division. Brigadier General Luigi Gherzi, commander of the 68th Infantry Division *Legnano*, was executed by the Germans in Cephalonia, on 22 September, aged 53.[43]

On Corfu all Italian officers were murdered by the Germans. On 4 October 1944 on the island of Kos in the Dodecanese about 2,500 Italians surrendered to the Germans. At least ninety-five Italian officers, including the garrison commander, Colonel Felice Leggio, were executed by their captors. On nearby Leros, the island's former Italian commander, Rear Admiral Luigi Mascherpa, was also murdered by the Germans.

In Sinj, near Split (in present-day Croatia), on 27 September 1943 three Italian generals and forty-six officers were massacred by elements of the German 7th Mountain Division *Prinz Eugen* after the surrender of the 15th Infantry Division *Bergamo*. The executed were 58-year-old Major General Alfonso Cigala-Fulgosi, Brigadier Generals Salvatore Pelligra and Angelo Policardi, five colonels, one lieutenant colonel, two majors, twenty-three captains, ten first lieutenants and five second lieutenants. Between 5 and 7 October in Kuç, southern Albania, after the surrender of the 151st Infantry Division *Perugia*, 118 officers were executed by the Germans, including Major General Ernesto Chiminello, the divisional commander. In Thessaly, in central Greece, the 24th Infantry Division *Pinerolo* surrendered to ELAS leftist guerilllas on the Pindus mountain range in north-western Greece. The remaining Greek-deployed Italian divisions (29th *Piemonte*, 36th *Forli*, 37th *Modena*, 56th *Casale* and 59th *Cagliari*) surrendered to the Germans on 23 September 1943.

IMPRISONING THE ENEMY

Lieutenant Generals Luigi Reverberi and Curio Barbasetti di Prun were arrested by the Germans in Italy and sent for detention to Nazi-occupied Poland. Reverberi had fought in Russia until late January 1943 with his 2nd Alpine Division *Tridentina* during the German invasion of the Soviet Union. In a battle near Valuyki, in western Russia, on 26 January 1943, during which Italian forces were encircled and destroyed by the Red Army, Reverberi evaded capture. Eight months later he was arrested by the Germans in Italy, after the downfall of Mussolini's regime and the Italian surrender to the Allies, and sent for detention to a POW camp in Posen, west-central Poland. Reverberi was liberated by the Red Army. He was briefly held by the Russians before he was repatriated. He died on 22 June 1954 following a heart attack in his home in Milan, aged 61.

Barbasetti di Prun commanded the XIV Army Corps in September 1943. He was also governor of Montenegro, then part of the Axis-occupied Yugoslavia. After the armistice between Italy and the Allies, di Prun was arrested by the Germans and sent to Oflag 64/Z, an officers' only POW camp at Schokken (present-day Skoki), in northern Poland. In early 1945, when the detainees were liberated by the Red Army, he remained in Soviet custody in Ukraine until October 1945, when he was released and repatriated. Di Prun died on 4 December 1953 at Orsara di Puglia, in the province of Foggia, in southern Italy, aged 68.

General Alberto Briganti was the last commander of the Italian air forces in the Dodecanese and Brigadier General Francesco Arena commanded the 36th Infantry Division *Forlì* that was stationed in Athens in September 1943. After the Italian armistice with the Allies, both surrendered to German forces. Following their refusal to collaborate by joining Mussolini's ISR, they were sent to Oflag 64/Z. In late January 1945 the POW camp was evacuated and most of the detainees had to move westwards. During a forced march, Briganti and Arena managed to escape and hide in a farm. They were discovered there on 28 January by two Russian soldiers, who mistook them for German collaborators and shot them on the spot. Fifty-five-year-old Arena was killed instantly. Briganti survived and was rushed to a hospital by Polish farmers with no fatal wounds, although he had been shot more than once. He was repatriated by the Russians in October 1945. Briganti died on 2 July 1997 in Rome, aged 100.

Carlo Geloso, a full general since October 1942 and commander of the Italian occupation forces in Greece, was also taken prisoner by the Germans and held in Schokken. When the camp was liberated by the Red Army, Geloso was imprisoned by the Russians in Kharkov in Ukraine until his release and repatriation in 1946. Geloso died on 23 July 1957 in Rome, aged 57.

Several Italian generals besides Geloso were detained by the Germans at Schokken after Italy's surrender to the Allies. Three of them, Lieutenant General Umberto di Giorgio, Major General Alberto De Agazio and Brigadier General Davide Dusmet, died there. Di Giorgio was responsible for the territorial defence of Rome on 28 September 1943 when he was arrested by the Germans and sent to Schokken. He died in the camp on 30 November of a heart attack, aged 61. De Agazio was commanding the artillery units of the Ninth Army in mid-September 1943 when he was arrested by the Germans. He died of a heart attack on the night of his arrival in Schokken, aged 55.

Dusmet was arrested by the Germans in mid-September 1943 in Dubrovnik, in present-day Croatia, while commanding the garrison of the city. On 2 October he was sent to Schokken, where he died on 24 November from pneumonia due to the lack of medical care, aged 62.

On 28 January 1945 six Italian generals who had been previously held in Schokken were murdered by SS guards at Kuźnica Żelichowska during a forced march. They were Lieutenant General Carlo Spatocco and Brigadier Generals Emanuele Balbo Bertone, Alberto Trionfi, Alessandro Vaccaneo, Giuseppe Andreoli and Ugo Ferrero.

Lieutenant General Renato Coturri organised the defence of Treviso on 8 September 1943 before going into hiding. Two days later he was arrested by the Germans and sent to Schokken. He was released after joining the ISR. In 1946 he was expelled from the Army and lost all decoration. Coturri died on 6 May 1961 in Genoa, in north-western Italy, aged 68.

The following generals were detained in Schokken until they were freed by advancing Soviet troops on 21 January 1945. Lieutenant General Alessandro Piazzoni, commander of the VI Army Corps, surrendered to the Germans in Dubrovnik in September 1943. He was sent to Schokken after refusing to collaborate by joining Mussolini's Italian Social Republic. He died on 14 May 1971 in Brescia, in northern Italy, aged 86.

Lieutenant General Umberto Mondino, commander of the XXV Army Corps, was arrested by German troops in Elbasan, in Albania. Freed by the Red Army. He was repatriated on 10 October 1946. He died on 22 July 1964 in Parma in northern Italy, aged 81.

On 8 September 1943, Lieutenant General Gervasio Bitossi was commanding the II Corps, headquartered in Siena in central Italy. He was arrested by the Germans in Vicenza a few days later and sent to Schokken. He was released and repatriated in May 1945. In June 1946, Bitossi retired from the army, refusing to swear allegiance to the (post-war) Italian Republic. He died on 26 June 1951 in Rome, aged 66.

Italian troops resisted briefly when German forces occupied La Spezia, north-western Italy, on 9 September. Their commander, Lieutenant General Carlo Rossi, was arrested and sent to Schokken, where he turned down offers to collaborate with Mussolini's new regime. He was freed by the Red Army in late January and repatriated on 6 October 1945. Rossi died on 21 April 1967 in Turin, aged 86.

Major General Attilio Grattarola was also detained in Schokken after his arrest by German troops in September 1943. He was freed on 26 January by advancing Soviet troops. Grattarola died on 8 October 1966, aged 84.

Major General Giulio Perugi was commanding the territorial defence of Udine, in north-east Italy, on 13 September 1943 when he was arrested by German troops and sent to Schokken. He was repatriated in October 1945. He died on 23 February 1949 in Rome, aged 62.

Lieutenant General Ercole Roncalia, commander of the XIV Army Corps, was arrested by the Germans in Podgorica, capital of present-day Montenegro, on 15 September 1945 and sent to Schokken. He was freed by the Red Army in late January 1945. His name was included in a list of war criminals formally issued in late 1945 by the post-war Yugoslavian government. Roncalia died in 1965 in Modena, northern Italy, aged 79.

Brigadier General Enrico Lugli was commanding the 4th Infantry Division Parma in Albania on 10 September 1943 when he was arrested by German troops and sent to

Schokken. He remained there until May 1945, when he was freed by the Red Army. After his repatriation, he was promoted to lieutenant general. Lugli died on 30 March 1967 in Rome, aged 78.

Lieutenant General Gino Pedrazzoli, commander of the 48th Infantry Division Taro in early September 1943, was arrested by the Germans and sent to Schokken. He was later transferred to a POW camp at Vittel, in north-eastern France. Pedrazzoli was released and repatriated in May 1945. He died on 1 January 1973 in San Giovanni del Doss, a municipality near Milan, aged 88.

General Michele Vaccaro, commander of the 2nd Infantry Division Sforzesca in early September 1943, was arrested by the Germans in Fiume in north-eastern Italy and sent to Schokken. He was released after accepting an offer to join the military of the Italian Social Republic. However, Vaccaro was never involved with the ISR after his repatriation. He died in 1980 in Rome, aged 92.

On 8 September 1943 Lieutenant General Armellini Chiappi's troops, including the 183rd Paratrooper Division *Ciclone*, resisted the advance of German forces towards Florence for four days. When the city was finally occupied, Chiappi was taken prisoner and sent to Schokken and later to a POW camp in Germany. He resisted all offers to join the Italian Social Republic in exchange for his release. Chiappi died in a POW camp at Wöllstein, near Mainz, on 4 November 1944, aged 64.

Brigadier General Guglielmo Barbò had led cavalry troops in the Russian Front. On 12 September 1943 he was arrested by German troops and after refusing to collaborate with Mussolini's Italian Social Republic he was imprisoned in San Vittore prison in Milan. He was later sent to Flossenbürg POW camp in Germany, close to the border with Bohemia, part of the present-day Czech Republic. Barbò died there from pleuritis on 14 December 1944, aged 56.

Brigadier Generals Alberto Murer, commander of the *Duca degli Abruzzi* barracks in Turin, and Constantino Salvi, commander of the military zone of Cuneo, in north-west Italy, also died in Flossenbürg. Murer was initially held in San Vittore prison in Milan.[44] He was then sent to Flossenbürg. On 6 September 54-year-old Murer was beaten to death by a kapo for hiding some potatoes. Salvi did not oppose the takeover of Cuneo by German troops on 8 September 1943. However, he then started collaborating with the local resistance groups. In August 1944 Salvi was arrested by the Germans and on 5 September he was sent to Flossenbürg. He died there on 17 January 1945, aged 58.

Mario Vercellino, a full general since October 1942, was commanding the Fourth Army in eastern France on 12 September 1943, when he was captured by German troops.[45] He was initially imprisoned in Toulon and later in Germany. Vercellino was released and repatriated in late 1945. He died on 11 July 1961 in San Remo, in north-west Italy, aged 82.

Lieutenant General Giuseppe Fabre, commander of an Alpini brigade, was arrested by the Germans in September 1943 in Saluzzo, a village in Piedmont, north-west Italy.[46] He remained detained in Germany until April 1945. Fabre died on 3 November 2007 in Saluzzo, three years before his 100th birthday.

Lieutenant General Alfredo Guzzoni was commanding the Axis forces in Sicily when the inland was invaded by the Allies in July 1943. Two months later, when the armistice of Cassibile was proclaimed, he was arrested by Mussolini's troops for treason. Guzzoni was spared execution thanks the intervention of high-ranking German officers. He died on 15 April 1965 in Rome, aged 88.

Major General Domenico Chirieleison, commander of the 4th Infantry Division *Livorno*, joined Mussolini's Italian Social Republic after the proclamation of the Italian armistice with the Allies. As of January 1944 he actively collaborated with the Allies and after the liberation of Rome he returned to the ranks of the Royal Italian Army. Chirieleison died in 1972 in Rome, aged 84.

Lieutenant General Carlo Ceriana-Mayneri was commanding the 216th Coastal Division on 12 September 1943 when he was arrested by German troops in Pisa, central Italy. He managed to escape and eventually reached an Allied-control area. He later joined the Italian Co-Belligerent Army. Ceriana-Mayneri died on 6 April 1960 in Rome, aged 74.

General Angelo Cerica, commander of the Carabinieri Corps, arranged Mussolini's arrest after the latter's interview with King Victor Emmanuel III. Later he led a battalion of cadets in a brief battle against German troops halfway between Rome and the seaport of Ostia. Cerica then went into hiding and later joined a partisan unit in Abruzzo, east of the Italian capital. He died on 11 April 1961 in Rome, aged 75.

In southern Croatia, the 32nd Infantry Division *Marche* tried to defend Dubrovnik. Their resistance was crushed by the Germans in late September. The division's commander, General Giuseppe Amico, was executed. Major General Ugo Buttà managed to evacuate from Montenegro to southern Italy with most of his 155th Infantry Division *Emilia* and have them surrender to Allied forces. He was held as a POW in England. Buttà died in 1949, aged 57.

In Sardinia and in Corsica, as well as in southern Italy's Calabria and Apulia, Italian troops were able to offer successful resistance and hold off the German forces until relieved by the arrival of the Allies. On 8 September 1943 54-year-old Brigadier General Ferante Vincenzo Gonzaka, commander of the 222nd Coastal Division, was shot dead near Eboli, southern Italy, by German troops after refusing to surrender. One day later in Foggia, southern Italy, Brigadier General Felice Caperdoni ordered troops under his command to surrender to the Germans and then shot himself in the head. The bullet did not kill him but left him permanently blinded. He was treated by German doctors initially and by Allied doctors later. Caperdoni committed suicide on 13 April 1955 in Mantù, a municipality south of Milan, in northern Italy, aged 65.

The disarmed Italian military personnel were confronted with the choice to continue fighting for Mussolini's puppet government, the Italian Social Republic, for the Wehrmacht as volunteers or otherwise be sent to detention camps in Germany. No more than 10 per cent agreed to enrol. The others were considered POWs. There was an initial and unsuccessful attempt to raise a force entitled 'Aviazione Legionaria Italiana'. Later, the new regime established by Mussolini as the Republica Sociale Italiana raised new armed forces based upon Italian prisoners then held in Germany, at the same time as some 90,000 Italian were recruited into German formations. Some 20,000 joined Waffen-SS units and a number of former paratroopers of the *Folgore* and *Nembo* divisions joined Luftwaffe's 4th Parachute Division.[47] Italian Military Internees (IMI) was the official name given by the German Army to the Italians, officers and soldiers who were captured, rounded up and deported in German-controlled territories. Of these, some 196,000 fled evading deportation. More than 13,000 lost their lives during deportation from Greek islands to the mainland.[48] Nine ships carrying Italian POWs were sunk by Allied ships or aircraft between September 1943 and June 1944. The ships were attacked near Rhodes (*Gaetano Donizetti*) on 22 September 1943, near Corfu (*Mario Roselli*) on 11 October, near Cephalonia (*Maria Amalia*) on 13 October, near Crete (*Sinfra*) on 20 October and near Cos (Aghios *Antonios*) on 19 November. Ships carrying Italian POWs also sank after being attacked by Allied naval vessels or aircraft near Amorgos (*Leda*) on 2 February 1944, near Crete (*Petrella*) on 8 February, near Milos (*Sifnos*) on 4 March, and near Crete (*Tanais*) on 9 June.

Earlier, on 12 February, *Oria*, a Norwegian steamboat, fell into rough seas and sank off the coast of eastern Attica. Some 4,095 Italian POWs, fifteen German soldiers and twenty-one crew members went down with the ship. This was one of the worst maritime disasters ever – probably the fourth worst loss of life caused by the sinking of a single ship and the worst in the Mediterranean Sea.[49]

Some 94,000 men including almost all the Blackshirts (the paramilitary wing of the National Fascist Party) decided to accept the offer to fight alongside the Germans. However, some 710,000 others were deported to Germany. In the spring of 1944 some 103,000 had declared themselves ready to serve in Germany or the ISR as combatant or auxiliary workers. Between 600,000 and 650,000 refused to continue the war alongside the Germans. The former Italian soldiers were sent into forced labour in war-related industries (35.6 per cent), heavy industry (7.1 per cent), mining (28.5 per cent), construction (5.9 per cent) and agriculture (14.3 per cent). Between 600,000 to 650,000 Italian soldiers remained in German labour camps, where between 37,000 and 50,000 of them perished. It is estimated that of the 700,000 Italians taken prisoner by the Germans, around 40,000 died in detention. At the end of the war, several thousand former IMIs ended up in the hands of the French, Russian and Yugoslavs and instead of being released were kept in captivity well after the end of the war.

After the proclamation of the armistice between Italy and the western Allies on 8 September 1943 several high-ranking officers of the Italian armed forces were involved in resistance activities against the German occupation forces. Most of them, including Generals Fenulli, Artale, Lordi and Armelini, Air Force Brigadier General Roberto Lordi and Army Colonel Lanza di Montezemolo, were organised in the so-called Clandestine Military Front (Fronte Militare Clandestino), a resistance organisation. Lanza di Montezemolo was the CMF's first commander. Fenulli, Lordi, Antale, Amico, Castaldi and Lanza di Montezemolo were captured, tortured and executed by the Germans.

Brigadier General Dardano Fenulli led units of his 135th Armoured Brigade Ariete II against German troops near Rome in early September 1943, when Italy changed sides. On 10 September, when a ceasefire was agreed in Rome between the Italian resistance and the German forces, he went into hiding. He carried on the resistance against the Germans as a leading member of Clandestine Military Front. Betrayed by an informer, Fenulli was arrested in February 1944. After a period of torture and detention in the Via Tasso prison, 54-year-old Fenulli was executed on 24 March during the Ardeatine massacre, in which 335 Italians were killed by an SS force as a reprisal for the killing of thirty-two SS soldiers by partisans. The Italian prisoners were taken to caves on the southern side of Rome and shot in the back of the neck in groups of five.[50]

Sabato Martelli Castaldi and Roberto Lordi, lifelong friends, rose to the rank of brigadier general in the Royal Italian Air Force (Regia Aeronautica) in 1933, but they were forced to resign from the military about two years later as their relationship with their country's fascist regime became strained. By the late 1930s they had found employment in a factory. After the Italian surrender to the Allies they fought against German troops near Porta, at San Paolo, south of Rome, before joining the Clandestine Military Front as prominent members. Before long they were forced to turn themselves in after the arrest of their employer, Ernesto Stacchini, by the SS, who bargained the industrialist's life with their surrender. After surrendering, the two men were held and tortured in the Italian capital's Via Tasso prison for sixty-four days before being executed.

Forty-seven-year-old Martelli Castaldi and 50-year-old Lordi were also among the 335 Italian resistance fighters and ordinary citizens, mostly hostages, who were slaughtered on 24 March 1944 by the Germans in the Ardeatine caves.

Army Colonel Lanza di Montezemolo was in charge of the Clandestine Military Front when he was arrested by the Germans on 25 January 1944. He had fought in North Africa with the 11th Armoured Engineers Group in late 1942 early 1943 and later against the German troops that occupied Rome on 10 September 1943. Forty-two-year-old Di Montezemolo was held and tortured by the SS in the Via Tasso prison for fifty-eight days before his execution in the Ardeatine caves. A last-minute proposal for Di Montezemolo's exchange with a number of equally important German prisoners was not even considered by Field Marshal Pietro Badoglio, the head of Italy's newly formed pro-Allied government.

Brigadier General Pietro Dodi was a First World War cavalry officer. After the proclamation of the armistice of Cassibile, he was involved in resistance against the German occupation forces in Rome. On 5 May 1944 he was arrested and held in the Via Tasso prison. On 6 June, while the Germans were retreating northward, 63-year-old Dodi was executed by SS troops in a hamlet north of Rome along with thirteen other high-profile prisoners.

Lieutenant General Mario Caracciolo di Feroleto dissolved his forces (Fifth Army) on 8 September 1943 and got involved in resistance fighting against the Germans with the Clandestine Military Front. In January 1944 he was captured by the Germans and sentenced to death by a fascist tribunal in Verona. The sentence was reduced to fifteen years. Di Feroleto was liberated from prison by partisans. He died on 21 December 1954 in Rome, aged 74.

Lieutenant General Mario Girotti commanded the 6th Alpine Division *Alpi Graie* in Yugoslavia from March 1942 to January 1943. After the Italian armistice with the Allies, he carried out resistance activities against the German occupation forces in Rome as a member of the Clandestine Military Front. He was arrested, tried and sentenced to death by firing squad. Rome was liberated by the US Fifth Army on 4 June 1944 before Girotti's sentence could be carried out. He was freed and later decorated by the post-war Italian government for his resistance activities. Girotti died on 3 November 1957 in Rome, aged 72.[51]

Forty-eight-year-old Brigadier General Giuseppe Perotti, army captains Franco Balbis and Giulio Biglieri, and army lieutenant Massimo Montano were arrested by the Germans in March 1944 and convicted of carrying out sabotage activities in the Piedmont region. They were executed on 5 April in Turin by a firing squad.

Admirals Inigo Campioni and Luigi Mascherpa were found guilty of high treason by a fascist court in Parma in May 1944. Campioni was the Governor General of the Italian

Aegean Islands (present-day Dodecanese in south-eastern Greece), headquartered in Rhodes. When the island was invaded by the Germans in September 1943 after the armistice of Cassibile, he was arrested and handed over to fascist authorities in German-occupied Italy.[52]

Rear Admiral Mascherpa was in charge of the Italian defences when German troops (including 600 paratroopers) invaded Leros in the Dodecanese on 12 November after the occupation of Rhodes. Three days later the Italian troops were forced to surrender, including Mascherpa, who was sent by the Germans to the Oflag 64/Z POW camp in Poland. He was then handed over to fascist authorities in German-occupied Italy, who jailed him initially in Verona and later in Parma, where Campioni was already held. On 13 May 1944, when Parma was bombed by the Allies and part of the San Francesco prison was hit, the two admirals refused to escape as many prisoners did. Campioni and Mascherpa were eventually tried for high treason and, after refusing to co-operate with Mussolini's puppet government, were sentenced to death. They were executed by a firing squad in Parma on 24 May. Campioni was aged 65 and Mascherpa 51.

Major General Giuseppe Amico commanded the 32nd Infantry Division *Marche* that was deployed in Axis-occupied Yugoslavia from 20 April 1941. His troops were involved in anti-partisan operations in southern Croatia. After the Italian surrender to the Allies, he was captured by the Germans for preventing with his troops the occupation of Dubrovnik in southern Croatia by the 7th SS Volunteer Mountain Division *Prinz Eugen*. Amico was summarily executed on 13 September 1943 near Slano, a village north-west of Dubrovnik, aged 52.

Lieutenant General Antonio Scuero was commanding the V Army Corps in Croatia when he was arrested by the Germans in Fume on the night of 9/10 September 1943. He was imprisoned by the Germans initially and later by the Italian fascists. Scuero was freed at the end of the war. He died on 25 July 1960 in Montechiaro d'Asti, near Turin, aged 74.

Italo Gariboldi, a full general, had fought in North Africa with the Tenth Army in 1942 and in southern Russia with the Italian Eighth Army in late 1942 and early 1943. He was in Italy on 8 September 1943 when King Victor-Emanuel III ousted dictator Benito Mussolini and then signed an armistice with the Allies. Like many other members of the Italian military, Gariboldi was made a POW by the Germans. He was released from prison by the Allies and died in Rome on 3 February 1970, aged 90.

Field Marshal Hugo Cavallero was imprisoned upon the fall of Mussolini's fascist regime.[53] Weeks earlier he had been dismissed as chief of the defence staff, blamed for the failure of the North African campaign and the setbacks suffered by the Italian Army in Russia.[54] In September 1943 Cavallero, who was fluent in German and English, was freed when Rome was occupied by the Germans. On the morning of 14 September he was found dead by a gunshot in the garden of a hotel at Frascati, near Rome. He was 62 years old. It is still up to debate whether he committed suicide or was assassinated by the Germans for refusing to continue collaborating with them by commanding the Italian forces still loyal to fascist ideals.

General Sebastiano Visconti Prasca led the Italian forces during the Greek campaign in late October 1940. In September 1943 he joined the Italian resistance against the Germans. Prasca was eventually captured and sentenced to death.[55] His sentence was commuted to life imprisonment. After his escape from a prison in Germany, Prasca fought with the Red Army. He took part in the final stages of the war in Europe, including the battle of Berlin. Prasca died on 25 February 1961 in Rome, aged 78.

Lieutenant General Mario Balotta was a convinced monarchist who commanded the 132nd Armoured Division *Ariete*, having fought in Albania, North Africa and Russia. In September 1943 he was arrested by the Germans and detained. Balotta was later detained by the partisans, too. He remained in the Army until 1946. He died of a heart attack in Viareggio, in central Italy, on 23 July 1963, aged 76.

Vice Admiral Bruno Brivonesi was in charge of the Sardinia Naval Command. He was arrested briefly on 14 September 1943 by the Germans, who were able to evacuate their forces from Sardinia to Corsica without difficulty. Furthermore, Luftwaffe bombers, using La Maddalena air base, sank the Italian battleship *Roma* off the north-western coast of Sardinia as it sailed to Malta to surrender to the Allies. Brinovesi died in 1970 in Rome, aged 84.

Lieutenant General Renzo Dalmazzo was commanding the Ninth Army in Albania when Italy capitulated to the Allies. He was captured by the Germans and remained in their custody until the end of the war. He died on 12 December 1959 in Turin, aged 73.

Lieutenant General Carlo Vecchiarelli was commanding the Eleventh Army in Greece in 1943. On 8 September he surrendered to the Germans and was sent to Poland for detention. Vecchiarelli was eventually handed over to the Italian Social Republic authorities. He was tried and sentenced to ten years in prison. He was released at the end of the war. Vecchiarelli died on 13 December 1948, aged 64.

On 8 September 1943 Full General Ezio Rossi was commanding Army Group East from his headquarters in Tirana, the capital of present-day Albania, when he was arrested by German troops. He was held in Schokken and Toruń concentration camps, in Poland, and then handed over to the Italian Social Republic authorities. Rossi was brought in front of a fascist tribunal in Brescia accused of treason, but was acquitted. He died on 19 July 1963 in Bologna, in northern Italy, aged 82.

Major General Bruno Malaguti had fought in Russia during the German invasion. When the armistice of Cassibile was proclaimed, he was commanding the 52nd Infantry Division *Torino*. His troops resisted a German attack at Gorizia, in north-western Italy, but were forced to surrender. Malaguti was sent to the Stalag XX-A POW camp, near Toruń in north-central Poland, and was then handed over to Italian fascist authorities in northern Italy. He was imprisoned in Verona, then in Venice and finally in Brescia. In January 1945 a fascist court sentenced him to death for high treason. Before the sentence was carried out, he was liberated by partisans. Malaguti was then transferred to Rome by order of the Allied military command. He was placed at the disposal of the Italian ministry of defence but his health had been compromised by the hardships endured in captivity. Malaguti died in a hospital in Rome on 2 December 1945, aged 57.[56]

Princess Mafalda of Savoy, Victor Emmanuel III's younger daughter, was arrested by the Germans, probably for not informing her German husband about her father's decision to surrender Italy to the Allies. Her husband, Philipp, Landgrave of Hesse, a Nazi Party member since 1930, was also arrested by the SS and detained initially in Dachau and later in Tyrol. Their four children were given sanctuary in the Vatican. Malfada was sent to the Buchenwald concentration camp, near Weimar in central Germany. She was seriously wounded when the camp was bombed by Allied planes on 24 August 1944, when 400 prisoners were killed. Mafalda died on the night of

26/27 August, aged 41. Her husband was liberated by US troops on 4 May 1945 but remained in Allied custody until 1947. Philipp died on 25 October 1980 in Rome, aged 83.

Victor Emmanuel III's eldest daughter, Princess Yolanda of Savoy, was married to Major General Giorgio Carlo Calvi di Bergolo, a cavalry officer.[57] He commanded the 131st Armoured Division *Centauro* in Libya until April 1943. After the armistice of Cassibile, di Bergolo participated in the negotiations for the surrender of Rome to General Albert Kesselring's German forces on 10 September 1943. He was then arrested and held initially in a hotel at Hirschegg, in south-western Austria, and then in his home in Italy. From there he managed to escape to Switzerland. After the abolition of the monarchy on 12 June 1946 di Bergolo left Italy and settled in Egypt. He returned to Italy in 1955. Di Bergolo died in Rome on 25 February 1977, aged 89.

Major General Bortolo Zambon, commander of the 27th Infantry Division *Brescia*, evaded being captured by the Germans in September 1943. He was arrested by Mussolini's Republican police near Como, in northern Italy, on 25 May 1944 and detained in San Vittore prison in Milan. Zambon managed to escape from there and take refuge in Switzerland. He returned to Italy in May 1945. Zambon died on 24 June 1967 in Milan, aged 87.

Umberto Pugliese was head of the Engineering Corps of the Royal Italian Navy.[58] He was the designer of the 35,000-ton battleships of the Vittorio class. In September 1943 he was arrested by the SS for being an Italian-Jew. Being persuaded that the information was not correct, Pugliese's captors let him go. He went into hiding until the end of the war. Pugliese died on 15 July 1951 in Sorento, in southern Italy, aged 81.

Brigadier General Giuseppe Garibaldi, a staunch opponent of the Mussolini regime, was the grandson of Giuseppe Garibaldi, who contributed to the unification of Italy in 1861. In September 1943 he was arrested by the Germans and held in the Regina Coeli prison in central Rome. After the war, he retired to private life. Garibaldi died on 19 May 1950 in Rome, aged 70.

Lieutenant Colonel Enrico Martini was captured by the Germans and detained at Apuania, in Tuscany, central Italy. He managed to escape from there and join the anti-fascist forces, contributing with his 1st Alpine Division Group to the liberation of cities in Piedmont, including the province's capital, Turin. Martini remained in the Italian Army until 1947, when he retired. He studied law at the University of Turin and later became a company executive. Martini died in a plane crash in Turkey on 17 September 1976, aged 65.

Vice Admiral Carlo Balsamo di Specchia-Normandia was the Kingdom of Italy's naval attaché in Tokyo from 1941, having been posted as naval attaché in Spain and Portugal in the mid-1930s. On 8 September 1943, when the armistice between and the western Allies was made public, he was arrested by the Japanese and remained imprisoned until Japan's surrender in September 1945.[59] He was repatriated in February 1946. Balsamo di Specchia-Normandia died on 22 May 1961 in Settignano, near Florence, in central Italy, aged 43.

SS Lieutenant General (SS-Obergruppenführer) Karl Friedrich Wolff headed the German delegation in the two-month secret negotiations with the western Allies in Bern, Switzerland, that resulted the surrender of the German forces still deployed in northern Italy. He was at the time the higher SS and police chief in Italy. On 26 April 1945 Wolff was captured by Italian partisans, but was freed soon enough by US Office of Strategic Services (OSS) executives.[60] Wolff was among the signatories of the instrument of surrender of the German forces in Italy. The surrender was signed at the Royal Palace in Caserta, on the edge of the Campanian plain, in southern Italy.[61] Eleven days later Wolff was arrested by the Allies and held in Kleist Park, at the Kammergericht court building, near Berlin. He escaped prosecution at the Nuremberg trials apparently because of his role in the surrender of the German troops in Italy. Wolff was later proven to be complicit in the deportation of 300,000 Italian Jews.[62] In 1964 he was convicted of genocide by a West German court and imprisoned until 1969.[63] He was given an early discharge due to poor health. Wolff died on 17 July 1984 at Rosenheim, in Bavaria, aged 84. Weeks before his death, Wolff converted to Islam.

Only SS-Lieutenant Colonel (SS-Obersturmbannführer) Herbert Kappler, the chief of the SS in Rome, was tried by an Italian tribunal after the war for crimes committed in German-occupied Rome by SS troops under his command, including the Ardeatine massacre of 24 March 1944.

Field Marshal Albert Kesselring, Colonel General (Generaloberst) Eberhard von Mackensen and Major General Kurt Mäzler were tried and convicted in Italy by British military tribunals for war crimes, including the Ardeatine massacre.

In 1948 Kappler was sentenced to life imprisonment. While in prison he converted to Catholicism. When his first wife divorced him, Kappler married a German nurse named Anneliese inside the prison, with whom he had started a mail correspondence. In 1977, while in hospital suffering from cancer, he was assisted by his second wife to escape and reach West Germany. An Italian request for his extradition was rejected by the West German authorities. Kappler died at home in Soltau, in Lower Saxony, six months after his escape, on 9 February 1978, aged 70.

Pietro Caruso was the chief of police (questore) in Rome in 1944. Together with General Kappler, he organised the massacre of Ardeatine as a revenge for an attack by Italian partisans the day before on a column of German soldiers in the Italian capital. Caruso was sentenced to death on 21 September 1944 and was executed (shot in the back) in the courtyard of the Forte Bravetta military prison in Rome.[64]

Another war criminal heavily involved in the Ardeatine massacre was SS-Captain (SS-Hauptsturmführer) Erich Priebke. He was in British custody in Rimini in 1946, when he escaped and fled to Argentina via Tyrol. He used a ratline in Rome run by a Roman Catholic bishop, the Austrian-born Alois Hudal.[65] Priebke lived in Argentina for almost fifty years. In 1996 Priebke was extradited to Italy, where he was convicted for war crimes and sentenced to fifteen years in prison. The sentence was eventually reduced to ten years because of his age and alleged ill health. Priebke died on 11 October 2013 in Rome, from natural causes, aged 100.

SS-Major Karl Hass was involved not only in the Ardeatine massacre, but also in the deportation of 1,000 Italian Jews to Auschwitz and the arrest of Princess Mafalda of Savoy, daughter of King Victor Emmanuel III. After the war he was not prosecuted for war crimes, presumably because he had been reportedly employed by the US Army's Counter Intelligence Corps (CIC) to spy on the Soviet Union. Hass was tried for war crimes as late as 1998. He was sentenced to life imprisonment. He died on 21 April 2004 of a heart attack in a rest home near Rome, where he had been serving a life sentence under house arrest. He was 92 years old.

Between July 1945 and May 1947 forty British trials were conducted in Italy of Italians suspected of war crimes.[66] There were eighty-one Italian defendants in all of the cases and twenty-nine (36 per cent) were found not guilty. Of the fifty-two found guilty, fifty-one saw their conviction confirmed upon review. Eight of these were condemned to death and two were duly executed. The sentences of four were commuted to life imprisonment. The other two condemned saw their sentences commuted to seven and to fifteen years' imprisonment, respectively.[67]

The trials were conducted in nine locations across Italy. Between February and April 1946 ten trials were conducted at several locations. The rest of 1946 saw sixteen trials conducted in six locations. Only thirteen trials took place in 1947. The causes of action were limited to offences against British and Commonwealth POWs and the number of cases involving each issue is as follows: unlawful killing, twenty-six; unlawful attempted killing, two; unlawful wounding, three; unlawful ill treatment, twenty-one.

General Nicola Belomo was one of the few Italians to be executed for war crimes by the Allies and the only one to be sentenced to death by a British military tribunal. Belomo was accused of killing a British POW and wounding his companion, both of whom had been recaptured after escaping from a POW camp within Belomo's command in 1941. He was found guilty of a war crime and executed by firing squad on 11 September 1945.

Captain Italo Simonetti was an officer of the 4th Alpine Division *Monte Rosa*. He was condemned by a British tribunal and executed on 27 January 1947 for his involvement in the shooting of an RAF airman who was captured after landing with his parachute.

General Mario Cartoni, following the 1943 armistice, was briefly imprisoned by the Germans. He was then appointed commander of the 4th Alpine Division *Monte Rosa*. He surrendered to Allied (Brazilian) troops on 29 April 1945, near Parma, in northern Italy, after the battle of Collecchio. In 1946 he was prosecuted for the murder of Lieutenant Alfred Lyth, a USAAF pilot, by *Monte Rosa* soldiers. He was demoted to the rank of colonel.

Pietro Koch was an Italian non-career military officer. He led a special detachment hunting down partisans for the German Army.[68] He was under the protection of SS-Lieutenant Colonel (SS-Obersturmbannführer) Herbert Kappler. Koch was arrested by the Allies, convicted of war crimes and executed at Forte Bravetta military prison on 4 June 1945, aged 26.[69] The trials were held in Italy under British Law and a request by the country's post-war government to allow an Italian judge to participate was denied on the grounds that Italy was not an Allied country when the Moscow Declaration was made on 30 October 1943.[70]

By 1949 British military tribunals had sentenced 230 Germans to death and another 447 to custodial sentences. None of the death sentences imposed between 1946 and 1949 were carried out.[71]

Tito Agosti was taken prisoner by the Allies twice. On 19 May 1941, as a colonel, he was captured by British troops in south Abyssinia (Ethiopia). He was repatriated later in an exchange of wounded POWs. After the armistice of Cassibile, Agosti joined the army of the Italian Social Republic, being promoted to major general. He fought against the US and French forces in north-western Italy, commanding the 2nd Grenadier *Vittorio*, one of the four divisions composed of former Italian prisoners in labour camps that were raised and trained in Germany. On 2 May 1945, after the second battle of the Alps, Agosti was captured by US troops and initially held in a POW camp at Coltano, 12km from Pisa. He was later transferred to Forte Boccea military prison in Rome, where he committed suicide on 27 January 1946, aged 56, while awaiting to be tried for war crimes.[72]

Air Brigade General Arrigo Tessari was one of the first to join Mussolini's Italian Social Republic. After the war, he was indicted for collaborating and sentenced to eight months in prison. He served his sentence in Forte Boccea. Tessari died on 5 September 1971 in Belluno, northern Italy, aged 74.

Brigadier General Francesco Amilcare Dupanloup commanded Port Militia, a branch of the Blackshirt forces tasked with guarding Italy's main ports. When the armistice of Cassibile was proclaimed, he joined the Italian Social Republic. On 25 April 1945 Dupanloup was arrested by Italian partisans in Pegli, near Genoa, and died while in their custody. According to another source, 56-year-old Dupanloup committed suicide with a gun when partisans showed up in his door.

Brigadier General Paolo De Maria led the 89th Blackshirt Assault Legion *Etrusca* in anti-partisan operation in Italian-occupied parts of Croatia. After Italy's armistice with the Allies, he raised an SS unit from Italian POWs and was given the rank of SS-colonel (SS-standartenführer). After the war, De Maria was tried in Savona, north-west Italy, for collaborationism and sentenced to one year and eight months in prison. He died on 17 February 1968 in Spoleto, near Perugia, aged 76.

Lieutenant General Enrico Adami-Rossi joined the Italian Socialist Republic after the armistice of Cassibile and was appointed commander of the territorial defence of Florence.[73] He was also the president of the military court in Milan in March 1944 that sentenced to death five suspected partisans for killing fascist sympathisers. One month later he was appointed head of the Piedmont Regional Military Command. In early May Adami-Rossi was arrested by US troops and detained in Coltano POW camp. The same month he was tried by a provisional (assizes) court in Florence and found guilty of collaborationism. His death sentence was later overturned by the Supreme Court. A second trial resulted in Adami-Rossi being sentenced to twenty-four years in prison, later reduced to two years. He was released in February 1948. Five years later Adami-Rossi was ultimately acquitted by the Supreme Court of Cassations. His name appears on a list of individuals wanted by Great Britain for war crimes that was issued in March 1947.[74] Adami-Rossi died on 12 July 1963 in Rome, aged 83.

Major General Giovanni Esposito was accused of crimes committed by troops under his command (5th Alpine Division *Pusteria*) in Montenegro and Bosnia, parts of Axis-occupied Yugoslavia, in 1941 and 1942. In mid-September 1943 he joined the Italian Social Republic and its Republican Army, having allowed German troops to control Trieste, in north-eastern Italy. More than 50,000 of Esposito's soldiers were disarmed and deported to Germany. On 14 June 1945 Esposito was arrested and imprisoned by the Allies. In April 1946 he was tried for collaboration and sentenced to thirty years in prison. In December 1948 a court of cassation halved his sentence to fifteen years. In January 1949 he was released from Civitavecchia prison in Rome following the amnesty that was declared on 22 June 1946 by the then minister of Justice and Italian communist party member Palmiro Togliatti. Esposito died on 3 June 1958 in Rome, aged 76.

IMPRISONING THE ENEMY

Major General Gioacchino Solinas and his 21st Infantry Division *Granatieri di Sardegna* briefly resisted the advance of German troops on Rome on 8 September 1943. He then joined Mussolini's Italian Social Republic, becoming regional commander of Lombardy. In July 1945 Solinas was arrested by partisans in Milan and brought to justice for collaborationism. On 11 July he was sentenced to twenty years in prison. He appealed the sentence and months later he was absolved by a court of cassation in Rome. Solinas died on 22 April 1987 in Sassari, on Sardinia, aged 94.

Major General Santi Quasimodo was arrested by the Germans after the Italian surrender. He was released as soon as he accepted the offer to serve the Italian Social Republic. He was appointed general of the Republican National Guard. Quasimodo was last seen in Brescia around 1 May 1945.

Lieutenant General Attilio Teruzzi was a former Minister of Italian Africa. When the armistice of Cassibile was proclaimed, he was the inspector-general of the Militia for National Security (Milizia Volontaria per la Sicuressa Nationale or MVSN), as the Blackshirts, the paramilitary wing of the National Fascist Party, were formally known.[75] Teruzzi then became one of the founders of the Italian Social Republic (ISR). After the war he was tried and sentenced to thirty years in prison. He was discharged earlier, on 6 April 1950. Teruzzi died twenty days after his release from prison on the island of Procida, off Naples, aged 67.

Brigadier General Ettore Del Tetto died inside Procida prison. A former regional commander of Naples, he was accused of collaborationism, having joined the ISR in September 1943. Del Tetto died in his cell on 18 April 1945, aged 55.

Lieutenant General Renato Ricci was the Commandant General of the MVSN until August 1944. He also commanded the Republican Police Force. After the war he was tried for war crimes and collaborationism and sentenced to thirty years in prison.[76] He was released earlier, in 1950, due to a general agreement. Ricci died on 22 January 1956 in Rome, aged 59.

Lieutenant General Archimede Mischi was involved in anti-partisan operation in Slovenia as commander of the Border Militia. In September 1943 he joined the ISR. On 25 April 1945, after Mussolini's execution, Mischi fled to Lecco, near Milan, where he attempted to commit suicide by cutting his wrists. After hospitalisation, he was held in Coltano POW camp near Pisa, and later was brought to justice for crimes committed by his troops in Piedmont. On 3 December 1947 he was sentenced to eighteen years in prison. He remained imprisoned in Forte Boccea until his early release in January 1950. Mischi died on 15 August 1970 in Forlì, northern Italy, aged 85.

On 26 July 1943 Lieutenant General Enzo Emilio Galbiati, the last chief of staff of the Blackshirts, ordered his troops in Viale Romania, north of the city centre of Rome, to hand over control to the Italian Army.[77] He was imprisoned for eleven months. Galbiati died on 23 May 1982 in Solbiate, near Como, in northern Italy, aged 85.

Major General (Blackshirt) Renzo Montagna had been arrested by the Royalists on 8 September 1943 but was released by the Germans a few days later. He joined the ISR and was one of the judges in the Verona trial, in which those who had voted against Mussolini in the Fascist Grand Council in July 1943 were sentenced to death. After the trial, Montagna was appointed commander of the Lombardy Regional Military command. At the end of the war he became a fugitive until he was amnestied by a provisional (assize) court in Como on 29 May 1947. Montagna died on 6 September 1978 in Voghera, near Pavia, in northern Italy, aged 84.

ITALIANS

Francesco Jacomini di San Savino, a career diplomat, was the Viceroy (Luogotente del Re) of Albania until March 1943. In March 1945 he was tried in Italy for war crimes committed in Albania and Slovenia and sentenced to twenty-four years in prison.[78] Di San Savino was released in June 1946 with the general amnesty issued by the Italian government.[79] He died on 17 February 1973 in Rome, aged 80.

Alberto Pariani, an army general since 1933,[80] had replaced di Savino as Viceroy of Albania. In early September 1943, after the proclamation of the armistice of Cassibile, he was arrested by German troops in the Royal Palace (Pallati Mbretëror) in the Albanian capital, Tirana. Pariani was eventually released by the Germans, but after the war he was arrested by the Italian authorities. He was tried for crimes allegedly committed while serving the fascist regime, but was acquitted. He died on 1 March 1955 in Malcesine, a municipality near Verona, in northern Italy, aged 79.

Italian atrocities

Fascist Italy's atrocities during the Second World War did not match Nazi Germany's or Japan's either in scale or in savagery, but did not lack notoriety. Italian war crimes were mainly committed in Abyssinia, Albania, Greece and Yugoslavia. In February 1937 thousands of civilians were murdered by Italian occupation forces in Addis Ababa, the capital of Abyssinia, as a reprisal for the attempted assassination of Field Marshal Rodolfo Graziani, viceroy of Italian East Africa. Five small bombs were thrown where Graziani and the other officials and attendees were standing on the stairs of the Royal Palace.[81] The viceroy was injured by shards of shrapnel to his legs. As a result of his wounds he was hospitalised for sixty-eight days.

Contemporary Italian figures of civilian deaths following the attack were anywhere between 600 and 2,000 but the most recent investigation of a British journalist based in Addis Ababa suggests that the death toll was much closer to the Ethiopian estimates (as high as 20,000). The unarmed victims were shot or bayonetted or stabbed to death with clubs or burned alive by flamethrowers. The perpetrators were ordinary soldiers or fascist militia, colonial troops (askari) and Italian gendarmes (carabinieri). The same day, sixty-two Abyssinian detainees were executed by Italian or Blackshirt troops in Addis Ababa's Alem Bekagn prison. Three months later, on 19 May, 297 monks and twenty-three laymen were shot during the assault of Italian troops on a Greek Orthodox (Coptic) monastery, the Debre Libanos of Ham, south-east of Asmara, capital of present-day Eritrea. The Addis Ababa massacre was attributed to Graziani but the order for the slaughter was given by Guido Cortese while the field marshal was heavily injured and unconscious for two days. Cortese was the Fascist Party secretary general in Addis Ababa.[82]

Of more than 1,200 Italians sought for war crimes in Africa and the Balkans, a relatively small number eventually faced justice. Britain and the US, fearful of bolstering communism in Italy and Yugoslavia, collaborated in this evasion. The punitive will of the western Allies towards Italian war criminals was extinguished after some initial trials by Anglo-Saxon courts and with the advancement of the Cold War.[83] The conspiracy succeeded in frustrating United Nations war crime investigations. The UN Commission of War Crimes had included 730 Italians in its lists of war criminals but was not to be a Nuremberg for Italian war criminals.[84]

Graziani was fascist Italy's highest-ranking war criminal to escape post-war justice.[85] He massacred entire communities in Abyssinia and Libya, and his troops posed for photographs holding several heads. US tanks rumbled into Milan and before long Graziani was arrested. He was transferred to North Africa for his safety as the communist partisans in Italy slaughtered every top fascist they could find. Graziani spent hardly four months in prison and was never convicted of anything. He was never even questioned in his lifetime about his responsibility for the atrocities and to this day Italy has never formally acknowledged them or apologised for them.[86] Graziani died on 11 January 1955 in Rome, aged 72.

Field Marshal Pietro Badoglio was also never tried for crimes committed before and during the war. His planes dropped 280kg bombs of mustard gas over Abyssinian villages in 1935 and reportedly even strafed Red Cross camps. The death and alleged torture of a downed Italian pilot, 26-year-old Lieutenant Tito Minnitti, by rebels near Dagehabur, in the Somali region of Abyssinia, on 26 December 1935 was used by the Italians as an excuse for the particular bombing. The British government, at the beginning of the Cold War, saw in Badoglio a guarantor of an anti-communist post-war Italy.[87] He died of old age in his bed on 1 November 1956, aged 85, and was buried with full military honours. His home town, Grazzano Monferrato, near Turin, in north-western Italy, was later named after him (Grazzano Badoglio).

Army General Mario Roatta and Cesare Maria De Vecchi, Commandant General of the Blackshirts, did not face justice as they managed to escape abroad and settle in Spain and in Argentina respectively. On 8 September 1943 De Vecchi forbade troops under his command, the newly raised 215th Coastal Division, to resist the invading German forces in the port of Piombino, near Florence, and in early October he went into hiding. Having voted against Mussolini in the Fascist Grand Council, De Vecchi was found guilty in the Verona Trial, albeit in his absence, and was sentenced to death. In 1947 he managed to escape to Argentina. He returned to Italy two years later, taking advantage of a general amnesty. De Vecchi died on 23 June 1959 in Rome, aged 74.

The Italian Second and Nineth Armies invaded Yugoslavia on 7 April 1941, along with German and Hungarian forces, and occupied large portions of present-day Slovenia, Croatia, Bosnia, Montenegro and Serbia. Mario Roatta commanded the Second Army. To suppress the resistance led by (mostly communist) partisans, he ordered summary executions, hostage taking, reprisals and internments, as well as the burning of houses and whole villages. Tens of thousands of Yugoslav civilians were murdered in reprisal. Thousands more were herded to their deaths in concentration camps lacking water, food and medicine. Roatta also ordered the deportation of 25,000 people in Slovene- and Croatian-inhabited parts of Yugoslavia. In June 1943 he returned to Italy to become chief-of-staff of the Army. Along with several other suspected Italian war criminals, Roatta was never tried for the atrocities committed by his forces in Yugoslavia. The British government frustrated such requests due to their attempt to bolster the anti-communist position of the post-war Italian government. On 5 March 1945 Roatta escaped from the Virgilio military hospital in Rome.[88] He fled to Spain, where he lived under the protection of the country's dictator Francisco Franco. In Italy he was convicted of war crimes in absentia and sentenced to life imprisonment. His sentence was overturned by the Italian High Court of Appeal in 1948. He returned to Italy eighteen years later and died in Rome on 7 January 1968, aged 80.

ITALIANS

Lieutenant General Gastone Gambara had a major role in the North African campaign and the repression of partisans in the Yugoslavian campaign. In early 1945 he was arrested and detained in Coltano POW camp, near Pisa. Gambara was never tried for war crimes.[89] In June 1945 he was dishonourably discharged by the Italian Army. Two years later he settled in Spain as a Francisco Franco's special guest. Gambara returned to Italy in 1952. He died on 27 February 1962 in Rome, aged 71.

In early July 1942, Italian troops were reported to have shot and killed near Fiume 800 Croat and Slovene civilians. They also burned down houses in Split, on the Dalmatian coast, in retaliation for the activity of the 1st Sisak Partisan Detachment, the first partisan armed anti-fascist resistance unit in Axis-occupied Yugoslavia. Massacres in this region included the infamous reprisal in Podhum, a village near Rijeka, where at least ninety-one civilians were executed on 12 July 1942. The village's 494 houses was burned down. Some 889 people, mostly the elderly, women and children, were detained in the Franchette concentration camp, close to Frosinone, near Rome.[90]

Lieutenant General Mario Robotti commanded the Italian 11th Infantry Division *Brennero* during their deployment in Slovenia and Croatia. He oversaw an ethnic cleansing policy that was applied by the Italian occupation forces in Axis-occupied Yugoslavia between 1941 and 1943. According to this policy, the political and ethnic frontiers in Yugoslavia should coincide.[91] In February 1943 Robotti was promoted to general and succeeded Roatta as commander of the Second Army in Yugoslavia. Following the armistice of Cassibile, he escaped to Venice and from there he disappeared from trace. Robotti was never even questioned by Allied or post-war Italian authorities about his alleged involvement in war crimes. He died in 1955 in Rapallo, near Genoa, in northern Italy, aged 73.

Alessandro Pirzio Biroli was an army general and won a silver medal winner in sabre fencing in the 1908 Olympics in London. He was not a fascist. As the commanding officer of the Ninth Army and military governor of Montenegro, Biroli ordered that fifty Montenegrins be executed for every Italian killed and ten for every Italian wounded. His brother married the daughter of Ulrich von Hassell, a diplomat and member of the German resistance against Hitler. Biroli was never convicted of war crimes. He died on 20 May 1962 in Rome, aged 84.

Fifteen Blackshirt officers of the Tiber Battalion were accused of killing numerous civilians in Matešić, central Croatia, in July 1942. Tens of thousands of Slovenians and Croatians were detained in concentration camps in Italy. Rab and Molat concentration camps were established on two islands off the Dalmatian coast. In Rab the conditions of internment were harsh and the death rate was 3,500 prisoners annually.[92] On Molat 200,000 Slovenes, Croats and Serbs were held by the Italian Army between 1941 and 1943. About 1,000 of them died or were shot. Renicci di Anghiari, in Tuscany, housed totally 10,000 prisoners, mostly Slovenes. The camp at Monigo, near Treviso, often surpassed its full capacity of 2,400 inmates. They were Slovenes and Croats. In November 1942 there were 2,122 detained in the camp, including 1,085 women and 466 children. Another camp for Slovenian and Croatian detainees (Gonars) was set up by the Italian Army near Friuli, in north-western Italy.

In Axis-occupied Greece the Italian Army committed atrocities in reprisal for the activity of resistance groups.[93] In December 1942 Italian troops burned two villages, Chryso and Mikro Horio, in eastern Crete, murdering most of their inhabitants.

On 12 March 1943 in Tsaritsani, north-west of Larissa, in central Greece, forty villagers were executed by the Italian Army and the houses were burned to ground. On 16/17 September 1943 elements of the 24th Infantry Division *Pinerolo* massacred 175 male inhabitants at Domeniko in Thessaly, in central Greece, before setting the village ablaze. In Kournovo, also in central Greece, 106 people were executed on 6 June 1943 by Italian troops in retaliation for the activity of Greek resistance groups in the region.

Ethiopia, Yugoslavia and Greece requested the extradition of some 1,200 Italian war criminals who were never brought to justice. Britain played a decisive role in ensuring that Ethiopia, in particular, was denied membership of the United Nations War Crimes Commission. As a result, the perpetrators of the Italian occupation were never held accountable for their crimes in Ethiopia. Only Major General Giuseppe Daodice was tried for war crimes perpetrated in Ethiopia. He was sentenced to fifteen years of forced labour, but did only five. Daodice died on 4 December 1952 in Bergamo, northern Italy, aged 70.

In August 1944 *L'Unità*, an Italian communist party newspaper, revealed macabre details of atrocities committed in Yugoslavia by Italian troops.[94] None of the Italians responsible for the many war crimes against Yugoslavs, including Generals Roatta and Rabotti and fascist commissar Emilio Grazioli, were ever brought to trial. After the war, in late 1947 and early 1948, Yugoslavia asked for the handover of forty-five 'presumed' war criminals. Yugoslavia publicly accused Italian high-ranking officers, including generals Ambrosio, Roatta, Robotti and Gambara, of war crimes and asked for their extradition, but Italy refused.

The fact that the country had liberated itself of fascism and was governed by an anti-fascist regime made it morally and materially capable of judging Italian citizens who may have committed crimes against human rights.[95] Italy therefore affirmed its complete competence to judge war criminals. The transfer of such competence to others would have signified a grave offence to national sovereignty. It was also believed in Italy that Yugoslavia would not offer the necessary guarantees for an impartial judgement.

In October 1946 Italy had presented a list of more than 150 'presumed' Yugoslav war criminals accused of atrocities against Italian soldiers during the period of occupation (1941–43). On the top of the list was the name of partisan communist chief and Yugoslavia's post-war strongman, Josip Broz Tito.[96]

In 1948 Athens and Rome signed a secret treaty, according to which Greece would abstain from prosecuting war criminals. Trials against war criminals for atrocities committed mainly on the Ionian Islands were initiated only in 1947 and were halted prematurely due to the passage of the statute of limitations for enforcement of the penalty.

Giovanni Ravalli was an Italian officer imprisoned for war crimes committed during the Axis occupation of Greece. He was the only Italian prosecuted by the special war criminals court in Athens. Ravalli was an infantry lieutenant of the 24th Infantry Division *Pinerolo*. He had surrendered to ELAS communist resistance fighters after his country's surrender to the Allies in autumn 1943. Ravalli was convicted of war crimes including the torture to death of Greek gendarme Isaac Sinanoglu, the execution of fifty civilians in Kozani, in northern Greece, as a punitive measure, the rape of women and the terrorising of civilians. His trial started on 18 February 1946 and ended on 10 June 1946. Ravalli was sentenced to three terms of life imprisonment. He served part of his sentence in prisons in Kozani and Thessaloniki, northern Greece. In 1959 he was pardoned by the Greek government and repatriated after Italy threatened to halt the payment of war reparations.[97] Ravalli died on 30 April 1998 in Rome, aged 88.[98]

JAPANESE

As five American soldiers surrounded General Hideki Tōjō's house in Tokyo on 11 September 1945, he shot himself with a pistol, but missed his heart.[1] Tōjō was the Empire of Japan's prime minister from 1941 until 1944 and minister of war from 1940 until 1944. After recovering from his wounds, he was transferred to Sugamo Prison in Tokyo. On 14 September Korechika Anami, Tōjō's successor at the ministry of war, signed Japan's surrender document with the rest of Admiral Kantarō Suzuki's government.[2] Early next morning, Anami committed suicide by performing seppuku, a form of ritualistic suicide by disembowelment that was initially practised voluntarily by medieval Samurai warriors who chose to die with honour than fall into the hands of their enemy.[3] Anami's suicide note reads: 'I – with my death – humbly apologise [to the Emperor] for the great crime [presumably that of Japan's military defeat and the consequently unconditional surrender to the Allies].[4]

General (since May 1945) Teiichi Yoshimoto, commander of the Eleventh Area Army, and Lieutenant General Chikahiko Koizumi, a Japanese military physician and welfare minister from July 1941 to July 1944, committed suicide on 14 September. Fifty-eight-year-old Yoshimoto slashed himself with a sword and then shot himself through the head with a pistol in his office in the Imperial Japanese Army (IJA) headquarters at Ichigaya in Tokyo. Sixty-one-year-old Koizumi dressed in a ceremonial kimono in his house, then slashed open his stomach with a short army sword and cut a jugular vein.[5]

One day later, 55-year-old Vice Admiral Matome Ugaki carried out a suicidal (kamikaze) mission against Allied forces. He wrote that he would fly one last mission to show the true spirit of bushidō. It means 'the way of the warrior' in Japanese and epitomises early Samurai values, including sincerity, frugality, loyalty, martial arts mastery and honour to death.[6]

On 15 August 56-year-old Lieutenant General Kumaichi Teramoto,[7] head of the Army aeronautical branch, and on 16 August, Vice Admiral Takijiro Ōnishi, vice-chief of the Imperial Japanese Navy general staff, committed seppuku in their quarters. Ōnishi did not employ another person (kaishakunin) to execute him by beheading, so he died of self-inflicted injury by sword over a period of fifteen hours. In his suicide note Ōnishi apologises to the approximately 4,000 Kamikaze,[8] the volunteer pilots he sent to suicide attacks against Allied (mostly US) naval vessels in the closing stage of the Pacific War.

Field Marshal Hajime Sugiyama and General (since September 1943) Shizuichi Tanaka committed suicide days later. Oxford-educated General Tanaka, commander of the Tokyo-headquartered Twelfth Area Army, shot himself through the heart with his pistol on 24 August in his office, aged 57. Sugiyama, two years younger, commanded the First Army. He shot himself in the chest with a revolver on 12 September while seated in his office in the IJA headquarters. At home, his wife also killed herself.

Hiroshima-born Lieutenant Colonel Tatsuji Suga was educated in the University of Washington, in Seattle, before becoming a military officer. He was also a Sindoist turned Roman Catholic. Suga was in charge of all POW camps in Borneo during the occupation of the Indonesian Archipelago by the Japanese forces. He committed suicide on the island of Labuan, part of present-day Malaysia, on 12 September 1945, while in Australian captivity.

Major General Toyoji Hiran, head of the military police (kempetai) of the Twenty-Fifth Army, committed suicide in Sumatra on 20 September. Lieutenant General Hitoshi Hamada, chief of staff of the Eighteenth Area Army, killed himself three days earlier in Thailand after his arrest by Allied troops.

General Baron (danshaku) Shikeru Honjō committed suicide while in US custody. He was accused of war crimes committed by troops under his command, the Kwantung Army, in Japanese-occupied Manchuria (Manchukuo) in the early 1930s. Honjō was arrested by the US occupation authorities although he had retired from the military in 1936. He committed suicide in his cell on 30 November 1945, aged 69.

Lieutenant Generals Seiichi Yamada, commander of the IJA's 5th Division, committed suicide on 18 August, aged 52, and Kiyotomi Okamoto, the Japanese military attaché to Switzerland, three days earlier.[9] Okamoto, who was one year younger than Yamada, had also been posted as military attaché to Berlin (1939–40). He was also the chief of Japanese Intelligence in Europe.[10]

Fifty-four-year-old Lieutenant General Mikio Uemura committed suicide on 23 March 1946 in Khabarovsk POW camp in eastern Siberia while in Soviet captivity. He had commanded the Fourth Army in Manchuria. General Rikichi Andō was the last Japanese governor-general of Taiwan. He committed suicide in Shanghai on 19 April 1946, aged 62, while in Chinese captivity.

A total of twenty-two generals and admirals of Japan's Imperial forces committed suicide in the final stages of the war or after the capitulation of their country. Fifty-four-year-old Fuminaro Konoe was a member of the government of Prince Naruhito Higashikuni on 16 December 1945, when he committed suicide by taking potassium cyanide poison at his home in Ogikubo, Tokyo. He came under suspicion of war crimes. Konoe had served as prime minister from 1937 to 1939 and from 1940 to 1941. His grandson, Morihiro Hosokawa, became Japan's prime minister fifty years later.

On 15 August 1945 Emperor Hirohito announced the country's surrender to the Japanese people in a nationwide radio broadcast.[11] Japan, shocked by the drop of the atomic bombs in Hiroshima on 6 August and Nagasaki three days later and by the Soviet intervention in the Pacific war on 8 August,[12] formally capitulated to the victorious Allies via a handful of Japanese diplomats and military officers on the deck of the battleship *USS Missouri* in Tokyo Bay on 2 September.[13] The British accepted formal capitulations in South-East Asia and in the East Indies, and the Soviets in Manchuria and northern Korea.

The entire Japanese military became POWs, most of them long enough to be disarmed. The number of those who surrendered in China is astounding: between 1.6 and 1.7 million men. This was just under half of the 3.5 million Japanese combatants left abandoned outside Japan.

On 30 August the US Eighth Army, commanded by General Robert L. Eichelberger, was deployed in Japan, assuming responsibility for occupying all the country. Japanese soldiers were rapidly disarmed and demobilised en masse. By December 1945 the Empire of Japan's forces across the country's home islands were fully dissolved.

Japanese citizens formed a self-help vigilante guard to protect women from rape by off-duty GIs.[14] US Army armoured vehicles were then ordered in battle array into the streets. Law-breaking GIs were arrested and tried, receiving long prison terms. Japan's occupation was overseen by US General Douglas MacArthur, who was appointed Supreme Commander for the Allied Powers (SCAP) by US President Harry S. Truman. He was ordered to exercise authority through the Japanese government machinery and the emperor.[15] Hirohito was allowed to remain on the throne after he agreed to replace the wartime cabinet with an administration acceptable to the Allies and committed to transforming Japan into a parliamentary democracy. The emperor was a living god to the Japanese people and MacArthur found that ruling via Hirohito made his job in running post-war Japan much easier than it otherwise would have been.[16]

America retained more than 70,000 Japanese POWs until early 1947. Japanese Surrendered Personnel (JSP) were used for labour purposes, including road maintenance, recovering corpses for reburial, cleaning and preparing farmland. They were used extensively to repair airfields and seaports damaged by Allied bombings during the war, as well as to maintain law and order until the arrival of Allied forces in a region.

The Japanese First General Army, headquartered in the Kantō region not far from Tokyo, remained active for several months after the surrender of Japan to help maintain public order in Honshu, the largest of the home islands, and oversee the final demobilisation and dissolution of the Imperial forces. POWs were also ordered by the Allies to dismantle the military facilities established by the IJA in Okinawa, in the Philippines and in other parts of the Pacific.

The British retained 113,500 of the approximately 750,000 Japanese POWs that were captured or surrendered in the Pacific and in South-East Asia. The last POWs captured in Burma and Malaya returned to Japan in October 1947.[17] Japanese prisoners were also used to help re-establish the French and Dutch colonies in South-East Asia and the Pacific.

In the early 1990s, after the end of the Cold War, Russian authorities published the names of 46,000 Japanese who had died in Soviet prison camps before and during the Second World War. Historian Yoshikuni Igarashi has doubled that figure, estimating that 100,000 Japanese perished while in Soviet captivity.

After Japan's unconditional surrender, MacArthur ordered the arrest of forty individuals, including all former members of the wartime Imperial government as they were suspected of war crimes. They were charged by the International Military Tribunal for the Far East (IMTFE) in Tokyo of waging a war against the United States, Great Britain, China and the Netherlands, as well as for war crimes, including the surprise attack on Pearl Harbor and the Bataan death march.

Some 132,134 POWs were taken by the Japanese from the British and the US forces alone, of whom 35,756 died in captivity.[18] Crimes committed by Imperial Japan before and during the Second World War were also responsible for the deaths of millions – some estimate between 3 and 14 million civilians – through massacre, human experimentation, starvation and forced labour that was either directly perpetrated or condoned by the Japanese military and government.

Suspected war criminals were tried by US tribunals in Japan (Tokyo and Yokohama), in the Philippines (Manila) and on the island of Guam. They were also tried by the British in Singapore and elsewhere, by the Australians in Rabaul (Papua New Guinea) and elsewhere, by the Dutch in Batavia (Dutch East Indies) and Manado (part of present-day Indonesia) and by the French in Saigon. Most trials (605) were held by the Chinese. The United States (456), the Netherlands (448), Great Britain (330), Australia (294), the Philippines (seventy-two) and France (thirty-nine) are included in the same list. Altogether, 2,244 war crime prosecutions were conducted in Asia and some 5,700 defendants were prosecuted. A total of 920 Japanese military personnel were convicted and sentenced to death,[19] although this total was 984 according to another source.[20] Some 3,419 defendants received various prison sentences and further 1,018 were acquitted. MacArthur was responsible for confirming and enforcing the sentences for war crimes handed down by the International Military Tribunal for the Far East (IMTFE).[21]

Tokyo, Yokohama and Guam trials

The International Military Tribunal for the Far East, also known as the Tokyo Trials, convened on 29 April 1946 and lasted for more than two and a half years – more than twice as long as the better-known Nuremberg Trials. The judges were two Americans (H.F. Stone and Major General M.C. Cramer), one British (W.D. Patrick), one Russian (Major General I.M. Zaryanov), one Chinese (J. Mei), one Canadian (E.S. McDougall), one Australian (W.F. Webb), one New Zealander (E.H. Northcroft), one Indian (R. Pal), one Frenchman (H. Bernard), one Dutch (B.V.A. Rölling) and one Filipino (D. Jaramilla).

Seven of the defendants were convicted as charged and sentenced to death, while sixteen received life imprisonment and two were given lesser jail terms. One defendant, Shūmei Ōkawa, was found mentally unfit for trial and the charges were dropped.[22] Ōkawa was a political philosopher who believed that Japan was destined to assume the mantle of liberator and protector of Asia against the United States and other Western nations. He had a sound knowledge of German, French, English, Indian (Sanskrit) and Arabic (having translated the Koran, the central religious text of Islam, into Japanese). Ōkawa, also known as the 'Japanese Goebbels', was diagnosed by a US Army psychiatrist as suffering from madness caused by syphilis. He was transferred to a mental institution, the Metropolitan Matsuzawa hospital in Tokyo, where he remained until 1948. Ōkawa died on 24 December 1957 in Tokyo, aged 71.

Two of the defendants in the IMTFE, Yōsuke Matsuoka and Marshal Admiral (Kaigun-genshui) Osami Nagano, died during the trial. Matsuoka was one of the architects of the Tripartite Pact that was signed in Berlin between Germany, Italy and Japan on 27 September 1940. He lived in the United States between 1891 and 1902[23] and also graduated from the law school of the University of Oregon.[24] He was also baptised Presbyterian Christian. In 1904 Matsuoka joined the Japanese foreign service. From July 1940 until July 1941 he served as foreign minister. Following the surrender of Japan, Matsuoka was arrested by the SCAP authorities and charged with war crimes and crimes against peace.[25] He died of natural causes in Sugamo prison on 26 June 1946, aged 66, before his trial came up before the IMTFE.

Marshal Admiral Osami Nagano was chief of the Imperial Japanese Navy (IJN) on 7 December 1941 when Japan launched a surprise air attack on Pearl Harbor in Hawaii. He reluctantly gave his approval for the attack after Admiral (later Marshal Admiral) Isoroku Yamamoto threatened to resign as combined fleet commander. Nagano rose to the rank of marshal admiral in 1943. In February 1944 he was replaced as chief of the IJN, becoming an advisor to the government. After the Japanese capitulation, he was arrested by the SCAP authorities and indicted of war crimes and crimes against peace. Nagano died of a heart attack due to complications arising from pneumonia in Sugamo prison on 5 January 1947, aged 66, before the conclusion of his trial before the IMTFE.

Of the defendants who received the death penalty, six were convicted of war crimes, crimes against humanity and crimes against peace. They were, Generals Hideki Tōjō, Seishirō Itagaki, Heitarō Kimura and Kenji Doihara, Lieutenant Generals Akira Mutō and Kōki Hirota.

Hirota, a career diplomat, was prime minister from 1936 to 1937. His contribution to the efforts that led to the signing of the tripartite pact between Germany, Italy and the Empire of Japan was considered significant.

Tōjō was prime minister from 1941 until 1944. His responsibility for the Japanese attack on Pearl Harbor was unquestionable.

Itagaki was commander of the Japanese Seventh Army on 12 September 1945 when he surrendered to British forces in Singapore. Troops under his command in Korea, Singapore and Malaya were involved in war crimes.

Kimura, commander of the Burma Area Army, was condemned for his laxity in preventing atrocities committed by his troops against Allied POWs in Burma.

Doihara, commander of the Twelfth Area Army, was convicted of overseeing war crimes carried out by his forces, mostly in Manchuria. Mutō was the chief of staff of the Fourteenth Army. He and his superior commander, General Tomoyuki Yamashita, were both convicted over atrocities committed by their troops in the Philippines between 3 February and 3 March 1945 against civilians and POWs.

One defendant, General Iwane Matsui, son of an impoverished Samurai, was convicted of crimes against humanity. Troops under his command, IJA's Central China Area Army, massacred between 40,000 and 300,000 Chinese civilians in Nanjin, then the capital of China, in December 1937. Matsui surrendered to the SCAP occupation authorities, on 6 March 1946.

The seven defendants who were sentenced to death were executed by hanging at Sugamo prison on 23 December 1948. Hirota and Matsui were 70 years old, Doihara 65, Tōjō and Itagaki 63, Kimura 60 and Mutō 56. The last thing Tōjō, Matsui, Kimura and Mutō did before they were hanged was to turn in the direction of the Imperial Palace and shout 'banzai' three times. It means 'ten thousand years' in Japanese and can be loosely translated as 'long live' in English.

The next mass execution was held almost two months later, on 12 February 1949, when eight officers had to climb the stairs of the gallows. They had been convicted of murdering Allied POWs. The last mass executions were carried out on 7 April 1950 when seven middle-ranking officers were hanged for the torture and murder of Allied POWs. The bodies of executed criminals were cremated and the ashes were scattered over the sea from aircraft.[26] Sugamo prison, in the Toshima district of northern Tokyo, was originally built in 1895. The buildings were not damaged during bombing by the US Army Air Force on the night of 9/10 March 1945. After the Japanese surrender, about 2,000 Japanese war criminals were held there, guarded by 500 US troops. Sugamo prison was also the site of the execution of Japanese convicted for war crimes and crimes against humanity during the Tokyo and the Yokohama Trials. The US Army handed over the facility to the Japanese authorities in 1952. On 31 May 1958 the last eighteen Japanese war criminals still serving sentences in Sugamo were paroled. Four years later the prison ceased to operate and in 1971 the buildings were dismantled.

The sixteen defendants who were sentenced to life imprisonment by the IMTFE were Baron Kiichirō Hiranuma, Field Marshal Shonruku Hata, Generals Baron Sadao Araki, Yoshijiro Umezu, Naoki Hoshino, Okinori Kaya, Marquis Kōichi Kido, Toshio Shiratori, Kuniaki Koiso, Jirō Minami, Admiral Shigetarō Shimada, Vice Admiral Takazumi Oka, Lieutenant Generals Hiroshi Ōshima, Kenryō Satō and Teiichi Suzuki, and Colonel Kingarō Hashimoto.

Hiranuma was prime minister from January to August 1939. Between 1940 and 1941, he served as interior minister. Hata commanded the Second General Army that was deployed in Hiroshima. He was one of the survivors of the atomic bombing.

Araki served as war minister and minister of Education. Umezu was war minister. He signed the instrument of the Japanese surrender during the ceremony on the battleship USS *Missouri* on behalf of the Imperial armed forces. Hoshino was minister of the economy in various governments. Hiroshima-born Kaya, a prominent bureaucrat, served as minister of finance from 1941 until 1944. Kido was the Lord Keeper of the Privy Seal and Emperor Hirohito's closest advisor. Shiratori served as ambassador to Italy between 1938 and 1940. Koiso, a former governor-general of Korea, was prime minister from 22 July 1944 until 7 April 1945. Minami commanded the Kwantung Army in Manchuria and later became governor of the Japanese-occupied Korea.

Shimada served as minister of the navy in the early 1940s and as chief of the IJN general staff from February until August 1945. Oka was in charge of naval ministry's naval affairs bureau and as of April 1945 member of the general staff of the IJN.

Ōshima was ambassador to Germany for a total of five years: in 1934, from 1938 to 1939 and from 1942 to 1945. He had been characterised more Nazi than the Nazis. Satō, a protégé of Prime Minister Hideki Tōjō, was the official spokesman for army policy and director of the Military Affairs Bureau.[27] Suzuki was cabinet minister and a close associate of Tōjō. Hashimoto was a radical thinker who was elected member of the Diet, Japan's national legislature, in 1944.[28] He was also involved in the Panay incident of 12 December 1937, when unprovoked Japanese bombers attacked and sank the US Navy gunboat USS *Panay* on the Yangtze River in China.[29]

Of the defendants who received life sentences Umezu, Shiratori and Koiso did not survive imprisonment. Umezu died from rectal cancer in his cell on 8 January 1949, aged 67. Shiratori passed away five months later, on 3 June, of natural causes, aged 61. Koiso's death, caused by oesophageal cancer, was on 3 November 1950. He was 70 years old.

Hiranuma was paroled in 1952. He died on 22 August 1952 in Tokyo shortly after his release from prison, aged 84. Kido, Araki, Suzuki, Ōshima and Hoshino were discharged after the end of the US occupation of Japan in 1952. Kido was released

A commandant of the Auschwitz death camp, forty-six-year-old former SS Lieutenant Colonel (SS-Obersturmbannführer) Rudolf Höss, is escorted to the gallows. He was convicted for crimes against humanity by a Polish tribunal and sentenced to be hanged. The execution was carried out on 16 April 1947 at Auschwitz, near Krákow, in southern Poland, next to the crematorium of the main camp (stammlager). (Stanisław Dąbrowiecki, historia.focus.pl/wojny/Rudolf-hoess-komendant-auswitz-naszubienicy-214)

Leading Nazi prisoners of war posing outside Mondorf's *Palace Hotel*, in Luxemburg, on 10 August 1945, prior to their transfer to Nuremberg to stand trial. In the center of the bottom row is former Marshal of the Reich Hermann Göring. Former Grand Admiral Karl Dönitz, former Field Marshals Wilhelm Keitel and Albert Kesselring, and former Colonel General (Generaloberst) Alfred Jodl can also be seen in the picture, along with Third Reich's Foreign Minister Joachim von Ribbentrop. (Public Domain)

Above: Hanna Reitsch (1912-1979) was a German aviator and test pilot. She flew several types of combat aircraft, including the *Junkers Ju 87 Stuka* dive bomber and the pulsejet-powered *Messerschmitt Me 328* fighter, and troop-carrying gliders, including the *DFS 230*. She was also the world's first female helicopter pilot. In the photograph, taken in March 1941, Reitsch is shown during an audience with Adolf Hitler in the presence of Marshal of the Reich Hermann Göring, the supreme commander of the Luftwaffe. After the German capitulation, she was arrested by the US Army, interrogated by intelligence officers and held for 18 months. (German Federal Archives (Deutsches Bundesarchiv)/B 145 Bild-FO51625-0295/CC-BY-SA 3.0)

Left: Princess Mafalda of Savoy, the second daughter of King Victor Emmanuel III of Italy, was arrested by the Germans in early September 1943, when her country surrendered to the western Allies. She was seriously wounded on 24 August 1944, when the Buchenwald concentration camp in which she was detained, was raided by Allied aircraft. Mafalda died two days later at the age of 41. Her German husband, Philipp, Landgrave of Hesse, whom she married in September 1925, was held by the Nazis in a POW camp near Flossenbürg, in Bavaria, until the end of the war. (Mondadori Publishers, Public Domain)

The public execution of Gerda Steinhoff, a female overseer at Stutthoff, in northern Poland, on 4 July 1946, along with three male kapos, Polish volunteer guards in the same Nazi concentration camp. They had been convicted for crimes against humanity and sentenced to death by a Polish tribunal. The executions were carried out in front of an enormous crowd of onlookers, at Biscupia Górka Hill, near Gdańsk, in northern Poland. (Stutthof Museum, Public Domain)

Lieutenant General Yoshihide Nayashi (1891-1978) passed the time tending a garden as a POW. He was the last commander of the Japanese 53rd Division. Nayashi had been convicted for war crimes during the Manila Trials and sentenced to life imprisonment. He was pardoned three years later by President Elpidio Quirino of the Philippines. (This photo (SE 6868) is from the collections of the Imperial War Museums, Public Domain)

This photo & caption is to be used for the dustjacket

Yoshiko Kawashima (1907-1948) was a Chinese (Manchu) princess who spied for the Japanese in Manchuria before and during the Second World War. She became known as "Mata Hari of the Far East". Kawashima, whose Chinese name was Din Bihui, was arrested by the Chinese Nationalists, in Beijing, in November 1945. Two years later, she was tried for treason and sentenced to death. Kawashima was executed on 25 March 1948 by a bullet shot in the back of the head. (Photographer unknown, Public Domain)

Imperial Japanese Army (IJA) Captain Gunkichi Tanaka (left) personally killed with his sword over 300 Chinese POWs and civilians, during the Nanjing massacre in 1937. IJA Second Lieutenants Tsuyoshi Noda (center) and Toshiaki Mukai (right) contested who could kill more Chinese with his sword in one day. Mukai won the contest after killing 106 Chinese – one more than Noda. On 28 January 1948, the three Japanese officers were convicted as war criminals by a Nanjing tribunal and executed. (chinaww2.com/2029/03/17/Nanjing-1948-the-reckoning/, Public Domain)

British-trained and -supervised German prisoners of war clear a minefield in Norway, after the country's liberation by the Allies in the summer of 1945. (This photograph is from the collections of the Imperial War Museums)

Prince Amedeo, 3rd Duke of Aosta (1898-1942), after his surrender to British and Commonwealth forces on 18 May 1941 at Amba Alagi, in East Africa. He was Italy's viceroy of Italian East Africa (Africa Orientale Italiana). Prince Amedeo died in a POW camp in Kenya at the age of 43. (This photograph (ID 007946) is from the collections of the Australian War Memorial, Public Domain)

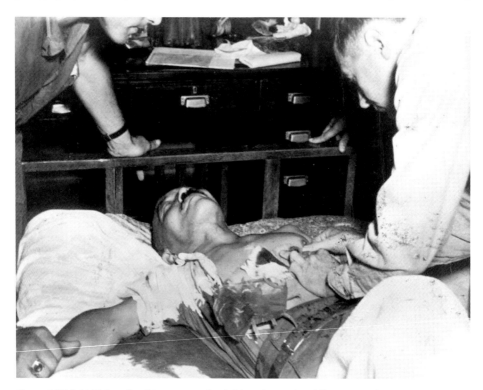

General Hideki Tōjō, after his attempted suicide, when US soldiers entered his house to arrest him on 11 August 1945. He was Japan's prime minister from 1941 to 1944 and his leadership was marked by extreme state-perpetrated violence in the name of Japanese ultranationalism. After recovering of his wounds, Hideki was convicted of war crimes by a US military tribunal and sentenced to death. He was hanged on 23 December 1948 in Tokyo's Sugamo prison at the age of 63. (US Army, Public Domain)

Irma Grese (1923-1945) and SS Captain (Hauptsturmführer) Josef Kramer in the prison cage of Celle, near Hanover. Grese, a camp overseer at Auschwitz and Bergen-Belsen, was nicknamed "hyena" because of her cruelty to female prisoners. Kramer served as commandant in both camps. They were later convicted of crimes against humanity and sentenced to death. Kramer and Grese were hanged on 13 December 1945 in Hamelin prison by British executioner Albert Pierrepoint. (Silverside (Sgt), No 5 Army Film & Photographic Unit. This photograph (BU 9745) is from the collections of the Imperial War Museums, Public Domain)

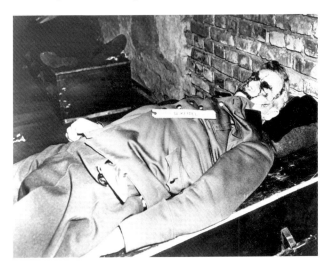

Keitel's body after execution. As the chief of Nazi Germany's armed forces, Field Marshal Wilhelm Keitel had signed a number of orders and directives that led to numerous war crimes. He was convicted, during the Nuremberg trials, and sentenced to death. Keitel was hanged on 16 October 1946, in the Nuremberg prison, at the age of 64. (US Army, Public Domain)

Ten Japanese officers and other ranks in the dock of the Singapore supreme court on 21 January 1946. Some of the defendants were convicted for the execution of POWs and others of maltreating and overworking Allied (mostly Indian) prisoners. (Vasey (Pilot Officer), Royal Air Force official photographer. This photograph (CF 1051) is from an Air Ministry World War II collection, Public Domain)

This photo & caption is to be used for the dustjacket

Among the German prisoners taken by the British army in Walcheren, a region in western Holland, was this Dutch woman. She is seen in the photograph with her husband, a Wehrmacht soldier, whom she refused to leave. The woman was allowed to march with him to the POW cage. (Goodwill A. (Pilot officer), Royal Air Force official photographer. This photograph (CL 1512) is from the collections of the Imperial War Museums, Public Domain)

Beate Köstlin (1919-2001), an aviator and test pilot, rose to the rank of captain (hauptmann) in the Luftwaffe. In late April 1945, she avoided being captured by the Red Army and managed to surrender to the western Allies. Köstlin was interrogated and detained in a POW camp for several months. She is posing in the photograph in front of a *Bücker Bü 131 Jungmann*, a German basic training by-plane. (Bücker Flugsdorf, Bradenburg, Public Domain)

SS-Brigadier (Brigadeführer) Franz Six (1909-1975) in Allied custody after the war. He would have dealt with the 300,000 British Jews had Great Britain been occupied by Hitler's forces. In 1941, he led one of the SS death squads in mass killings of Jews in Smolensk, in German-occupied Russia. Six, a former university professor, was tried for war crimes in Nuremberg, in 1948 and sentenced to twenty years' imprisonment. He was released from Landsberg prison four years later. (Six-franz-nuremberg.jpg/1 January 1948)

SS female overseers in custody, after the liberation of the notorious Bergen Belsen concentration camp by British troops, on 19 April 1945. In the photograph can be seen Hildegard Kanbach (first from left), Magdalene Kessel (second from left), Irene Haschke (centre, third from right), Elisabeth Volkerath (second from right, partly obscured) and Herta Bothe (first from right). Volkerath was convicted as a war criminal and hanged in Hamelin prison eight months later. Bothe and Hasckke were also convicted and imprisoned for ten years each. (Oakes, H. (Sgt), No 5 Army Film & Photographic Unit. This is a photograph (BU 4065) from the collections of the Imperial War Museums, Public Domain)

Ilse Koch was an SS camp overseer. She was nicknamed "Beast of the Buchenwald" because of the atrocities she was involved in during her service at the particular concentration camp. In 1947, she was convicted as a war criminal by a US tribunal in Dachau and sentenced to life imprisonment. Her sentence was commuted to four years and two years later, Koch was released from Landsberg prison. She was then arrested by West German authorities and tried for war crimes. In January 1951, Koch was sentenced to life imprisonment by an Augsburg court. She hanged herself in her cell, at Aichach women prison, in September 1967, at the age of 60. (US Army Signal Corps, Public Domain)

Austrian-born Maria Stromberger (1898-1957) served at Auschwitz as a nurse for the camp's SS personnel. After the war, she was arrested as a war criminal but was soon acquitted after it was testified in court by former detainees that she had been secretly providing food and medicine to prisoners. The photo is from Stromberger's Auschwitz ID card. (Harald Walser. Auschwitz-Birkenau State Museum. Public Domain)

Japanese high-ranking officers involved in the Nanjing massacre are photographed before their trial by a Kuomintang (Nationalist Chinese) military tribunal. (This image is a work of a US military officer identified as Lieutenant Rob. The image was taken as a part of his official duties. As a work of the US federal government, the image is in the Public Domain in the United States)

Three Japanese generals in a British POW camp. They are photographed while playing a game called "Go". From left to right can be seen Lieutenant Generals Masaki Honda (1889-1964) and Yoshihide Hayasi (1891-1978) and Major General Tomotoki Koba (1890-1963). (Morris W. A. (Sgt), No 9 Army Film & Photographic Unit. This photograph (SE 6866) is from the collections of the Imperial War Museums, Public Domain)

This woman has just been informed by a repatriated German POW that her son died in captivity in Russia. She was taking part in a demonstration, ten years after the end of the war, for the release of German prisoners still held in prisons and forced labour camps in the Soviet Union. (US National Archives & Records Administration, Public Domain)

Colonel General (Generaloberst) Alfred Jodl after his arrest by British troops, on 23 May 1945, in his home, near Flensburg, in northern Germany. He was the chief of operations staff of the German armed forces high command (Oberkommando der Wehrmacht) throughout the war. In the photograph Jodl is under guard by elements of the Cheshire Regiment. (Oakes (Sgt), No 5 Army Film & Photographic Unit. This photograph (BU 6701) is from the collections of the imperial War Museums, Public Domain)

Sugamo prison, a facility near Tokyo, housed some 2,000 convicted war criminals, after the Japanese surrender. It was also the site of execution by hanging of numerous generals, admirals and high-ranking officials of Japan's militaristic regime, who had been sentenced to death by the International Military Tribunal for the Far East. The prison closed down in 1962 and the building complex was demolished nine years later. (Gekkan-Okinawa Sha Publishing, Public Domain)

Rudolf Hess, Adolf Hitler's deputy (from 1933 until May 1941), is awaiting trial, after the German surrender. He is photographed in his cell, in Landsberg prison, on 24 November 1945, while reading "Jugend", a book written by a Belgian, Ernest Claes. Hess was sentenced to life imprisonment at Nuremberg. He hanged himself in his cell, at Spandau prison, on 17 August 1987, at the age of 93. (Library of Congress, Public Domain)

Captured German female POWs in a camp near Regensburg, in eastern Bavaria. Half-a-million women volunteered as auxiliaries in Nazi Germany's armed forces (Wehrmacht) during the Second World War. The photograph was taken on 22 April 1945, whilst the war was still going on further north with Berlin being already under attack my Soviet forces. (National Archives & Records Administration, Public Domain)

The *Tudor Vladimirescu* Division enters Bucharest in August 1944 at the head of the Soviet forces. They were one of the formations made up of former Romanian POWs and used by the Red Army to drive German troops out of Romania and later enforce the establishment of a communist regime in the country. Below: Romania's King Mihail I (1921-2017) is reviewing the troops of the *Tudor Vladimirescu* Division. He is followed by the divisional commander, Brigadier General Nicolae Cambrea (1899-1976), who had also been in Soviet captivity before his collaboration with his captors. King Mihail was forced to abdicate and leave Romania on 30 December 1957. (CIA.gov/library/centre-for-the-study-of-intelligence/csi-publications/Public Domain)

Nissen huts were broadly used for the accommodation of Axis POWs by the British during the Second World War. Designed and patented in 1916 by a British army officer, Major P. N. Nissen of Royal Engineers, it was a prefabricated steel structure made from a half-cylindrical skin of corrugated iron. The particular hut was conceived to meet military demand for accommodation in Great Britain and in many Commonwealth countries. It was also used for family housing in the post-war period in Great Britain and abroad. (The photograph is from the collections of the Imperial War Museums)

Hermann Göring, Rudolf Hess and other Nazi top officials were confined, during their trial in Nuremberg, in this corridor of a prison ran by the US Army at the city's Palace of Justice. The guards posted at each cell are watching the prisoners through a small window day and night. They were former members of the Latvian Legion, who had surrendered to the western Allies, after fighting along with Germans against the Red Army. The guards wear blue helmets and white belts. (US Army (Photo: OMTPJ-P-25), Public Domain)

in 1953 because of health problems. Like other Japanese peers, he was stripped of his hereditary peerage upon the abolition of the Kazoku. The 1947 Constitution ended the use in Japan of all titles of nobility outside the immediate Imperial Family.[30] Kido died of cirrhosis of the liver on 6 April 1977 in the Imperial Household Hospital in Tokyo, aged 81.

Hata, Minami and Hashimoto were paroled in 1954. Hata died on 10 May 1962 in Tokyo, aged 82. He was the last surviving military officer with the marshal's rank. Minami died in Tokyo not long after his release, on 5 December 1955, aged 81. Hashimoto was paroled in 1954 but released from Sugamo prison one year later.[31] He died while suffering from lung cancer on 29 June 1957 in Tokyo, aged 67.

Araki, Suzuki, Ōshima, Kaya and Shimada were released in September 1955; the first for health reasons. Araki died on 2 November 1966 at Yoshino, in Honshu, aged 89. Suzuki died on 15 July 1989 at Shibayama, in the Chiba prefecture of Honshu, aged 100. He was the last surviving defendant of the main Tokyo/Nuremberg Trials, as Rudolf Hess had committed suicide at Spandau prison in Berlin, five years earlier (26 April 1984), aged 93.[32] Ōshima was paroled and three years later he was granted clemency by the Ichirō Hatoyama government. He died on 6 June 1975 in Tokyo, aged 89. In 1958 clemency was also granted to Hoshino. He died on 16 January 1978 in Tokyo, aged 85.

Kaya died on 9 May 1977 in Tokyo, aged 88. He was the last surviving full admiral of the Second World War period. Oka and Satō, both sentenced to life imprisonment, were paroled in 1956.[33] Oka died on 4 December 1973 in Tokyo, aged 83 and Satō, two years later, on 6 February 1975, also in Tokyo, aged 80.[34]

Two former foreign ministers who were among the defendants during the Tokyo Trials received shorter prison terms. Shigenori Tōgō and Mamoru Shigemitsu were imprisoned for twenty and seven years respectively. Tōgō was foreign minister from 1941 until 1942, having previously served as ambassador to Berlin and Moscow. In early 1945 he was appointed governor-general of the Japan-occupied Korea. Tōgō died of cholecystitis (inflammation of the gallbladder) in Sugamo prison on 23 July 1950, aged 67.[35]

Shigemitsu became foreign minister three times. On 2 September 1945 he signed along with General Yoshijiro Umezu, as representatives of the Prince Higashikuni Naruhiko administration, the Japanese Instrument of Surrender, on board the *Missouri*. Shigemitsu was convicted as a war criminal by the IMTFE and received a seven-year prison term. He was paroled in 1950. He died on 26 January 1957 of a myocardial infarction in his summer house at Yugowara, in the Kanagawa prefecture of Honshu, aged 69.

General Hayao Tada, who commanded the North China Area Army until July 1941, was indicted of war crimes. He testified as a witness for the prosecution against Generals Iwane Matsui, Seishirō Itagaki and Kenji Doihara. Tada died of stomach cancer on 18 December 1948 in his home at Tateyama, some 70km from Tokyo, aged 66. After his death, it became known that all charges against him had been dropped by the SCAP occupation authorities.

A total of 996 Japanese, mostly military officers, were tried in Yokohama from late 1945 throughout 1949 accused of acts of atrocity. These defendants, compared to those brought in front of the INFE in Tokyo, were characterised as lesser cases,[36] although

124 of them received death sentences. Of these sentences, only fifty-one were carried out; all at Sugamo prison. The sentences were served also at Sugamo.

The most notable of these defendants were Lieutenant General Tasuku Okada and Imperial Japanese Army (IJA) Captain Kaichi Hirate. Okada was convicted of the execution of at least thirty-eight American airmen who had been shot down during combat missions over Japan.[37] Hirate was convicted of the mistreatment and murder of American POWs held in a camp under his command at Hakodate, on Hokkaido, Japan's second largest island. Both were executed at Sugamo. Hirate was hanged on 10 May 1946, aged 37, and Okada was executed by firing squad[38] on 17 September 1949, aged 59.

In 1949 Major General Yoshitaka Kawane and Colonel Kuratano Hirano, who had been convicted of ordering the ten-day Bataan Death March, were executed. Some 3,000 Filipinos and Americans died in March 1945 during the forcible transfer of 76,000 Allied POWs by the Japanese military after the Battle of Bataan in the Philippines in April 1942.

Lieutenant General Eitarō Uchiyama was also convicted of the execution of downed American airmen between April and August 1945. He was sentenced to thirty years in prison. In April 1958 he was paroled and died on 25 December 1973, aged 86.

Lieutenant General Isamu Yokohama commanded the Eleventh Army in 1943 and the Sixteenth Army in 1944. He was convicted during the Yokohama Trials over medical experiments carried out by the IJA at the Kyushu Imperial University on unwilling American POWs, mostly downed airmen. He was sentenced to death in 1948, but his sentence was later commuted to life imprisonment. Yokohama died in Sugamo prison on 21 April 1952, aged 63.

Lieutenant General Masazumi Inada was also convicted over medical experiments performed on American airmen. He was sentenced to seven years in prison. In 1951 he was released from Sugamo. Inada died on 24 January 1986, aged 89.

Lieutenant General Takaji Wachi was convicted of using Red Cross ships to transfer troops and munitions unlawfully to the Philippines. He was sentenced to six years' hard labour. Wachi was released on parole in 1950. He died on 30 October 1978, aged 85.

In 1958 those still serving prison sentences from the Yokohama trials were all paroled.

Lethal experiments on live prisoners were carried out between 1937 and 1945 by '731', a covert biological and chemical warfare research and development unit of the IJA. It was based in the Ping-fang district of Harbin, the capital of Manchukuo, the puppet state of the Empire of Japan in Manchuria from 1932 until 1945 (now part of north-east China). The unit is estimated to have killed between 200,000 and 300,000 prisoners during experimentation.[39]

Dr Shirō Ishii, a lieutenant general (surgeon general) of the IJA, who was in charge of the unit, received immunity from the prosecution of war crimes after the Japanese surrender in exchange for germ warfare data and other scientific information gathered by the '731'.[40] Ishii died on 9 October 1959 from laryngeal cancer in a hospital at Shinjuku, a borough of Tokyo, aged 67. He converted to Catholicism shortly before his death.[41]

Lieutenant General (Surgeon General) Masaji Kitano was Ishii's second-in-command in the '731'. After the Japanese surrender, he was detained in a POW camp in Shanghai. Kitano was repatriated in January 1946 and was never brought to justice for war crimes, having also received immunity by the US occupation authorities for the scientific data gathered by his unit. Kitano died on 17 May 1986 in Tokyo, aged 91.

On 27 May 1949, exactly five years after murdering an American POW, IJN Lieutenant Commander Kaoru Okuma was executed by hanging in Sugamo prison. US Army Air force Second Lieutenant Robert E. Thorpe was captured by the Japanese on 27 May 1944, after his Republic P-47D Thunderbolt fighter-bomber developed an engine problem and ditched in the sea north of Kairiru Island, off the north coast of New Guinea. Thorpe was picked up from the sea and transferred to the 27th Special Naval Base, where he was beaten up by his captors and wounded in the leg during shooting practice. Okuma then used his sword to behead the prisoner. Thorpe's murderer was convicted in Yokohama on 6 July 1948 and Okuma was sentenced to death. Four of his colleagues who participated in Thorp's execution were defendants in the same trial. Four junior and petty officers (Yutake Odazawa, Naotada Fujihira and Tsunehiko Yamamoto) were sentenced to life imprisonment with hard labour, while IJN Captain Kiyohisa Noto received twenty years' hard labour.[42] Rear Admiral Shiro Sato, the commander of the base in which Thorpe was murdered, had committed suicide at war's end.

Trials were held on the island of Guam, in Micronesia, by the War Crimes Commission of the US Navy for crimes committed by the Japanese military in the Mariana, Marshall and Gilbert, Palau, Bonin and Caroline Islands. The commission, headed by Captain (later Rear Admiral) John D. Murphy, functioned like a grand jury from 1945 until 1949. Guam, the largest of the Mariana Islands, an unincorporated territory of the United States since 1898, was occupied by the IJA from 8 December 1941 until 21 July 1944. Japanese Army collaborators, mostly members of the Chamorro tribe, indigenous people in parts of Micronesia, were among the defendants in the Guam trials. Seven accused Japanese committed suicide rather than face trial or sentencing.[43] One of them, Colonel Aritsune Miyazaki, took potassium cyanide after his arrest in Tokyo. He was to be charged over the murder of twelve captured US airmen and six Jesuit missionaries at Ngatpang, in Palau, on 4 September 1944. Miyazaki was the head of the military police (kempeitai) in Palau, an island group in the western Pacific. Lieutenant Colonel Toroji Ito also killed himself before facing trial while in US custody.

On Guam the 114 defendants were charged with murder, torture, cruelty, assault, mistreatment, starvation and other crimes. Two defendants were convicted of cannibalism and seven others for the mutilation of dead POWs. Two lieutenant generals and as many rear admirals were among those convicted. Thirty-six death sentences and sixteen life sentences were handed out. Of the death sentences, twenty were commuted to life imprisonment and one to sixteen years in prison. Two defendants, Captain Kazaharu Yamamoto and Second Lieutenant Yokichi Ichikawa, were sent to prison for twenty-five years. Twenty-four defendants were sentenced to ten to fifteen years of hard labour and the remnant received lesser prison terms. Of the 114 charged, eight were acquitted.

Those sentenced to death were executed either by a firing squad or by hanging.[44] At the beginning of the trials, US Navy was not adequately prepared to conduct executions by hanging. A US Army official hangman was then assigned to train naval personnel to carry out such duties. Thirteen death sentences were carried out by hanging at the Marianas HQ, US Pacific Fleet. Convicted men were sent to Sugamo prison.

Of the defendants in the Guam trials, Lieutenant General Yoshio Tachibana was the most notable. He commanded the 109th Division that was deployed on Chichijima, the largest of the Bonin (present-day Ogasawara) Islands, 620 miles (1000km) south-southeast of Tokyo. Tachibana was sentenced to death by hanging for his role in the murder of eight captured US airmen. He was also convicted for acts of torture and cannibalism committed by his troops in Chichijima. Tachibana was executed on 24 September 1947 in Asan-Maina, a village on the western shore of Guam, aged 57.

Rear Admiral Shigematsu Sakaibara was convicted over the murder of ninety-eight US civilians on the atoll of Wake, in the western Pacific, on 5 October 1943. Sakaibara was commanding the Japanese garrison on Wake Island.

Rear Admiral Shimpei Asano and commander Chisato Ueno, a naval doctor, were found guilty of torturing to death four US POWs at Chuuk, also known as Truk, part of Micronesia in the southern Pacific Ocean.[45] They were also convicted for having allowed medical experiments to be carried out on live prisoners and mutilation of the bodies of POWs. Asano and Ueno were hanged on Guam on 31 March 1947.[46]

Earlier, on 23 May 1946, the Navy War Crimes Commission determined that Vice Admiral Abe Kōsō ordered and supervised the beheading of nine US Marine commandos on Kwajalein, an atoll of the Marshall Islands. He was hanged on 19 June 1947 on Guam.

Captain Hiroshi Iwanami, a naval doctor, was found guilty of murdering ten US POWs in July 1944 and allowing medical experiments to be carried out on live prisoners. He was the commanding officer of Japan's stronghold at Chuuk. After his arrest, he tried unsuccessfully to kill himself with a sharp pencil.[47] He was executed by hanging on 16 July 1947 on Guam.[48]

Vice Admiral Chūchi Hara was the last commander of Truk. He was surrendered to US forces on 2 September 1945. Hara was convicted of war crimes at his trial on Guam and sentenced to six years in prison. He was released from Sugamo prison on 19 April 1951. He died on 17 February 1964 in Tokyo, aged 74.

Manila Trials

Japanese war criminals were also brought before Allied military tribunals in the Philippines. In late 1945 a war crimes commission was created by General Douglas MacArthur to try high-ranking officers who were involved in atrocities committed during the invasion and occupation of the Philippines by the Imperial Japanese forces. Of the 169 defendants, 133 were found guilty as charged. Twenty-five were given the death sentence and sixteen were sent to prison for life. General Tomoyuki Yamashita, Lieutenant Generals Masaharu Homma, Takeshi Kono, Hikotaro Tajima and Hong Sa-ik, and Major General Mashatoshi Fujishige were sentenced to death.

Yamashita surrendered to Allied forces near Luzon in the Philippines on 2 September 1945. On 15 February 1942 his Twenty-Fifth Army had seized Singapore, capturing about 80,000 British and Commonwealth troops. On 26 September 1944 Yamashita became military governor of the Philippines. His trial before a US military tribunal lasted from 29 October 1945 until 23 February 1946. Yamashita was charged in relation to the Manila massacre, during which at least 100,000 civilians were killed between 3 February and 3 March 1945.[49] He was also accused over two massacres that were carried out by his troops in the Alexandra Barracks Hospital and at Sook Ching following the fall of Singapore. He was also accused of the mass murder of 139 US POWs on 14 December 1944 at Palawan, western Philippines. Yamashita denied ordering these crimes. He claimed that he would have punished those responsible for the massacres if he had that knowledge. However, he was found guilty and sentenced to death by his judges, three major generals (L. Donovan, R.B. Reynolds and J.A. Lester) and two brigadier generals (M.H. Harwerk and E.F. Bullens).

The decision, called command responsibility or 'Yamashita standard', set a precedent in that a commander can be held accountable before the law for the crimes committed by his troops even if he did not order them. The doctrine of command accountability has been added to the Geneva Convention and has been adopted by the International Criminal Court established in 2002.

An appeal for clemency was denied by US President Harry S. Truman. Yamashita was hanged on 23 February 1946 at Los Baños prison camp, 30 miles (48km) south of Manila, aged 60.[50]

Homma led the Fourteenth Army during the Japanese invasion of the Philippines on 8 December 1941. After the Japanese surrender he was indicted on war crimes committed by troops under his command near Manila Bay between 7 January and 9 April 1942 during and after the Battle of Bataan. On 11 February 1946 Homma was convicted of all counts (including his responsibility for the Bataan Death March) and sentenced to death.[51] Homma's wife appealed to General MacArthur to spare her husband's life. Her pleas were denied although the verdict changed and Homma was ordered to be shot rather than sent to the gallows, the latter being considered the greatest dishonour among military officers. Homma was executed by a US-Filipino firing squad at Los Baños POW camp on 3 April 1946, aged 58.

Kono, commander of the 77th Brigade, was convicted for the massacre of at least 2,500 Filipino civilians on Panay Island, on the central part of the archipelago.

Tajima, commander of the Bataan garrison, was convicted over the murder of three captured US naval aviators in May 1944.

Korean-born Hong Sa-ik joined the IJA in 1910 and four years later he graduated from the Japanese military academy. He rose to the rank of lieutenant general. Sa-ik was in charge of all camps holding Allied POWs in the Philippines from March 1944. He converted to Christianity while in Allied custody after the Japanese surrender. During the Manila trials, Sa-ik was convicted of atrocities committed by troops under his command against Allied prisoners. He was hanged on 26 September 1946 in the Los Baños POW camp, aged 57.

Fujishige, commander of the 17th Infantry Regiment, was convicted of the murder of 25,000 Filipino civilians in the Batangas province on Luzon Island. Tajima, Hong and Fujishige were executed on 17 July 1946 and Kono one year later.

Colonel Satoshi Oie, after his death sentence for war crimes, was transferred to Tokyo to testify in another trial. His death sentence was carried out after completing his obligation as a court witness. On 23 October 1948 Oie was transferred in a bus to a firing range near Sugamo prison. It became known that, before falling dead, Oie thanked, one after the other, everyone involved in his execution, including the six-man firing squad.[52]

In 1948 the convicts who had not been executed were all transferred to Filipino custody. They were released in 1953 under an amnesty by President Elpidio Quirino.[53] It was an unexpected decision by the leader of a nation that had lost 530,000 to a million people, mostly civilians, in the Second World War, during the Japanese invasion and occupation.[54]

Trials against 155 Japanese military officers indicted of war crimes were conducted in Manila between 1947 and 1949 by the National War Crimes Office (NWCO) of the newly independent Republic of the Philippines. Most of the trials mainly covered war crimes ranging from murder and torture to rape and looting. Of the defendants, 138 were convicted, seventy-nine were sentenced to death and thirty-one were sent to prison for life.

Only fifteen executions of Japanese war criminals were carried out on the gallows of the New Bilibid prison, at Muntilupa, a borough of Manila. In March 1949, Lieutenant General Shizuo Yokohama and Rear Admiral Takesue Furuse were sentenced to death by musketry. Their sentence was commuted to life imprisonment in July 1953. They were pardoned on 28 December 1953. Yokohama was pardoned although he had been convicted of the murders of Quirino's wife and three of his children during the Battle of Manila. Yokohama died on 6 January 1961, aged 71.

IJN Lieutenant Commanders Somin Ogawa, Shisuhiko Mineo and Yamasu Kose were sentenced to death by hanging in February 1949. Their sentence was commuted to life imprisonment on 2 July 1953 and they were pardoned on 23 December that year.

Lieutenant Generals Yoshihide Nayashi and Shigenori Kuroda were sentenced to life imprisonment in July 1949. Kuroda, who commanded the Fourteenth Army during the country's occupation by Japanese forces, was pardoned in December 1951. He was repatriated in early 1952 and died on 30 April the same year in Tokyo, aged 64. Nayashi was pardoned six months later. He died on 5 February 1978, aged 86.

Major General Kiyotake Kawaguchi was the last commander of the Tsushima garrison on two so-named islands situated halfway between Kyushu and the Korean Peninsula. On 14 November 1949 he was convicted of war crimes committed by his forces in 1942 in the Lanao province in the Philippines, including complicity in the execution of the Philippine's Supreme Court Chief Judge José Abad Santos. Kawaguchi was sentenced to six years in prison but was pardoned on 4 July 1953. He died eight years after his repatriation, on 16 May 1961, aged 68.

On 4 July 1953 President Quirino pardoned 105 Japanese convicts awaiting their executions or serving their sentence. Quirino also pardoned 323 Filipino collaborators with the Japanese Army and Navy.

British military tribunals

From 1946 to 1948 some 330 war crimes trials were organised by the British in Singapore, Kuala Lumpur, Rangoon, Hong Kong and Borneo. Of these trials, 131 were conducted at eight military tribunals in Singapore,[55] most of them in the Supreme Court building on St Andrew's Road. More than 400 accused linked to the Japanese military were tried by the British for various war crimes in these eight tribunals and a further four throughout Asia.

In the first trial, held from 21 January to 1 February, ten Japanese defendants were convicted of ill-treating 520 Indian prisoners in a POW camp, named Pileliu or Pililiou, part of the Palau Islands in Micronesia, resulting in the death of 118 men. One of the defendants, Lieutenant Nakamura Kaniyaki, was sentenced to death for beheading one prisoner. Seven of the other defendants were given prison sentences ranging from two to twelve years, while two were acquitted. On 15 March 1946 Kaniyaki was among the first three convicted of war crimes to be executed in Singapore. A middle-rank officer, Captain Mitsuo, and an NCO, Sergeant Major Jijima, were the other two.

Lieutenant General Kawamura Saburō and Lieutenant-Colonel Oishi Masayuki were convicted over the purge of 25,000–50,000 civilians, who were mostly ethnic Chinese, in Singapore between 18 February and 3 March 1942, in what went down as the Sook Ching massacre. At the time Saburō was commander of the recently occupied city and Masayuki was in charge of the military police (Kempeitai). They were sentenced to death on 2 April 1947 by a British military tribunal.[56] Saburō was hanged on 2 June 1947, aged 51.[57]

On 18 March 1946 in the Supreme Court building in Singapore the trial of seventeen Japanese and five Chinese interpreters (also known as 'the Double Tenth Trial') began. They were accused of torturing fifty-seven civilians and Allied POWs, resulting in the death of fifteen, who had been unfairly suspected by the Japanese of assisting British and Australian commandos in a raid on Singapore Harbour on 10 October 1943.[58] After a hearing lasting twenty-one days, eight of the defenders were sentenced to death. They were Lieutenant Colonel (then Major) Sumida Haruzō, Warrant Officer Tadamori Morai, Sergeant Majors Masuo Makizono, Takao Terada, Shigeo Tsujio and Shozo Morita, Sergeant Toichira and Chinese interpreter Toh Swee Koon. Three defendants, Warrant Officer Shigeru Sakamoto and Sergeants Hideo Kasahara and Masayoshi Nigo, were sentenced to life imprisonment. Interpreter Kasuo Miyaki received a fifteen-year prison sentence. Sergeant Kozo Sugimoto and Interpreter Chan Eng Thian were sent to prison for eight years. Of the defendants, seven were acquitted.[59] Toh was not executed. On account of his British citizenship, he was later tried by a civilian (district) court. On 8 October 1946 Toh was sentenced to four years' 'vigorous' imprisonment.[60]

On 19 February 1946 four NCOs and one private were convicted of war crimes committed during the Japanese occupation. They were Warrant Officer Atsusi Hirazawa and Sergeant Shigetoshi Shin, who were sentenced to death and executed by hanging. Private Yoshitarō Murata was sent to prison for fourteen years and Corporal Ryosoku Hase was sentenced to five years' imprisonment.

On 22 August 1946 two Japanese and eight Korean-born Imperial Japanese Army (IJA) privates were convicted over war crimes committed in Singapore. Lieutenant Kishio Usuki, Sergeant Major Aitaro Hiromatsu and three of the Koreans, (listed as Japanese names) Kinzo Motoyama, Mitsui Tokuyama and Taikyo Iwaya, were sentenced to death and hanged. IJA Korean privates Meizan Matsumoto, Kinei Morimoto and Shyunshyaku Minaka were sentenced to life imprisonment. IJA Korean privates Eiji Kumoi and Yugei Tomotoma were sent to prison for fifteen and ten years, respectively. The death sentences of Motoyama and Tokuyama were later commuted to life imprisonment.

Earlier, on 26 February 1946, Lieutenant Akuni Yamaguchi, Sergeant Major Mitsugi Matsumoto and Sergeants Susumi Uekihara and Timohei Shimomura were convicted for torturing three Singaporean citizens, resulting in the death of two of them. The four defendants were sentenced to death and hanged.

Major Ichikawa, who commanded a battalion of the 215th Infantry Regiment, was the first to be tried as a war criminal in Rangoon (present-day Yangon), in Burma (present-day Myanmar). He was convicted of murdering, with thirteen of his men, 600 inhabitants of Kalaga village, east of Moulmenin (present-day Mawlamyine).

First Lieutenant Hiroshi Abe was accused in connection with the death of hundreds of workers during construction of part of the Burma railway at Songkurai, in eastern Thailand close to the border with Burma. More than 12,000 Allied POWs and Korean workers had been under his supervision. Abe was sentenced to death by hanging, as a 'B' Class war criminal, but his sentence was commuted to fifteen years' imprisonment. In 1947 he was released from Changi prison in eastern Singapore. In 1995 Abe testified against the Japanese government in a lawsuit seeking compensation for Koreans in Japan during the Second World War. His whereabouts ever since are not known.

Field Marshal (Gensui) Hisaichi Terauchi, commander of the Southern Expeditionary Army Group, was responsible for the mistreatment of labourers during the construction of a railway linking Burma with Siam (present-day Thailand). He had also ordered that all Allied POWs in his command area were to be massacred if Japan's home islands were invaded.[61] Terauchi surrendered his sword to the British in Saigon as a token of defeat on 30 November 1945. He was never tried for war crimes as he died of a stroke on 12 June 1946 at Renggam, a town in the south of the Malay Peninsula, while being transferred to a POW camp. He was 66 years old. Terauci's wakizashi, an original Samurai short sword has been kept ever since at Windsor Castle in England.

Lieutenant General Hatazō Adachi commanded the Eighteenth Army on the island of Papua New Guinea. On 11 September 1945 he surrendered to elements of the Australian 6th Division at Cape Wom. He was mainly accused after the war over an order he issued in October 1944 that gave his officers the power of summary field executions.[62] During his trial in front of an Australian military tribunal, Adachi took responsibility for the crimes committed by his subordinates. On 12 July 1947 he was found guilty as charged and sentenced to life imprisonment. Adachi killed himself in his cell with a paring knife on 10 September that year in a prisoners' compound in Rabaul, a township in the New Britain province of Papua New Guinea, aged 57.

Lieutenant General Renya Mutaguchi commanded the Fifteenth Army in mid-1944 during the invasion of India, which was disastrous for the Japanese. In December 1945 he was arrested and extradited to Singapore as a suspected war criminal. Mutaguchi evaded a conviction for war crimes and was released from prison three years later. He died on 2 August 1966 in Tokyo, aged 77.

Lieutenant General Masatane Kanda became commander of the Seventeenth Army in September, replacing Lieutenant General Harukichi Hyakutake, who had suffered a debilitating stroke. Kanda surrendered his forces to the Australian II Corps on 8 September 1945 on Bougainville, an island that was part of Papua New Guinea.[63] He was later convicted of war crimes by an Australian military court and sentenced to fourteen years in prison. He was released in 1952. Kanda died on 15 January 1983, aged 92. Hyakutake remained hidden in the jangle. He was transferred to Japan for medical treatment as late as February 1946 and died on 10 March 1947 in Tokyo, aged 58.[64]

Lieutenant General Masaki Honda surrendered his Thirty-Third Army to Allied forces in southern Burma in August 1945. He remained in British custody until 1947. Honda was never charged over any war crimes. He died on 17 July 1964, aged 75.

JAPANESE

Australian military tribunals

Lieutenant General Baba Masao commanded the Thirty-Seventh Army in Borneo from 26 December 1944. On 10 September 1945 he surrendered to the Australian 9th Division. On 28 May 1947 he was brought in front of an Australian military tribunal in Rabaul accused of war crimes, including leading death marches during which 2,200 Australian POWs perished.[65] Eight days later Masao was found guilty and sentenced to death. He was hanged on 7 August 1947, aged 47. Captain Hoshi Susumu, who was a defendant in the same trial, also received a death sentence and was executed.[66]

General Hitoshi Imamura commanded alternately the Sixteenth and Seventeenth Armies during the Pacific War. He was tried for war crimes by an Australian military tribunal in Rabaul from 1 to 16 May 1947. Imamura was convicted over the execution of Australian POWs in Java, one of the main islands of the Indonesian Archipelago. He was found guilty and sentenced to ten years' imprisonment. Imamura was released from Sugamo Prison in 1954. As he found that his sentence was too light, he had a replica of a prison built in his garden in Tokyo and stayed in there until his death on 4 October 1968, aged 82.[67]

Captains Tacuo Takakuwa and Genzō Watanabe, co-commandants of the Santakan POW camp in north Borneo, were convicted in March 1946 during a Labuan trial over the death march of 536 Australian and British POWs in May–June 1945. Most of the 183 survivors were later executed.[68] Takakuwa and Watanabe were sentenced to death and hanged in Rabaul on 6 April 1946.[69]

Some 300 trials of Japanese war criminals were conducted by the Australian military between 1945 and 1951 in Darwin, northern Australia, and in several locations in the Asia-Pacific region. These trials were held in Rabaul (190), Manus Island (26), Singapore (25), Morotai Island (25), Labuan (16), Hong Kong (13), Darwin (3) and Wewak (2).[70] A total of 812 Japanese were tried. Some 137 were convicted, sentenced to death and executed; far more were sentenced to terms of imprisonment. Of the 643 guilty sentences, 130 (or 20 per cent) were mitigated, commuted or not confirmed. Australian, British and American victims were represented in seventeen, five and two trials respectively as the overwhelming majority of the victims in most cases were Indian or Chinese POWs.

In April 1946 two Imperial Japanese Army (IJA) NCOs and seven IJA Formosan soldiers were found guilty by an Australian military tribunal in Rabaul of the execution of sick Chinese POWs. Four of the convicted, two NCOs and two soldiers, were hanged on 17 July 1946 in Rabaul.

The average number of defendants tried in any of the trials by Australian military tribunals was three. In one case the defendants numbered ninety-one. They had been guards in Tantoei POW camp on Ambon Island, 800km north of Australia, and were accused of maltreating prisoners. In July 1942 forty-three Dutch POWs were beaten for two hours and four months later twenty-five Australian POWs were beaten and tortured (some of them for as long as eleven days). Of the defendants, thirty-six were found guilty, forty-four were acquitted and eleven were released due to insufficient evidence. The Japanese convicts were placed in purpose-built compounds, which were administered by the Australian Army and Navy. The compounds were guarded by detachments from the Papua New Guinea civilian police force.[71] Those imprisoned were held at Rabaul

(1945–49) and at Manus Island (1949–53). Thereafter all remaining Japanese convicts were repatriated to serve their sentences in Sugamo Prison.

Imperial Japanese Navy (IJN) Lieutenant Paul Hideo Katayama, a devout Christian, was sentenced to death by an Australian military tribunal at Morotai Island on 28 February 1946.[72] He was convicted for his participation in the execution of Allied POWs, having been in command of a Japanese firing squad. Katayama was a member of Ginza Church, part of the United Church of Christ in Japan, in downtown Tokyo. He had also studied English Literature at Tokyo University. An uncle of his was married to an English woman. Katayama was executed by a firing squad in Rabaul on 23 October 1947.[73]

Rear Admiral Kyosho Hamanaka, a defendant in the same trial, was found guilty of ordering the murder. He was sentenced to death and executed by shooting on 15 January 1946.[74] Lieutenant General Sakurai Shōzō surrendered his Twenty-Eighth Army to the Allied forces in September 1945 at Moulmein, 90 miles (300km) southeast of Rangoon. He was held in a POW camp until June 1947. Shōzō died on 7 July in Tokyo, aged 96.

Lieutenant Commander Baron Masamitsu Takasaki was suspected of committing war crimes by Australian and Dutch military authorities. Between 11 and 12 January 1946, he was tried on Morotai Island in the Dutch East Indies (present-day Indonesia) by an Australian military tribunal, accused of the murder of two Australian POWs on 19 June 1945 at Sarlon, near Manado, in north Celebes. Takasaki, who was educated at St Catherine's College, Cambridge, was acquitted. He was later tried for war crimes by a Dutch military tribunal and was again acquitted, despite strong circumstantial evidence connecting him to several war crimes committed against Allied POWs. It is believed that Takasaki escaped punishment because of his wealth, his social position, his willingness to cooperate with investigators and a hiatus in the war crimes trials.

Dutch military tribunals

The Dutch East Indies (DEI) authorities faced a number of obstacles in preparing for war crimes trials. Many Japanese nationals who had committed such crimes there were no longer available. Some were dead, some were missing, and some had already been repatriated to Japan and consequently were beyond the reach of the Dutch. Despite that as many as 448 military tribunals were convened in the DEI from 6 March 1946 until 24 September 1947 in which a total of 1,038 Japanese were tried for war crimes.[75] Of those convicted, about 200 were sentenced to death and executed.

In the DEI the largest number of war crimes' trials were held in Batavia, present-day Jakarta. Suspected war criminals were also tried in various locations, including: Balikpapan, Banjarmasin, Morotai and Pontianak, in Borneo; Manado, in North Celebes; Macassar, in South Celebes; Medan, in north Sumatra; Ambon, part of the Maluku Islands; Hollandia, in New Guinea; and Kupang, in Timor.

About one third of the Japanese indicted of war crimes were members of the army's military police (Kempeitai) or its naval equivalent (Tokkeitai). The first who were tried, in December 1946, were 200 Japanese and Koreans who had served as guards in POW and civilian internment camps. The defendants before the Dutch military tribunals were accused of various crimes, including atrocities, murder, torture and rape. Some of them were accused of forcing at least thirty-five interned European (mostly Dutch) women, including little girls, to serve as 'comfort women' in brothels licensed by the Japanese military. The consent for the particular programme was given by Lieutenant General Shinshichiro Kokubu. He was the chief-of-staff of the Sixteenth Army that was stationed in Batavia at the time. Kokubu later commanded the Timor garrison, headquartered at Kupang. He was never charged with any crimes. Kokubu died in 1984 in Japan, aged 90.

Major General Seiji Nojaki, who commanded the 152nd Infantry Division, was also responsible for enforcing prostitution, having served as commandant in Semarang, east of Batavia, in central Java. He was never charged either. Nojaki died on 8 November 1974, aged 84.

Vice Admiral Marquis Tadashige Daigo commanded IJN's Sixth Fleet from May to September 1945. After the Japanese surrender, he was arrested in Japan by the US occupation authorities and extradited to the DEI to be tried as a war criminal. Daigo was convicted in Batavia over the involvement of troops under his command in the massacre of 21,000 civilians, including women and children, at Pontianak, the largest city of Kalimantan in Borneo, between April 1943 and June 1944. Daigo was sentenced to death and executed on 6 December 1947 at Pontianak with a rifle shot to his stomach, aged 56.

Rear Admiral Koichiro Hatakeyama had ordered the mass execution of at least 100 Australian and Dutch POWs on Ambon Island on 7 February 1942,[76] as well as the execution of 312 Australian and Dutch defenders of Laha airfield, Java, on 24/25 February 1942.[77] Hatakeyama was never tried for these atrocities as he was killed in a plane crash in China in 1945. The officer who was ordered to lead the death squads in both incidents, IJN commander Kunito Hatakeyama, was convicted by a Dutch court martial, after the war. He was sentenced to death and hanged.

Lieutenant General Masaomi Yasuoka, a tank officer, participated in the 1939 Soviet–Japanese border wars before becoming the military governor of Surabaya, a port city in east Java.[78] He was arrested on 2 September 1945 and charged by a Dutch military court with unspecified war crimes.[79] Yasuoka was found guilty and sentenced to death. He was hanged in Surabaya on 12 or 14 April 1948, aged 61.

Captain (Taisa) Toyoaki Horiuchi commanded the Yokosuka 1st Special Naval Landing Force, IJN's first paratrooper unit, which was activated on 20 September 1941.[80] On 12 January 1942 he led his unit on a combat jump in north Sulawesi, in the DEI. Some of his men killed thirty of the surrendered Dutch, who were mostly officers, using swords. On 6 January 1947 Horiuchi was arrested and detained in Sugamo prison, and then extradited to the DEI to be tried as war criminal. On 28 January 1948 he was indicted for his involvement in the murder of the Dutch POWs. Horiuchi was found guilty of the killings by a Dutch military tribunal although he did not order them. He was sentenced to death. On 25 September 1948 Horiuchi was executed by hanging in Manado, aged 48.

Lieutenant General Moritake Tanade assumed command of the Twenty-Fifth Army in April 1943. After the war he was convicted by a Dutch military tribunal in Medan for war crimes committed by his troops in Sumatra and sentenced to death. He was executed on 10 July 1949, aged 60.

IJA Captain Kenichi Sone served as commandant in three POW and civilian internment camps in the DEI. On 2 September 1946 he was convicted of the maltreatment of prisoners, particularly during his tenure (April 1944–June 1945) at the all-women

Tzideng internment camp near Batavia. He was sentenced to death and held in Glodok prison until his execution by firing squad on 7 December 1946, aged 36 or 37.

Major General Toshinari Shōji was the last commander of the Fifth Area Army. After the Japanese surrender, he was arrested by the US occupation authorities and extradited to the DEI. Shōji was convicted in Batavia for crimes committed on Allied POWs and civilians during the invasion of the DEI by Japanese forces in January 1942. He was arrested by Allied occupation authorities in April 1948. Nine months later Shōji was sentenced to death, but his sentence was later commuted to ten years' imprisonment. He was released earlier from Sugamo prison. Shōji died on 10 December 1974, aged 84.[81]

Lieutenant General Seisaburō Okazaki was the last Japanese to be tried for war crimes by the Dutch authorities. He was arrested in Japan in April 1948 by the US occupation authorities and extradited to the DEI. In March 1949, in Batavia, he was charged over atrocities committed by troops under his command during the invasion of the DEI. Okazaki, then a major general, was chief-of-staff of the Sixteenth Army that was involved in cases of mass murder, murder, torture, rape and mistreatment of POWs in Java and Borneo. On 16 March Okazaki was acquitted of all charges. It is believed by some that he was found not guilty despite the existence of sufficient evidence to support a guilty verdict. Okazaki was released from prison in March 1950. He died on 27 May 1979, aged 86.

Saigon trials

Between January and May 1946 Nationalist Chinese troops in northern Indochina repatriated 400 suspected war criminals to Japan, probably on US orders. They also transported 160 more to Guangzhou, also known as Canton, in southern China, for a separate war crimes trial. American officers, likewise, conducted an investigation on suspected war criminals in Indochina, independently from the French, until 1947. At the same time, in early 1947, the US military authorities helped French representatives to extradite Japanese suspected of war crimes to Saigon from various parts of the Pacific and the Far East. By June 1947 France had identified more than 933 Japanese suspected to have committed war crimes in French Indochina during the Second World War. Trials were conducted in Saigon by the French Permanent Military Tribunal from October 1946 until March 1950. In thirty-nine trials a total of 239 defendants were indicted. They were B- and C-grade war criminals, leaving to the Tokyo trials the prosecution of the A-grade war criminals. Of the defendants in the Saigon trials, sixty-three were sentenced to death, 130 others received prison sentences, including twenty-three verdicts for life imprisonment, and thirty-one were acquitted. A further 228 people were condemned in absentia. Those condemned were incarcerated in the Poulo Island and Chí Hòa prisons. Of the death sentence verdicts, sixty-three were carried out.

On 3 March 1945 Japanese forces across Indochina took the French colonial forces by surprise and had them disarmed in order to strengthen Japan's control in the peninsula. During the operation, known as Meigō Sakusen, one French general was arrested and beheaded and 300 French soldiers were murdered after their surrender in the Saigon-Cholon region in north-east Indochina. Colonel Shizume and three captains were later convicted over the execution of the soldiers, in what became known as the Lang Son massacre. They were accused of taking the prisoners into a small courtyard in groups of twenty and having them shot and bayonetted in cold blood. In January 1950 the four defendants were sentenced to death and executed.

Imperial Japanese Army (IJA) Captain Yoshio Fucuda was accused by the French permanent military tribunal in Saigon of the execution of General Émile René Lemonnier, the military commander of Lang Son, a city close to the border with China.[82] Lemonnier was beheaded by his captors for refusing to sign the documents for the surrender of his troops. Fucuda, who gave the order for the execution, was convicted and sentenced to death. He was executed on 19 March 1951.

On 14 February 1947 forty-nine members of the Saigon-based Japanese military police (Kempeitai) were charged with torturing sixty French arrestees. They were convicted of the torture of at least sixty French soldiers in the Saigon-Cholon region on 3 March 1945. Thirteen of the defendants, including four convicted in absentia, received the death penalty, twenty-seven were given prison sentences of various lengths ranging from seven years to life imprisonment and nine were acquitted.

Lieutenant General Yuitsu Tsuchihashi, commander of the Thirty-Eighth Army, served as governor-general of Indochina from 9 March until 28 August 1945. He was then taken prisoner in Saigon by Nationalist Chinese troops and held in a POW camp in Guangdong (formerly romanised as Canton), a coastal province in southern China. In January 1948 Tsuchihashi was transferred to French custody in Saigon, where he remained imprisoned until his release in July 1949. He was never charged with war crimes. Tsuchihashi was repatriated in June 1950. He died on 31 May 1972 in Japan, aged 81.

The final executions of convicted war criminals by the French military authorities in Indochina were carried out on 11 May 1951. Most of those handed prison sentences had been transferred from various detention facilities in Indochina to Sugamo prison by mid-1950.

Chinese and Soviet military tribunals

The western Allies tried 5,707 Japanese, of which 4,524 were convicted.[83] Little data is available regarding Japanese prosecuted for war crimes by the Communist Chinese and Soviet authorities after the war. The Nationalist Chinese (Kuomintang) tried 883 Japanese, of whom 504 were convicted. Of those convicted, 149 (or roughly 30 per cent) received death sentences. These trials related only to crimes committed against Chinese.

In the trials conducted by the Nationalists in Nanjing (also known as Nanking), China's capital at the time, for the massacre of 40,000 to 400,000 civilians in early December 1937, the defendants were General Yasuji Okamura and Lieutenant Generals Hisao Tani and Rensuke Isogai. Other Japanese generals involved in the particular massacre were not tried by the Chinese. General Iwane Matsui had been tried by the International Military Tribunal for the Far East in Tokyo, while Prince Yasuhiro Asaka had been granted immunity by General MacArthur as a member of the Imperial family. General Kesago Nakajima, Lieutenant General Heisuke Yanagawa and Prince Kan'in Kotohito had died in 1945; Yanagawa on 22 January of illness, aged 65, Prince Kan'in on 21 May of an infection caused by inflamed haemorrhoids, aged 79, and Nikajima on 28 October from natural causes, aged 64.

Okamura and Tani were tried in Nanjing along with IJA Captain Gunkichi Tanaka and Second Lieutenants Toshiaki Mukai and Tsuyoshi Noda. On 13 December 1937 Mukai and Noda allegedly competed over who could kill 100 people faster using a sword.[84] In this outrageous contest Mukai was the winner with 106 kills, leaving Noda second with one fewer. During the massacre Tanaka killed about 300 Chinese on his own. After the Japanese surrender, Tanaka, Mukai and Noda were arrested by the American occupation authorities and held in Sugamo prison before their extradition to China.[85] They were convicted of crimes against humanity by a Kuomintang military tribunal in Nanjing and sentenced to death. They were executed on 28 January 1948 in the mountains of the Yuhuatai region. Tanaka was 42, Mukai 35 and Noda 35 years old.

Tani was convicted on 16 February 1947 over the Nanjing massacre and sentenced to death. He was executed publicly by shooting on 26 April 1947 outside the south gate of Nanjing, aged 64.[86]

General Okamura, although convicted of war crimes in July 1948, was protected by Nationalist Chinese leader Chiang Kai-shek, who retained him as a military advisor. He died on 2 September 1966 in Tokyo, aged 82.

Lieutenant General Takashi Sakai had led the Japanese troops during the invasion and occupation of Hong Kong in February 1942. He was arrested by the American occupation authorities and extradited to China. On 27 August 1946 he was convicted by a military tribunal in Nanjing over the extrajudicial execution of Chinese civilians and sentenced to death. Takashi was executed on 30 September 1937 by firing squad, aged 58.

Lieutenant Generals Rensuke Isogai and Hisakazu Tanaka were tried by the Nationalist Chinese for crimes committed in Hong Kong during their tenure as military governors. Isogai served in Hong Kong from 1942 to 1944 and Tanaka from February 1945 until the end of the war. Tanaka was convicted of the murder of an American POW and sentenced to death by a US military court in Shanghai in 1946. He was then turned over to the Chinese nationalists to be tried for crimes against humanity. Tanaka was found guilty of atrocities, including executions, torture and rape, committed in Hong Kong by Japanese troops. He was sentenced to death and was publicly shot in Canton on 27 March 1947, aged 58.

Isogai was convicted by a Kuomintang military court in Nanjing and sentenced to life imprisonment. He was released from prison and repatriated in August 1952. Isogai died on 6 June 1967 in Japan, aged 80.

On 24 May 1945 Lieutenant General Takeo Itō was sentenced to death by an Australian military tribunal in Rabaul for the murder of Chinese civilians. The sentence was not carried out and three months later he was extradited to Nationalist Chinese authorities. In 1948 he was tried in Hong Kong and convicted of war crimes. Itō was sentenced to twelve years in prison.[87] He died on 24 February 1965, aged 75.

Lieutenant General Sasaki Tōichi was also involved in the Nanjing Massacre. He was captured by the Red Army and handed over to the Chinese Communists. Tōichi was interned in the Fushun war criminals' management centre, where he died in 1955 aged 69.

The Fushun prison primarily housed Japanese prisoners who were 'gifted' by the Russians. In July 1950 the Soviet Union sent to the newly established People's Republic of China (PRC) 969 Japanese POWs to judge. The PRC sponsored official trials in the cities of Taiyuan, in the Shanxi province, and Shenyang, in Liaoning province. In total, in the early 1950s there were 1,109 Japanese in PRC custody. Forty-seven of them died in prison. A further forty-five defendants were given long prison sentences in the summer of 1956, when they were tried for war crimes. More than a thousand more were convicted of similar crimes. When it came to those convicted of the most serious war crimes, the Communist Chinese authorities were more lenient than the western Allies, the Soviets and the Nationalist Chinese in eschewing capital punishment and life imprisonment as punishments.[88] Summary executions of Japanese prisoners were carried out though in former Manchuria, mostly after unofficial 'people's trials'. Estimates place the number of executed Japanese POWs at possibly 3,500 individuals. In the PRC the formal policy was to have the war criminals transformed by inculcating in them a sense of remorse and bringing them closer to communist ideology. The convicted Japanese were kept imprisoned in China until 1964. Chinese collaborators, as well as Nationalist (Kuomintang) prisoners, were released after twenty-five years; as late as the mid-1970s.

General Jun Ushitoku, commander of the Third Army, attempted to oppose the Soviet invasion of Manchukuo (Manchuria). By 13 August 1945 his troops were largely shattered and he surrendered to the Red Army on 21 August. He spent more than a decade as an internee in the Soviet Union. He was released and repatriated on 26 December 1956. Ushitoku died on 24 November 1973 in Tokyo, aged 89.

General Seiichi Kita commanded the Sixth and the Twelfth Armies during the Second World War. He fought unsuccessfully with the First Area Army against the Red Army, when the Soviet Union invaded Manchukuo. Together with his surviving soldiers, he became a POW. Kita was never repatriated. He is thought to have died in a POW camp on 7 June 1952, aged 66.

Lieutenant General Shōjiro Iida invaded Thailand at the head of the 25th Army. He later invaded Burma at the head of the Fifteenth Army. In 1945 Iida assumed command of the Thirtieth Army in Manchukuo just before the Soviet invasion. He was taken prisoner by the Red Army and held as a POW in the Soviet Union from 1945 until 1950. Iida died on 23 January 1980 in Tokyo, aged 91.

General Otozō Yamada became a POW in the Soviet Union after Japan's surrender. He was tried for war crimes at Khabarovsk, the largest city in the Soviet Far East, 500 miles (800km) from Vladivostok. During the trial, which lasted from 25 until 31 December 1949, he admitted to authorising the use of Ishii bombs, fragile porcelain grenades containing typhus and bubonic plague bacteria.[89] He was also found guilty of encouraging biochemical weapon experimentation on involuntary human subjects, resulting in the torture and murder of thousands of people. Yamada was convicted as charged and sentenced to twenty-five years in a labour camp.

Lieutenant Generals Kajitsuka Ryuji and Takahashi Takaatsu, Major Generals Kawashima Kiyoshi and Shunji Satō and Lieutenant Colonel Toshihide Nishi were also tried in Khabarovsk over the use of biological weapons against Soviet forces. On 31 December 1949, Ryuji Takaatsu and Kiyoshi were convicted and sentenced to twenty-five years in a labour camp. Satō and Nishi were also found guilty and sentenced to twenty years in labour camp.

Two officers and as many non-commissioned officers were also convicted in Khabarovsk over the use of biological weapons. Senior Sergeants Karasawa Tomio and

Mitomo Kazuo were sentenced to eighteen and fifteen years in prison respectively. The verdict for Major Onue Masao and Lieutenant Hirazakura Zansaku was twelve and ten years in prison respectively. Lighter prison terms (up to three years) were imposed on further two defendants by the same military court. Yamada, Ryuji, Takaatsu, Kiyoshi, and Satō were sent to Camp No. 48, a facility in Ivanovsky Region in which the detainees were high-ranking officers.[90] Those who received shorter sentences served the full term of their time in labour camps. Takaatsu died in Soviet custody on 24 September 1951, aged 63.

On 13 December 1956 the convicted war criminals became subject to the Declaration of the Presidium of the Supreme Soviet of the USSR on amnesty for Japanese citizens convicted in the USSR and were deported to their homeland.[91] Their repatriation coincided, in a way, with the normalisation of the Soviet–Japanese relations.[92] Yamada died on 18 July 1965 in Tokyo, aged 83. Ryuji died in 1976, aged 88. Satō died on 2 January 1977, aged 80.

Fugu Plan

Colonel Norihiro Yasue and Imperial Japanese Navy (IJN) Captain Koreshige Inazuka were involved in the Fugu Plan, aimed at taking Jews from Europe to Japanese-occupied territories of China in Manchukuo. Until 1942, when the scheme fell apart as the Japanese aid to Jews could not be tolerated by its ally, Nazi Germany, some 24,000 European Jews were able to emigrate to Japan, thus escaping the Holocaust. Yasue was captured in August 1945, when the Red Army invaded Manchuria. He died in a POW camp in Khabarovsk on 4 August 1950, aged 64. Inuzuka did not face any charges by the Western Allies in Japan after his country's capitulation. He died on 19 February 1965, aged 74.

Setsuzo Kotsuji, a Japanese orientalist, was at the time the only Japanese who could speak and read Hebrew. The son of a Shinto priest, Kotsuji converted to Christianity in his youth. He later helped Jews to emigrate from Europe and settle in Japanese-occupied Shanghai. When his activities became known, Kotsuji was released from detention by the American occupation authorities. He converted to Judaism in 1959, taking the name of Abraham. Kotsuji died on 31 October 1973 in the United States, aged 74.

Abraham J. Kaufman was a Russian-born medical doctor and Zionist who emigrated to Harbin, China, in 1912. He helped tens of thousands of Jews seeking safe havens in Kobe in Japan and Shanghai in Japanese-occupied China. In 1945, days before the end of the war, Kaufman was kidnapped by the Russians and charged with collaboration with foreign forces. He was held in a Gulag labour camp for eleven years. Kaufman was released in 1956. Five years later Kaufman emigrated to Israel. He died there on 25 March 1971, aged 86.

Never charged

Forty-two suspects, such as Nobosuke Kishi, who later became prime minister, and Yoshisuke Aikawa, head of Nissan, were imprisoned by the Supreme Command of Allied Powers (SCAP) authorities in the expectation that they would be prosecuted at a future Tokyo tribunal but they were never charged. They were released in 1947 and 1948 respectively.

General Toshizō Nishio was the governor of Tokyo from 1944 until the end of the war. He was arrested by the SCAP authorities and imprisoned but formal charges for war crimes were never brought. He was eventually released from prison. Nishio died on 26 October 1960 in Tokyo, aged 78.

General Yasuji Okamura who served mostly in Burma during the war, was imprisoned after the Japanese surrender but never charged with war crimes. He was eventually released. Okamura died on 2 September 1966 in Tokyo, aged 82.

Admiral Sankichi Takahashi was imprisoned as a war crimes suspect but was never charged. He was freed in December 1948. Admiral Soemu Toyoda was the last commander of the Imperial Japanese Navy. He was interrogated and held in Sugamo prison as war crimes suspect. In 1948 he was charged of violating the laws and customs of war but was finally acquitted.

General Nobuyuki Abe was the last governor of Japanese-occupied Korea and a previous (1939–40) prime minister of Japan. Abe was arrested by the Americans after the Japanese surrender. He was not charged with any war crimes and was soon released from prison.

Lieutenant General Rikichi Tsukada commanded Teishin Shudan, the Imperial Japanese Army's paratrooper forces. After the Japanese defeat in the Philippines, he ordered the remnant of his troops to carry out guerrilla-type missions in the mountains, west of Clark airfield. The Alamo Scouts, the reconnaissance unit of the US Sixth Army, were assigned to capture him, but he escaped. Tsukada turned himself in after the formal surrender of Japan. He was eventually released and never charged with war crimes. Tsukada died on 19 May 1958, aged 65.

Colonel Hiromichi Yahara was a senior staff officer of the Thirty-Second Army in charge of operations. During the American invasion of Okinawa, he evaded arrest. He mixed with local civilians disguised as an English-language teacher. Yahara was eventually recognised by the US military authorities and detained in a POW camp. He was later released as he was never charged with war crimes.

The Imperial family

Members of Japan's Imperial family involved in the conduct of war were not brought before the International Military Tribunal for the Far East for prosecution after the country's capitulation. For politico-strategic and geopolitical reasons General Douglas MacArthur decided to support the Imperial Family and to grant immunity to all its members, with one exception. They and their children lost their imperial status and privileges and became ordinary citizens (commoners) following the abolition of the collateral branches of the Japanese Imperial family. The abolition was announced by the US occupation authorities on 14 October 1947. The members of the Imperial family and their sons were purged from holding any political and public office because they had been officers in the Imperial forces.

Prince Nagahisa Kitashirakawa was a field artillery captain of the Imperial Japanese Army (IJA). He died in a plane crash on 4 September 1940, aged 30, while on duty in Mengjiang, in present-day Mongolia, thus becoming the first member of the Imperial family killed during the Second World War. Nagahisa was posthumously promoted to major.

Field Marshal (Gensui) Nashimoto Morimasa was the only member of the Imperial family arrested for war crimes by the US forces. On 2 December 1945 General MacArthur, the governor of Japan during the US occupation, ordered the arrest of Nashimoto as a 'Class A' war criminal, largely for his role in supporting state Shintoism. He was released from Sugamo prison on 14 October 1947 after four months' imprisonment. Nashimoto, a graduate of the St Cyr military academy in France, had been a field marshal since 1932. He died on 2 January 1951 in the Shibuya-ku borough of Tokyo, aged 76.

Prince Naruhiko Higashikuni was an IJA general and also a St Cyr graduate. He was the only member of the Imperial family and the last military man to become prime minister. He was premier for fifty-four days, from August to October 1945. Naruhiko died on 20 January 1990 in Tokyo, aged 102.

Prince Yasuhiko Asaka was considered a war criminal for his role in the Nanjing Massacre in December 1937 in which an estimated 40,000 to more than 300,000 Chinese were murdered.[93] He allegedly issued the order 'kill all captives'. Nanjing was at the time the capital of China. Yasuhiko was a general of the IJA from 1931. He was only interrogated by the occupation authorities about his involvement in the Nanjing massacre. He was exonerated from criminal prosecutions before the Tokyo tribunal by order of General MacArthur. In December 1951 Yasuhiko converted to Catholicism.[94] He died on 12 April 1981 in Atami, central Honshu, aged 93.

Prince Kaya Tsunenori was a lieutenant general of the IJA. He was appointed as the Emperor's personal envoy to Nanjing following the 1937 massacre. Kaya died on 3 January 1978 in Chiba, in the Kantō region of Honshu, aged 77.

Prince Kan'in Haruhito was a major general who assumed command of the 4th Armoured Division in the Kantō region of Honshu on 21 May 1945. After Japan's capitulation, he was tasked with visiting Saigon as a formal representative of Emperor Hirohito to ensure the compliance of the Southern Army Group to surrender. Can'in died on 14 June 1988 in Tokyo, aged 85.

Prince Fushimi Hiroyasu was a graduate of the Imperial German naval academy (1892–95). He was also educated in England (1907–10). He served as chief of staff of the Imperial Japanese Navy (IJN) from 1932 until 1941. Fushimi died on 16 August 1946 in Tokyo, aged 70.

Prince Tsuneyoshi Takeda was a lieutenant colonel of the IJA. He held executive responsibilities over Unit 731, which conducted biological weapons research using unwilling Allied POWs in experiments. After Japan's capitulation, he was sent to Sinkyo, in Manchukuo, as a formal representative of Emperor Hirohito to ensure the Kwantung Army's compliance with the surrender order. Tsuneyoshi died on 11 May 1992 in Chiba, 40km south-east of Tokyo, aged 83.

Prince Takahito Mikasa, a cavalry officer and a major since 1941, was a staff officer in the Imperial General Headquarters. He died on 17 December 2022 in Tokyo, aged 100.[95]

JAPANESE

The 'Mata Hari of the Far East'

Yoshiko Kawashima was a Qing dynasty Manchu princess who spied for the Japanese during the Second Sino–Japanese War (7 July 1937–2 September 1945). She undertook undercover missions, mostly in Manchuria, always in disguise and often wearing male clothing. For a time, Kawashima (whose Chinese name was Jin Bijui) was the mistress of General Hayao Tada, who commanded the Japanese forces in North China until July 1941. On 11 November 1945 she was arrested in Beijing by the Chinese nationalists (Kuomintang authorities) and brought to trial at Hebei, a northern province of China. On 20 October 1947 she was convicted as hanjian (traitor). On 25 March 1948 40-year-old Kawashima was executed in Beijing by a bullet to the back of the head.[96] Her body was later put on public display.

PART TWO
DETAINEES (II)

In June 1941 the great majority of the countries of south-eastern Europe were allied to Nazi Germany: Romania, Hungary, Bulgaria, Slovakia, and Croatia. All except Bulgaria sent contingents of their own forces to fight either on the Russian Front or as security troops in the Balkans.

Romanians

The Kingdom of Romania joined the Tripartite Pact of Germany, Italy and the Empire of Japan on 23 November 1940. The country was at the time a military dictatorship under General Ion Antonescu, with King Mihail I a figurehead with no effective political power. Two Romanian Armies, the Third and the Fourth, took part in the German campaign against the Soviet Union. In Stalingrad alone the Romanian casualties were 109,000 men. By the end of the war the number of Romanian POWs in the Soviet Union was significant.

Up to 100,000 Romanian soldiers were disarmed and taken prisoner by the Red Army after the Royal coup d'état of 23 August 1944, when Romania switched its alliance from the Axis powers to the Allies. Before that date almost 165,000 Romanian soldiers were reported missing, with most of them assumed to be POWs. At least 140,000 Romanians were taken prisoner by the Red Army after the Axis defeat in Stalingrad.

The Soviet authorities generally used POWs as a workforce in labour camps.[1] From late 1943 to early 1944 Romanian POWs were present in several 'production camps' ran by the Soviet authorities. Some 6,740 Romanians worked in Spassky POW camp, at Karlag, Karaganda Oblast, in the Kazakh Soviet Socialist Republic (SSR), now part of Kazakhstan.[2] Spassky was the largest POW camp in the region. Some 900 Romanian POWs died in Stalinist camps in central Kazakh SSR between 1941 and 1950 due to harsh conditions.[3]

At least 140,000 uniformed Romanians, including four army generals, were taken prisoner by the Red Army in 1941–44. Thousands more, including several generals and admirals, were imprisoned after the war when the communists seized power, turning their country into another People's Republic and part of the Eastern Bloc. The high-ranking officers in particular were considered either supporters of Romania's previous pro-Axis regime or enemies of the communist ideology, or both. They were also held accountable for their participation in Nazi Germany's invasion of the Soviet Union. Of the condemned generals in the post-war period, fourteen died in prison or during their confinement in one of the forced labour camps set up across the Danube-Black Sea Canal.

Romania switched sides, joining the Allies in the fight against Germany, after Antonescu's downfall on 23 August 1944. Lieutenant General Constantin Sănătescu, commander of the Fourth Army, was named prime minister.[4] Having led Romanian troops in the battle of Stalingrad as an ally of Hitler's forces, he was now tasked not only with consolidating the coup, but – more importantly – with repelling the attacks by the German troops still deployed in the country. In the battles fought between 24 and 31 August a large portion of Romania was liberated with the support of the Red Army, but the country was, in fact, under Soviet occupation.

Some Romanian prisoners volunteered to fight for the Soviets. They went on to form the *Tudor Vladimirescu Division* under Nicolae Cambrea in October 1943, but it did not go into action until after King Mikhail I led Romania to join the Allies. Some 22,411 Romanian detainees took part in forming Romanian volunteer divisions of the Red Army and about 50,000 more remained in labour camps. In April 1946 61,622 Romanian POWs were repatriated from USSR. The last Romanian prisoners were freed in 1956. Many were arrested again by communist Romanian authorities after returning home for 'waging war on the Soviet Union' and sent to prisons and labour camps.

Three Romanian high-ranking officers were led to captivity in Russia. These were General Mihail Lascăr, Major General Georghe Cosma and Brigadier General Nicolae Cambrea. Lascăr, who commanded Romania's Third Army during the battle of Stalingrad, was taken prisoner by the Russians on 22 November 1942. Cosma was captured on 24 August 1944 at Tângu Neamț, in northern Romania, part of present-day Moldavia.[5] He was held by the Red Army at Bistriocioara, in western Romania. Cambrea was taken prisoner in 1943. He collaborated with the Soviet authorities and was eventually put in charge of the *Tudor Vladimirescu*. This unit was at the head of the Soviet forces that liberated Bucharest, Romania's capital, on 31 August 1944.[6] The *Tudor Vladimirescu* Division was also part of the Soviet forces that won the battle of Debrecen, in Hungary, against German and Hungarian troops in October 1944.[7]

The only high-ranking Romanian officer who did not fall into Soviet hands was Brigadier-General Platon Chirnoagă. He was in German custody from mid-1944.[8] On 8 May 1945, when Nazi Germany was defeated, he was released from a POW camp. Then he was arrested by the US Army and detained at the Glasenbach POW camp, near Salzburg. He was freed in April 1947. Chirnoagă settled in Austria and then moved to France. In 1968 he settled in Stuttgart, West Germany, where he died in 1974, aged 80.[9]

After the downfall of the Antonescu regime, the 250,000-strong Romanian Army was involved in fighting on the Allied side against German and Hungarian forces. On 12 September, in Bucharest, Antonescu was placed under house arrest. A few days later a former commander of the Romanian 1st Mountain Brigade was captured by the Red Army in western Romania while fighting with the German Army. He was Major General Artur Gustav Phleps, who had resigned from the Romanian Army in 1940 to join Nazi

Germany's Waffen-SS as a standartenführer (colonel).[10] When he was captured by Soviet troops in Şimand village near Arad, he had the rank of SS-obergruppenführer (lieutenant general). On 21 September 1943 Phleps was shot dead by his guards while trying to escape.[11] He was 62 years old.

On 3 March 1945 Romanian Army general Gheorghe Avramescu was killed during an aerial attack near Jászberény, central Hungary. When it happened, he was in Soviet custody. Sixty-one-year-old Avramescu had been arrested for interrogation by NKVD state security agents while leading Romanian troops against retreating German and Hungarian forces.

Only two Romanian generals were killed in action during the Second World War. They were Major General Alecu Ioan Sion and Brigadier General Grigore Bălan. Sion was fatally wounded on 24 November 1942 at Bolshaya Doshchika fighting against the Red Army near Stalingrad.[12] Bălan was wounded by a German artillery shell on 9 September 1944 during the siege of Sfântu Gheorghe in central Romania. Bălan died from his wounds three days later, aged 48.[13]

On 7 December 1944 Lieutenant General Nicolae Rădescu became Romania's last pre-communist prime minister. He was forced to resign on 1 March 1945; five days later the first communist-dominated government of Romania took office. Petru Groza, the leader of the Ploughmen's Front, a leftist agrarian political organisation, became prime minister. A month later the Russians raised, at Kotovsk (present-day Podilsk), near Odessa, in southern Ukraine, a second division made up of Romanian prisoners of war. A Romanian general who was also in Soviet custody, Mihail Lăscar, was named divisional commander. The new formation was baptized *Horia, Cloşca and Crişan* division (after the names of the leaders of a 1784 peasant revolt in Transylvania against Hungarian landowners of the region). This formation, along with the *Tudor Vladimirescu* division, became a key instrument with which Moscow was able to establish complete communist control of post-war Romania. Lăscar served as minister of defence in 1946–47.[14] Cambrea, the commander of the *Tudor Vladimirescu* division, was promoted to general in 1949, before being assigned the command of Romania's 2nd Military Region. Cambrea died in Bucharest on 5 February 1976, aged 76 or 77.

Joseph Stalin was reluctant to allow the use of armed POWs in operations with the Red Army because of the way the problems it had faced after arming POWs in Poland. Two years after the massacre of 22,000 Polish officers by the NKVD in the Katyn forest in April and May 1940[15] Stalin permitted the raising of an 80,000-strong force with the aim of fighting the Germans alongside the Soviet forces.[16] However, unable to support the Polish force, the Soviets decided to deport its members. In March 1942 the Poles made their way through Iran, Iraq and Palestine, becoming a major tactical and operational formation under the British high command. The Polish II Corps, commanded by a Polish lieutenant general, Władysław Anders, fought bravely in the Italian theatre of operations. Only 310 members of the force returned voluntarily to Poland in 1947.

Meanwhile, Antonescu had been handed over to the Soviet occupation forces. He was transferred to Moscow and held in Lubyanka prison. In spring 1946 he was sent back to Romania. Antonescu was charged with high treason and sentenced to death. He was executed by firing squad on 1 June, along with five prominent members of his regime. Days later Prime Minister Rădescu fled to Cyprus and from there to the United States. He died in New York on 16 May 1953, aged 79. On the last day of 1947 King Mihail

I was forced to abdicate and he was allowed to leave the country. Romania was formally declared a People's Republic by the country's new pro-Moscow administration.

Before long, some 30 per cent of the country's officer corps had been purged from the military due to fears of monarchist loyalties or anti-communism. They were dismissed en masse without pension. Several others, including army generals, admirals and air force generals, were arrested and imprisoned. A number of them were sentenced to death or to many years' imprisonment. Thirteen high-ranking officers died during their confinement in prison or at a forced labour camp.

A number of Romanian officers had been decorated by Nazi Germany for their bravery during Hitler's campaign against the Soviet Union. Lieutenant General Petre Dumitrache was awarded in 1942 the Knight's Cross in the Class of Knight, the highest order of the Third Reich. Two generals, M. Lascăr and Petre Dumitrescu, and one major general, Corneliu Teodorini, were honoured with the most prestigious Knight's Cross of the Iron Cross with Oak Leaves. Twelve officers were Knight's Cross of the Iron Cross recipients. They were four generals: M. Lascăr, Petre Dumitrescu, Ioan Mihail Racoviţă and Edgar Rădulescu; two lieutenant generals, Corneliu Dragalina and Nicolae Tătăranu; two major generals, Georghe Manoliu and Leonard Mociulschi, and one brigadier general, Radu Korne.

Other recipients of the same order were two air force generals, Ermil Gheorghiu and Emanoil Ionescu, and one vice admiral, Horia Macellariou. Two officers, General G. Avramescu and Major General L. Mociulschi, were awarded in 1942 the German Cross in Gold.

Finally, four generals were recipients of the Iron Cross: P. Dumitrescu, I.M. Racoviţă, Edgar Rădulescu and M. Lascăr; two lieutenant generals, C. Dragalina and Ilie Şteflea; two major generals, L. Mociulschi and N. Tataranu; and one brigadier general, Vladimir Constantinescu.

Another officer, David Popescu, was decorated with fascist Italy's Order of the Crown. Lieutenant General Popescu, Vice Admiral Nicolae Păis and Major General Dimitru Dămăceanu were graduates of Modena Italian military academy and a further two, General I.M. Racoviţă and Lieutenant General Aurel Aldea, had attended a German military academy in Hanover.

Popescu was dismissed and put in the reserves after returning from Odessa in August 1941. Following the August 1944 coup he was rehabilitated and promoted to corps general. In 1950 he was denounced as a 'deadly enemy of communism'. Popescu was then arrested and detained in Jilava prison. He was released on 4 July 1953 as he was acquitted of all charges. Popescu died two years later, aged 68.

Aldea was instrumental in the coup that resulted in the arrest of Antonescu and Romania's switching allegiance from the Axis powers to the Allies.[17] He was arrested on 27 May 1946 and tried by a people's court, charged with resistance activities. Found guilty of plotting against the state, Aldea was sentenced to life imprisonment. He died in Aiud prison, in central Romania, on 17 October 1949, aged 62.

The majority of these officers were persecuted, condemned and imprisoned by Romania's communist authorities. The charges they faced varied between 'high treason', 'conspiracy against the state', 'waging war on the Soviet Union' and 'war crimes'. Thirteen of them died in prison or in a forced labour camp. They were the generals N. Ciupercă and I. M. Racoviţă; the lieutenant generals A. Aldea and H. Cihoski; the brigadier generals Constantin Eftimiu, R. Korne, Constantin Petrovicescu, Ioan Popovici and R.R. Rosetti; the major generals Ioan Arbore, Radu Baldescu, and Constantin S. Constantinescu-Claps; and a vice admiral, Nicolae Răis. In Aliud prison died: Lieutenant General A. Aldea (1949) and brigadier generals R. Korne (1949), C. Petrivesescu (1949) and C. Eftimiu (1950). In Sighet prison died: General I.M. Racoviță (1954), Lieutenant General H. Cihoski (1950), Vice Admiral N. Păis (1952) and Brigadier General I. Popovici (1953).

With the exception of Rosetti, who had seen combat as back as the First World War and had only ideological differences with the newly established communist regime, the rest had fought in Stalingrad, the Caucasus and Crimea against the Red Army.

Cihoski was a member of the Supreme Court of the National Defence from 1943 until 1944. He was arrested in 1945 and sent to Sighet prison, where he died on 18 May 1950, aged 79.

Petrovicescu was known for his pro-Nazi ideology and anti-Semitism. He served as interior minister during the Antonescu regime until the summer of 1941, when he was arrested and sentenced to five years in prison. Following the 1944 coup Petrovicescu was arrested and held in the prisons of Alba Iulia, in western Romania, and Sibiu. In 1946 he was tried (simultaneously with Antonescu) before the first of a series of Romanian people's tribunals as war criminal. He was sentenced to life imprisonment. Petrovicescu died in Aliud prison on 8 September 1949, aged 66.

Păis had led Romanian war vessels of the Black Sea Fleet to support Axis ground forces fighting in Crimea. When he died, aged 65, Vice Admiral Păis was buried in a mass grave. Rosetti died in his cell, aged 73, having served only five months of a two-year prison sentence.

General Raconiță, Lieutenant General Cihoski, Brigadier Generals Korne and Popovici, and Major General Baldescu were sent to prison without a trial. Korne was beaten severely in Jilava prison and left with a broken spine. He died in Văcăresti prison on 28 April 1949, aged 53.

General N. Ciupercă died in his cell on 25 August 1950, aged 68, due to failing health. Baldescu was arrested in 1951 and died in his cell three years later. Popovici was 83 years old at the time of his arrest in 1948. He died in prison five years later. Life imprisonment was the sentence for Aldea, Eftimiu, Petrovicescu, twelve years for Ciupercă, ten years for Arbore and Constantinescu-Claps, three years for Păis and two years for Rosetti.

Aldea, Korne, Eftimiu and Petrovicescu died in Aliud prison, in central Transylvania. Racoviță, Cihoski, Păis and Popovici died in Sighet prison, northern Romania. Ciupercă, Constantinescu-Claps, Arbor and Rosetti died in Văcăresti prison, near Bucharest. Baldescu died in Bucharest's Gilava prison.

In 1950, following the establishment of the communist regime, Leontin Sălăjan was named general and five years later defence minister. His only experience with military matters were the two years of his national service in a broadcasting unit in the mid-1930s. He remained in this post until his death eleven years later. Sălăjan died during a failed ulcer operation on 28 August 1966, aged 53.

Lieutenant General Nicolae I. Dăscălescu fought in the battle of Stalingrad. When Romania switched sides in August 1944, he led the Fourth Army in battles against retreating German forces in Czechoslovakia. On 25 March 1945 he was wounded during the battle of Banska Bystrica in central Slovakia. In 1946 Dăscălescu was put on trial as a war criminal but the court dismissed the accusations. In 1951 he was thrown in Jilava prison for his involvement in an alleged agricultural sabotage. Dăscălescu was released in 1955. He died on 28 September 1969, aged 85.

Major General Gheorghe Cosma was taken prisoner by the Red Army on 24 August 1944 in Târgu Neamt, western Moldavia. He had fought in Crimea and Stalingrad. In late 1944 he was released and led Romanian mountain troops in the fight against German forces. In 1955 Cosma was tried at the military tribunal in Iași by the communist authorities for his role on the Eastern Front. He was found not guilty and acquitted. Cosma died on 1 July 1969, aged 67.[18]

General Ioan Mihail Racoviță commanded the Cavalry Corps. He was tasked with rebuilding the Romanian Fourth Army after the Axis forces' crushing defeat at Stalingrad. On 1 January 1944 he led his forces in defensive battles in the Caucasus area against the advancing Red Army. After the 1944 coup Racoviță was appointed minister of defence in the pro-Allies government of Constantin Sănătescu. On 20 May 1946 Racoviță was promoted to general. From 20 May 1946 until 30 June 1947 he commanded the First Army. On 1 September 1947 Racoviță retired from the army. In June 1950 he was arrested and imprisoned at Sighet prison, in northern Romania, where he died on 28 June 1954, aged 65.

General Gheorghe Avramescu commanded the Fourth Army during the Crimea campaign. After the 1944 coup, he fought on the side of the Red Army against the retreating German and Hungarian forces. On 2 March 1945 Avramescu was arrested on the Slovakian front by NKVD agents. He died a day later, while in Soviet custody, aged 61. On 3 March 1945 his wife (Adela) and his daughter (Felicia) were arrested back home and sent to Siberia. On their way there, on 6 March, his daughter committed suicide.

Lieutenant General Nicolae Ciupercă commanded Romania's Fourth Army in the operations that led to the occupation of Odessa by German and Romanian forces from 8 August to 16 October 1941. Three years after the end of the war Ciupercă was arrested by the communist authorities and brought in front of a people's tribunal. He was sentenced to twelve years imprisonment for invading the Soviet Union. Ciupercă was held at Jilava prison before being transferred to Văcăresti prison. He died in his cell on 25 May 1950, aged 68, due to failing health.

Lieutenant General Gheorghe Gialăk fought with the Cavalry Corps on the East Front. In October 1944 he was arrested and detained in Malmalson prison, Bucharest. He was released in February 1945, but arrested again on November 1951. He was charged with crimes against humanity committed in Soviet territories. He was held in Jilava prison until his release in 1955. Gialăk died in 1977 in Bucharest, aged 109.

Brigadier General Corneliu Carp fought in the East Front at Odessa. He was arrested in 1950 and condemned to twelve years imprisonment by a people's court. Carp was released in 1955. He died in 1982, aged 87.

Brigadier General Vladimir Constantinescu commanded the 8th Cavalry Division during the Caucasus campaign. After the war he was imprisoned at Aiud from October 1948 to July 1950. He was sent for some time to the Albă forced labour colony at the Danube-Black Sea Canal. Major General Emanoil Bărzotescu commanded Romanian VI Corps on the Eastern Front. In 1950 he was sent to a forced labour camp ay the Danube-Black Sea Canal. Bărzotescu died in 1968, aged 79.

Lieutenant General Ion Dumitrache commanded the 2nd Mountain Division during the Caucasus Campaign. He was awarded the Knight's Cross of the Iron Cross for capturing Nalchik, the furthest point of the Axis military advance into the Caucasus. In February 1949 Dumitrache was arrested for presumed war crimes. He was held at Aiud, Jilava and Văcăreşti prisons. In October 1950 he was released for lack of evidence. Dumitrache died on 6 March 1977, aged 87.

Major General Gheorghe Manoliu also fought on the Eastern Front alongside German and Italian forces. He commanded the 4th Mountain Division from March 1942. In February 1949 Manoliu was condemned to forty-five years in prison as a war criminal. He was detained at Aiud prison (1950–52) and at Jilava prison (1952–54). He was released in 1954. Manoliu died in Bucharest in 1980, aged 92.

General Petre Dumitrescu led Romanian forces, mostly in Crimea. By October 1941 his Third Army had captured 15,565 Soviet POWs. In 1946 Dumitrescu was put on trial for war crimes, but was acquitted because of a lack of evidence. He died of natural causes in Bucharest on 15 January 1950, aged 67.

In September 1951, with the communist regime already established in Romania, General Constantin Constantinescu-Claps was arrested and incarcerated at Văcăresti prison, near Bucharest. In September 1954, he was condemned to fifteen years in prison for ordering the execution of four Soviet partisans during Romania's participation in the German campaign against the USSR. One year later Constantinescu-Claps was exonerated and released. He died in June 1961 at Bacău, in western Moldavia, aged 77.

Major General Dumitru Carlaont took part in the siege of Odessa. After the war he was arrested twice accused of war crimes and crimes against humanity committed on Soviet territories, but was acquitted. In 1951 Carlaont was arrested again. He was tried and sentenced to twelve years in prison. He was released in 1955, but four years later he was arrested for antisocial activities and condemned to seven years in prison. Carlaont was released from Jilava prison in 1960. He died in Bucharest ten years later, aged 81.

Rear Admiral Horia Macelariu commanded the Royal Romanian Navy's Black Sea fleet from early 1943 and distinguished himself in the evacuation of Axis (mostly German) troops from Crimea from 15 April to 14 May 1944. He was arrested by his country's communist authorities on 19 April 1948 and held in the Jilava prison. Macelariu was then convicted by a people's court and sentenced to life imprisonment with hard labour. His sentence was later reduced to twenty-five years with hard labour. In April 1958 he was transferred to Râmnisu Sărat prison in eastern Romania. Macelariu was released from Cherla prison on 29 July 1964. He died on 11 July 1989 in Bucharest, aged 95.

General Gheorghe Mihail never fought against Soviet forces. In January 1947 he was sentenced by a people's court to twelve years' imprisonment. He passed through the prisons of Văcăresti, Pitesti, Ocnele Mari, Sighet and Jilava. He was released in October 1960. Mihail died on 31 January 1982 in Bucharest, aged 94.

General Constantin D. Nicolescu was one of the participants in the 1944 coup that brought down Antonescu's regime. He was at the time the military commander of Bucharest. Nicolescu never fought against Soviet forces. In January 1948 he was removed from the army. Later in the year he was arrested by the communist authorities and tried by a people's court for plotting an uprising. He was sentenced to seven years' imprisonment. Nicolescu served his term at Jilava and Aiud prisons. His family was evicted from his home and were persecuted. He was released from prison in 1955. Nicolescu died on 6 July 1972, aged 84.

Colonel Gheorghe Arsenescu was wounded during the Axis campaign in Crimea. In 1946 he was involved in anti-communist activity. He remained in hiding until 1 February 1960, when he was arrested by Securitate, Romania's security forces. In February 1962 Arsenescu was convicted by a military tribunal and sentenced to death. He was executed on 29 May 1962 in Jilava prison, aged 54.

Major General Leonard Mociulschi was commanding the 1st Mountain Division in August 1944 when Romania changed sides in the war. He and his troops then joined the Soviet 337th Infantry Division in fighting in eastern Czechoslovakia against the retreating German forces. On 12 August 1948 he was arrested by his country's communist authorities in Codlea, central Romania, and sent without trial to penal colonies at the Danube-Black Sea Canal (Castelu), Onești and Târgu Ocna, in western Romania. In 1955 a military tribunal dropped the case against him and assigned him to forced domicile in Balș. He was rehabilitated in 1964 and died in Brașov in 1979, aged 90.

Horia Agarici was a Royal Romanian Air Force captain and a Second World War flying ace.[19] He shot down in combat ten enemy, mostly Soviet, aircraft, flying a British-made Hawker Hurricane Mk.I fighter. On 23 June 1941, when he was a senior lieutenant, Agarici achieved three kills in a single combat, gunning down Soviet Ilyushin DB-3 bombers near the port of Constanța in eastern Romania. In 1943 he was promoted to captain and assumed command of the 58th Fighter Squadron. In early April 1944, during a raid on Bucharest by US and British RAF aircraft, he made his last kill of an enemy (western Allied) plane. His fighter was then hit and Agarici had to make a forced landing. After the communist takeover, he was dismissed from the military and deported to Neatâmarea village in eastern Romania. In 1955 he was convicted of fabricated charges by a military court, which stripped him of his rank and sentenced him to twenty-five years' imprisonment with hard labour. Nine years later Agarici was released from Aiud prison. The same year his rank of air force captain was reinstated. Agarici died on 13 July 1982 in Constanța, aged 71.

Hungarians

The 209,000-strong Hungarian Second Army participated in the German campaign against the Soviet Union. By the end of the war 600,000 Romanians and Hungarians, including 400,000 officers and soldiers were detained in about 2,000 POW and labour camps, many of them (158) located in the Baltic States. Some 48,000 Hungarians died in Soviet captivity.[20] According to other estimations, 200,000 Hungarians, including interned civilians and detained POWs, perished in transit or captivity in the Soviet Union during and after the war.[21]

Colonel General (Vezérezredes) Béla Miklós de Dánlok was prime minister of Hungary until 17 October 1944, when he defected to the Russians. He then made a plea for the commanding officers of the First Army to defect with their units to the Red Army. With the exception of a regimental commander, no other officer responded to de Dánlok's plea. He died in Budapest on 21 November 1948, aged 58. Despite his collaboration with Moscow, he was buried without military honours.

Ferenc Szálasi, an extreme right politician and a former army major, became prime minister on 15 October 1944 when the Germans removed by force Admiral N. Horthy de

Nagybánya, who was serving as a regent to the Kingdom of Hungary. Szálasi's government was dissolved on 7 May 1945, a day before Nazi Germany's surrender in Berlin.

Colonel General Vitéz Lajos Csatay de Csataj was commanding the Third Army. On 15 October 1944 he was arrested by the Gestapo. A day later, 58-year-old de Csataj committed suicide, along with his wife.

Colonel General János Vörös had fought on the Eastern Front. On 19 March 1944, when the Germans occupied Hungary, he was chief of staff of the army. Vörös was a member of the delegation that signed the armistice convention in Moscow on 15 October 1944. In 1945 he retired from the army. Four years later, on his 58th birthday, Vörös was arrested by the post-war Hungarian authorities on a charge of spying. He was convicted and sentenced to life imprisonment by a military court. He was released from prison in 1968 and died on 23 July the same year in Balatonfüred, central-west Hungary, aged 77.

The Soviet influence over the Hungarian military began to increase rapidly in November 1948, when hundreds of military 'advisers' were assigned to the Hungarian army from the top all the way down to regimental level.[22] Colonel General Gusztáv Jány commanded the Second Army during the battle of Stalingrad. After the war, he was found guilty of war crimes by a Hungarian military tribunal and sentenced to death. Jany was executed by a firing squad on 26 November 1947 in Budapest, aged 64. He was posthumously exonerated by the Supreme Court of Hungary in 1993.[23]

Meanwhile, Szálasi was arrested by US troops at Mattsee, a market town in northwest Austria, and extradited to Hungary. He was convicted of war crimes and treason by the People's Tribunal in Budapest. During his relatively brief rule between 10,000 and 15,000 Hungarian Jews were murdered.[24] Szálasi was sentenced to death and hanged on 12 March 1946 in Budapest along with two of his ministers, Colonel General Károly Beregfy (defence) and Gábor Vajna (Interior). Beregfy, who had previously commanded the Third Army, was captured by US troops in Austria on 30 April 1945 and was extradited to Hungary.

Colonel General Döme Sztójay served as prime minister from 22 March until 29 August 1944. In April 1945 he fled to Germany. In October 1945, after his arrest by US troops, Sztójay was extradited to Hungary. He was convicted of treason and war crimes by the People's Tribunal in Budapest. He was sentenced to death and was executed by firing squad in Budapest on 22 August 1946, aged 63.

The Third Army, commanded by Colonel General Jozsef Heszlényi, was surrounded by the Soviet Forty-Sixth Army some 40km to the west of Budapest and was destroyed on 25 March 1945. The remnant of the Hungarian troops, including their commander, retreated towards southern Austria and on 8 May 1945 surrendered to US forces. Fifty-four-year-old Heszlényi was handed over to the Russians. On 2 June, while in Soviet custody, he committed suicide by cutting his wrists with a razor blade. On 19 June in Budapest a military tribunal posthumously demoted Heszlényi and had him dishonourably discharged from the Hungarian army.

Lieutenant General (Altábornagy) Vitéz Jenö Rátz de Nagylak was chief-of-staff of the Royal Hungarian Army in the late 1930s, when he also served as defence minister. On 22 March 1944 he was appointed deputy prime minster. After the war, de Nagylak was sentenced to death by the People's Tribunal in Budapest. His sentence was reduced to life imprisonment. De Nagylak died in his cell in Theresian prison, at Vác, 22 miles (35km) north of Budapest, on 21 January 1952. He was 69 years old.

Colonel General Jenő Major commanded the Second Army for thirteen days in November 1944. After the defeat of his forces during the battle of Debrecen, he fled to Germany. Major avoided extradition to Hungary after the war. He settled at Sonthofen, in Southern Bavaria. Major died there on 13 January 1972, aged 80.

Colonel General Károly Bartha de Dálnokfalva was defence minister until 24 September 1942. He played a role in the Hungarian participation in atrocities committed by Axis forces in the Vojvodina region, now part of Serbia, including the massacre of 50,000 civilians. After the war, he managed to leave the country and emigrate to Venezuela, where he worked as a railway construction engineer. De Dálnokfalva died on 22 November 1964 during a trip to Linz, Austria, aged 80.

Colonel General Vilmos Nagy de Nagybaczon was defence minister from 1942 until his resignation on 8 June 1943. He was in favour of a separate peace with the western Allies. On 16 November 1944 he was arrested by the Hungarian Gendarmerie (Csendörök) at his home in Pilicsaba, some 15 miles (24km) from Budapest. He eventually managed to escape. On 1 May 1945 Nagy was arrested by US troops at a farm in Bavaria. He was not extradited. In 1946 he returned to Hungary on his own decision. Three years later his property was confiscated by the state and he had to live in poverty. He died on 21 June 1976 in Pilicsaba, shortly after his 92nd birthday.

Colonel General Gusztáv Hennyey served as foreign minister for a month in 1944. In the mid-1930s he was chief of the military intelligence and later commanded the II Army corps. In late 1944, he was arrested by Hungarian ultra-rightists, held in the Theresian prison and then taken to Bavaria. After the war the pro-Moscow Hungarian authorities demanded his extradition, but he remained in US custody. After his release Hennyey settled in Munich. He died there on 14 June 1977, aged 88.

Lieutenant General Géza Lakatos de Czikszentsimon had served as prime minister from 29 August 1944 to 16 October 1944. He commanded the Second Army in 1943 and the First Army from 1 April 1944 until 15 May 1944. After the war, Lakatos was interned by the Hungarian authorities in Theresian prison until January 1945. His military pension was revoked and his property was confiscated by the state.

Lieutenant General Lajos Veress de Dálnok commanded the Second Army until 16 October 1944. He was then arrested by the Germans, who suspected him of favouring a separate agreement between Hungary and the western Allies. He was detained in Sopronkőhida prison, 5km south of the Austrian border, from where he managed to escape. After the war, he was sentenced to life imprisonment by the People's Tribunal in Budapest. During the 1956 uprising Lakatos and de Dálnok were released from prison and allowed to leave the country. Lakatos went to Australia to live with his daughter who had emigrated there. He died on 21 May 1967 in Adelaide, in South Australia, aged 77. De Dálnok left Hungary on 3 November 1956 and settled in Great Britain. He died on 29 March 1976 in London, aged 86.

Spaniards

División Azul (Blue Division) was a unit of volunteers from Francoist Spain within the German Army. They fought on the Eastern Front during the Second World War, identified (designated) by the Germans as 250th Infantry Division. In 1941 the strength of the division was 18,000 men. Through rotation as many as 47,000 Spaniards served on the Eastern Front.[25] Notably, the Spaniards participated in the siege of Leningrad but their force was withdrawn from the front after Spanish pressure in October 1943 and was returned to Spain soon afterwards. Some 3,000 non-returners were voluntarily incorporated into the German 121st Infantry Division as the short-lived Blue Legion, and eventually into the Waffen-SS. The casualties included 4,954 men killed and 8,700 wounded. Another 372 members of the Blue Division/Blue Legion were taken prisoner by the Red Army. According to Soviet records, the number of Spaniards who became POWs in USSR was 452.[26] Seventy died while in Soviet custody and 382 were released from POW camps and repatriated. Of these men, 286 remained in captivity until 2 April 1954, when they were allowed to leave USSR on an International Red Cross ship. Some 1,900 Spaniards are buried in a cemetery in Veliky Novgorod, between Moscow and St Petersburg.

Blue Division was commanded by General Agustín Muñoz Grandes until December 1942, when he was replaced by General Emilio Esteban Infantes. In 1962 General Grandes was appointed deputy prime minister of Spain by Francisco Franco.

An estimated 159 Portuguese volunteers fought for the Axis in the Second World War, mainly in the Spanish Blue Division. They were mostly veterans of the Spanish civil war, the so-called Viriatos, and were essentially adventurous mercenaries or fascist nationalists fighting the communist and Bolshevik threat.

Two Spaniards and a Gibraltarian were arrested on Gibraltar by the British authorities on sabotage charges. In August 1943 José Martín Muñoz, a Spaniard working on the Rock, was convicted over an explosion and fire at a large fuel tank on Coaling Island, off Gibraltar. In mid-1943 another Spaniard, Luis López Gordón-Cuenca, was convicted over his membership of a German military intelligence service (Abwehr) network. Both were sentenced to death and hanged the same day, 11 January 1944, in Gibraltar by British executioner Albert Pierrepoint.

In late 1942 a Gibraltarian, José Kay, was executed in HM Prison Wandsworth, near London. He had been arrested in March 1942 by the British authorities and convicted of gathering information on military movements for the Abwehr. According to British Intelligence, 183 Spaniards and Gibraltarians were involved in espionage and sabotage operations against the fortress of Gibraltar during the Second World War.[27]

Conscripted

Austrian, Czech and Slovakian nationals had to serve in Nazi Germany's army before and during the war, after their countries became by force part of the Third Reich. In Czechoslovakia, in particular, significant changes were carried out in the military in 1948, when the country's communist party seized power. More than half of the officers began to experience persecution and many were forced to leave. The political process focused mainly on personnel who fought in Eastern Europe against the Red Army. Paradoxically, there was also persecution of officers and non-commissioned officers who had fought the war on the western Front. The armed forces in post-war Czechoslovakia came fully under the power of the Communist Party and in 1950 there was a major reorganisation on the Soviet model.

PRO-AXIS PUPPET GOVERNMENTS

Yugoslavia and Albania became, one way or another, protectorates of Axis forces in the Balkans during the Second World War. Josip Broz Tito's 800,000-strong communist partisans were able to expel the Axis from Serbia in 1944 and from the rest of Yugoslavia by mid-1945. The Soviet Red Army provided limited assistance with the liberation of Belgrade, the Yugoslav capital, and withdrew, after the war was over, leaving Tito in control of the country and determined to lead an independent communist state in unified Yugoslavia.

By 14 May 1945 the British V Corps accepted, in southern Austria, the surrender of tens of thousands of retreating Croatian Ustaše and Slovene Home Guard members who had been fighting under German command during the Second World War.[1] They were fleeing the Soviet forces and Tito's partisans.[2] The surrendered, including elements of the German 7th SS Division *Prinz Eugen*, were detained at the Viktring POW camp, near Krumpendorf, in the Austrian state of Carinthia.

Croatians

The Independent State of Croatia or Nezavisna Država Hrvatska or ISC was a puppet state established by Germany and Italy on 10 April 1941. It extended over parts of present-day Croatia, Slovenia, Serbia, and Bosnia-Herzegovina, and was governed, as a one-party state, by the fascist Ustaše or Ustaša, a political organisation. The Ustaše was found in 1929 by Ante Pavelić, who headed the ISC from 1941 until 1945.

Croatia, as a newly independent state, could not send its own forces, but provided three 'legions of volunteers'.[3] The first legion was formed with three four-company infantry battalions, an anti-tank company and a heavy weapons company. One battalion was raised entirely from Muslims in Bosnia-Herzegovina. A naval legion and an air force legion were also raised. The first legion was designated 369th Croatian Reinforced Infantry Regiment. They were attached to the German 100th Jäger Division, then deployed on the southern sector of the Eastern Front.

The Croatian legion was annihilated in Stalingrad. Very few of the Croat volunteers were evacuated, the remainder being killed or captured. By mid-1944 three Croatian divisions had been raised and they were commanded by the Germans to fight Tito's communist partisans in Yugoslavia.[4] On 14 May 1945, at the Carinthian border town of Bleiburg, the British Army refused the surrender of a fleeing column numbering 25,000 to 30,000 Ustaše troops, among them several civilian refugees. They were directed the following day to Tito's partisans, on the other side of the border. By 24 May all

Croatian and Slovenia prisoners held by the British in the Viktring POW camp were also extradited to Yugoslavia. Tens of thousands of the forcibly repatriated POWs were executed by Tito's partisans and the remnant were taken to forced labour camps in Yugoslavia or in the Soviet Union.

In November 1945 Josef Stalin mentioned in a conversation with Polish communist leader Władysław Gomułka that the Yugoslav partisans had shot 24,000 of some 34,000 Croatian captives.[5] According to the estimate of Joso Tomasevich, a Croatian-American historian, the Croatian victims in the particular massacres numbered 70,000.[6] According to an estimate by the British Army, a total of 26,339 people were extradited to Yugoslavia from Bleiburg and Viktring POW camps, including 12,196 Croats, 8,263 Slovenes, 5,480 Serbs and 400 Montenegrins.[7] The exact number of deaths in the forced marches within Yugoslavia and during the detention of the extradited POWs in various camps ranges between 50,000 to 200,000.[8] Yugoslav communist guerrillas have also been blamed for the massacre of Croatian captives and civilians in a mine near Pečovnik, in present-day Slovenia, and in Tezno, near Maribor, in present-day Slovenia. Up to 12,000 people, including pro-German Slovene Home Guards, Croat POWs, Serbian and Montenegrin collaborationists, and a small number of German and Italian POWs, were executed in March 1945 at Kosevški Rog, in south-eastern Slovenia, also by Tito's communist forces.

Jewish-born Andrija Bethlehem was the first casualty among the ISC leaders. A prominent member of the Croatian Assembly and a deputy prime minister, he was captured by communist partisans near Rasinja, a municipality in northern Croatia, in November 1943. Bethlehem was summarily executed, aged 63 or 64.

Ante Pavelić, a fascist and ultra-nationalist politician, was the leader of the ISC from day one (10 April 1941). He was prime minister (1941–43) and defence minister (January–September 1943). His policies resulted in the death of 100,000 Serbs, Roma and Jews[9] in concentration camps that were established and run in his puppet state.[10] In 1943 Pavelić appointed Nikola Mandič as prime minister. In May 1944, he ordered the arrest of his foreign minister Mladen Lorković. He was charged with making secret contact with British and US officials and was sentenced to death. Lorković was executed by firing squad in Lepoglava prison, northern Croatia, in late April 1945, aged 36.

In May 1945, following the surrender of Nazi Germany, Pavelić ordered his forces initially to keep fighting and later to surrender to British forces in Austria. He fled through Austria to Argentina, where he became an advisor to President Juan Perón. In mid-1956 he settled in Francoist Spain. In December 1949 Pavelić was wounded during an assassination attempt by a Serb immigrant, who shot him with a pistol. He died of his wounds on 28 December, aged 70.

Bosnian-born Nikola Mandić became ISC's prime minister in September 1943. On 1 March 1944 he met Hitler in Salzburg.[11] On 15 May 1945 he surrendered to British forces in Austria. Three days later he was extradited to Yugoslavia. On 6 June Mandić was convicted of treason and war crimes by a military tribunal in Zagreb and sentenced to death. He was executed by hanging in Zagreb one day later, aged 76.

On 7 June Mile Budak was hanged in Zagreb after his conviction as war criminal by a military court. He was the chief ideologist of the Croatian fascists and the ISC's chief propagandist. Budak also served as education minister in 1941 and foreign minister in

1943. On 18 May 1945 he was arrested in Austria by British troops and handed over to Tito's partisans. Budak was executed, aged 55.

Field Marshal (Vojskovoda) Slavko Kvaternik was defence minister until January 1943, when he retired from the military. His Jewish wife Olga Frank had committed suicide in late 1941 reportedly because of the anti-Semitic policies of the Ustaše regime in Croatia, for which her husband was also responsible. In May 1945 Kvaternik was captured by US troops in Austria.

Bosnian-born Miroslav (Friedrich) Navratil had retired from the air force as a colonel in 1940. He was brought back into active service with the establishment of the ISC. Navratil rose to the rank of lieutenant general and served as minister of the armed forces from September 1943 to late January 1944. He then moved to Vienna with his family. After the war, he was arrested by US troops in Zell am See, in the Austrian state of Salzburg.

Kvaternik and Navratil were both extradited to Yugoslavia, where they were convicted of war crimes and sentenced to death. They were executed by hanging in Zagreb on 7 June 1947. Kvaternik was 68 and Navratil 53 years old.

Bosnian-born Andrija Aktuković, as interior minister (1941–42) ordered the establishment of detention camps for Serbs, Jews and Roma and as justice minister (1942–43) signed the racial laws that characterised the Ustaše regime. After the war, he escaped to the United States, where he stayed until 1986. Then his extradition to Yugoslavia was ordered by a US court.[12] Aktuković was tried in Zagreb as a war criminal and sentenced to death. The sentence was not carried out due to his age and poor health. Aktuković died of natural causes in a prison hospital in Zagreb on 16 January 1988, aged 88.

Bosnian-born Adem-aga Mešić, a First World War military officer, served as deputy prime minister. He headed a narrow circle of Germanophile Yugoslav Muslims supporting the Ustaše movement. After the war, Mešić escaped to Austria, where he was arrested by British troops and extradited to Yugoslavia. Mešić was tried in Zagreb and convicted of treason and war crimes. He was sentenced to life imprisonment. Mešić died in prison in Zagreb on 1 July 1945, aged 77.

The Croatian Air Force Legion's Colonel Franjo Džal was captured by communist partisans in northern Croatia while trying to surrender to Allied forces. He was summarily executed.

Slovenians

Leon Rupnic, a Slovenian army general, served as chief inspector of the Slovenian Home Guard (H.G.), a collaborationist militia force, from September 1944 to May 1945. On 5 May 1945 he fled to Austria, where he was arrested by British troops on 23 July. Six months later Rupnik was extradited to Yugoslavia. He was convicted of treason by a military court and sentenced to death. Rupnik was executed by firing squad in Ljubljana on 30 September 1946, aged 66. His son, Major Vuk Rupnik, led units of the H.G. during Yugoslavia's Axis occupation. Before the communist takeover, he crossed the border with Austria at the head of a Slovene militia battalion. He later moved to Argentina and settled in Castelar, near Buenos Aires. Rupnik died there on 14 August 1975, aged 63.

Franc Frakelj was involved in the murder of sixty Serbs and Roma in the winter of 1943–44. The massacre was carried out south of Ljubljana by a murderous militia detachment under his command called Black Hand (Črna Roka). Frakelj evaded capture by Tito's forces and escaped abroad. It is believed that he emigrated to Canada, where he disappeared without a trace.

Among Slovenia's notable collaborationists during the Axis occupation of Yugoslavia were three Roman Catholic bishops. Aloysius Stepinac, archbishop of Zagreb, was arrested on 18 September 1946 by Tito's communist authorities and charged with high treason and collaboration with the enemy. Convicted by a court in Zagreb, Stepinac was sentenced to sixteen years' imprisonment. He served five years in Lepoglava prison, in northern Croatia, until December 1951. Then, he was transferred to a house in Kračić, near Zagreb, to serve the rest of his sentence under guard. Stepinac died of thrombosis on 10 February 1960, aged 61.

Gregorij Rožman, archbishop of Ljubljana, and Ivan Šarić, archbishop of Vrhbosna (Bosnia and Macedonia) with see in Sarajevo, evaded capture following the communist takeover in Yugoslavia. Both fled to Austria in October 1946 and stayed in Klagenfurt, Carinthia, the southernmost Austrian state. Šarić later moved to Madrid, where he died on 6 July 1960, aged 88. Rožman moved to Switzerland and from there emigrated to the United States. He died on 16 December 1959 in Cleveland, Ohio, aged 76.

Serbian anti-communists

Dragolijub 'Draža' Mihailović, a Serb army general, was captured by Tito's partisans on 13 March 1946.[13] He was the leader of the Chetniks, a Serbian royalist/nationalist movement and guerrilla force that was established in Axis-occupied parts of Yugoslavia. The Chetniks engaged in tactical or selective collaboration with Axis forces,[14] including the puppet Government of National Salvation in Belgrade. They also used terror tactics against Croats, Muslims and communists in many parts of Serbia and Bosnia-Herzegovina. Mihailović was tried in Belgrade by a military tribunal and found guilty of treason and war crimes. He was sentenced to death and executed by firing squad on 17 July 1946, aged 53.

Three of the Chetnik area commanders were also captured by Tito's forces at the end of the war. They were Lieutenant Colonel Dragutin Kaserović and Majors Vojislav Lukašević and Jesdimir Dangić. Kaserović and Lukašević were convicted of war crimes and sentenced to death by firing squad.[15] Lukašević was executed on 14 August, aged 36 or 37, and Kaserović, three days later, aged 48.

Dangić was sent to Stryi POW camp, in south-eastern Poland, in early 1944 after his arrest by German troops in Serbia. In August 1944 he escaped and joined the Polish resistance. In early 1945 Dangić surrendered to Soviet forces, who extradited him to Tito's communist authorities in Yugoslavia. He was convicted as a war criminal by a military tribunal in Sarajevo and sentenced to death. Dangić was executed by firing squad on 28 August 1947, aged 50.

Three Chetnik area commanders were captured by Ustaše forces.[16] They were Zaharije Ostojić, Petar Baćović and Pavle Đurić, who were summarily executed on 20 April 1945 in Jasenovac concentration camp, at the confluence of the Sava and Una rivers in Croatia.

Two Chetnik area commanders, Dobroslav Jevdević and Momčilo Dujič, managed to evade capture and escape to Italy. Jevdević was detained by the Allies briefly in Grottaglie POW camp, near Taranto. He died in Rome in October 1962, aged 66.

Dujić surrendered to Allied forces in southern Italy. He was held in POW camps initially in Italy and later in Germany. In 1947 Dujić was convicted of war crimes in absentia by a military court in Belgrade. Between 1947 and 1949 he lived in Paris. He then emigrated to the United States. Dujić died on 11 September 1999 in San Diego, California, aged 92.

Major Zvonimir Vušković was one of the closest associates of Mihailović. He avoided capture, after the communist takeover in Yugoslavia, by fleeing to Bari, Italy. Vučkovič later moved to Paris, and from there to the United States. He died in California on 21 December 2004, aged 88.

Colonel Velimir Piletić commanded the Chetnik forces in eastern Serbia. Marko Mesić, a Croatian general, had been captured by the Red Army after the Battle of Stalingrad. He was later sent to Yugoslavia by the Soviets to command Yugoslav communist troops. In September 1944, near Kladovo, in eastern Serbia, communist forces led by Mesić captured Piletić and had his men killed. During his transfer by train to Belgrade to be tried for war crimes, the Chetnik prisoner managed to escape and flee to Austria. Piletić lived in Paris until his death on 3 July 1972, aged 66.

Albanians

From April 1939, when Italian troops occupied the country, Albania was a protectorate and dependency of Italy. The Germans started to occupy the country in September 1943, when Balli Kombëtar, Albania's National Front, formed a puppet government in the capital, Tirana. Balli Kombëtar was a nationalist anti-communist movement, which collaborated with the Germans. Ekrem Libohova and Rexhep Mitrovica served as prime ministers in Albania during the Italian and German occupation respectively. Italophile Libohova left Albania in September 1943 prior to the country's occupation by the German Army. He went to Rome, where he lived until his death on 7 June 1948, aged 66. Mitrovica was prime minister until June 1944. He escaped to Croatia prior to the communist takeover, and from there to Turkey. Mitrovica died on 21 May 1967 in Istanbul, aged 79.

Major General Prenk Pervizi, who became minister of defence on 23 October 1943, opposed the recruitment of Albanian volunteers by German Waffen-SS units. However, on a number of occasions nationalist partisans, all members of Balli Kombëtar, fought alongside German troops against Albanian communist partisans. Atrocities, including burning villages and executing civilians, were also committed against Albania's Serb and Greek minorities.[17] Albania was liberated by the communist-dominated National Liberation Army (NLA) by 30 November 1944, being the only country in Europe to have done so without assistance by Allied forces.

Austrian-educated Spiro Moisiu, who commanded the NLA, was dismissed from the Albanian military in 1946 by Enver Hoxha's regime for favouring the Soviet model of government in Albania. Moisiu died on 12 April 1981 in Tirana, aged 80. His son Alfred became President of Albania in 2002.

PRO-AXIS PUPPET GOVERNMENTS

Meanwhile, in August 1944, Pervizi left Tirana and took refuge in the mountains in southern Albania until 1946, when he escaped to Greece. In 1965 Pervizi moved to Italy and a year later to Belgium. He died on 6 September 1977 in Jolimont, aged 80. His mother, his wife and his three children died while in prison and labour camps of Hoxsa's regime.

Safet Butka, a high school teacher, was a co-founder of Balli Kombëtar along with Mid'hat Frashëri and Ali Bey Këlcyra. He organised partisan groups that liaised with the British SOE (Special Operations Executive). In April 1944 Captain (later Colonel) David Smiley parachuted into Albania on a special assignment with nationalist partisans.[18] Although a staunch nationalist, Butka tried to cooperate with Albania's communist-dominated Liberation Front. On 19 September 1943, upon hearing the first clashes between communist and nationalist partisan, Butka killed himself at Melçan, in Kolonje, in south-eastern Albania, aged 42. Frashëri and Këlcyra fled to Italy on 18 October 1944, after seeing the overwhelming advance of the communist guerrilla forces. Frashëri later emigrated to the United States. He died of a heart attack in a New York hotel on 3 October 1949, aged 69.

Këlcyra was arrested by the British when he arrived in Italy and was detained for about two years. He stayed on in Italy after his release. Këlcyra died in Bari on 24 September 1963, aged 72.

Muharrem Bajraktari, Vasil Andoni and Hasan Dosti also evaded capture. On 23 October 1944, with the communists on the brink of victory in Albania, they escaped to southern Italy. Bajraktari later moved to Brussels in Belgium. He died on 21 January 1982, aged 92. Andoni, a high school teacher, was an anti-communist. He had also opposed collaboration with the Germans. Andoni died on 7 October 1994 in Rome, aged 92. Dosti emigrated to the United States after five years in Italy. He died on 29 January 1991 in Los Angeles, aged 96. Seven of his children back home spent several years in Enver Hoxha's prisons and labour camps. Victor Dosti was 19 years old when he was imprisoned and 65 when he was released in 1990, with the collapse of Albania's communist regime.

Several Axis collaborators, including an Austrian general, were captured in Albania by the communists and tried by the Special Court for War Criminals and Enemies of the People that was held in Tirana between 1 March and 13 April 1945.[19] They were convicted of treason and collaboration and given death or long prison sentences. General Akif Përmeti, who was minister of defence during the Italian occupation, was sentenced to death. He was executed by firing squad on 14 April 1945 in Tirana, aged 60. Bahri Omari, Fejzi Alizoti and Kol Tromara, cabinet ministers in various collaboration governments, were sentenced to death and executed near Tirana on 14 April 1945. Omari, a former foreign minister and Hoxha's brother-in-law, was 56; Alizoti, a former finance minister, was 70; and Tromara, who had returned from the United States in 1939 and served as culture minister, was 62 or 63 years old, when they had to stand in front of a firing squad. Alizoti's son, Riza, was later convicted as a spy and saboteur in the service of foreign forces.[20] He was sentenced to death and executed by hanging in Tirana on 10 October 1947, aged 32.

Italo-Albanian Terenzio Tocci, who served as speaker of the parliament during the Italian occupation, was sentenced to death. He was executed in Tirana on 14 April 1945, aged 65. Turkish-educated Kemal Vrioni, a former finance minister, was sentenced to death, but his sentence was commuted to ten years' imprisonment. Vrioni died in Burrel prison in 1952, aged 66 or 67. Costaq (Koço) Kotta and Ibrahim Biçakçiu, two collaborationist prime ministers, were sentenced to life imprisonment. Kotta died in Burrel prison, in north-eastern Albania, on 1 September 1947, aged 61. Biçakçiu was released from prison in 1962. He died on 4 January 1977 in Elbasan, central Albania, aged 71.

Ismet Kryeziu and Sokrat Dodbiba, both ministers in collaborationist governments, were sentenced to thirty years in prison with hard labour. Kryeziu died in Burrel prison in 1952, aged 63. Turkish-educated Dodbiba died in the same prison on 20 October 1956, aged 58.

Austrian-educated Mihal Zallari, who had served as speaker of the parliament during the Axis occupation, was also sentenced to thirty years in prison with hard labour. He was released in 1962. Zallari died in Albania on 17 March 1976, aged 81.

Tefik Mborja was the general secretary of the Albanian Fascist Party that was founded within a month of the Italian invasion in 1939. He was sentenced to twenty years in prison during the trial of collaborators. Mborja was reportedly poisoned while in Burrel prison and died on 1 July 1954, aged 62.

Greek-educated Gjergj Bubani, the Radio Tirana director during the Axis occupation, was sentenced to fifteen years' imprisonment with hard labour. He was released five years later. Bubani died on 28 February 1954 in Tirana, aged 55.

One of the defendants in the trial of collaborators by the special court in Tirana was Austrian General Gustav von Myrdacz. He had joined the newly formed Royal Albanian Army (RAA) in 1920, after his retirement from the Austrian Army. Nine years later, he rose to the post of chief-of-staff of the RAA. When Italy occupied Albania, von Myrdacz lost his position, but did not leave. He stayed on even after the communist takeover. In October 1944 he was arrested by the communists and imprisoned. During the trial of Albanian collaborators, von Myrdacz was convicted as a fascist and enemy of the Albanian people. He was sentenced to death and executed on 11 July 1945 near Tirana, aged 70.

Greeks

Greeks, like Albanians, did not volunteer to join German Wehrmacht or Waffen-SS units during their country's occupation by Axis forces as occurred elsewhere in Western and Eastern Europe. Greece's collaborationist government only provided a number of security battalions that aided the Germans in the fighting against communist (mostly) resistance organisations. These battalions were involved in numerous atrocities, mostly against civilians both in urban centres and in the countryside.

Their commander and the defence minister of the collaborationist government, Greek Army Major General Georgios Bakos, an ardent Germanophile, was arrested after the country's liberation and imprisoned.[21] He had tried unsuccessfully to raise a Greek volunteer unit to fight along the Wehrmacht on the Eastern Front. While waiting to be tried for collaboration and war crimes, Bakos was abducted by communist guerrillas in mid-December 1944, when they briefly seized the Averoff prison in Athens. He was summarily executed by his captors on 6 January 1945, aged

PRO-AXIS PUPPET GOVERNMENTS

52, a few days before the failure of the communists to seize power in Greece's capital by force of arms.

The collaborationist governments of Greece were led by Lieutenant General Georgios Tsolakoglou, Konstantinos I. Logothetopoulos and Ioannis Rallis, who presided over what was in effect a puppet regime. Tsolakoglou had signed the unconditional surrender of the Greek forces in Albania in April 1941. He was appointed prime minister of a puppet government in Athens by the Germans on 30 April 1941. On 2 December 1942 he was replaced by Logothetopoulos, a German-educated gynaecologist and a university professor. Logothetopoulos was married to the niece of German Field Marshal Wilhelm List,[22] who commanded the Twelfth Army in the invasions of France, Yugoslavia and Greece.

On 7 April 1943 the German- and French-educated Rallis became the third and last collaborationist prime minister during the Axis occupation of Greece. During Rallis's tenure, hundreds of Greek Jews were arrested in several parts of the country and transferred to concentration and death camps in Germany and German-occupied Poland. After the country's liberation, Tsolakoglou was arrested, tried for collaboration with the enemy and sentenced to death. His sentence was ultimately commuted to life imprisonment. Tsolakoglou died of leukaemia in prison on 22 May 1948, aged 62.

When the Germans left Greece in October 1943, Logothetopoulos went with them to Nazi Germany. After the German capitulation, he was arrested by US troops in Vilshofen an der Donau, a small town in Bavaria, where he was practising medicine.[23] Logothetopoulos was extradited to Greece, where he was convicted of collaboration and sentenced to life imprisonment. He was released from prison in 1951. Logothetopoulos died on 6 July 1961 in Athens, aged 82. Rallis was also convicted of collaboration after the country's liberation and sentenced to life imprisonment. He died on 26 October 1946 in his cell in the Averoff prison, aged 67 or 68. Thirty-four years later his son, Georgios Rallis, a centre-right politician, became Greece's prime minister.

Xenophon Giosmas led a collaborationist paramilitary formation that was active in and around Thessaloniki in northern Greece during the country's occupation by German, Italian and Bulgarian forces. In 1945 he was convicted of collaboration and war crimes and sentenced to death. Seven years later Giosmas was pardoned and released from prison. He died on 14 January 1969, aged 69.

Sotirios Gotzamanis served as minister of finance from 1941 to 1943. He left Greece with Italian troops in October 1941. From Italy he later moved to Nazi Germany. In 1945 Gotzamanis was sentenced to death in absentia for collaboration by a tribunal in Athens. He returned to Greece nine years later after being pardoned. Gotzamanis died of a stroke in Thessaloniki on 28 November 1958, aged 73.

Major General Charalambos Katsimitros, who had distinguished himself previously as a military commander during the Italo-Greek war, served in collaborationist governments as minister of labour and as minister of agriculture. In 1945 he was sentenced to five years in prison for collaborationism. Four years later Katsimitros received a royal pardon. He was released from prison and promoted to lieutenant general. He died in 1962 in Athens, aged 75 or 76.

Lieutenant General Panagiotis Demestichas was court-martialled in 1946 for serving as interior minister in the first collaborationist government. He was dismissed from the army. Demestichas died on 14 November 1960, aged 75.

Nikolaos Bourantas commanded a 700-strong motorised police unit that carried out operations against communist guerrillas and sympathisers in the greater area of Athens during the Axis occupation. He was accused of collaboration and war crimes in November 1945 but was acquitted. Bourantas was later appointed chief of Greece's police force. He died 16 January 1981 in Athens, aged 81.

Konstantinos Kollias served as an attorney general from 1941 to 1944. He was tried for collaboration after the country's liberation but was acquitted. Kollias served as prime minister from April to December 1967 during the country's rule by a military junta. He died on 13 July 1998 in Athens, aged 96 or 97.

VOLUNTEERS AND COLLABORATORS I

Tens of thousands of foreign volunteers in Europe and Asia joined the fight alongside the Germans, mostly, and the Japanese also, forces during the Second World War. Anti-communism was the cardinal reason behind the decision of these men to betray their countries by so doing and at the same time to put their lives into danger. There were legions of volunteers from western European states, including German-occupied France and Belgium, in the Wehrmacht. Eventually the Waffen SS would absorb personnel from other countries in western Europe, including the Netherlands, Norway and Denmark.

French

On 7 May 1945 thirteen Frenchmen serving in a Wehrmacht unit were captured by US forces near the German town of Bad Reichenhall, a spa town in northern Bavaria. One of them was identified as Waffen-SS Untersturmführer (Second Lieutenant) Serge Hermann Louis Krotoff.[1] One day later they were brought in front of French General Philippe Leclerc de Hauteclocque, commander of the Free French 2nd Armoured Division, who accused them of treason for wearing German uniforms. Infuriated with a comment about his US Army uniform made by one of the prisoners, probably Krotoff, Leclerc ordered the execution of the prisoners. Twelve of them were shot hours later without trial. One was spared for belonging to a Wehrmacht and not to a Waffen-SS unit like the rest. The bodies of the executed were left unburied for three days at Leclerc's orders.

The Légion des Volontaires Française, or LVF, fought on the Eastern Front as a component of the German Army, listed as the 638th Reinforced Infantry Regiment. Composed of two battalions, the LVF initially fielded 181 officers and 2,271 other ranks, all French volunteers.[2] They were initially commanded by Roger Henri Labonne, a former French army officer who was given the rank of oberst (colonel) by the Germans. Labonne was arrested by Allied troops in Germany after the war and handed over to the French authorities. He was tried and condemned for collaborationism. On 25 November 1946 Labonne was sentenced to life imprisonment, but was discharged earlier. He died in 1960, aged 79.

The most prominent French fascist leader, Jacques Doriot, a politician and former communist, co-founded the LVF in 1941 along with Marcel Déat. Doriot joined the LVF as an NCO (sergeant major) and rose to the rank of oberleutnant (senior lieutenant). He espoused pro-German and anti-communist propaganda on Radio Paris. Doriot was killed on 22 February 1945 near Mengen, in Württemberg, Germany, aged 46, when his car was strafed by Allied aircraft.

Almost half of the LVF men were killed in combat on the Eastern Front or because of wounds inflicted during battle. French volunteers also served in a Grenadier regiment that was raised by the German Army in 1943. In March 1942 Colonel Edgar Puaud replaced Debonne in the command of the LVF. On 17 March 1945 Puaud was wounded near Neustrelitz, in north-eastern Germany, during combat against the advancing Red Army. He was left behind with other wounded soldiers by his retreating troops[3] and his fate is not known.

Monsignor Mayol de Lupé, a Roman Catholic priest, was wounded and captured by the Germans during the First World War, when he served as chaplain of the French 1st Cavalry Division. He was detained in a POW camp for two years. In late 1941, after Hitler's invasion of the Soviet Union, his fanatical anti-communism led him to openly collaborate with the Germans. Initially de Lupé joined the LVF and later became chaplain of the German 638th Infantry Regiment, also known as 33rd Waffen-SS Division *Charlemagne* that was made up of French volunteers. De Lupé was featured on the front page of *Signal*, Nazi Germany's propaganda magazine.[4] He was arrested by Allied troops inside a convent near Munich in April 1945 and was later handed over to the French authorities. De Lupé was convicted of treason and sentenced to fifteen years' imprisonment. He remained in jail, although severely ill, for four years. He was released in 1951. De Lupé died in his home near Versailles, outside Paris, on 28 June 1955, aged 82.

The Phalange Africain (initially listed as *Légion Impériale*) was raised in North Africa by the Germans in November 1942. Some 450 French volunteers who wanted to serve alongside German and Italian forces joined the unit that saw some combat at the Tunisian front as a component of the German 334th Infantry Division. The Phalange Africain was dissolved in early May 1943 with the surrender of the Axis forces in North Africa to the Allies.

The commander was Colonel Simor P. Cristofini, who was a supporter of the Union of Corsica with Italy. He was captured in Corsica by Allied troops and handed over to Free French authorities. Cristofini was tried in November 1943 in Algiers by a French court for high treason and collaboration with the enemy. After being sentenced to death he tried to kill himself. Cristofini was executed by firing squad while suffering from his wounds, aged 52. His wife (Marta Renucci) was sentenced to fifteen years in prison for collaborating with Italian fascism.

Rear Admiral Charles Platon and Jean-Marie Perrot were executed for collaboration by French communist partisans. Platon was in charge of the colonial ministry of the Vichy puppet government. He was arrested at home on 22 July 1944 and executed after a summary trial six days later in Valojulx, south-west France, aged 54. Platon's last wish, which was approved by his captors, was to give the firing squad the order to shoot. Earlier, on 12 December 1943, Perrot was assassinated, also by French communist partisans, in Scrignac, north-west France, aged 66. He was a Roman Catholic priest and a Breton nationalist.

General Charles Marion and Jeanne Coroller-Danio were assassinated by non-communist partisans. Marion served as a prefect for the collaborationist government of Vichy. He was also a horse rider and participated in the 1928 (Amsterdam) and

VOLUNTEERS AND COLLABORATORS I

1932 (Los Angeles) Summer Olympics in the team dressage event. In 1944 Marion was tried and sentenced to death by a proper court, but while waiting execution he was kidnapped and murdered by partisans on 16 November in Annecy, south-eastern France, aged 57.

Jeanne Coroller-Danio, a Breton nationalist, had allegedly been involved in anti-resistance activity. On 13 July 1944 she was kidnapped by partisans in Penguily, north-west France. Coroller-Danio was eventually stabbed and beaten to death. She was 52 years old.

Pierre Pucheu, a fascist and former interior minister of the Vichy government, was arrested and tried in Algiers by a Free French court. On 20 March 1944 he was sentenced to death for collaboration and executed by firing squad in Algiers, aged 44.[5] Pucheu was allowed to give the firing squad the order to fire himself.

In January 1944 Milice Française, a paramilitary organisation, was raised by the Vichy regime to help fight French resistance groups. Milice Française was led by Joseph Darmand, a decorated soldier in the First World War and in the early Second World War.[6] In September 1944 he fled to Germany, where he was arrested by British troops. Darmand was handed over to the French authorities, who charged him with treason. He was sentenced to death on 3 October 1945. Seven days later he was executed by firing squad in Fort de Châtillon, south of Paris, aged 48.

Earlier, on 28 June 1944, two months before the liberation of Paris, Philippe Henriot was assassinated by partisans in Paris, aged 55. As a cabinet member in a Vichy government, he directed propaganda broadcasts.

After the liberation, France was swept for some time by a wave of official trials (epuration legal) of collaborationists. Executions without trial and other forms of so-called people's justice resulted the death of at least 10,000 people.

Tens of French collaborators, including cabinet members and officials of the Vichy regime, were eventually arrested by France's post-war authorities and tried for treason. Marshal Philippe Petain headed France's collaborationist regime from 11 July 1940 until 20 August 1944. French Vichy is often described as a German puppet government, although it has also been argued that it had an agenda of its own. In late April 1945 Pétain surrendered to the French authorities on the Swiss–French border after an eight-month stay in Germany. He was tried by the High Court and found guilty of collaboration with the enemy and other crimes, including the obligatory transportation of French labourers to Nazi Germany and the deportation of French Jews to concentration camps in Germany and German-occupied Poland. At least 72,000 French Jews were killed in Nazi concentration camps. On 15 August 1945 Pétain was sentenced to death. He was also stripped of all military ranks and honours, including the distinction of Marshal of France. The sentence was later commuted due to Petain's age to life imprisonment. He remained in prison until 8 June 1951, when the sentence was commuted to confinement in hospital due to health issues.[7] Pétain, who had commanded France's troops during the First World War,[8] died in a private home on Ile de Yeu, a small island off the French Atlantic coast, on 23 July 1951, aged 95.

Pierre Laval was the head of government and foreign minister of the Vichy regime. He provided French labourers to Germany and organised the deportation of French Jews.[9] After the liberation of France he was imprisoned by the Germans until April

1945. Then he fled to Francoist Spain. When he returned to France, Laval was arrested and charged with treason, collaboration with the enemy and crimes against humanity. In October 1945 he was sentenced to death. He attempted to commit suicide by taking poison before the sentence could be carried out. However, poison was so old that it proved ineffective. Laval was executed by firing squad on 15 October in Fresnes Prison, 7 miles (11km) south of Paris, aged 62.

Georges Suarez, a biographer of Marshal Pétain, supervised the French newspapers that were controlled by the Germans. He was convicted of collaboration by a French court and executed by firing squad on 9 November 1944 in Fort de Montrouge, at Arcueil, 3.3 miles (5.3km) south of Paris, aged 54.

Jean-Pierre Mourer, an Alsatian autonomist, had his name Germanised to Hans Peter Murer. In August 1945 he was arrested in Munich by the Allies and handed over to the French authorities. Mourer was tried for collaboration with the enemy and sentenced to death. He was executed by firing squad on 10 June 1947 at île Napoléon in Alsace, close to the German border, aged 50.

Henri Devillers and Pierre Paoli were arrested as spies. Devillers was detected spying for Nazi counter-espionage (Abwehr III). He was summarily tried and executed by the partisans on 19 June 1942 in Lyon, aged 28. Paoli spied for the Gestapo and caused the arrest of 300 people. He was also involved in torturing prisoners. Paoli obtained the rank of scharführer (SS squad leader) and was given German citizenship. On 16 May 1945 he was arrested by British troops at Flensburg, northern Germany, and handed over to the French authorities. He was tried for high treason and war crimes and sentenced to death. Paoli was executed on 15 June in Bourges, central France, aged 24.

Belgians

A few thousand Belgians volunteered to fight alongside the German forces, during the Second World War. The French-speaking volunteers joined the 2,000-strong Wallon Legion (Légion Wallonie) with roughly a thousand Dutch-speaking Belgians becoming members of the Flemish Legion (Vlaams Legionen). Both units were raised by the Wehrmacht in July 1941, a few weeks after the German invasion of the Soviet Union, and were involved in military operations on the Eastern Front. They struggled to find sufficient recruits in Belgium to replace their persistently heavy losses, estimated at 1,337 killed.[10]

The Walloon Legion's most notable commander was Belgian national Léon Degrelle. He rose to the rank of SS-colonel (SS-standartenführer) as his unit was later integrated into a Waffen-SS formation. In October 1943 some 200 Belgian volunteers who refused to swear allegations to Hitler were transferred to penal units of the German Strafbataillon. Men of this unit were assigned mine-clearing duties and suicidal missions.

The SS-Assault Brigade Wallonia (Sturmbrigade Wallonien), as it was listed in June 1943, was almost decimated by Soviet forces near Korsun, present-day Cherkasy, central Ukraine, in mid-February 1944. The surviving members of the Belgian collaborationist unit managed to surrender to the British Army at Lübeck, northern Germany, and escaped capture by the Red Army. Meanwhile, Degrelle managed to flee to German-occupied Norway and from there flew to Francoist Spain. Having been sentenced to death in absentia back home in late 1944 and formally stripped of his citizenship, Degrelle remained in exile until his death. He died of cardiac arrest in a hospital in Málaga on 31 March 1994, aged 87.[11]

The Flemish Legion, constantly commanded by German officers, was later integrated into a Waffen-SS unit, listed as SS Volunteer Legion Flanders (SS-Freiwilligen Legion Flandern). They sustained heavy casualties on the Eastern Front in fighting in and around the besieged Soviet city of Leningrad. The remnant of the unit surrendered to Soviet forces at Mecklenburg, north-eastern Germany, on 3 May 1945.

Belgian volunteers also joined the Walloon Guard (Garde Wallon) and the Flemish Guard (Vlaamsche Wacht), two collaborationist paramilitary formations that were raised in November 1941 to serve as an auxiliary police force in German-occupied Belgium. In June 1944 the 3,000-strong Flemish guard was transformed by the Wehrmacht into a flak brigade.[12] Belgian volunteers were involved in fighting in the Netherlands in 1944 as elements of various German Army units, including the 27th SS Volunteer Grenadier Division and the SS-Assault Brigade *Langemarck*. They later withdrew into Germany and fought in the Rhine defences and finally in Bavaria.

Jef François, who had served as first lieutenant (SS-obersturmführer) in the 27th SS Volunteer Division *Langemarck* was convicted of treason and war crimes after the liberation of the Netherlands and sentenced to death.[13] His sentence was commuted to life imprisonment. In 1952 he was released from prison. François died in 1996 in Belgium, aged 94 or 95.

Only three notable Belgians were executed for collaborationism.[14] A total of 48,298 defendants received prison terms ranging for life imprisonment (2,955) to 'less than five years' (30,244). In 1965 only three convicted collaborationists were still in Belgian prisons. René Lagrou fought on the Eastern Front with Waffen-SS units. He was captured in France by Allied troops but managed to escape and reach Francoist Spain. In 1947 he made it to Argentina. Lagrou died from cancer in Barcelona on 1 April 1969, aged 64. Albert Luykx, another Waffen-SS trooper, was convicted and sentenced to death in 1948. He managed to escape from prison before the death sentence could be carried out and fled to Ireland, where he remained in hiding. Luykx died in Dublin in 1978, aged 60 or 61.

Dutch

On 5 September 1945 three Dutch and one Belgian Nazi sympathiser were arrested in Lydd, in Kent, England, spying for Germany. Two of the Dutchmen, Karl H. Meier and Charles A. van der Kiebon, and the Belgian, Josef R. Waldberg, were convicted of espionage at the Old Bailey and sentenced to death.[15] The third Dutchman, Sjoerd Pons, was acquitted. Meier and Waldberg were hanged at Pentonville Prison, London, on 10 December 1940.[16] Both were 25 years of age. Van der Kiebon, also 25, was executed in the same prison seven days later.[17]

In the Netherlands, after the country's occupation by German forces in May 1940, Anton Mussert, the leader of the pro-German National Socialist Movement (NSB in Dutch from Nationaal Socialistische Beweging), was named 'leader of the Dutch people' and appointed head of a puppet government, which was in fact a marginal body with little or no power. Folkert Posthuma was Mussert's minister of agriculture and trade. He was assassinated on 3 June 1943 at Vorder, eastern Netherlands, by the Dutch resistance, aged 69.

Johan van Lom betrayed Dutch resistance members to the German occupation forces. In early March 1945 he was abducted by Resistance members and sentenced to death by poisoning. After refusing to drink the poison, 26-year-old van Lom was executed on 6 March in Amsterdam with a shot to the neck.

Between 800 and 1,000 Dutchmen are known to have served in Wehrmacht and Waffen-SS units during the war. At one time it was intended to deploy four battalions, totalling nearly 3,000 Dutch-speaking Belgian volunteers, in defence of Flemish territories in Belgium against the Allied advance. Most of them were later sent to join the (Belgian–Flemish) 27th SS Volunteer Grenadier Division on the Eastern Front. Some 1,500 Dutch volunteered and served in the German Navy, where 300 Belgian-Flanders had already been recruited.[18]

Andries Jan Peters served as a lieutenant (untersturmführer). He was convicted in 1951 of crimes against Dutch civilians committed by thirty men under his command. Peters was sentenced to death and executed by firing squad near the Hague on 21 March 1952, aged 36.

Mussert, the head of the collaborationist government, was arrested in his office on 7 May 1945 a day after the country's liberation by Allied forces. On 28 November he was convicted of high treason by the Special Court of Justice (Bijzonder Gerechtshof). On 12 December Mussert was sentenced to death. He was executed by firing squad on 7 May 1946 at Waalsdorpervlake, near the Hague, where hundreds of Dutch citizens had been killed by Nazi occupation forces.[19] He was 51 years old.

Cornelis van Geelkerken, who co-founded the NSB along with Mussert in 1931, was convicted by the Special Court of Justice and sentenced to life imprisonment. He was released from prison in 1959. Van Geelkerken died on 27 March 1976 in Ede, in the central Netherlands, aged 75.

Anna van Dijk, the daughter of a Dutch Jewish couple, was convicted for betraying 145 people, including her family, to the occupation authorities. Some eighty-five of her victims, including Anne Frank, died later in Nazi concentration camps. Frank was the Jewish girl who kept a diary in which she documented life in hiding under Nazi persecution. Van Dijk was arrested in June 1945. She was sentenced to death on 24 February 1947 by a special court in Amsterdam. Van Dijk was executed by firing squad on 14 January 1948 in Weesperkarspel, a municipality near Amsterdam. The night before her execution van Dijk converted to Roman Catholicism.

Some 51,419 'unpatriotic citizens' suffered punishment by the authorities in one or another form in the post-war Netherlands. They were sentenced for collaboration or war crimes to prison terms ranging from life imprisonment (268 defendants) to five years or less. In Belgium and the Netherlands, in the case of convicted and war criminals, however light the sentence it was almost always accompanied by other sanctions such as a fine, confiscation of personal goods, police supervision after the prison term and the obligation to reside in a specific town.[20]

Danes

Some 6,000 Danes, including seventy-seven officers of the Royal Danish Army (RDA), joined the Free Corps Denmark (Frikorps Danmark) after the German occupation of their country. They were one of the four national legions that were raised in 1941 by

VOLUNTEERS AND COLLABORATORS I

the Waffen-SS in Belgium, Holland, Denmark and Norway to participate in fighting on the Eastern Front. The Free Corps Denmark (FCD) was commanded by Knud Børge Martinsen, a former captain of the RDA, who rose to the rank of SS-lieutenant colonel (SS-Obersturmbannführer). Danish volunteers were recruited later by German units, including the 3rd SS Panzer Division *Totenkopf* and the 5th SS Division *Viking*.

In the winter of 1943–44, the Danish-officered 1,000-strong Schalburgkorps was raised by the SS to combat the country's resistance organisations. Danish volunteers also joined the HIPO Corps (HIPO-korpset), an auxiliary police force that was established by the Gestapo in September 1944. Landstormen, a 200-strong paramilitary militia, and Lorenzen Group (Lorenzengruppen), an armed paramilitary organisation subordinate to the HIPO Corps, were also raised by the Germans in January and in December 1944 respectively. Peter Group (Petergruppen) was a paramilitary organisation that was formed with Nazi sympathisers to also combat the Danish resistance.

Martinsen, the first commander of the FCD, was arrested in his home on 5 May 1945. Four years later he was tried by a Danish court for high treason and other crimes and sentenced to death. Martinsen was executed by firing squad in Copenhagen on 25 June 1949, aged 43.

His successor in the command of the FCD, Christian P. Kryssing, was later transferred to SS units, including the 5th SS Division *Viking*, consisting of volunteers from Denmark, Norway, Sweden and Iceland. He rose to the rank of brigadier general (generalmajor) of the Waffen-SS. In May 1945, Kryssing surrendered to the British, who handed him over to the Danish authorities. He was convicted of treason and collaborationism and sentenced to four years' imprisonment. Kryssing was released from prison early, in May 1948. He died on 7 July 1976 in Haderslev, southern Denmark, aged 85.

Up to 300 members of the HIPO Corps were prosecuted by the post-war Danish authorities. At least ten of them were convicted of treason and war crimes, sentenced to death and executed. Several of the accused received death sentences that were later commuted to prison terms. The leader of the Landstormen militia, Max Johannes Arildskov, was sentenced after the country's liberation to eight years in prison. However, on 9 May 1948 he was pardoned. Arildskov died in 1986, aged 90.

Ten members of the Lorenzen Group were convicted and sentenced to death. Four of them, including their commander Jørgen Lorenzen, were executed in May 1949. The sentences of the rest were commuted to life imprisonment. The last of those who received a life sentence was released from prison in 1959.

In April 1947 seven members of the Peter Group were convicted by a Danish court of fifty-seven murders and 116 sabotage events. They were sentenced to death and executed by firing squad in the Bådsmandsstraede Barracks, Copenhagen, on 9 May 1947, including their commanders, Kai Henning and B. Nielsen.

Between November 1947 and November 1950 101 men and two women were sentenced to death for treason or war crimes by the Copenhagen Municipal Court (Københavns Byret). Forty-six men were executed. The death sentence of thirty-men and the two women were commuted to life imprisonment. The two women were Grethe Bartram and Anna Lund Lorentzen. Bartram was a Gestapo informer during her country's occupations. Because of her, at least fifty-three people, including her brother, were arrested, tortured and deported, and a number of them were executed. She was arrested on 10 May 1945 and seventeen months later she was convicted by a criminal court in Aarhus and sentenced to death. Her sentence was commuted to life imprisonment in December 1946. Ten years later, in October 1956, she was released from prison. Bartram then moved to Sweden. She died in Vessigebro, south-west Sweden, in January 2017, aged 92. Lorentzen was also released from prison in October 1956.

Norwegians

Norway was occupied by German troops in April 1940 and ten months later a collaborationist government took over in Oslo. Before long, hundreds of Nazi sympathiser Norwegians joined military and police formations and units that were raised in Norway by the Wehrmacht, the SS and the Gestapo voluntarily. Some 500 Norwegians volunteered and served in the German Navy (Kriegsmarine).[21] The 1,900-strong Norwegian Legion (Norske Legion) was formed in June 1941 and took part in military operations near Leningrad during the German invasion of the Soviet Union, assigned mostly rear defence tasks. Until March 1943, when the Legion was disbanded, their casualties totalled 180 men. The remnants of the formation were transferred to various units, including the 5th SS Division *Viking* and the SS Ski Jäger Battalion *Norwegen*.

Vidkun Quisling, the self-proclaimed and Nazi-backed prime minister of Norway during the German occupation, turned himself into the police on 9 May 1945 immediately after the liberation of Oslo by British troops. He was imprisoned in Akershus fortress, in Oslo, until his trial three months later. On 10 September Quisling was convicted of high treason and sentenced to death. The man whose name became a synonym for traitor or collaborator with the enemy was executed by firing squad in Akershus fortress on 24 October 1945, aged 58.[22]

Reidar Haaland and Olav Aspheim were members of the Statspolitiet, a Nazi-type armed police force that was raised in German-occupied Norway in June 1941. Haaland was convicted after the liberation of Norway of treason and for the maltreatment of prisoners. He was sentenced to death by the Supreme Court of Norway and executed on 17 August 1945, aged 26. Aspheim was a member of the firing squad that executed twenty resistance fighters in Oslo on 9 February 1945. After the liberation of Norway, he was tried for treason and wrongful execution and sentenced to death. Aspheim was executed on 9 March 1948, aged 26. The execution of Haaland and Aspheim was carried out by firing squad in the Akershus fortress.

Of the forty Norwegians who were sentenced to death for treason or war crimes, twenty-five were executed – all by firing squad except one. Erich Hoffmann was tried under British law for the execution of seven civilians and hanged on 15 Nay 1946 in Hamelin prison, Germany, aged 46.[23]

Sophus Kahrs rose to the rank of SS major (SS-sturmbannführer) while in command of the SS Ski Jäger Battalion *Norwegen*. After the war, he was sentenced by a Norwegian court to ten years' imprisonment with hard labour. In July 1947 Kahrs managed to escape from prison and flee to Argentina. He died in Buenos Aires on 18 November 1986, aged 68.

Arthur Qvist had won a silver medal as a horse rider in the Berlin Summer Olympics in 1936. During the German occupation of Norway, he served voluntarily in various SS units, rising to the rank of major. After the war Qvist was convicted of treason and collaborationism and sent to prison for eight years. He was discharged earlier. Qvist died on 20 September 1977, aged 77.

Finn Kjelstrup served in various units with the rank of SS-major until December 1942, when he resigned. In 1947 he was arrested and convicted of treason. A year later Kjelstrup was pardoned and released from prison. He died on 5 December 1961, aged 77.

Fredrik Jensen served with distinction in various Waffen-SS units, rising to the rank of SS-major. In mid-1945 he was arrested by US troops in Vienna and transferred to the Norwegian authorities. He was tried for treason and sentenced to three months' imprisonment and loss of citizen's rights for ten years. After his release from prison Jensen moved to Sweden and from there to Spain. He died on 31 July 2011 in Málaga, Spain, aged 90.

British and Commonwealth collaborators and spies

In 1943 thirty British, British Dominion and Commonwealth prisoners of war detained in various POW camps were persuaded by the Germans to join a newly raised Wehrmacht unit, the British Free Corps (Britische Freikorps). The idea for the unit came from John Amery, a British fascist, who did a lot of propaganda work for the Nazis from Berlin. The British Free Corps (BFC) never had a commander per se as it was the intention of the SS (Schutzstaffel) to appoint a British one when a suitable officer came forward. The only British officers to volunteer for recruitment were William Shearer and Douglas Berneville-Clay, who apparently failed to meet the standards set by the Germans. As a result the BFC was assigned to three (one at a time) German Waffen-SS officers, who acted in a liaison capacity between BFC and the central command of the SS.

William Shearer, a second lieutenant in the 4th Seaforth Highlanders, suffered a mental breakdown in March 1943 after his recruitment to the unit. He was eventually repatriated to Great Britain by the Red Cross. Shearer was never charged with treason and collaboration as he was proved unfit for trial. He died on 9 July 1995 in Northamptonshire, aged 78.

Berneville-Clay was a second lieutenant in the West Yorkshire Regiment. He was captured in Tunisia by the Afrika Korps and detained in POW camps in Italy and Germany. In mid-April 1945 he left the BFC and, heading westward in a stolen vehicle, reached Allied lines. After the war, Berneville-Gray was never court-martialled for treason and collaboration. After going to prison condemned for other crimes, he emigrated to Australia. He died of cancer in 1975 in Campbelltown, New South Wales, aged 58.

The BFC was regarded battle ready in March 1945 when they, members of a Waffen-SS unit by now, were deployed near Neustrelitz on the west bank of the Order River in eastern Germany. They were not involved in any fighting against Allied forces. By 2 May most of the personnel had surrendered to western Allied troops. After the war some members of the BFC were prosecuted. Those who had been serving in the armed forces were court-martialled, while the merchant seamen and other civilians were tried in the Old Bailey.

Roy N. Courlander, a British-born New Zealand soldier, was captured by the Germans in Calamata, southern Greece, in April 1941. On 3 September 1943, after his recruitment to the BFC, Courlander escaped to Belgium. He joined the Belgian resistance in the fighting against retreating German forces. On 3 October 1945 Courlander was tried for treason and collaboration by a New Zealand court martial at Westgate-on-sea, Kent, in southern England. On 3 October Courlander was sentenced to fifteen years in prison. In May 1950 his sentence was reduced to nine years. He was released from prison on 2 October 1951. Courlander died on 1 June 1979 in Lethbridge Park, New South Wales, Australia, aged 64.

William Charles Brittain, a lance corporal in the British Army's Royal Warwickshire Regiment, was captured during the Battle of Crete in May 1941. He was recruited to the BFC by the Germans during his detention in a POW camp. In 1946 Brittain was sentenced to ten years' imprisonment by a military court in Colchester. Two months later he was released on health grounds suffering from an incurable form of Crohn's disease.

A. Minchin and Kenneth Berry were the BFC's first recruits. They were merchant seamen who became POWs after the sinking of their ships by the Germans. Alfred Minchin, a junior corporal (SS sturmmann) of the Waffen-SS, was convicted at the central criminal court in London on 5 February 1946 of conspiring to assist the enemy. He was sentenced to seven years' imprisonment. Minchin died in Somerset in February 1998, aged 81.

Berry received a nine-month prison sentence at Bow Street Magistrates' Court. On 10 May 1947, after his release, Berry married in Cornwall his German girlfriend, Carola Schwartz, with whom he had six children. He died on 22 November 1992 in Falmouth, in south-west England, aged 67.

Thomas Haller Cooper was half German, having a British father and a German mother. He was also a member of the British Union of Fascists and fluent in German. Cooper was not allowed to serve in the British armed forces. In the summer of 1939 he went to Germany and about a year later, in July 1940, he was recruited by the Waffen-SS. Cooper, who fought on the Eastern Front, is the only Briton to receive the 'wound budge in silver', a Wehrmacht combat decoration, after being hurt in action. In January 1945 after his conviction by the Central Criminal Court in London for high treason and collaboration with the enemy, Cooper was sentenced to death by hanging.[24] His sentence was commuted to life imprisonment on the grounds that he was a follower rather than a leader in treason. He was released from prison in 1953. Cooper emigrated to Japan, where he worked as language teacher. He returned to England in early 1987. Cooper died in the late 1990s, aged 67.[25]

Edwin Barnard Martin was a private in the Essex Scottish Regiment of the Canadian Army when he was captured during the Allied raid on Dieppe, France, in August 1942. After the war he was court-martialled by the Canadian Army for becoming a member of the BFC and sentenced to twenty-five years in prison. Martin was pardoned in 1954. He died on 16 August 1987 in Riverside, Ontario, aged 68.

Henry A. Symonds was a private in the British Army's Princess Louise's Kensington Regiment. He was captured by the Germans in Italy on 4 October 1943 and joined the BFC two months later. After the war Symonds was court-martialled in England for treason and collaboration with the enemy and sentenced to fifteen years in prison. He died in June 1994 in Vale Royal, Cheshire, aged 70.

VOLUNTEERS AND COLLABORATORS I

George F. McLardy, a British Army soldier and former member of the British Union of Fascists, was captured by the Germans in northern France in May 1940. He was recruited to the BFC after three years in various POW camps. In April 1945 McLardy fled to Belgium, where he joined the Belgian resistance in the fighting against retreating German forces. He surrendered to US troops and was later handed over to the British military authorities. In early January 1946 McLardy was court-martialled at Blacon Camp, near Chester, and sentenced to life imprisonment.[26] While in prison, he acquired an external degree in chemistry from Cambridge University. In 1953, when he was pardoned and set free, McLardy emigrated to Germany. There he married a German woman and worked as a pharmacist. He died on 16 December 1981 in Ingelheim am Rhein, near Mainz in Rhineland-Palatinate, aged 66.

Philip Jackson, a 36-year-old gunner in the British Army, was arrested by an undercover security service officer posing as a Nazi spy offering information related to targets of importance for German bombers. In February 1942 he was court-martialled and sentenced to death by firing squad. His sentence was commuted to life imprisonment.

Theodore Schurch, a British soldier and member of the British Union of Fascists, was captured by the Germans in North Africa in 1942. He was released after agreeing to work for German and Italian intelligence. In March 1945 Schurch was arrested in Rome by western Allied troops and eventually convicted by a special court in London on nine charges of treachery. Six months later he was sentenced to death. He was hanged, aged 27, on 4 January 1946, at Pentonville prison, London, by chief executioner Albert Pierrepoint. Schurch, who had a Swiss father and a British mother, was the only British soldier executed for treachery during the war. He was also the last convict in Great Britain executed for an offence other than murder.

Schurch was convicted according to the Treachery Act, an Act of Parliament that became law in May 1940 to facilitate the prosecution and execution of enemy spies. The Treachery Act was also employed against citizens during and immediately following the war. Between 1940 and 1946, nineteen people, including five British subjects, were executed for treachery in Great Britain. Those executed, besides Schurch, were John Johnson Armstrong, Duncan Scott-Ford, Oswald John Job and a Gibraltarian, Jose Estelle Key.

The first to be executed under the Act was John Johnson-Armstrong. A marine engineer by occupation, he was convicted in 1941 in London for his conduct with the German consulate in Boston, Massachusetts, and sentenced to death.[27] Johnson-Armstrong was hanged by executioner Albert Pierrepont on 10 July 1941 in Wandsworth Prison, London, aged 39.

Duncan Scott-Ford, a merchant seaman, was convicted of treachery after selling to an enemy agent for £18 (about £900 in 2023) in Portuguese currency naval secrets related to the crossing of the Atlantic by British convoys. On 16 October 1942 Scott-Ford was sentenced to death and on 3 November he was hanged by Pierrepoint in Wandsworth, aged 21.[28]

Oswald John Job was born in London's East End to German parents. He was found guilty in court as an informer to the enemy.[29] He was sentenced to death and executed in Pentonville on 23 March 1944 at the hands of Pierrepoint, aged 58.[30]

Between 1939 and 1945 seventy British men and women were convicted – mostly in secret trials – of working for Nazi Germany.[31] They spied, committed acts of sabotage and provided assistance to Berlin from the safety of their homes and offices throughout Great Britain. William Gutheridge and Wanda Penlington cut telephone wires to obstruct the emergency services; Albert Munt, a London schoolboy, lit fires to guide German bombers to their targets; Edgar and Sophia Bray tried to smuggle plans for a new tank to Berlin; Irma Stapleton stole experimental munitions and handed these to a man believed to be a Nazi spy. Most of them, called fifth columnists by Winston Churchill, were ardent fascists, while others were paid in cash for their treachery.[32]

Four of those convicted were sentenced to death, with two being executed. Dorothy O'Grady, aged 42, a petty criminal and former prostitute, was the first British woman to be sentenced to death for treachery, although she was tried as a saboteur. She was caught cutting military telegraphic wires on the Isle of Wight. She was also in possession of detailed maps of defences across the south coast of the island. On 17 December 1940 O'Grady was convicted in a secret trial at Winchester assizes and sentenced to death. Two months later her sentence was commuted to fourteen years' penal servitude. She served nine months. In 1950, after her release, O'Grady settled in Lake on the Isle of Wight. She died there on 11 October 1985, aged 87.

Declassified MI5 and government files show that during the war hundreds of British fascists were interned without trial on specific evidence that they were spying for Nazi Germany.[33]

VOLUNTEERS AND COLLABORATORS II

Around one-and-a-half million Soviet citizens of various ethnicities served the Germans in some capacity during the war, with the bulk of them being recruited by non-Russian nationalities, including Estonians, Latvian, Lithuanians, Ukrainians and Georgians.[1]

Russians

There were at least 427,000 Russian volunteers who fought on the Eastern Front against Stalin's forces.[2] Those integrated to military units constituted the Battalions and the Legions of the East (Ostbataillonen and Ostlegionen). Red Army deserters and Soviet prisoners of war were also used by the Wehrmacht mostly as drivers, cooks and medical orderlies. At the beginning of 1944 seventy-two Eastern battalions were deployed in Western Europe.[3] Brigadier General Heinz Hellmich commanded initially German Army's Eastern troops. In January 1944 he was replaced by Major General Ernst Köstring, who had served as military attaché in Moscow until the German invasion of the Soviet Union. He surrendered to US troops on 4 May 1945 and was detained for two years. Köstring died on 20 November 1953 in Unterwössen, in the south-eastern part of Bavaria, aged 77.

The Eastern battalions, including one air force regiment, about equal numerically to thirty Wehrmacht-type divisions, were also called Russian Liberation Army (Russkaya Osvoditelnaia Armiia) or RLA and were commanded, as of January 1944, by Russian General Andrei Vlasov, a former lieutenant general of the Red Army. He was commanding the Soviet 2nd Shock (Assault) Army on 12 July 1942 when he was captured near Leningrad by German troops. While in Soviet custody, Vlasov proposed the formation of the RLA, which was raised in September 1944. Due to lingering fears of a betrayal en masse, it was decided in Berlin to send these volunteers to German-occupied territories in western and southern Europe.[4] Since most of these men had volunteered to fight communism, their deployment to the west resulted a blow to their morale.[5] The RLA's only combat against Soviet forces took place on 11 December near the River Oder. The collaborationist Russians were forced to retreat and march southward to Prague, in German-controlled Bohemia. RLA troops (1st Division) then took part in the Prague uprising against the Red Army alongside Czech resistance fighters. Under the Yalta Agreement the Western Allies promised to Josef Stalin any Soviet collaborator who fell into their hands.

On 7 May 1945 Lieutenant Colonel Vladimir Boyarsky was captured by Czech communist partisans near Příbram, a town located 29 miles (46km) south-west of

Prague. He had co-signed with Vlasov the proposal for the raising of the RLA. Boyarsky was hanged on the spot after slapping in the face the Soviet officer, Captain Smirnov, who was in charge of the Czech partisans. One day later Vlasov was captured near Plzeň by elements of the Soviet 25th Tank Corps, after the rejection of his offer by the US Army to surrender to them. He was sent to Moscow, where he was confined to Lubyanka prison. On 30 July 1946 Vlasov was tried for treason and other crimes and sentenced to death. He was executed by hanging in Moscow on 1 August 1946, aged 44.

Major General Vasily F. Malyshkin was Vlasov's deputy. On 24 October 1941 he was commanding a brigade of the Nineteenth Army when he was captured by German troops near Vyazma, a town south-west of Moscow. On 9 May 1945 Malyshkin surrendered to US forces. Ten months later he was handed over to the Soviet authorities. On 18 April 1946 he was tried in Moscow for treason and other crimes. Found guilty as charged, he was sentenced to death. Malyshkin was hanged on 1 August (the same day as Vlasov) in Butyrka prison, aged 49.

Brigadier General Sergei Bunyachenko was arrested by Romanian troops in December 1942 near Vladikavkaz, in the north Caucasus region while commanding the Soviet 59th Rifle Brigade. In February 1944, after collaborating with the Germans, he was promoted to major general and seven months later assumed command of the RLA's 1st Division, also known as the Wehrmacht's 600 (Russian) Infantry Division. On 15 May 1945 Bunyachenko surrendered to US troops, who handed him over to the Soviet military authorities. He was confined in a Moscow prison (Butyrka) until his trial. On 30 July 1946, 43-year-old Bunyachenko was tried with eleven other officers of the RLA. All were sentenced to death and executed by hanging on 1 or 2 August 1946.[6]

Finnish-born Brigadier General Boris A. Smyslovsky was an émigré Russian anti-communist officer who organised twelve battalions of collaborationist troops using mostly émigré Russian volunteers. In March 1945 this 10,000-strong force was unified, becoming the Wehrmacht's 1st Russian Army with Smyslovsky as their commander. Two months later, 462 men of the formation evaded captured by the Red Army by crossing the border into Liechtenstein. Among them was Smyslovsky, who later moved to Argentina along with a number of his men. In 1975 he returned to Liechtenstein. Smyslovsky died in Vaduz, the capital of the country, on 5 September 1988, aged 90.

Liechtenstein was the only European country to turn down Moscow's requests after the war for the repatriation of Soviet citizens in compliance with the provisions of the Yalta inter-Allied conference. The former Red Army soldiers who chose to stay on in Liechtenstein were permitted to do so by the country's authorities and were taken care of. Two hundred others who chose to be repatriated were put on a train for the journey home. During a stop in Hungary, the refugees were reportedly taken off the train and summarily executed by NKVD agents, members of an agency tasked with conducting police work in the Soviet Union and overseeing the country's prisons and labour camps.

Vladimir Ilitch Boyarsky and Bronislav Kaminski were executed during the war. Boyarsky, born to a Polish family in Berdetskoye, near Kiev, in the Soviet Union, had co-signed with Vlasov the appeal to the German high command for the raising of Russian collaborationist troops. He formed the Russian People's National Army

(RPNA) in March 1942 and assumed their command six months later. The 4,000-strong unit was made up of White (anti-communist) émigrés, who were assigned mostly anti-partisan missions in the rear of German forces. By 1943 the RPNA had ceased to exist and most of the personnel were transferred to the Wehrmacht or to SS formations in western Europe. Boyarski was captured by Czech partisans on 5 May in 1945, near Příbram, a town in the central Bohemian region in the present-day Czech Republic. Two days later he was executed, aged 44.

Kaminski was a Russian anti-communist and Nazi collaborator. He raised a brigade-size private force that was involved in atrocities committed mostly during the sixty-three-day (1 August–2 October) Warsaw Uprising. He was arrested by the Gestapo and charged with stealing property of the Third Reich. He was executed on 28 August 1944 in Litzmannstadt, present-day Łódź, in Poland, aged 45. His private army was disbanded.

In August 1941 an entire Cossack regiment with their officers deserted to the Germans.[7] They fought under the command of Major (later Major General) Ivan N. Kononow. The 1st Cossack Division was formed by April 1943 and fought mostly against Josip Broz Tito's communist partisans in German-occupied Yugoslavia. Kononow was the only Cossack commander who escaped forced repatriation to the Soviet Union after the war. He remained in West Germany out of sight and eventually managed to emigrate to Australia. Kononow died on 15 September 1967 in Adelaide, aged 67.

Pyotr N. Krasnov, a former Ataman (commander) of the Don Cossacks, was a lieutenant general in the Czarist army in 1917, when the communist revolution erupted in Russia. Two years later he fled to France, where he became one of the leaders of the anti-communist White Movement. Although a Nazi collaborator since 1941 and head of the Berlin-based Cossack government in exile, Krasnov refused to join forces with the RLA because he disliked the fact that their commander was a former Red Army general. At the end of the war he surrendered to British forces in Austria. On 28 May 1945 Krasnov was handed over to the Russians. He was taken to Moscow and confined in Lubyanka prison.[8] He was tried for high treason and other crimes and sentenced to death. Krasnov was hanged in Moscow on 17 January 1947, aged 77.

All the major Eastern volunteer units of the Wehrmacht and the Waffen-SS, including the Cossack Cavalry Corps and the 1st Division RLA, attempted to surrender to the western Allied forces at the end of the war. Practically all the major units were handed back to the Soviet military authorities by the western Allied forces, often amid the most heart-breaking scenes.[9] It must be noted that many of the Cossacks were accompanied in their deployments by their women and children and none of them had any illusion about the fate that awaited them at Stalin's hands. Hundreds of thousands of men and many members of their families disappeared into the appalling embrace of the NKVD. Nearly all the ringleaders of the volunteers were executed, beginning with General Vlasov. Most of the officers and men were executed. The survivors were swallowed up by the Gulags, from which only a few returned.[10]

On 25 February 1945 a German officer, Lieutenant General Helmuth Pannwitz, was elected feldataman (supreme commander) of XV SS Cossack Cavalry Corps by the officers and men of the formation.[11] He had been with them, typically as a liaison officer, since 21 April 1943, when the Cossacks first became a component of the German military as the Cossack Cavalry Brigade. Von Pannwitz led these anti-communist warriors in anti-partisan operations, initially in Ukraine and Belarus and later in German-occupied Yugoslavia. On 11 May 1945 he surrendered to British forces near Völkermarkt, in south-east Austria. His troops, according to the provisions of the Yalta Conference, were handed over to the Soviet Union. As a German national, von Pannwitz could have preferred British custody. Instead, he chose to have the same fate with his troops and surrendered to Soviet military authorities at Judenburg, in south-east Austria. He was tried for war crimes in Moscow by a military tribunal and sentenced to death. Von Pannwitz was executed on 16 January 1947, aged 48.[12]

Major Semyon Bychov, a Soviet pilot, was taken prisoner by the Germans when his fighter plane was shot down on 10 December 1943. After agreeing to collaborate, Bychov was assigned combat missions by the Germans. He also led the 1st Aircraft Regiment of the Russian Liberation Army. Bychov carried out air raids against Red Army and partisan targets around Dvinsk, in south-east Latvia. In April 1945 he surrendered to the US Army in Cherbourg, France. They turned him over to the Soviet military authorities. On 24 August 1946 Bychov was tried in Moscow for treason and other crimes and was sentenced to death. He was executed by firing squad on 4 November, aged 28.

Ukrainians, Georgians, Caucasians and Armenians

The only units of Eastern volunteers that formed part of the Wehrmacht at the beginning of the German invasion of the Soviet Union were two Ukrainian battalions, which had been raised by the Germans in Poland in the spring of 1941. These units were made up of members of the country's Ukrainian minority.[13] Ukrainian volunteers joined the 180,000-strong Ukrainian Liberation Army. One battalion, the 643rd, was posted by the Germans on Guernsey and Jersey during the German occupation of the Channel Islands.[14]

Only in the final stages of the war did the Ukrainian volunteers find an effective leader in Pavlo Shandruk. He was a former officer of the Russian Imperial Army and the Polish Army. After refusing to join Vlasov's Russian Liberation Army (RLA), Shandruk was permitted by the Germans to raise the Ukrainian National Army (UNA) in early 1945. He assumed their command in April. Two divisions were battle ready by May 1945.[15] The UNA's 1st Division saw some action in Yugoslavia and Austria and the 2nd in Czechoslovakia. On 8 May Shandruk and 1,300 men of the 1st Division surrendered to US forces in Austria. The remnant of the UNA's 2nd Division surrendered to British forces near Udine in northern Italy. As Polish pre-war citizens, most of the Ukrainian volunteers were not passed over by the Allies to the Soviet authorities. Shandruk lived in West Germany and later emigrated to the United States. He died on Trenton, New Jersey, on 15 February 1979, aged 89.

A large number of Ukrainian volunteers who had deserted en masse from the 14th SS-Division managed to fight their way through the Soviet lines to safety in the US zone of Germany, where they arrived in the winter of 1946–47.[16]

In February 1945 Colonel Petro Dyachenko, one of the commanders of the Ukrainian Liberation Army, raised and led the Free Ukraine Brigade. They fought with distinction in Poland as part of the German Army Group Centre, capturing 300 Soviet POWs. Dyachenko was promoted to lieutenant general on 7 May 1945. He surrendered to the

US Army and was not handed over to Soviet military authorities, being a former Polish (and not Soviet) citizen. He eventually emigrated to the United States. Dyachenko died in Philadelphia, Pennsylvania, on 23 April 1945, aged 70.

Brigadier General Ritter von Niedermayer, who was also a Berlin university lecturer before the war, could speak fluent English and Russian, and passable Arabic, Turkish and Farsi (Persian). During the First World War, he carried out intelligence assignments in Persia and Afghanistan. In 1943 he raised and led a division made up of Caucasian, Georgian and Armenian volunteers. The formation was involved in fighting in Italy in May 1944, when von Niedermayer was replaced in the command. He was later arrested by the Gestapo, court-martialled for defeatism and sent to Torgau prison in eastern Germany. After the German capitulation, von Niedermayer was arrested by the Red Army and transferred to Moscow to be tried for war crimes. He was sentenced to twenty-five years' imprisonment. He died suffering from tuberculosis in Vladimir prison, 120 miles (200km) east of Moscow, on 25 September 1948, aged 63.

The Georgians who served in the German armed forces numbered at least 30,000. They were Georgian émigrés living in western Europe and Georgian POWs. They were raised in December 1941 and trained by the German Army in western Ukraine. These anti-communist volunteers comprised the Georgian Legion (Georgische Legion) and part of the North Caucasian Legion. Their units became operational in autumn 1942. One battalion of Georgian volunteers, the 823rd, was deployed on Guernsey and Jersey during the German occupation of the Channel Islands.[17] Some components of the Georgian Legion later fell under the operational control of the Waffen-SS. A Germanophile anti-communist and monarchist émigré Georgian, Shalva Maglakelidze, was appointed commander of the Georgian Legion. He was a jurist with a PhD from Berlin university who had lived in Germany since 1938. In 1944 Maglakelidze was forced to resign after disagreeing with the systematic deployment of Georgian units in western Europe. On 5 April 1945, with the western Allies driving into Germany, the 822nd Georgian Battalion that was stationed on the Dutch island of Texel revolted against their German overlords and held their positions until 20 May, past the German surrender. In accordance with inter-Allied agreements, the Georgian volunteers who surrender to western Allied forces had to be handed over to the USSR as they were Soviet citizens. They were treated as traitors in military tribunals in the USSR and received long prison sentences. Many were sent to labour camps and gulags in Central Asia and Siberia.[18] Maglakelidze lived in Italy after the war and later moved to West Germany. In 1954 he was kidnapped by Soviet agents and transferred to the USSR. He was imprisoned but never charged with treason or collaborationism. Maglakelidze was released from prison, after making a public confession in which he denounced the Georgian émigrés as US and British agents. He died in 1976 in Tbilisi, the capital of the Georgian SSR, aged 83.

The first volunteers to become regular members of the German Army came from the Asiatic and Caucasus peoples of the Soviet Union.[19] They were grouped into two battalions, one Turkoman and Caucasian, both integrated into the German 444th Security Division (Sicherungdivision). Five East Legions (Ostlegionen) were later raised in the greater Caucasus region. These were the Turkestan, Muslim-Caucasian, North Caucasian, Volga Tartar and the Armenian Legions.

The number of Armenians who volunteered to fight against the Red Army alongside Wehrmacht forces was estimated at 33,000, although those placed in field units were no more than 11,000. These volunteers were either former POW camp detainees or anti-communist Armenians of a diaspora who came from abroad to join the Armenian Legion. Of the eight battalions of the formation, the first, the 812th, was raised in 1942. Drasatmat Kanayan was made commander of the Armenian Legion. He collaborated in the hope of freeing Armenia of Soviet control in the event of Nazi Germany's victory over the USSR.[20] Kanayan, also known as General Dro, was a military commander and politician (a prominent member of the US-based Armenian Revolutionary Federation). His troops initially participated in the occupation of the Crimea Peninsula by Axis forces. They were later deployed in German-occupied France, taking part mostly in the defence of Toulon. In May 1945 Kanayan was arrested by US troops in Heidelberg, south-west Germany, but was soon released. He later emigrated to the United States. Kanayan died in Boston, Massachusetts, on 8 March 1956, aged 71.

Estonians

Only weeks after the German invasion of the USSR volunteers from newly liberated Latvia and Estonia were recruited into indigenous security detachments.[21] The twenty-six security detachments raised by the Germans in Estonia in late 1941 were eventually upgraded to three battalions – the 658th, the 659th and the 660th. By March 1942 the number of battalions had risen to sixteen.[22] The Estonian Legion was made up of 500 volunteers in October 1942 as part of the Waffen-SS. Their number rose to 1,280 by the spring of the following year. Estonian volunteers also joined the Special Purpose Division 300 (Div.zbV.300), also known as the Estonian Frontier Guards Division, and the German–Scandinavian 5th SS Panzer Division *Viking*. At least 30,000 Estonians were conscripted to serve in the German and Finnish armies.

On 24 January 1944 the Estonian Legion was re-formed into the 13,700-strong 20th Grenadier Division (1st Estonian) of the Waffen-SS. A former Estonian army officer, Alfonse Rebane, was eventually appointed their commander, rising to the rank of SS-Colonel (SS-Standartenführer). The division fought on the Russian front, with Rebane emerging as one of the most decorated of the German Army Baltic officers. He received medals for his bravery and his combat skills. Most of his troops were later captured by the Red Army in Czechoslovakia. Rebane managed to reach the British occupation zone and later joined the Secret Intelligence Service (MI6) as an expert on the Baltic states.[23] The Nuremberg Trial ruled later that the 30,000 Estonians who had served in units raised by the Germans were conscripts, not volunteers. They were defined as freedom fighters protecting their homeland from a Soviet occupation, and as such they were not considered true members of the Waffen-SS.[24]

Two Estonian collaborators, Aleksander Laak and Karl Linnas had been commandants in Nazi concentration camps that were established in Estonia. About 5,000 Jews and Roma who had been deported from various west European countries were killed in these camps, located in Jägala, near Tallinn, and near Tartu. Lieutenant Laak, the commandant in Jägala, fled to Canada after the war. He eventually became a naturalised Canadian citizen. On 6 September 1960 Laak was found hanged in the garage of his home in Winnipeg, central Canada, aged 53.[25]

Linnas was the commandant of the Tartu concentration camp, located 187km south-east of Tallinn, the present-day capital of Estonia. He followed the German troops when they withdrew from the Baltic states in 1944. In 1951 Linnas emigrated to the United States and six years later he became a US citizen. In 1981, when his Nazi past was revealed, Linnas was stripped of US citizenship and deported to the Soviet Union. He was sentenced to death in Leningrad, but his sentence was commuted to life imprisonment due to poor health. Linnas died three months later in the prison hospital in Leningrad, aged 67.[26]

Alfred Käärmann was an anti-communist resistance fighter and had nothing to do with collaborationism. He fought against Soviet troops after the invasion and occupation of Estonia by the Red Army in June 1940. In 1941 he went into hiding in a forest. In October 1944 Käärmann was wounded in a skirmish with Soviet troops and went into hiding again. He was captured by KGB agents in 1952. He was tried and sentenced to twenty-five years' hard labour. Käärmann spent fifteen years in a camp in the Ural Mountains. In 1967 he was released and allowed to return to Estonia. Three months later Käärrmann was expelled from his home country and banned from working. He lived in absolute poverty until 1975, when he was permitted to return to Estonia. Käärmann, a heroic figure to his people since the collapse of communism three decades ago, died in Hargla, southern Estonia, on 4 February 2010, aged 88.

Evald Mikson headed the police force in Tallin/Harjumaa between 1941 and 1944 and was allegedly involved in war crimes against Jews and Roma. When the German forces withdrew from Estonia, he tried to escape to South America along with other collaborators, but their ship was stranded off the coast of Iceland. Mikson did not go on with the effort to reach Venezuela. He settled in Reykjavík, the capital of Iceland, until his death on 27 December 1993, aged 82. Mikson had played football for the national team of Estonia between 1934 and 1938. His sons played professional football, Jóhannes Eðvaldsson with Celtic in Scotland and Atli Eðvaldsson with Borussia Dortmund in Germany. Atli later coached Iceland's national team.

Latvians

On 6 June 1940, after the invasion of his country by Soviet forces, 52-year-old General Ludvigs Bolšteins, commander of the Latvian Border Guards, killed himself in his office in Riga, Latvia's capital, to evade capture.

General Žanis Bahs and Colonel Jānis Puriņs had fought against the Red Army after the proclamation of the Republic of Latvia in November 1918. When the country was invaded, occupied and annexed by the Soviet Union, Hitler's ally at the time, both were arrested. Bahs was deported to Moscow, where he was tried on 18 July 1941 and sentenced to death. He was executed on 16 October at Kommunarka, a shooting range near Moscow, aged 56. Puriņs was imprisoned, after his arrest and then disappeared. He is presumed to have been executed.

In Latvia, after 'liberating' the country from the Soviet occupation, the Germans organised six regiments consisting of volunteers. They became the nucleus of the Latvian Legion (Latviešu Leģions in Latvian) that was formed in January 1943. By

July 1944 the formation comprised 87,000 men. A further 23,000 Latvian volunteers joined the Wehrmacht as auxiliaries. Each Latvian regiment averaged 2,700 men, who were sent to the front almost at once. They were engaged in the two-year-long siege of Leningrad and in various battles including the one in Berlin in the final stage of the war in Europe.

The Latvian Legion's poorly equipped and worse-trained troops were so badly mauled by the Red Army around Dünaburg, present-day Daugavpils, in south-west Latvia and Pickau-Ostrów, in west-central Poland, that their units were gradually disbanded between July and September 1944.[27] The most serviceable survivors joined two formations, the 19th Waffen Grenadier Division (2nd Latvian) and the 15th Waffen Grenadier Division (1st Latvian).[28] The commanders of the Wehrmacht and the Waffen-SS Latvian units were German-officered.

Two Latvians, Vilis Janums and Kārlis Lobe, became regimental commanders in the 15th Waffen Grenadiers (1st Latvian) and the 19th Waffen Grenadier (2nd Latvian) Divisions respectively. They rose to the rank of SS-colonel (SS-standartenführer). Janums surrendered to US troops on 26 April 1945 near Lindau, in Saxony-Anhalt. He was detained until 1946. He then settled in West Germany. Janums died on 6 August 1981 in Münster, in North Rhine Westphalia, aged 87. Lobe commanded the infantry units of the 19th Waffen Grenadier Division (2nd Latvian). In the final phase of the war he surrendered to British troops in Germany. After his release a year later, he settled in Sweden. Lobe died on 9 July 1985 in Stockholm, aged 90.

Two harassment squadrons (störkampfstaffel) of the Luftwaffe, known also as Luftwaffen-Legion Lettland, were formed in March 1944. They consisted of Latvian volunteer, flying Arado Ar 66 and Gotha Go 145 single-engine, two-seater biplanes. They were commanded by Latvian Lieutenant Colonel Jānis Rucels. The 12th Night Combat Group (Latvian) (Nachtschlachtruppe 12, Lettisch) flew 6,150 sorties with the loss of six pilots. In October 1944, when the unit was disbanded for lack of fuel and spares, several men fled to neutral Sweden, crammed four to a plane, thus evading capture by advancing Red Army forces.[29]

Mārtiņs Grundmanis had won a gold medal with the Latvian national side in the 1st Eurobasket basketball championship in 1935. He was conscripted in the Latvian Legion, but in mid-1944 he was captured by the Red Army. On 30 November Grumandis committed suicide in a POW camp at Sarkandaugava, a neighbourhood of Riga, aged 31.

Pēteris Dzelzītis fought against the Red Army as a trooper of the 19th Waffen Division (2nd Latvian) and as a guerilla fighter after the withdrawal of the German forces from his country. On 2 February 1948 Dzelzītis was captured by Soviet troops. He was tried and sentenced to death. He was executed on 16 February 1948, aged 27.

Kurts Fridrihsons was a painter, illustrator and stage designer. In October 1944 he joined the Latvian Legion, but soon became a deserter. In 1951 Fridrihsons was arrested in Latvia by the communist authorities and convicted of anti-Soviet activities and nationalism. He was sentenced to twenty-five years in prison and sent to a Gulag camp in Omsk Oblast, in south-western Siberia. Fridrihson was released in 1956. He died on 31 January 1991 in Riga, aged 79.

French-educated Emanuels Grīnbergs was a mathematician known for Grīnbergs' theorem. Because he joined the Latvian Legion, he was sent to a labour camp in Kurtaisi, west of Tbilisi, in present-day Georgia. He also lost his teaching job at the University in Riga. After his release, Grīnbergs could only find a job as a factory worker. In 1954 he was allowed to return to Riga and teach at the university. He died in 1982 in Riga, aged 71.

In 1939 Alfons Bērziņš became a European champion in the long-track skating competition. In 1944, after joining the Latvian Legion, he served as a platoon commander in an anti-aircraft unit. In May 1945 Bērziņš was captured by the Red Army after the capitulation of the Courland Pocket. He was sentenced to ten years' hard labour. After his release, Bērziņš was allowed to return to Latvia and work as a skating coach. He died on 16 December 1987 in Riga, aged 71.

Edgars Vinters, a painter, was recruited into the Latvian Legion in 1944 and taken prisoner by the Soviet troops in early 1945. He was detained in a POW camp near Moscow. In 1947 Vinters was released and allowed to return to Latvia. He worked as a painter and taught art lessons in schools. He died on 29 April 2014 in Riga, aged 94.

Vilis A. Hāzners, a former officer of the Latvian army, led an anti-communist guerrilla force between early 1941 and early 1943. He then joined the 15th Waffen Grenadier Division (1st Latvian) as a regimental commander. He rose to the rank of major. On 26 January 1945 Hāzners was wounded in battle and sent to German-occupied Denmark for recovery. After the German capitulation, he was held by the western Allies in a POW camp at Zedelgem in Belgium. After his release, Hāzner emigrated to the United States, where he died on 12 May 1989, aged 84.

Oskars Perro, a medical doctor and writer, was conscripted into the 19th Waffen Grenadier Division (2nd Latvian) as an SS senior lieutenant (SS-obersturmführer). He was wounded five times in combat before being taken prisoner by western Allied troops in Germany on 12 May 1945. After his release, Perro returned to his studies in Germany and later to Canada. He died on 2 May 2003 in Canada, aged 84.

Francis Rudolph, a painter, served briefly in the Latvian Legion before becoming a deserter. In 1947 he managed to reach England and later became a notable painter. Examples of Rudolph's work have been exhibited in the Ashmolean Museum in Oxford and in the Gregynog Hall in mid-Wales. He died in 2005 in London, aged 84.

Valdemārs Baumanis was the Latvian head coach in the Eurobasket of 1938 and a lieutenant in the Latvian army. In 1943 he was conscripted into the Latvian Legion, rising to the rank of captain. Baumanis was later transferred to the 15th Waffen Grenadier Division (2nd Latvian). In March 1945 he led 4,000 Latvian soldiers to the western Allied lines, thus evading being captured by the Red Army. Baumanis was detained in a POW camp at Putlos, northern Germany. After his release, he lived in France, where he worked as coach for the CEP Lorient basketball club for four years. In 1954 he emigrated to the United States. He died in Chicago on 24 April 1992, aged 87.

Arajs Kommando (Arāja Komanda in Latvian) was a notorious 1,500-strong (its maximum size) unit of Latvian auxiliary police consisting of pro-Nazi volunteers in early July 1941. Members of this unit participated, along with German SS troops, in massacres of Jews and Roma. Between 30 November and 8 December 1941 almost half of the country's Jewish 26,000 population were murdered at Rumbula, a forested area near Riga, the Latvian capital. Five months earlier Arajs Kommando members were involved in the massacre of 5,700 Jews and Roma near Liepāja, on the western coast of Latvia. The Arajs Komando was also assigned to anti-partisan operations and served as guards at the notorious Salaspils concentration camp, south-east of Riga. The unit, commanded by Victors Arājs, was disbanded in late 1944 and most of the personnel were transferred to the Latvian Legion. Viktors Arājs, a law graduate and former policeman, led the Latvian Security Group, as Arājs's Kommando was initially named. He rose to the rank of SS-major. After the war, he was in British custody for four years. In 1949, after his release, Arājs worked in a printing company in Frankfurt under the false name Victor Zeibots. On 21 December 1979 he was arrested by the West German authorities and charged with crimes against humanity. He was sentenced to life imprisonment by a court in Hamburg. Arājs died on 13 January 1988 in Kassel-Wehlheiden prison, central Germany, aged 78.

Herbert Cukurs, a long-distance aviator, was Arājs's deputy in the command of the unit.[30] He is known as 'the Butcher of Latvia' because of his role for in atrocities, including the Rumbula massacre and the burning of Jewish synagogues in Latvia.[31] Cukurs retreated with the German forces to Germany and from there fled to Brazil. He was assassinated or extrajudicially executed, according to Israeli comments, in Shangrilá, near Montevideo, in Uruguay, by agents of Mossad, Israel's intelligence and special operations agency.[32]

In Soviet-controlled Latvia, 365 former members of the Arajs Kommando were arrested after the war. They were persecuted and convicted. Forty-four of the defendants were sentenced to death, of whom thirty were executed. The rest received prison sentences with hard labour, ranging from ten to twenty-five years.

Karlis A. Ozols was a senior lieutenant in the Nazi-controlled Latvian auxiliary police. He later led a unit of the Latvian Security Service in war crimes committed in Minsk, the capital of present-day Belarus. In the spring of 1945 Ozols escaped from Riga by sea. He lived in West Germany until 1949, when he emigrated to Australia. Seven years later he became an Australian citizen. Ozols was never charged with war crimes. In 1956 he was Australia's chess champion. Ozols had won the bronze medal in the unofficial Chess Olympiad in Berlin in 1936. He died on 26 March 2001 in Australia, aged 89.

Konrāds Kalējs was an official of the Latvian security police during Nazi rule. In 1945 he fled to Denmark and five years later he emigrated to Australia. Kalējs became an Australian citizen in 1957. He later moved to the United States. When his Nazi past was revealed by the press, Kalējs was deported to Canada. In 1999 he was deported to England and from there to Australia. His extradition to Latvia to be tried for war crimes was eventually ordered by a Melbourne court but it was never carried out because Kalējs was suffering from dementia and had prostate cancer. He died on 8 November 1981 in Melbourne, aged 88.

About a thousand former members of the Latvian Legion were employed by the US Army after the war to guard top Nazi officials during their trial in Nuremberg. Baltic (mostly Latvian) former POWs were also employed to guard US military installations in West Berlin during the 323-day blockade of the non-communist zone of the city by the Soviet forces between June 1948 and May 1949.

On 15 March every year veterans of the Latvian Legion, as well as Nazi sympathisers, parade in Riga, carrying flags and posters, and then lay wreaths at the Monument of Freedom. In 2019, the number of those who paraded, estimated at a thousand, was larger than in years past.[33]

Lithuanians

The lack of volunteers for a pro-German 'Legion' in Lithuania led to a compromise: the formation of 3,000-strong engineering unit (Litauische Bau-Bataillonen) consisting of five battalions and a number of auxiliary air defence battalions. The short-lived Lithuanian Territorial Defence Force (LTDF), made up of conscripts, was raised in 1943. After brief engagements against Soviet and Polish (Home Army) partisans, the 10,000-strong force was disbanded. Many of the men either joined other Nazi auxiliary forces or started forming anti-Soviet resistance groups.

Lieutenant General Petras Kubiliūnas had fought against the Red Army from August until December 1919 during the Lithuanian–Soviet War. He was the highest-ranking Lithuanian in the country's German administration between 1941 and 1944. After the German withdrawal from his country, Kubiliūnas fled to Germany and managed to reach the British occupation zone. In December 1945 he was kidnapped from a farm in Schleswig-Holstein, northern Germany, by Soviet (NKVD) agents and transported to Moscow. He was tried for treason and other crimes by a military tribunal and sentenced to death. Kubiliūnas was executed on 22 August 1946 in Moscow, aged 52.

Major Jonas Semaška and Captain Jonas Noreika also fell into Soviet hands after the war. Semaška had been wounded fighting against the Red Army while commanding the 13th Battalion of the LTDF. After the capitulation of Nazi Germany on 8 May 1945, Semaška returned to Lithuania and joined the anti-communist partisans. On 15 April 1946 he was arrested in Telšiai, in north-west Lithuania. He was charged with treason and collaborationism and sentenced to death. Semaška was executed on 21 January 1947 in Vilnius, aged 39. His wife and his 9-year-old son were exiled to Siberia.

Noreika was a former Lithuanian army captain who collaborated with the Nazis. He organised and led the Lithuanian Activist Group, a paramilitary force that was involved in atrocities, including the massacre of 1,800 Jews in Plungé, in north-west Lithuania, on 3 August 1941. He was later appointed governor of the Šiauliai district in northern Lithuania. In March 1943 Noreika was arrested by the SS for failing to raise a Waffen-SS division from the local population and sent to concentration camps in Poland. In late 1944 he was liberated by Soviet forces and in early May 1945 he was drafted into the Red Army. On 18 March 1946 Noreika was arrested, charged with collaboration and war crimes and sentenced to death. He was executed by firing squad on 26 February 1947 in Vilnius, aged 36.

Aleksandras Lileikis was chief of the Secret Police in Vilnius. He was suspected of the murder of thousands of Jews and Roma. Lileikis fled to Germany and before emigrating to the United States in 1955 he did some work for the CIA. In 1976 he became a naturalised American citizen. In 1994, when his Nazi past was revealed, Lileikis was stripped of US citizenship.[34] Four years later he returned to Lithuania. On 6 February 1998 Lileikis was charged with genocide and imprisoned. He died of a heart attack on 26 September 2000 in Vilnius, aged 93.

General Povilas Plechavičius commanded the LTDF. On 15 May 1944 he was arrested by the Red Army and detained in Salaspils concentration camp in Latvia. After his release in July 1944, Plechavičius escaped to the west. Five years later, he emigrated to the United States. Plechavičius died in Chicago on 19 December 1973, aged 83.

Kazys Škirpa was appointed premier of a provisional government by the Germans. In June 1944 he was arrested by the Gestapo and detained briefly. Škirpa fled to the west, evading capture by the advancing Soviet forces, and reached Ireland via Paris. He taught Russian in Trinity College, Dublin, until 1949, when he emigrated to the United States. Škirpa died on 18 August 1979 in Washington, aged 84.

Arabs and Indians

Arab volunteers were organised by the German Army in German-occupied France, Iraq and Tunisia. In May 1941 in Iraq, after a revolt led by pro-German Rashid el Galiani, the Germans raised Sonderverband 287, a unit consisting of Iraqi and Palestinian volunteers. After the collapse of the revolt, the unit was deployed near Athens in Greece.[35] The German-officered Sonderverband 287 eventually reached the strength of three battalions.

The Free Arab Legion (FAL), the North African Legion (NAL) and the African Phalange (AP) were formed in 1943. The FAL was made up of Arabs from various countries in the Middle East; the NAL was raised from Muslims resident in German-occupied France; while the PA (Phalange Africaine in French) was made up of 300 Vichy French and 150 North African Muslims. Arab and Muslim units of the German Army fought in the Caucasus, Yugoslavia and North Africa. Five battalions of the 5th Panzer Army in Tunisia were made up of Arab and Muslim volunteers.

Amin Al-Husseini was a Palestinian Arab nationalist and Grand Mufti of Jerusalem. He was also a Muslim leader in Mandatory Palestine. During the war, he collaborated with Germany and Italy by making propagandist radio broadcasts and by helping Nazis and fascists to recruit Bosnian Muslims for the Waffen-SS. After the war, he sought protection in Cairo to avoid prosecution as war criminal. He died on 4 July 1974 in Beirut, aged 79.

The Free India Legion (FIL) was made up of British Indian soldiers captured by the Axis forces in North Africa and of Indian expatriates in Europe. It was led by Subbas Chandra Bose, an extremist nationalist Indian, and was intended to serve as a liberation force for British-ruled India. He fled his country as he was wanted by the British authorities for his political activities and reached Berlin through Afghanistan and the USSR. Bose persuaded the Germans to raise the FIL. By the end of the year the three-battalion unit had about 2,000 men. From August 1944 to May 1945 the FIL was a component of the Waffen-SS. It was stationed initially in France (Bordeaux) and later in Germany. Indian volunteers did not engage in direct combat until the end of the war.

In 1943 Bose travelled to Japanese-occupied Singapore in German U-boat *U-180* to help organise the parallel Indian National Army (INA) recruited from Indian prisoners in Japanese hands.[36] Two divisions were raised in October 1943. The 43,000-strong INA were engaged in operations, mostly in Burma. Bose died from his injuries on 18 August 1945 when the Japanese plane he was travelling in crashed near Taihoku, present-day Taipei, in Formosa (now Taiwan). He was 48 years old.

In Europe, after the German surrender the rest of the FIL members tried to reach neutral Switzerland over the Alps but were captured by US and French troops. A total of 7,600 Indians were taken prisoner in Europe and shipped to India to face charges of treason. Nearly 16,000 Indians surrendered to British and Commonwealth forces in Burma and Singapore in August 1945.[37] They were also shipped to India, where they were interrogated and detained for at least three months. About 11,000 were released and the rest were accused of treason, but their trials, which began in November 1946, were never completed.

Major Generals Prem Sahgal, Mohammed Zaman Kiani and Shah Nawaz Khan, who commanded formations of the INA, were accused of treason and imprisoned for several months but were not convicted. They were dismissed from the British Indian Army and banned from serving in the post-war armies of India and Pakistan. This condition, enforced by the British in the agreement for the independence of the two countries, applied to all FIL and INA officers and other ranks. Sahgal died on 17 October 1992 in India, aged 75. Kiani died on 4 June 1981 in Pakistan, aged 70. Khan died on 9 December 1983 in India, aged 69.

An Indian battalion was raised in Italy in July 1942. The unit, consisting of Indian POWs, was Italian-officered. A long-term Indian resident of Rome, Mohammad Iqbal Shedai, an activist, was appointed political commissar of the Battaglione Azad Hindustan. They did not see any combat. In November 1942 the unit was dissolved following a mutiny and the 400 men were sent back to POW camps. Shedai evaded capture when Rome was occupied by Allied forces in 1944 by fleeing north and later leaving Italy. In 1947 he settled in Lahore, north-east Pakistan, with his French wife. In the 1950s Shedai taught Hindu in the University of Turin. He died on 13 January 1974 in Lahore, aged 86.

Chinese and White Russians

The Japanese set up several puppet regimes in occupied Chinese territories, including Manchukuo (1932), Mengkukuo (1936), Wang Kemin (1938) and Wang Jingwei (1940). The Manchukuo Imperial Army could field up to 220,000 men. The military forces of these regimes, known collectively as the Collaborationist Chinese Army, numbered more than one million at their height, although other estimates put the number at 2 million conscripts. This number included the 600,000-strong National Revolutionary Army or Peacekeeping National Army. The four infantry and two cavalry divisions of the Inner Mongolian Army were also a collaborationist force. Both formations were destroyed by the Red Army in August 1945, as well as the Asano Detachment, a unit made up of White Russian volunteers living in Manchuria. At various times the detachment numbered from 300 to 3,000 men.[38] They were part of the 162nd Rifle Regiment of the Japanese armed forces in Manchukuo. The Russians were perhaps the only Europeans to fight for Japan in the Second World War. They were anti-communists hoping to overthrow the Soviet regime[39] and fought directly against the Red Army.

Ethnic Boyats who had left the Soviet Union and Outer Mongolia because of the Stalinist purges in the 1930s were also conscripted into the Japanese Army. After the Japanese surrender, most of the Russian volunteers were taken prisoner by the Red Army and taken to the Soviet Union en masse. Their more senior figures were executed, while others were sent to forced labour camps of the Gulag system for up to fifteen years.

IMPRISONING THE ENEMY

Urzhin Garmaev, a former junior officer of the Russian White Army, left the Soviet Union during the civil war. He was employed by the Manchukuo Imperial Army, eventually rising to the rank of lieutenant general. He led Buryat-Mongolian collaborationist troops in battles against the Red Army in the Khalkhyn Temple in 1935 and near the Khalkhyn Gol River four years later. In September 1945 Garmaev was captured by Soviet forces and sent to Moscow. He was convicted of treason and executed on 13 March 1947, aged 59.

The survivors of these forces were detained after the war in Soviet POW camps or in rehabilitation camps of the Chinese communist regime. Some 300,000 to 500,000 Chinese collaborationists voluntarily joined the Japanese military, mostly as auxiliary personnel. In the Imperial Japanese Navy (IJN) they manned surface units conducting coastguard missions. In IJA and IJA aviation units they were only assigned transport missions. Following the Japanese surrender, most of the survivors joined the fight against Soviet and Chinese communist forces in various parts of China. Others were detained in Soviet POW camps or in the rehabilitation camps of China's post-war communist regime.

Three Chinese generals defected to the Japanese during the Japanese invasion of Manchuria in 1931. They were Zhang Jinghuei, Zhang Shiyi and Xi Qia. When he collaborated, Zhang Jinghui was governor of Harbin, in north-east China. From 1935 to 1945 he served as prime minister of the Japanese puppet regime of Manchukuo. Zhang Shiyi was governor of Liaoning province at the time of the Japanese invasion. As a collaborator he held the largely ceremonial post of Speaker of the Senate in Manchukuo. Xi Qia was in command of the Kirin provincial army in north-east China. After his defection, he became the minister of finance (1934) and interior (1936) in Manchukuo cabinets. All three were captured by the Red Army in late August 1945 following the Soviet invasion of Manchuria. They were held in a Siberian prison for five years and then extradited to the newly founded People's Republic of China (PRC). They were detained at the Fushun war criminals' management centre in Liaoning province, in the north-eastern part of the PRC. Xi Qia died in Fushun months later, aged 67. Zhang Shiyi died of illness in Fushun on 13 November 1956, aged 72. Zhang Jinghui also died in Fushun three years later, on 11 January 1959, aged 88.

The fate of the various commanders of the collaborationist National Revolutionary Army (NLA) in the summer of 1945, after their capture by or surrender to Chinese nationalist (Kuomintang) or Chinese communist forces, varied. General Yang Kuiyi was executed by Chinese nationalists and Generals Sun Dianying and Bao Wenyue died in a communist prison. Lieutenant General Xiao Shuxwan was killed while resisting arrest and Lieutenant General Ye Peng was executed by Chinese Nationalists.

General Yang Kuiyi was the governor of Hubei province in central China. He was tried for treason in Nanjing, then capital of China, by a Kuomintang tribunal and sentenced to death. He was executed in October 1945, aged 60.

General Sun Dianying commanded a 600,000-strong force of the NLA. He was captured on 2 May 1947 by elements of the (communist) People's Liberation Army. He died in prison at Wu'an in northern China on 1 October 1948, aged 61.

General Bao Wenyue served as war minister in the Nanjing collaborationist government of Wang Jingwei. In the summer of 1945 he was arrested by Kuomintang troops and convicted of treason. The death sentence handed down by a Nanjing court was never carried out. He was later transferred to a prison in Formosa and remained in custody until 1975. He died five years later in Taipei, the capital of Formosa, aged 88.

Lieutenant General Xiao Shuxwan was killed in 1945 while resisting arrest, aged 51. Lieutenant General Ye Peng was a member of the Nanjing collaborationist government. After his capture in 1945 by Chinese nationalists, he was initially spared and later allowed to serve under Chiang Kai-shek's Kuomintang administration. However, on 18 September 1947 Ye Peng was arrested and convicted of treason. He was sentenced to death and executed, aged 50.

General Pang Bingxuan commanded the 24th 'Army Group' of the NLA. In August 1945 he surrendered himself and his troops to Kuomintang forces in Nanjing. He was later allowed to serve Chiang Kai-shek. In 1948 he followed the Nationalist leaders to Formosa. Pang Bingxuan died on 12 January 1963 in Taipei, aged 83.

General (warlord) Ren Yundao had organised a 20,000-strong collaborationist army during his country's Japanese occupation. At the war's end he fled to the British-controlled Hong Kong and from there emigrated to Canada.[40] Ren Yundao died in Canada in 1980, aged 90.

The Empire of Japan started recruiting volunteers from several occupied regions of the Far East and the South-East Asia during the war, particularly when its human resources were stretched thinly and its military needed additional troops. It is estimated that a total of 207,182 Formosans served in the Japanese armed forces during the war. From 1937 to 1945 more than 207,000 Formosans were employed by the Japanese military. At least 27,000 of these volunteers were killed or presumed killed in action.[41] The 5,000-strong Tagasago Volunteers were soldiers of the IJA recruited from Formosan indigenous peoples. They were trained to carry out special operations and anti-guerrilla missions.

Koreans

On 9 May 1942 the Japanese colonial government of Korea announced that, beginning in December 1944, Korean men would be drafted into the IJA. It was decided when the tide of war turned against Japan and took about thirty months from the initial announcement to the enlistment of the first Koreans. Until then only 18,000 Koreans had passed the tests for induction into the IJA. The Gando Special Force (GSF) was an independent battalion within the Manchukuo army composed primarily of ethnic Koreans.[42] (Gando in Korean means eastern Manchuria.) By the end of the war about 110,000 conscripts served with the Japanese military. According to another estimate, up to 200,000 Korean males were inducted into the IJA. The Japanese did not normally trust Koreans on combat missions and they were mostly used as service troops. Many of the commandants and armed guards in POW camps were Korean. They were sometimes more cruel than the Japanese.[43] A further 400,000 Korean labourers were involuntarily sent to Japan to support its war effort.

Korea produced seven generals and numerous field grade offices (colonels, lieutenant colonels and majors) during thirty-five years of colonial governance by Japan, despite institutionalised discrimination. Lieutenant General Honk Sa-ik was one of them. He was arrested by the US Army in September 1945 and indicted for war crimes, having been in charge of POW camps in the southern part of the Philippines during the Japanese occupation. Honk was found guilty as charged by a US military court during the Manila trials and sentenced to death on 18 April 1946. He was executed by hanging on 26 September, aged 59. His wife and his son lived a nightmare in postwar Korea. They could not get any employment and lived in poverty until they were allowed to emigrate to the United States.

Japanese-educated Yi Un was the imperial crown prince of Korea until the annexation of his country by the Japanese in 1910. He made a career in the Japanese Army, rising to the rank of lieutenant general. From July 1943 to April 1945 Yi Un (also known as Eun) commanded the Japanese First Air Army. After the war he lost his royal status and was permitted to return to Korea in the 1960s on health grounds. Yi Un died on 1 May 1970 in Seoul, aged 72.

Kim Suk-won, an ethnic Korean and a 1913 graduate of the Imperial Military Academy in Tokyo, was an IJA colonel when Japan surrendered to the Allies. He was then commissioned by the military of the US-controlled Republic of Korea (ROK). He took part in the Korean War and retired in 1956 as a brigadier general. Kim died on 6 August 1978 in Seoul, aged 84.

Chung Il-kuon, a Russian-born ethnic Korean, assumed a Japanese name (Ikken Nakajima) and made a career in the IJA as a cavalry officer. He rose to the rank of colonel. In August 1945, following the Soviet invasion of Manchuria, Chung was held briefly by the Red Army. In 1946, after moving to the US-controlled southern part of the Korean Peninsula, he was commissioned by the army of the ROK. Chung was promoted to major general during the Korean War, aged 33. He retired from the military in 1957 and seven years later he became prime minister of the ROK. Chung died on 17 January 1994 in the United States, aged 76. He had been hospitalised in Hawaii suffering from lymph cancer.[44]

Japanese-educated Korean Jang Do-young served in the Japanese Army as a lieutenant during the Second World War. In 1945 he enrolled in the military of the ROK and later commanded troops during the Korean War. Jang rose to the rank of lieutenant general. In May 1961 he was made prime minister following a military coup. Three months later he was brought down and forced into exile. He died on 3 August 2012 in Orlando, in the United States, aged 89.

Baik Sun-yup commanded Japanese units, mostly in Manchuria. He also led troopers of the Gando Special Force in several missions against Chinese Communist forces in Jiandao, eastern Manchuria. In December 1945, still a colonel in the IJA, he fled southward, evading capture by the Red Army or by Korean communist troops. After reaching the US-controlled part of the Korean peninsula, Baik joined the army of the ROK and later fought during the Korean War. After his retirement in 1960, he served as his country's ambassador in many countries, including France, Spain and Belgium. Baik died on 10 July 2020 in Seoul four months short of his 100th birthday.

After the war, 173 Formosans and 148 Koreans (mostly charged with Class B and Class C war crimes) were tried as war criminals. Of them, twenty-three Koreans and twenty-six Formosans were sentenced to death.[45] Of the Formosans convicted of war crimes, twenty-one were sentenced to death and executed. Of the remainder, 147 received prison sentences.[46] Collaborationist armies were also raised in the Japanese-occupied territories of Dutch East Indies (present-day Indonesia), Burma (present-day Myanmar) and Malaysia. The Defenders of the Motherland (Pembela Tanah Air or PETA) was made up of 57,000 Nationalists in the Dutch East Indies, split into sixty-nine daidan (battalions). The Burmese National Army (BNA) was established in December 1941 by Aung San as a collaborationist force. Within five months its strength had risen to 23,000 men. In March 1945 the BNA switched sides and started fighting against the retreating Japanese troops.[47] In Japanese-occupied Malaysia, a 2,000-strong a collaborationist force consisting of Malays and Indians, the Malayan Volunteer Army, emerged in April 1944.

In these territories the collaborators did not face such problems as was the case in Asia and Europe after the withdrawal of the occupation forces. They joined the struggle for their countries' independence and many of them, mostly officers, later formed the core of the fledging Indonesian, Malaysian and Burmese military.

Propaganda broadcasters

Hans Fritzsche, a popular radio commentator and head of the news division of the Nazi Propaganda Ministry, was acquitted at Nuremberg because the court was not prepared to accept that his broadcasts were intended to incite the German people to commit atrocities or conquer other peoples.[48] However, he was later classified as a major offender by a West German denazification court, which sent him to prison for eight years.[49] Fritzsche died on 27 September 1953 in Cologne, aged 53.

After the war, a number of foreign nationals were arrested for willingly broadcasting Nazi propaganda from Germany, Italy and Japan. They were convicted of treason. Two Nazi sympathisers, Paul Ferdennet and Jean Hérold-Paquis, were convicted in France for carrying out propaganda work for the Germans during their country's occupation by Axis forces. Ferdennet, a French journalist, worked for Radio Stuttgart until 1942. He broadcast propaganda aiming at demoralising French soldiers and civilians.[50] Hérold-Paquis, another French journalist, broadcast propaganda from Paris. In early 1945 Ferdennet was arrested, tried and convicted of treason. He was sentenced to death and executed on 4 August, aged 44.

Hérold-Paquis had fought with nationalists during the Spanish civil war. He headed the propaganda mechanism of France's collaborationist Vichy administration. Hérold-Paquis also broadcast daily news as well as comments in which he called for the destruction of Great Britain.[51] After the liberation of France, he fled to Germany and went from there to Switzerland. In mid-1945 Hérold-Paquis was handed over by the Swiss to the French authorities, who charged him with treason and sentenced him to death. He was executed in the fort at Châtillon on 11 October 1945, aged 33.

John Amery was a British Nazi collaborator. The idea of raising the British Free Corps to fight alongside German forces on the East Front came from him. A stout anti-communist, Amery left England in 1936 and settled in Paris. After the German occupation of France, he moved to Berlin, from where he broadcast and wrote Nazi propaganda. In 1944 Amery moved to Italy. On 25 April 1945 he was captured near Como by Italian partisans, who turned him over to the Allied military authorities in Milan. He was then transferred to London. In November 1945 Amery was tried and, to general astonishment, he pleaded guilty to eight charges of treason. He was sentenced to death. Amery was hanged by Albert Pierrepoint in Wandsworth Prison on 19 December 1945, aged 33.[52]

Norman Baillie-Stewart was a British citizen who also broadcast propaganda for the Nazis. He was a junior officer (subaltern) in the Seaforth Highlanders Regiment in 1933 when he was arrested and court-martialled for passing military information to German agents. Four years later, after his release from prison, Baillie-Stewart went to Germany via Austria. In August 1937 he was employed by the Reich broadcasting corporation.[53] In mid-1945, after the German capitulation, Baillie-Stewart was arrested by Allied troops at Altaussee, in central Austria. He was later convicted in England of treason and collaboration with the enemy and sentenced to five years' imprisonment. The relatively light conviction was due to the fact that he was by then a naturalised German citizen and had formally denounced his British citizenship. In May 1949, after his release from H.M. Prison Pankhurst, Baillie-Stewart moved to Ireland. He died of a heart attack in a pub in Harmstown, near Dublin, on 7 June 1966, aged 57.[54]

Raymond Davies Hughes also recorded propaganda broadcasts for the Germans. He was an RAF airman whose Lancaster bomber was shot down over north-eastern Germany on 17 August 1943 during a raid on the Peenemünde rocket installations. Davies Hughes was parachuted to safety. He was later captured and detained in a POW camp. He was spared the detention when he agreed to make propaganda broadcasts in Welsh for the Nazis. In mid-1944 his broadcasting activity came to an end and Davies Hughes was sent back to the POW camp. In early 1945 the camp was liberated by the Red Army and the airman was handed over to British military authorities. In August 1945 Davies Hughes was court-martialled at RAF Uxbridge and sentenced to five year's hard labour for collaboration. His sentence was subsequently reduced to two years following an appeal for clemency. He died on 4 April 1999 in Cheltenham, aged 76.

US-born William Brooke Joyce, nicknamed Lord Haw-Haw, was a prominent English language propaganda broadcaster in Nazi Germany during the war. He was a member of the British Union of Fascists (BUF) under Sir Oswald Mosley from 1931. In 1937 he moved to Berlin, where he was employed by the Nazi broadcasting corporation in September 1939, three days after the declaration of war between Great Britain and Nazi Germany. As of the summer of 1942 he became a commentator, calling on the British to surrender. His British wife, Margaret Cairns Joyce, a typist and former dancer, also worked in the broadcasting house (Rundfunkhaus) as a newsreader. She was nicknamed Lady Haw-Haw. After the war, Lord Haw-Haw was arrested by British troops at Flensburg, a north-German city close to the border with Denmark. He was shot wounded during his arrest.[55] Joyce was later tried at the Old Bailey on three counts of high treason and sentenced to death. He was hanged on 3 January 1946 at Wandsworth Prison, aged 39. His wife was not charged with anything. After being detained for some time in Holoway Prison, she was released. Margaret Cairns Joyce died in London, in 1972.

Three American journalists were arrested, tried and convicted after the war for broadcasting propaganda from Nazi Germany. They were Robert Henry Best, Douglas Chandler and Herbert J. Burgman. Best was a Vienna-based correspondent for the United Press. He started commenting on German state radio on April 1942 under the pseudonym 'Mr Guess Who'. Best was arrested by British troops on 29 January 1946 in Carinthia, the southernmost state of present-day Austria. He was handed over to the US military authorities. Chandler had lived in Germany since 1931. He broadcast propaganda from Berlin under the pseudonym 'Paul Revere' and made his last broadcasts from Munich in February 1945. Three months later Chandler was arrested by US troops at his home in Durach, in Bavaria. He was released, but arrested again in June 1946.

Best and Chandler were sentenced to life imprisonment by the Boston Federal District Court, Massachusetts, on 6 June 1947[56] and on 16 April 1948 respectively. Best died of a brain haemorrhage on 16 December 1952 in the medical centre for federal prisoners in Springfield, Missouri, aged 56.[57] Chandler's life sentence was commuted sixteen years later. He was released from prison on the condition that he leave the country immediately. After his discharge, Chandler went to West Germany. He died in the 1970s in West Germany or in the Canary Islands.

Burgman was also convicted of broadcasting propaganda from Berlin during the war. He married a German national in 1924 and was later employed by the US embassy in Berlin. Burgman was arrested at his home in Rumpenheim, near Frankfurt, in November 1945. He was convicted of treason on 11 November 1949 by the Washington D.C. District Court[58] and sentenced to ten years' imprisonment. Burgman died in the medical centre for federal prisoners in Springfield on 16 December 1953, aged 59.

Frederick Wilhelm Kaltenbach, an American journalist of German ancestry, was another Nazi propaganda broadcaster. A post-graduate of the University of Berlin, he settled in the German capital after his marriage to German national, Dorothea Peters. He did a lot of propaganda work for the Nazis, including broadcasting. Kaltenbach was arrested in his house in Berlin by the Red Army. He died in Soviet Special Camp 2 in Buchenwald in October 1945, aged 50.[59]

Slovenian-born Lyenko Urbanchich was a Nazi collaborator who broadcast anti-communist propaganda on Radio Ljubljana from late 1941 until early 1944. When Josip Broz Tito's communist forces won the war in Yugoslavia, Urbanchich fled to Austria. He remained in British custody until May 1948. Two years later he was able to emigrate to Australia. Urbanchich died on 22 February 2006 in Sydney, aged 84.

The first woman to be convicted of treason against the United States was Mildred Elizabeth Gillars, known as Axis Sally, who did propaganda work as an announcer for the Reichs-Rundfunk-Gesellschaft (RRG), the German state radio. On 10 March 1949 she was sentenced by a US court to thirty years in prison. However, she was released on 10 June 1961. She died on 25 June 1988 of colon cancer in Colombus, Ohio, aged 87.[60]

Rita-Luisa Zucca, an Italian-American, was tried by an Italian military tribunal on charges of collaboration. She had broadcast propaganda from Rome and Milan during the war. On 29 March 1946 Zuca was sentenced to four-and a-half years in prison. She was released after nine months when the Italian government declared a general amnesty for collaborators. She died in Italy as she was stripped of the US citizenship in 1941, and because of her collaboration past she was barred from returning to the United States. Zucca died in 1998, aged 85 or 86.

Iva Toguri D'Aquino was an American citizen who freely participated in English-language radio broadcasts on the Zero Hour radio show, transmitted for propaganda purposes by Radio Tokyo. She became known to the Allied soldiers in South-East Asia and the Pacific as "Tokyo Rose". After the war, D'Aquino was arrested in Yokohama and tried for treason in San Francisco Federal District Court. On 29 September 1949 she was sentenced to ten years in prison. On 28 January 1956 she was paroled after six years and two months in a federal prison for women in Alderson, in west Virginia. Twenty-one years later, D' Aquino received a pardon from President Gerald Ford. The pardon restored her US citizenship, which had been abrogated as a result of the conviction.[61] She died on 26 September 2006 in Chicago, aged 90.

American journalist Jane Anderson was captured and tortured by Republican fighters in Spain in September 1936 while covering the country's civil war for the *London Daily Mail*. She was released one month later following a formal intervention by the US government. Between 1940 and 1945 Anderson transmitted Nazi propaganda from Berlin under the pseudonym Georgia Peach. On 2 April 1947 she was arrested by US troops in Salzburg, northern Austria. On 27 October 1947 the US Department of Justice dropped all charges against her for lack of evidence.[62] The fact that she took Spanish citizenship by marriage before the war possibly affected the decision. Anderson was released from US custody in Salzburg in early December 1947.[63] She moved to Madrid, where she died on 5 May 1972, aged 84.

PART THREE
RELEASE AND REPATRIATION

By September 1946, more than a year after the end of the war in Europe, 402,000 German prisoners of war (POWs) were still held in camps across Great Britain.[1] Many of them had been transferred from POW camps in the United States and Canada. For several reasons prisoners were not repatriated immediately after the end of hostilities in Europe. Great Britain could not afford to let go a cheap labour force, which was saving the population from starvation. Their labour was required to grow food and repair the war damage done.[2] In March 1947 170,000 POWs (all Germans because the last Italians had gone by late 1946) were working in agriculture, helping farmers bring in the harvest. Furthermore, German prisoners swept up the rubbish after the VE (Victory in Europe) Day celebrations and helped construct Wembley and other infrastructure for the Summer Olympics that were hosted in London in 1948. The Ministry of Agriculture argued against the repatriation of working German prisoners since they made up 25 per cent of the land workforce and it wanted to continue having them work in Great Britain until 1948.

In the United States some 14,000 repatriations were delayed in 1946 so prisoners could be used in the spring farming season. Certain Congressmen wanted POW labour extended beyond June 1946, but President Harry Truman rejected their proposal. After the war, German POWs were also used in several west European countries, including France, Belgium, Holland, Denmark and Norway, to de-mine and perform other dirty post-war tasks.[3] It was estimated by the French authorities that 2,000 prisoners were being killed or wounded each month by the end of 1945 while clearing minefields.[4] In Norway, the last available casualty record from August 1945 shows that by that time 275 German POWs had been killed and further 392 injured while performing de-mining tasks.

International law stipulated that POWs should be repatriated after a peace treaty was signed. However, with Germany occupied, the signing of a peace treaty was a remote possibility. In Germany there was a severe food shortage since fields had not been planted in 1945 and the entire infrastructure had been blown to pieces. Germans lived on rations of 1,500 to 1,750 calories per day until 1948. Shipping POWs back too early would be like sending them to starve. Germany, a country in ruins and split into zones of occupation, was simply unable to receive them. The practical use of arranging transports also hindered plans.

Furthermore, repatriating ardent Nazis among the POWs was considered imprudent. In Canada and the United States German prisoners were roughly labelled either black, grey or white, depending on their level of remaining indoctrination with Nazi ideology as judged on the basis of interviews. Those classified as white were given priority for release and repatriation.[5] In Great Britain they had been graded as to their attitude to the Nazi beliefs. Those who still thought that Hitler was right were graded 'C'. Those opposed to Nazism were graded 'A'. Those in a state of uncertainty were graded 'B'. Those graded 'A' were given priority in the release and repatriation procedure. Former Waffen-SS personnel and U-boat officers were graded 'C' and 'C+' and were among the last to be repatriated. Most of them were transferred to Oldham, a POW camp with a reputation for dealing with hard cases. The C-graded remained in British custody until 1949. In political screening carried out at Camp 668 at Aliwal in Wiltshire on 11 and 12 July 1945, twenty-five POWs out of 559 were given 'C'.[6] The rest were graded 'A' (ninety-four), 'B+' (one), 'B' (419) and 'B-' (twenty). Priority for repatriation was given by the review boards to German POWs who were builders, farmers, drivers, mechanics, etc.

The repatriation of German POWs from Great Britain began in September 1947. Those who were ill or had battle wounds had left earlier. All Germans had been sent home by 1948 except for about 25,000 who were given the opportunity to stay on. They preferred to remain where they had made a new life to returning to a war-damaged and divided country. Many of this group had married British women. Initially, there was a ban not only on 'romantic liaison', but also on fraternisation between Axis POWs and the local population. In Canada, five girls even faced charges under the Defence of Canada Act regulations. They were put on probation for their love letters to German POWs that had been intercepted.[7] On Sunday, 15 December 1946 it was announced by the BBC that the British government had lifted the ban on fraternisation with German prisoners.[8] Once the ban was lifted 736 marriages between German POWs and British women took place almost immediately.[9] More such marriages would follow. One English bride was Mary from Wellington, who married Wolfgang, a detainee at the Cluddley POW camp in 1946.[10] When she was asked about why she married a German, she always said: 'I did not marry a country, I married a man!' By late 1947, all restrictions on German POWs were almost completely removed. Those who applied to remain in Great Britain were interviewed to see whether they were suitable. If accepted, in accordance with the Geneva Convention, they were sent to Münsterlager (present-day Münster), in north-western Germany, to be officially discharged from their country's armed forces. Then, as civilians, they were given ration books, money and travel warrants to visit their families. They were allowed to stay in Germany for a month before returning to Great Britain.[11]

Eberhard Wendler was captured in June 1944 near Saint-Lô in Normandy. He was one of the 25,000 Germans who were allowed to stay on in Great Britain. He married Kathleen and became a British subject. Wendler worked as an electrical engineer.[12]

Of the German prisoners who stayed on in Great Britain, Sergeant (feldwebel) Bernd Trautmann, a former paratrooper, found his way from POW camp 50, near Wigan, to football glory as a goalkeeper for Manchester City. He fought on the Eastern and the Western fronts, was captured by Soviet and French troops and managed to escape on both occasions. As the war drew to a close, Trautmann was taken prisoner by British troops.[13] He was detained in POW camps in Belgium (Ostend) and England (Essex, Cheshire and Lancashire). He was released in 1948 and permitted to remain in the country. One year later, after playing amateur football for a non-league team in St Helens, north-west England, Trautmann signed for Manchester City, a first division club. In 1950, having already de-Germanised his Christian name from Bernd to Bert,[14] he married Margaret Friar. They went their separate ways in 1972. Trautmann played for City in 545 matches during a fifteen-year period between 1949 and 1964. In 1956 he won the Football Writers' Association Footballer of the Year award. Four years earlier City had turned down an offer from West German football club Schalke 04 to transfer him. Trautmann died at his home in Spain on 19 July 2013, aged 89, having suffered two heart attacks earlier in the year.[15]

Because of repatriation the number of German prisoners held on British soil declined as follows. In December 1946 the total number of German POWs was 355,200. In March 1947, they numbered 305,800; in June 267,250; in September 220,000; and in December 155,000. By the end of 1947 around 250,000 German prisoners had been repatriated. In March 1948 there were 82,000 German prisoners still living in Great Britain and three months later there were only 2,790 left. The last German POWs were repatriated in November 1948.

Up to a million repatriated prisoners stayed in camps along the Rhine River, the so-called Rheinwiesenlager.[16] For some time after their arrival home food was scarce for most of the repatriated German prisoners; the conditions were overcrowded and treatment was generally rough.[17] Many of them did not survive the harsh conditions of having to camp outdoors without a shelter for months. In Friedland, near Göttingen, in central Germany, 1,000 former German POWs who had arrived from England were exchanged for an equal number of prisoners released by the Red Army.[18] Only through a specific procedure were former POWs able to switch zones in Germany, from the Russian to the western Allied and vice versa, and unite with relatives. A number of German prisoners committed suicide prior to their repatriation because they did not want to live under communism in Eastern Germany. On 25 June 1946, in Braham Castle (Camp 109), near Dingwall, Ross-shire, in the Scottish Highlands, Fritz Saalbach, a German POW, hanged himself in the bathroom of the prisoners' compound.[19] At Fort Dix POW camp, near Trenton, in New Jersey, in the United States, three Russians committed suicide on 29 June 1945, fifty-two days after the fighting in Europe ended.

First Lieutenant Feoktist Kalinin, Second Lieutenant Ignatz Nasarenko and Private Felip Spotow were deserters from the Red Army who had been taken prisoner by western Allied troops, fighting as members of a German battalion. They hanged themselves while facing repatriation to the country they had betrayed.

In Egypt, repatriation began in 1946 with the first group of 6,000 German prisoners being shipped home. The pace of repatriation was remarkably slow due to a shortage of ships, however it was mostly complete by the end of 1948. A point of contention was that the repatriated were not allowed to take out of Egypt more than £10 worth of goods, when many had saved their tiny wages for months and years to take foodstuffs back home to their families.[20] Due to a lack of shipping the repatriation of prisoners from Australia also proved difficult. The main problem was that Great Britain, which controlled the majority of Empire shipping, needed the ships to return troops from Asia. Consequently, most of the Italian POWs had to wait at least six months to be repatriated from Australia.

A total of 2.8 million German Wehrmacht personnel were held as POWs by the USSR at the end of the war, according to Soviet records. Soviet captivity meant labour camps and re-education for up to ten years or death.[21] Quite a large number of German POWs had been released by the end of 1946.[22] The first to be released and repatriated were anti-Nazi prisoners, with the weakened, the chronically ill and the disabled to follow. In 1948 there were about 840,000 German POWs still held in the USSR.[23] At the time of the creation of a communist state in the Soviet-occupied zone of Germany, the German Democratic Republic or GDR, in October 1949 all but 85,000 POWs had been released and repatriated. Most of those still held had been convicted as war criminals and many were convicted to long terms (usually twenty-five years) in forced labour camps. It was not until 1956 that the last of these 'war convicts' (kriegsverurteilte), about 15,000 men, were repatriated following the intervention of West German chancellor Konrad Adenauer in Moscow.

Prisoners of war who were not returned to their homelands by 1956 were declared criminals by the Soviet authorities and transferred to forced labour camps or to special regime prisons. They were usually members of the SS, high-level officers, or POWs who had violated a regulation while under control of the Main Administration of Prisoners of War and Internees. This administration, better known in the Soviet Union under its initials in Russian, GUPVI, was shut down by 1956. Among the last to be released and repatriated was Colonel Erich Hartmann, the highest-scoring (352 victories) fighter ace in the history of aerial warfare.[24] He had been declared guilty of war crimes but without due process.

By 1953 about 2,356 Europeans who had been captured by the Red Army while fighting as volunteers with German Army or Waffen-SS units had also been released from POW camps and repatriated to their countries of origin.[25] According to the same (Russian) source, they comprised: 145,790 Austrians, 65,954 Czech and Slovaks, 57,149 Poles, 21,811 French, 20,354 Yugoslav (mostly Croatians), 4,530 Dutch, 1,833 Belgians, 421 Danes, 382 Spaniards and eighty-three Norwegians. Some 10,085 Italian prisoners were repatriated between 1945 and 1954. Most of these were allowed to return home in 1945–46. In 1946 a group of Italian officers were accused of war crimes and sentenced to many years of forced labour. After the death of Stalin, the accusations were proved to be false and they were released in 1954. In 1945 61,662 Romanian POWs were repatriated from the Soviet Union.[26] The last Romanian and Hungarian POWs were repatriated in 1956. A number of Second World War prisoners of various European nationalities did not return to their countries until the collapse of the Soviet Union in the early 1990s. Others who had settled and started families opted to remain.[27]

The repatriation of Japanese POWs from the USSR began in 1946 – ten years before the normalisation of relations between the Soviet Union and Japan. The repatriated prisoners numbered 18,616 in 1946, 166,240 in 1947 and about 175,000 in 1948. By late 1949 about 97,000 had been repatriated and a further 971 had been transferred to the People's Republic of China. The repatriated figure given for 1950 is 1,585. The Japanese who chose to stay in the Soviet Union after their release from captivity numbered 2,988. Beginning in 1949, there were reports of returnees being

RELEASE AND REPATRIATION

uncooperative and hostile upon returning to Japan, owing to communist propaganda they had been subjected to during their imprisonment. These incidents resulted in the Japanese public gaining a more negative perception of the returning soldiers and increased the hostility of the country's occupation authorities towards the left wing in post-war Japan.

Japanese POWs held in Communist China were released between 1956 and 1964. The Manchukuo and Kuomintang prisoners were released between 1959 and 1975. They were held mostly at Fushun War Criminal Management Centre, also known as Liaoning No. 3 Prison, in Liaoning, a coastal province in north-east China. The Kuomintang prisoners were incarcerated by the communist regime for twenty-five years. They were never put on trial. The People's Republic of China permitted them to go to Taiwan, where they were refused entry. The Taiwanese authorities did not want to let them in as they believed that they had been brainwashed by the communists.

In January 1945 192 US and 227 Japanese ships were employed for the repatriation of Japanese POWs from overseas. The repatriation of the Japanese who were held in New Zealand began in late 1945. At least 800 prisoners were transported in two trains from Featherstone to Wellington. They left for Japan on two American tank landing ships, LST-273 and LST-275, on 30 December.[28] They arrived home on 4 February 1946 after making stops at the islands of Guam and Guadalcanal.

Andras Tomas, a Hungarian army conscript, was probably the last Second World War POW to be released. He was repatriated aged 75 after five decades in Soviet forced labour camps, gulags and psychiatric hospitals.[29] He had been captured by the Red Army in autumn 1944 during the defence of Nyíregyháza, north-east Hungary, by German and Hungarian troops. Toma was hidden from sight in a mental hospital in Kotelnich, 600 miles east of Moscow. He was flown home on 11 August 2000 in a wheelchair as he had a leg amputated.[30]

Korean-born Private Yang Kyoungjong is a case of his own. He fought for Japan, the USSR and Nazi Germany during the Second World War and was also detained in Soviet, German and American POW camps. In 1938 the Japanese made him fight with their army against Soviet forces in Manchuria. After his capture by the Red Army, Kyoungjong was persuaded to join the Soviet military and fight against the Germans. After his capture by the German Army, he was persuaded to join the Wehrmacht and fight against the Allies. Elements of the American 101st Airborne Division caught him after D-Day in Normandy in summer 1944 and put him in a POW camp. According to another source, the Korean soldier of the Wehrmacht was taken prisoner by British troops, who handed him over to the US Army.[31] After the war, Kyoungjong was permitted to emigrate to the United States. He died there in 1992, aged 72. Antony Beevor[32] and Steven Zaloga[33] regard Kyoungjong's existence a fact, but information about him is very limited worldwide.

BIBLIOGRAPHY AND RECOMMENDED READING

Adam, Thomas, *Admiral Graf Spee, Germany and the Americas*, ABC-CLIO, 2005
Adam-Smith, Patsy, *Prisoners of War. From Gallipoli to Korea*, Penguin, 1992
Ahrenfeldt, Robert H., *Psychiatry in the British Army in the Second World War*, Routledge, 2018
Allen, Louis, *Burma: The Longest War 1941–1945*, Phoenix Press, 2000
Aliko, Tomor, *Genocide of the Intellectual Elite of the Albanian Nation under Communist Terror*, Shtypshkronja Maluka, 2007
Annas, George J., *The Nazi Doctors and the Nuremberg Code*, Oxford University Press, 1995
Andreyev, Catherine, *General Vlasov and the Russian Liberation Movement*, Cambridge University Press, 1987
Antill, Peter D., *Crete 1941: Germany's Lightning Airborne Assault*, Osprey Publishing, 2005
Arad, Yitzak, *Belzec, Sobibór, Treblinka: The Operation Reinhard Death Camps*, Indiana University Press, 1987
Arendt, Hannah, *Eichmann in Jerusalem: A Report on the Banality of Evil*, Penguin Books, 1963
Axelrod, Alan, *Real History of The Second World War. A New Look of the Past*, Sterling Publishing, 2008
Axworthy, Max; Şerbanescu, Horia, *The Romanian Army of The Second World War*, Osprey Publishing, 1991
Bahm, Karl, *Berlin in 1945: The Final Reckoning April 1945*, Motorbooks International, 2001
Bailey, Ronald H., *Partisans and Guerrillas (The Second World War)*, Time-Life Books, 1979
Bailey, Ronald H., *Prisoners of War*, Time-Life Books, 1981
Baker, David, *Adolf Galland: The Authorised Biography*, Windrow & Green, 1998
Baratieri, Daniela; Edele, Mark; Finaldi, Giuseppe, *Perspectives of the Nuremberg Trial*, Routledge, 2013
Barnet, Corelli (ed.), *Hitler's Generals*, Phoenix, 1989
Barret, David, *Chinese Collaboration with Japan 1932–1945. The Limits of Accommodation*, Stanford University Press, 2002
Bartov, Omer, *The Eastern Front 1941–1945: German Troops and the Barbarization of Warfare*, Palgrave Macmillan, 2001
Bartrop, Paul R.; Totten, Samuel, *Dictionary of Genocide*, Greenwood, 2008

BIBLIOGRAPHY AND RECOMMENDED READING

Battistelli, Pier Paolo, *The Balkans 1940–1941. Mussolini's Blunder in the Greco-Italian War*, Bloomsbury Publishing, 2021
Baumel, Judith; et al, *Holocaust Encyclopedia*, Yale University Press, 2001
Beevor, Antony, *Crete: The Battle and the Resistance*, Westview Press, 1994
Beevor, Antony, *Stalingrad, The Fateful Siege 1942–1943*, Penguin Books, 1999
Beevor, Antony, *The Second World War*, Little Brown & Company, 2012
Bergström, Christer, *The Ardennes: Hitler's Winter Offensive 1944–1945*, Casemate Publishing, 2014
Bessel, Richard, *Germany 1945: From War to Peace*, HarperCollins, 2009
Bird Keith, *Erich, Raeder: Admiral of the Third Reich*, Naval Institute Press, 2013
Bishop, Chris, *Waffen-SS Divisions: 1939–1945*, Amber Books, 2017
Bix, Herbert P., *Hirohito and the Making of Modern Japan*, HarperCollins, 2000
Bloxham, Donald, *The Final Solution: A Genocide*, Oxford University Press, 2009
Boer, Sjoerd J. de, *Escaping Hitler's Bunker. The Fate of the Third Reich's Leaders*, Frontline Books, 2021
Borch, Fred L., *Military Trials of War Criminals in the Netherlands East Indies 1946–1949*, Oxford University Press, 2017
Bosworth R.J.B., *Mussolini's Italy: Life Under Fascist Dictatorship 1915–1945*, Penguin Books, 2005
Brescia, Maurizio, *Mussolini's Navy: A Reference Guide to the Regia Marina 1930–1945*, Seaforth, 2012
Brown, Archie, *The Rise and Fall of Communism*, HarperCollins, 2009
Brown, Daniel Patrick, *The Camp Women. The Female Auxiliaries Who Assisted the SS in Running the Nazi Concentration Camp System*, Schiffer Military History, 2001
Brown, David, *The Royal Navy and the Mediterranean*, Routledge, 2002
Bungay, Stephen, *The Most Dangerous Enemy. A History of the Battle of Britain*, Aurum Press, 2000
Burgwyn, James H., *Mussolini Warlord: Failed Dreams of Empire 1940–1943*, Enigma Books, 2012
Campbell, Ian, *The Addis Ababa Massacre: Italy's National Shame*, Oxford University Press, 2017
Campbell, Valery, *Camp 165 Watten. Scotland's Most Secretive Prisoner-of-War Camp*, Whittles Publishing, 2008
Carradice, Phil, *Hitler and his Women*, Pen & Sword, 2021
Carruthers, Bob, *German Paratroopers 1939–1945 – The Fallschirmjager*, Pen & Sword, 2013
Cartier, Raymond, *La Seconde Guerre Mondiale*, Larousse-Paris Match, 1965
Cervi, Mario, *The Hollow Legions. Mussolini's Blunder in Greece 1940–1941* (Storia della Guerra di Grecia 1940–1941), Chatto and Windus, 1972
Cesarani, David, *Final Solution: The Fate of the Jews 1933–1945*, St Martin's Press, 2016
Clodfelter, Micheal, *Warfare and Armed Conflicts. A Statistical Encyclopedia of Casualty and Other Figures 1492–2015*, McFarland, 2017
Collier, Richard, *The War in the Desert*, Time-Life Books, 1977

Collins, D.J.E.; Prasad, Bisheshwar, *History of the Royal Indian Navy 1939–19. The Official History of the Indian Armed Forces in the Second World War*, Orient Longmans, 1964

Conti, Flavio Giovanni, *I Prigionieri di Guerra Italiani 1940–1945*, Il Mulino, 1986

Darman, Peter, *A–Z of the SAS. The battles, the weapons, the training and the men*, Sidgwick & Jackson, 1992

Deane, Hugh, *The Korean War: 1945–1953*, China Books & Periodicals, 1999

Dear, I.C.B. (ed.); Foot, M.R.D. (ed.), *The Oxford Companion to the Second World War*, Oxford University Press, 1995

Dénes Bernád, *Romanian Aces of The Second World War*, Osprey Publishing, 2003

Dębski, Jerzy, *Death Books from Auschwitz: Remnants*, K. G. Saur, 1995

Devlin, Gerald M., *Paratrooper! – The Saga of Parachute and Glider Combat Troops During The Second World War*, Robson Books, 1979

Doherty, M.A., *Nazi Wireless Propaganda: Lord Haw-Haw and British Public Opinion in the Second World War*, Edinburg University Press, 2000

Dorrian, James G., *Storming Saint-Nazaire: The Gripping Story of the Dock-Busting Raid March 1942*, Naval Institute Press, 1998

Dorril, Stephen, *MI6: Inside the Covert World of Her Majesty's Secret Intelligence Service*, Simon & Schuster, 2002

Dower, John W., *Embracing Defeat. Japan in the Wake of The Second World War*, W.W. Norton & Company, 1999

Dupuy, Ernest R.; Dupuy, Trevor N., *The Collins Encyclopedia of Military History*, BCA, 1994

Dupuy, Trevor N., *Encyclopedia of Military Biography*, I.B. Tauris, 1992

Ellis, John, *The Second World War Data Book: The Essential Facts and Figures for All the Combatants*, Aurum, 1993

Ellis, Major Lionel F., Warhurst, Lieutenant-Colonel A.E., *Victory in the West. The Defeat of Germany. History of the Second World War*, Naval & Military Press, 2004

Elsie, Robert, *A Biographical Dictionary of Albanian History*, I.B. Tauris, 2012

Engel, David, *Facing a Holocaust: The Polish government-in-exile and the Jews 1943–1945*, UNC Press, 1993

Erickson, John, *The Road to Berlin*, HarperCollins, 1985

Evans, David C.; Peattie, Mark R., *Kaigun: Strategy, Tactics and Technology in the Imperial Japanese Navy 1887–1941*, Naval Institute Press, 1997

Evans, Richard J., *The Third Reich in History and Memory*, Oxford University Press, 2015

Ezergailis, Andrew, *The Holocaust in Latvia 1941–1944. The Missing Center*, Historian Institute of Latvia/The US Holocaust Memorial Museum, 1996.

Farrell, Nicholas, *Mussolini: A New Life*, Phoenix, 2004

Feldon, Mark, *Guarding Hitler: The Secret World of the Führer*, Pen & Sword Military, 2014

Fest, Joachim, *Inside Hitler's Bunker: The Last Days of the Third Reich*, Farrar Strauss & Giroux, 2004

Fielding, Steve, *Pierrepoint: A Family of Executioners*, John Blake Publishing, 2008

Ford, Ken, *The Rhine Crossings 1945 (Campaign)*, Osprey Publishing, 2007

Frank, Richard, *Downfall: The End of the Japanese Empire*, Penguin Books, 1999

BIBLIOGRAPHY AND RECOMMENDED READING

Friedlander, Henry, *The Origins of Nazi Genocide: From Euthanasia to the Final Solution*, University of North Carolina Press, 1995

Fuller, J.F.C., *The Second World War 1939–1945. A Strategical and Tactical History*, Da Capo Press, 1993

Fuller, Richard, *Shōkan: Hirohito's Samurai*, Arms & Armour Press, 1992

Galante, Pierre; Silianoff, Eugene (ed.), *The Voices from the Bunker: Hitler's Personal Staff Tells Story of the Führer's Last Days*, Anchor, 1990

Giangreco, D.M.; Moore, Kathryn; Polmar, Norman, *Eyewitness D-Day: Firsthand Accounts from the Landing at Normandy to the Liberation of Paris*, Barnes & Noble, 2004

Gooch, John, *Mussolini and his Generals: The Armed Forces and Fascist Foreign Policy 1922–1940*, Cambridge University Press, 2007

Hájková, Anna, *The Last Ghetto. An Everyday History of Theresienstadt*, Oxford University Press, 2020

Hamilton, Charles, *Leaders and Personalities of the Third Reich*, James Bender Publishing, 1996

Hand, Linda, *The Secret Agenda: The US Government, Nazi Scientists and Project Paperclip 1945–1990*, St Martin's, 1991

Heberer, Patricia; Matthäus Jurgen, *Atrocities on Trial: Historical Perspectives on the Politics of Prosecuting War Crimes*, University of Nebraska Press, 2008

Hébert, Valery, *Hitler's Generals on Trial: The Last War Crimes Tribunal in Nuremberg*, University of Kansas Press, 2010

Heiber, Helmut; Glantz, David M., *Hitler and his Generals: Military Conferences 1942–1945*, Enigma Books, 2005

Heller, Kevin John, *The Nuremberg Military Tribunals and the Origins of the International Criminal Law*, Oxford University Press, 2011

Heyde, Werner, *Who's Who in Nazi Germany*, Routledge, 2001

Holmes, Richard, *The Oxford Companion to Military History*, Oxford University Press, 2001

Hunt, Michael, *The World Transformed: 1945 to the Present*, Oxford University Press, 2013

Husel, Dieter K., *Peenemünde to Canaveral*, Prentice Hall, 1960

Irving, David, *Hitler's War* (Translated into Greek), Govostis, 2003

Itoh, Keiko, *The Japanese Community in Pre-War Britain. From Integration to Disintegration*, Routledge, 2013

Jardim, Tomaz, *The Mauthausen Trial – American Military Justice in Germany*, Harvard University Press, 2012

Jewell, Brian, *Over the Rhine – The Last Days of War in Europe*, Spellmount, 1985

Jowett, Philip S.; Andrew, Stephen, *The Italian Army 1940–1945*, Osprey Publishing, 2000

Kater, Michael H., *Doctors Under Hitler*, University of North Carolina Press, 1989

Junge, Traudl, *Until the Final Hour: Hitler's Last Secretary*, Arcade Publishing, 2004

Jurado, Carlos Caballero, *Foreign Volunteers of the Wehrmacht 1941–1945*, Osprey Publishing, 2001

Keegan, John, *The Second World War*, Pimlico, 1997

Keegan, John, *The Times Atlas of the Second World War*, The Times, 1994

Kennan, George F., *Russia and the West. Under Lenin and Stalin*, 1960
Kershaw, Ian, *Hitler: A Biography*, Norton & Company, 2008
Krivosheev, Grigoriy F., *Soviet Casualties and Combat Losses in the Twentieth Century*, Greenhill Books, 1997
Langbein, Hermann, *People in Auschwitz*, University of North Carolina Press, 2005
Lepre, George, *Himmler's Bosnian Division: The Waffen-SS Handschar Division 1943–1944*, Schiffer Publishing, 1997
Levene, Mark; Roberts, Penny, *The Massacre in History*, Bergham Books, 1999
Lichtblau, Eric, *The Nazis Next Door: How America Became a Safe Haven for Hitler's Men*, Houghton Mifflin Harcourt, 2014
Liddell Hart, Basil H., *A History of the Second World War*, Weidenfeld & Nicolson, 1970
Lifton, Robert Jay, *The Nazi Doctors: Medical Killing and the Psychology of Genocide*, Basic Books, 1986
Lingen, Kerstin von, *Allen Dulles and Nazi War Criminals: The Dynamics of Selective Prosecution*, Cambridge University Press, 2013
Lingen, Kerstin von, *Kesselring's Last Battle: War Crimes and Cold War Politics 1945–1960*, University Press of Kansas, 2009
Linton, Suzannah, *Hong Kong's War Crimes Trials*, Oxford University Press, 2013
Littlejohn, David, *Foreign Legions of the Third Reich*, Bender Publishing, 1987
Littlejohn, David, *The Patriotic Traitors*, Heinemann, 1972
Longerich, Peter, *Heinrich Himmler: A Life*, Oxford University Press, 2012
Lu, David Jon, *Agony of Choice: Matsuoka Yōsuke and the Rise and Fall of the Japanese Empire 1880–1946*, Lexington Books, 2002
MacArthur, Douglas, *Reminiscences of General of the Army Douglas MacArthur*, Bluejacket Books, 2015
Maga, Timothy P., *Judgement at Tokyo: The Japanese War Crimes Trials*, University of Kentucky Press, 2001
Magargee, Geoffrey, *Inside Hitler's High Command*, University Press of Kansas, 2000
Mallett, Derek R., *Hitler's Generals in America: Nazi Prisoners of War and Allied Military Intelligence*, University Press of Kentucky, 2013
Manvell, Roger; Fraenkell, Heinrich, *Göring: The Rise and Fall of a Notorious Nazi Leader*, Skyhorse, 2011
Maurois, André, *Histoire de la France* (History of France) (in French), Dominique Wapler, 1947
Mazower, Mark, *Hitler's Empire: How the Nazis Ruled Europe*, Penguin Press, 2008
Mazower, Mark, *Inside Hitler's Greece. The Experience of Occupation*, Yale University Press, 1993
McDonough, Frank, *After the Reich: The Brutal History of Allied Occupation*, Basic Books, 2007
McMillan, Richard, *The British Occupation of Indonesia 1945–1946*, Routledge, 2006
Milazzo, Matteo J., *The Chetnik Movement and the Yugoslav Resistance*, John Hopkins University Press, 1975
Miller, Michael; Andrea Schultz, *Gauleiters: The Regional Leaders of the Nazi Party and their Deputies*, R. James Blender Publishing, 2017
Miller, Michael, *Leaders of the SS and the German Police*, James Bender, 2006

BIBLIOGRAPHY AND RECOMMENDED READING

Moore, Bob; Fedorowich, Ken, *'Family down under: Italian Prisoners of War in Australia, 1931–1943'*, in the British Empire and Italian POWs, Palgrave Macmillan, 2002

Moreno, Jonathan, *Undue Risk: Secret State Experiments on Humans*, Psychology Press, 2001

Moseley, Ray, *Mussolini: The Last 600 Days of Il Duce*, Taylor Trade Publishing, 2004

Mueggenberg, Brent, *The Cossack Struggle Against Communism 1917–1945*, McFarland, 2019

Murray, Williamson; Millett, Allan R., *A War to be Won. Fighting the Second World War*, Belknap Press of Harvard University, 2007

Murphy, Sean, *Letting the Side Down. British Traitors in the Second World War*, The History Press, 2005

Naftali, Timothy, *The CIA and Eichmann's Associates*, University of Virginia, 2005

Nesbit, Roy Conyers; Acker, Georges van, *The Flight of Rudolf Hess: Myths and Reality*, Stroud History Press, 2011

Newland, Samuel J., *Cossacks in the German Wehrmacht 1941–1945*, Frank Cass, 1991

Neville, Peter, *Mussolini*, Routledge, 2004

Nicholls, David, *Adolf Hitler: A Biographical Companion*, ABC-CLIO, 2000

Orpen, Neil, *East African and Abyssinian Campaigns. South African Forces in The Second World War*, Purnell, 1968

Overy, Richard J., *Interrogations: The Nazi Elite in Allied Hands*, Viking, 2001

Page, Neil, *Day Fighter Aces of the Luftwaffe 1943–1945*, Casemate Publishers, 2020

Paskuly, Stevan (Ed.), *Rudolf Höss. Death Dealer: The Memoirs of the SS Kommandant at Auschwitz*, Da Capo Press, 1996

Patai, Raphael, *The Jews of Hungary: History, Culture and Psychology*, Wayne State University Press, 1996

Paxton, Robert O., *Vichy France: Old Guard and New Order 1940–1944*, Alfred A. Knopf, 1972

Pearson, Owen, *Albania in Occupation and War: From Fascism to Communism 1940–1945*, I.B. Tauris, 2006

Perez, Luis G. (Ed.), *Japan at War. An Encyclopedia*, ABC-Clio, 2013

Peterson, Edward N., *The American Occupation of Germany. Retreat to Victory*, Wayne State University Press, 1977

Piccigalo, Philip R., *The Japanese on Trial: Allied War Crimes Operations in the East 1945–1951*, University of Texas Press, 1979

Pringle, Heather-Anne, *The Master Plan: Himmler's Scholars and the Holocaust*, Hyprerion, 2006

Pyle, Christopher, *Extradition, Politics and Human Rights*, Temple University Press, 2001

Rashke, Richard, *Useful Enemies: America's Open-Door Policy for Nazi War Criminals*, Open Road Media, 2013

Read, Anthony, *The Devil's Disciples: Hitler's Inner Circle*, W.W. Norton & Company, 2004

Reed, Anthony; Fisher, David, *The Fall of Berlin*, Pimlico, 2002

Reid, P.R., *Colditz: The Full Story*, Pan/Macmillan, 2011

Reybrouck, David van, *Revolusi: Indonesia and the Birth of the Modern World*, De Besige Bij., 2020

Rhodes, Richard, *Masters of Death: The SS-Einsatzgruppen and the Invention of the Holocaust*, Vintage Books, 2002

Richter, Heinz A., *Greece in The Second World War* (in Greek), Govostis, 1988

Rigg, Bryan-Mark, *Hitler's Jewish Soldiers: The Untold Story of Nazi Racial Laws and Men of Jewish Descent in the German Military*, University Press of Kansas, 2002

Roberts, Andrew, *The Storm of War. A New History of the Second World War*, Allen Lane, 2003

Rolling, B.V.A.; Cassesse, *The Tokyo Trial and Beyond*, The Polity Press, 1993

Ryan, Allan A., *Yamashita's Ghost – War Crimes, MacArthur's Justice and Commander Accountability*, University Press of Kansas, 2012

Salter, Michael, *Nazi War Crimes. Intelligence and Selective Prosecution at Nuremberg: Controversies Regarding the Role of the OSS*, Routledge, 2007

Scianna, Bastian Matteo, *The Italian War in the Eastern Front 1941–1943: Operations, Myths and Memories*, Palgrave Macmillan, 2019

Searle, Alaric, *Wehrmacht Generals. West German Society and the Debate on Rearmament 1949–1959*, Praeger Publishers, 2003

Sebag-Montefiore, Hugh, *Enigma: The Battle for the Code*, Wiley, 2004

Segev, Tom, *Soldiers of Evil: The Commandants of the Nazi concentration Camps*, Crafton Books, 1988

Selley, Lore, *Auschwitz: The Nazi Civilization*, University Press of America, 1992

Seymour-Jones, Carole, *She Landed by Moonlight: The Story of Secret Agent Pearl Witherington*, Hodder & Stoughton, 2013

Spitz, Vivien, *Doctors from Hell: The Horrific Account of Nazi Experiments on Humans*, Sentient, 2005

Stahel, David, *Joining Hitler's Crusade: European Nations and the Invasion of the Soviet Union 1941*, Cambridge University Press, 2018

Stein, George H., *The Waffen-SS*, Cornell University Press, 1984

Stockings, Craig; Hancock, Eleanor, *Swastika Over the Acropolis. Reinterpreting the Nazi invasion of Greece in The Second World War*, Brill, 2013

Tanner, Stephen, *Refuge from the Reich: American Airmen and Switzerland during the Second World War*, Da Capo Press, 2001

Takemae, Eiji, *Inside GHQ: The Allied Occupation of Japan and its Legacy*, Continuum International, 2002

Thacker, Toby, Joseph Goebbels: Life and Death, Palgrave Macmillan, 2010

Theotokis, Nikolaos, *Airborne Landing to Air-Assault, A History of Military Parachuting*, Pen & Sword Military, 2020

Tolstoy, Nikolai, *The Secret Betrayal*, Charles Scriber's Sons, 1977

Tomasevich, Jozo, *War and Revolution in Yugoslavia 1941–1945: The Chetniks*, Stanford University Press, 1975

Towle, Philip; Kosuge, Margaret; Kibata, Yōchi (ed.), *Japanese Prisoners of War*, A. & C. Black, 2000

Trumble, Tom, *Tomorrow We Escape. One man's extraordinary story of courage and survival from Tobruk to the prison camps of occupied Europe*, Penguin, 2015

Vinogradov, V.K., *Hitler's Death. Russia's Great Secret from the Files of the KGB*, Chancer Press, 2005

BIBLIOGRAPHY AND RECOMMENDED READING

Wachsmann, Nikolaus, *KL: A History of the Nazi Concentration Camps*, Farrar, Straus & Giroux, 2015

Walker, Andrew, *The Nazi War Trials*, CPD, 2006

Weale, Adrian, *Army of Evil: A History of the SS*, NAL Caliber, 2012

Weidling, Paul J., *Nazi Medicine and the Nuremberg Trials: From Medical War Crimes to Informed Consent*, Palgrave Macmillan, 2004

Wellfield, John, *Empire in Eclipse: Japan in the Post-War American Alliance System*, Bloomsbury Publishing, 2012

West, Nigel, *MI5: The True Story of the Most Secret Counterespionage Organisation in the World*, Stein & Day, 1981

Wilmot, Chester, *The Struggle for Europe*, Fontana, 1952

Winstone, Martin, *The Dark Heart of Hitler's Europe: Nazi Rule in Poland Under the General Government*, Bloomsbury Publishing, 2014

Wistrich, Robert, *Who's Who in Nazi Germany*, Routledge, 1995

Wittman Rebecca, *Beyond Justice: The Auschwitz Trial*, Harvard University Press, 2012

Wright, Edmund, *Vichy Government: A Dictionary of World History*, Oxford University Press, 2006

Yerger, Mark C., *Allgemeine-SS: The Commands, Units and Leaders of the General SS*, Schiffer Publishing, 1997

Zentner, Christian; Bedürftig, Friedmann, *The Encyclopedia of the Third Reich*, Da Capo Press, 1991

Zweig, Ronald W., *The Gold train: The Destruction of the Jews and the Looting of Hungary*, Harper Collins, 2002

Various Sources (Reports, Articles, etc)

Ceber (North in English) magazine, 'Finnish Prisoners-of-War during The Second World War' (in Russian), No. 11–12, 2002

CIA, *Information Report-Rumania-Aiud Prison* (PDF), 11 January 1954

Conti, Flavio Giovanni, *Prigioneri De Guerra Italiani Negli Stati Uniti 1942–1946* (Italian prisoners of war in the United States 1942–1946) (PhD thesis), Roma Tre University, 2010/2011

Connor, Stephen, 'Side-stepping Geneva: Japanese troops under British control 1945–1947', *Journal of Contemporary History*, 45 (2), 2010

Evans, Roly, 'Lessons from the Past. The Rapid Clearance of Denmark's Minefields in 1945', *Journal of Conventional Weapons Destruction*, Vol. 22, Issue 1, Article 4, JMU Scholarly Commons, April 2018

Focardi, Philippo; Klinkhammer, Lutz, 'The question of Fascist Italy's war crimes: The construction of a self-acquitting myth 1943–1948', *Journal of Modern Italian Studies*, 2004

Hand, Linda, 'US Coverup of Nazi Scientists', *Bulletin of the Atomic Scientists*, 41 (4), April 1985

International Committee of the Red Cross, Report No. 1397, POW Camp Sutton Bridge, Lincolnshire, 28 August 1948

Japanese War Crimes in the Pacific. Australia's Investigations and Prosecutions, National Archives of Australia, 2019

Judgement of the International Military Tribunal for the Trial of German Major War Criminals, 'The Invasion of Belgium, the Netherlands and Luxembourg', London, 1951

Koninklijke Bibliotheek (www.kb.nl), 'German prisoners of war clearing mines'

Kuznetsov, S.I., 'The Situation of Japanese POWs in Soviet Camps', *Journal of Slavic Military Studies*, 8/1995

Law Reports of Trials of War Criminals, United Nations War Crime Commission, His Majesty's Stationery Office (London), 1947

Lewis, George G.; Mehwa, John, History of Prisoner of War Utilization by the US Army 1776–1945, Center of Military History, US Army, 1982

Madsen, Chris, 'Victims of Circumstance: The Execution of German Deserters by Surrendered German Troops under Canadian Control in Amsterdam May 1945', *Canadian Military History*, vol. 2, issue 1, article 8, 1993

McFarlane, Ian, *Italian Prisoners of War*, The Companion to Tasmanian Society, Centre for Historical Studies, 2006

Nawyn, Kathleen J., 'Neutralizing the hard centre of German militarism: US military government and the Wehrmacht elite officers 1945–1948', US Center of Military History, *Army History*, No. 77, Fall 2010

Padaliu, Effie, 'Britain and the 'turn-over' of Italian war criminals to Yugoslavia 1945–1948', *Journal of Contemporary History*, Vol. 39, No. 4, 2004

Records of the United States Nuremberg War Crimes Trials, US Government Printing Office, District of Columbia, 1950

Smith, Arthur L., Churchill's German Army: Wartime Strategy and Cold War Politics 1943–1947, vol. 54, Sage Library of Social Research, 1977

The Pacific War Research Society (Ed.), *Japan's Longest Day – Surrender: The last twenty-four hours through Japanese eyes*, Kadansha International, 1973

Thomas, Roger J.C., *Prisoner-of-War Camps 1939–1948*, National Monuments Record Centre, Public Archive of English Heritage, 2003

NOTES

Introduction

1. *BBC History Magazine*, April 2017.
2. capitalpunishment.org/hameln.htm
3. Charles Hamilton, *Leaders and Personalities of the Third Reich*, Vol. 1, R. James Bender Publishing, 1984, p.110.
4. Katrin Himmler, *The Himmler Brothers: A German Family History*, Pan/Macmillan, 2012, p.275.
5. ZDF-Dokumentation, 13 June 2021.
6. James P. O'Donnell, *The Bunker*, Da Capo Press, 2001, p.293.
7. Williamson Murray; Allan R. Millett, *A War to be Won. Fighting the Second World War*, The Belknap Press of Harvard University Press, 2001, pp.557–558.
8. encyclopedia.uia.org/en/problem/prisoners-war
9. The Canadian Encyclopedia, *POW camps in Canada*.
10. Robert Harvey, *American Shogun. MacArthur, Hirohito and the American Duel with Japan*, John Murray, 2006, p.236. Also, Andrew Roberts, *The Storm of War. A History of the Second World War*, Allen Lane, 2009, p.275.
11. Roberts, p.276.
12. George MacDonald Fraser, *Quartered Safe Out Here. A Harrowing Tale of World War II*, (Autobiography), Skyhorse, 2014, pp.283–285.
13. Hermann F. Meyer, *Von Wien nach Kalavryta. Die blutige Spur der 117.Jäger-Division durch Serbien und Griechenland* (Translated into Greek), Labyrinthos, 2022, p.633.
14. Dirlewanger, Oscar, *The Holocaust Encyclopedia*, Yale University Press, 2001, p.150.
15. Hamburger Algemeine Zeitung, 11 May 1949.
16. Arthur L. Smith, *Churchill's German Army: Wartime Strategy and Cold War Politics*, Vol. 54, Saga Library of Social Research, 1977, p.79.
17. Otto Skorzeny, *Meine Kommando Unternechem* (translated into Greek), Eurobooks, 2007, p.504
18. S.P. McKenzie, 'The treatment of prisoners of war in World War II', *The Journal of Modern History*, Vol. 66, No. 3, September 1994, p.487.
19. Murray and Millett, pp.557–558.
20. Andrew Roadnight, 'Sleeping with the Enemy. Japanese Troops and the Netherlands East Indies 1945–1946', *History*, Vol. 87, Issue 2086, 2002.
21. Niall Ferguson, *The War of the World. Twentieth Century Conflict and the Descent of the West*, Penguin Press, 2006, p.497.

22. Murray and Millett, p.543.
23. Ibid., p.569.
24. historynet.com/german-pows-and-the-art-of-survival

PART ONE – DETAINEES (I)

Germans

1. Roger Manvell; Heinrich Fraenkel, *Hess: A Biography*, Granada, 1971, pp.101–105.
2. William L. Shirer, *The Rise and Fall of the Third Reich*, Simon & Schuster, 1960, p.835.
3. Roy Conyers Nesbit; Georges van Acker, *The Flight of Rudolf Hess: Myths and Reality*, History Press, 1999, p.71.
4. Nesbit & van Acker, p.97. Also, Manvell & Fraenkel, p.173.
5. Richard J. Evans, *The Third Reich at War*, Penguin, 2008, p.141.
6. Evans, p.509 and p.724.
7. Manvell and Fraenkel, pp.320–325.
8. Ian Kershaw, *Hitler: A Biography*, Norton & Company, 2008, p.964.
9. Sky 'H' History (history.co.uk/history-of-ww2/prisoners-of-war)
10. Lloyd Clark, *Blitzkrieg. Myth, Reality and Hitler's Lightning War – France 1940*, Atlantic Books, 2017, p.9.
11. Ben Shepherd, *Hitler's Soldiers: The German Army in the Third Reich*, Yale University Press, 2016, p.519.
12. David M. Crowe, *Crimes of State Past and Present: Government-sponsored Atrocities and International Legal Responses*, Routledge, 2013, p.87.
13. Werner Masser, *Nüremberg: Tribunal der Sieger* (in German), Verlag Antaios, 2005, pp.349–350.
14. Robert Wistrich, *Who's Who in Nazi Germany*, Routledge, 1995, p.135.
15. CIA-Kent School, The Last Days of Kaltenbrunner. Also, David Cesarani (ed.), *The Final Solution: Origins and Implementation*, Routledge, 1994p. pp.81–82.
16. Enzo Biagi, *La Seconda Guerra Mondiale. Una Storia Due Uomini* (in Italian), Fabbri, 1983, p.2743.
17. Biagi, p.2757.
18. Northern Star, New South Wales, 'Allies capture Nazi pagan philosopher', 22 May 1945.
19. Martyn Housden, *Hans Frank: Lebensraum and the Holocaust*, Palgrave Macmillan, 2003, p.218.
20. The Flash (A fortnightly edition published by the Royal Welsh Fusiliers), 10 December 1945.
21. Henry Pitt papers (1941–45), United States Holocaust Museum. Major Henry Pitt was in charge of the US 101st Airborne Division detachment that arrested Julius Streicher on 24 May 1945 in Waidring, in western Austria.
22. Richard J. Overy, *Interrogations: The Nazi Elite in Allied Hands 1945*, Viking, 2001, p.205. Also, Roger Manvell; Heinrich Fraenkell, *Göring: The Rise and Fall of a Notorious Nazi Leader*, Skyhorse, 2011, p.393.
23. Biagi, p.2743.
24. Keith Bird, *Erich Raeder: Admiral of the Third Reich*, Naval Institute Press, 2013, ISBN 978-1612513751.

NOTES

25. David T. Zebecki, *Dönitz: A Defense*, Merriam Press, 2007, pp.14–17 and pp.95–96.
26. Andrew Walker, *The Nazi War Trials*, CPD, 2006, p.145.
27. Jochen von Lang, *The Secretary: Martin Bormann. The Man who Manipulated Hitler*, Random House, 1979, p.432.
28. Lang, p.417.
29. Michael Miller, *Leaders of the SS and German Police*, vol. 1, James Bender, 2006, p.154.
30. Peter Longerich, *Heinrich Himmler: A Life*, Oxford University Press, 2012, p.1 and p.736.
31. Alan Wykes, *Himmler*, Pan Books, 1973, p.158.
32. Wykes, p.159. Also, Bend Bulletin, '*Heinrich Himmler Kills Himself in British Prison*', 24 May 1945.
33. Leard Rapport; Arthur Northwood; A.L.S. Marshall, *Rendezvous with Destiny: A History of the 101st Airborne Division*, Infantry Journal Press, 1948, pp.741–744.
34. Gitta Sereny, *Albert Speer: His Battle with Truth*, Macmillan, 1995, p.573.
35. The Avalon Project of Yale Law School, Chapter of the International Military Tribunal, Article 6. Also, avalon.law.yale.edu/imt/judlawre.asp
36. Tulby H. Edmondson, *Comparative Memories: War, Defeat, and Historical Memory in the Post-Civil War American South and Post-World War II Germany* (thesis), Department of History, Appalachian State University, May 2013, p.44.
37. Kathleen J. Nawyn, '*Neutralizing the hard centre of German militarism: US military government and the Wehrmacht's elite officers 1945–1948*', US Center of Military History, Army History, No. 77, Fall 2010, p.28.
38. Edmondson, p.43.
39. Albrecht Lehmann, *Gefangenchaft und Heimkehr: Deutsche Kriegsfangen in der Sowjetunion*, Beck, 1986, p.10.
40. Charles B. MacDonald, *The Battle of the Huertgen Forest*, Lippincott, 1963, p.372.
41. Corelli Barnet (ed.), *Hitler's Generals*, Phoenix, 1989, p.329.
42. Robert S. Wistrich, *Greim, Robert Ritter von, Who's Who in Nazi Germany*, Routledge, 2001, p.84.
43. Samuel W. Mitcham Jr, *Hitler's Field Marshals and their Battles*, Guild Publishing, 1988, p.281.
44. Kerstin von Lingen, *Kesselring's Last Battle: War Crimes Trials and Cold War Politics 1945–1960*, University Press of Kansas, 2009, pp.110–118.
45. Von Lingen, pp.160–162.
46. Ronald M. Smelser; Edward J. Davies, *The Myth of the Eastern Front: The Nazi-Soviet War in American Popular Culture*, Cambridge University Press, 2008, pp.64–67.
47. Von Lingen, pp.242–243 and p.248.
48. jewishvirtuallibrary.org/dachau-war-crimes-trials
49. Mango Melvin, *Manstein: Hitler's Greatest General*, Weidenfeld & Nicolson, 2010, pp.425–431.
50. Benoît Lemay, *Erich von Manstein. Hitler's Master Strategist*, Casemate, 2010, pp.467–468.
51. James Lucas, *Alpine Elite: German Mountain Troops of World War II*, Jane's Publishing, 1980, p.218.

52. Don Williams, '*Did Kiwis Killed a Field Marshal?*', The Volunteers. New Zealand Military History Society, 46 (3), pp.39–48.
53. David Nicholls, *Adolf Hitler: A Biographical Companion*, ABC-CLIO, 2000, pp.35–36.
54. Geoffrey P. Magargee, *Inside Hitler's High Command*, University Press of Kansas, 2000, p.172.
55. Samuel W. Mitcham Jr, *Hitler's Field Marshals and their Battles*, Crafton Books, 1989, p.125.
56. Valerie Hebert, *Hitler's Generals on Trial: The Last War Crimes Tribunal in Nuremberg*, University Press of Kansas, 210, p.150.
57. Hebert, p.95.
58. Mitcham, p.268.
59. Gregory Liedtke, '*Lost in the mud: The (nearly) forgotten collapse of the German Army in the western Ukraine in March and April 1944*', The Journal of Slavic Military Studies, pp.218–219.
60. Samuel Mitcham; Gene Meuller, *Hitler's Commanders: Officers of the Wehrmacht, Luftwaffe, Kriegsmarine and Waffen-SS*, Rowman & Littlefield, 2012, p.252.
61. Charles Messenger, *The Last Prussian: A Biography of Field Marshal Gerd von Rundstedt 1875–1953*, Pen & Sword, 2011, p.153.
62. Douglas Martin, 'Manfred Rommel, Son of German Field Marshal, Dies at 84', *New York Times*, 9 November 2013.
63. William L. Shirer, *The Rise and Fall of the Third Reich, Simon & Schuster*, 1990, pp.1076–1077.
64. Generalfeldmarschall Maximilian Freiherr von Weichs, lexikon-der-wehrmacht.de
65. Helmut Heiber; David M. Glantz, *Hitler and his Generals: Military Conferences 1942–1945*, Enigma Books, 2005, p.211.
66. Daniela Baratieri; Mark Edele; Giuseppe Finaldi, *Perspectives of the Nuremberg Trial*, Routledge, 2013, p.57.
67. Joachim Fest, *Plotting Hitler's Death*, Phoenix House, 1997, p.380.
68. Earl F. Ziemke, *Stalingrad to Berlin: The German Defeat in the East*, Center of Military History, US Army, 2002, p.137.
69. Valerie Hebert, *Hitler's Generals on Trial: The Last War Crimes Tribunal in Nuremberg*, University Press of Kansas, 2010, p.219.
70. Johannes Hürter, *Hitler's Army Leaders – The German Commanders-in-Chief in the War against the Soviet Union 1941–1942* (in German), Oldenbourg Wissenschaftsverlag, 2007, p.635.
71. Hebert, pp.216–217.
72. Ibid., p.218.
73. David Stahel, *The Battle of Moscow*, Cambridge University Press, 2015, p.28.
74. Hebert, p.209 and p.218.
75. Ibid., p.3.
76. Ibid., p.151.
77. George Lepre, *Himmler's Bosnian Division: The Waffen-SS Handschar Division 1943–1944*, Schiffer Publishing, 1997, p.271.
78. Peter Longerich, *Heinrich Himmler: A Life*, Oxford University Press, 2011, p.330.
79. Thomas Adam, *Admiral Graf Spee. Germany and the Americas*, ABC-CLIO, 2005, p.45. Also, Dudley Pope. '*Langsdorff shoots himself*'. *The Battle of the River Plate*, Secker & Warburg, 1987, p.194.

NOTES

80. Walther-Peer Fellgiebel, *The Bearers of the Knight's Cross of the Iron Cross 1939–1945* (in German), Podzun-Pallas Verlag, 1986, p.199.
81. Antony Beevor, *Stalingrad*, Penguin Books, 1999, pp.365–366. Also, Samuel W. Mitcham Jr, *Panzer Legions: A Guide to the German Army Tank Divisions of World War II and their Commanders*, Stackpole Books, 2007, p.134.
82. Rolf Stoves, Die Gepanzerten und Motorisierten Grossverbände 1935–1945 (in German), Pozdun-Pallas Verlag, 1986, pp.130–133.
83. Kobus, Generalleutnant Arthur, lexicon-der-wehrmacht.de
84. Howard D. Grier, *Hitler, Dönitz and the Baltic Sea: The Third Reich's Last Hope 1944–1945*, Naval Institute Press, 2007, pp.81–88.
85. Christian Goeschel, *Suicide in Nazi Germany*, Oxford University Press, 2009, p.152.
86. *Irish Times*, 27 May 1947.
87. Samuel W. Mitcham Jr, *Rommel's Desert Commanders: The Men who Served the Desert Fox. North Africa 1941–1942*, Stackpole Books, 2008, p.43.
88. J.F. Cody, *The Battalion. Official History of New Zealand in the Second World War 1939–1945*, Historical Publications Branch, 1953, p.135.
89. Mitcham, p.44.
90. Henrik O. Lunde, *Hitler's Pre-Emptive War: The Battle of Norway*, Casemate, 2010, p.220.
91. Sven T. Ameberg; Hosar Christian, *Vi dro mot nord: Felttoget I Norge I April, skildret av tyske soldater of offisever*, Aventura, 1989, p.62.
92. Jerry Scutts, *Lion in the Sky: The US Air Force Fighter Operations 1942–1945*, Stephens, 1987, p.58.
93. David T. Zabecki (ed.), *The German War Machine in World War II*, ABC-Clio, 2019, p.329.
94. E.R. Hooton, *Luftwaffe at War: Gathering Storm 1933–1936*, vol. I, Chevron/Ian Allan, 2007, p.65.
95. Kurt Braatz, *Werner Mölders – Die Biographie* (Werner Mölders – The Biography) (in German), Moosburg, 2009, pp.350–351.
96. Peter Stockert, *Die Eichenlaubträger 1939–1945*, Band 1 (The Oak Leaves Bearers 1939–1945, Vol. I) (in German), Friedrichshaller Rundblick, 2012, p.2.
97. John English, *Amazon to Ivanhoe: British Standard Destroyers in the 1930s*, British Ship Society, 1993, p.120.
98. 'U-39 The First U-boat to be Sunk in World War II', HMS *Firedrake*.com, p.20.
99. Paul Kemp, *U-boats Destroyed – German Submarine Losses in the World Wars*, Arms & Armour, 1999, p.60.
100. The Observation Post, South African Modern Military History, 17 January 2016. Also, samilhistory.com/the-first-german-general-to-surrender-in-wwii-surrendered-to-the-south-africans
101. Dirlewanger, Oskar, *The Holocaust Encyclopedia*, Yale University Press, 2001, p.150. Also, Walter Stanoski Winter; Walter Winter; Stuan Robertson, *Winter Times: Memoirs of a German Sinto who Survived Auschwitz*, University of Hertfordshire Press, 2004, p.139.
102. George H. Stein, *The Waffen-SS*, Cornell University Press, 1984, p.266. Also, Christian Ingrao, *The SS Dirlewanger Brigade – The History of the Black Hunters*, Skyhorse Publishing, 2011, p.71.
103. Robert S. Wistrich, *Who's Who of Nazi Germany*: Dirlewanger, Oskar, Routledge, 2001, p.44.

104. Richard Evans, *The Third Reich at War*, Penguin Group, 2008, p.724.
105. *Hamburger Allgemeine Zeitung*, 11 May 1949.
106. Peter Hohnen; Richard Guilliatt, *The Wolf – The True Story of an Epic Voyage of Destruction in World War One*, Bantam Press, 2009, p.298.
107. alchetron.com/Hans-Cramer
108. R.C. Mowat, *Ruin and Resurgence 1939–1966*, Blandford Press, 1966, p.67.
109. Andrew Roberts, *The Storm of War. A New History of the Second World War*, Allen Lane, 2009, p.470.
110. Helen Fry, *The Walls Have Ears*, Yale University Press, 2019, p.100.
111. Michael Parrish, *The Lesser Terror: Soviet State Security 1939–1953*, Praeger Press, 1996, p.129.
112. Antony Beevor, *Berlin: The Downfall 1945*, Viking-Penguin Books, 2002, p.386.
113. Samuel W. Mitcham, *Panzer Legions: A Guide to the German Army Tank Divisions in World War II and their Commanders*, Stackpole Books, 2007, p.121.
114. Thomas Fischer, *Soldiers of the Leibstandarte*, J.J. Fedorowicz Publishing, 2008, pp.42-43
115. James P.O'Donnell, *The Bunker*, Da Capo Press, 1978, pp.325–330.
116. Beevor, p.244.
117. J.W. Monahan, *The Containing of Dunkirk (PDF), Canadian Participation in the Operations in North-West Europe*, Historical Section, Canadian Military Headquarters, 1947, para 86–87.
118. pegasusarchive.org/pow/cB_FeatherstonePk.htm
119. Earl F. Ziemke, *Stalingrad to Berlin: The German Defeat in the East*, Center of Military History, US Army, 2002, p.385.
120. specialcamp11.co.uk/Generalmajor%20Bernhard%Lossberg.htm
121. Samuel W. Mitcham, *German Order of Battle*, Vol. 2, Stackpole Books, 2007, pp.263–264.
122. 'Falltöter von rechts', Der Spiegel, 20 December 1961.
123. Hermann F. Meyer, *Die blutige Spur der 117.Jäger-Division durch Serbien und Griechenland* (in German), Bibliopolis, 2002, p.641.
124. Jonathan Bernstein, *P-47 Thunderbolt Units of the Twelfth Air Force*, Bloomsbury Publishing, 2012, p.11.
125. George Lepre, *Himmler's Bosnian Division: The Waffen-SS Handschar Division 1943–1944*, Schiffer Publishing, 1997, p.313.
126. Samuel W. Mitcham, *Panzer Legions: A Guide to the German Army Tank Divisions in World War II and their Commanders*, Stackpole Books, 2007, pp.113–114.
127. Paul Kemp, *U-Boats Destroyed. German Submarine Losses in World Wars*, Arms & Armour, 1999, p.214.
128. Kathleen J. Nawyn, '*Neutralizing the Hard Centre of German Militarization* (PDF), Army History, US Army Center of Military History, Fall 2010.
129. Heinz Hohne, *Canaris: Hitler's Master Spy*, Doubleday, 1979, p.377.
130. Spealcamp11.co.uk/Generalmajor%20Georg%20Benthack.t
131. David Lester, *'Who committed suicide?', Suicide and the Holocaust*, Nova Publishers, 2005, p.11.
132. Eliane Crocé et al, *Les Troupes de Marine 1622–1987*, Charles Lavauzelle, 1986, p.431.

NOTES

133. warfarehistorynet.com/article/a-hidden-massacre-in-belgium
134. Christian Zentner; Friedemann Bedürftig, *The Encyclopedia of the Third Reich*, Da Capo Press, 1991, p.197.
135. Louis Snyder, *Encyclopedia of the Third Reich*, Da Capo Press, 1994, p.66.
136. Danny S. Parker, *Hitler's Warrior. The Life and Wars of SS Colonel Jocken Peiper*, Da Capo Press, 2014, p.134.
137. Jens Westemeier, *Joachim Peiper: A Biography of Himmler's SS Commander*, Schiffer Publications, 2007, p.171.
138. Alex Kershaw, *Avenue of Spies: A True Story of Terror, Espionage, and One American Family's Heroic Resistance in Nazi-Occupied Paris*, Crow/Archetype, 2015, p.91. Also, Charles Glass, *They Fought Alone*, Penguin Press, 2018, pp.257–258.
139. Sara Helm, *A Life in Secrets,* Talese, 2005, pp.278–279 and p.331.
140. Roger Ford, *Five from the Forest*, Cassel Military Paperbacks, 2004, pp.108–109.
141. Andrew Ezergailis, *The Holocaust in Latvia 1941–1944*, Historical Institute of Latvia, 1996, p.296.
142. Sarah Helm, *A Life in Secrets: Vera Atkins and the Missing Agents of World War II*, Doubleday, 2005, pp.216–219.
143. Rita Krammer, *Flames in the Field: The Story of Four SOE Agents in Occupied France*, Michael Joseph, 1995, pp.115–116.
144. Michael D. Miller; Andreas Schulz, *Gauleiter: The Regional Leaders of the Nazi Party and their Deputies*, R. James Bender Publishing, 2012, p.484.
145. Miller & Schulz, p.488.
146. Richard Bessel, *Germany 1945: From War to Peace*, HarperCollins, 2009, p.62.
147. capitalpunishmentuk.org/USWCH.html
148. Charles Hamilton, *Leaders and Personalities of the Third Reich*, Vol. 2, James Bender Publishing, 1996, p.66.
149. Charles Hamilton, *Leaders and Personalities of the Third Reich*, Vol. 1, James Bender Publishing, Vol. I, p.158.
150. Ibid., p.161.
151. Ronald M. Smelser; Edward J. Davies, *The Myth of the Eastern Front. The Nazi-Soviet War in Popular Culture*, Cambridge University Press, 2008, p.737.
152. Anthony Read, *The Devil's Disciples: Hitler's Inner Circle*, W. W, Norton & Company, 2004, p.917.
153. Samuel W. Mitcham, *The Rise of the Wehrmacht*, Vol. I, ABC-Clio, 2008, p.146
154. David Owen, *Dogfight: The Supermarine Spitfire and the Messerschmitt Bf 109*, Pen & Sword, p.288.
155. *Chillicothe Daily Tribune*, 2 June 1942.
156. Helen Fry, *The Wall Have Ears*, Yale University Press, 2019, p.194.
157. Lexikonder-Wehrmacht.de/Personnenregister/D/DesslochO.htm
158. E.R. Hooton, *Luftwaffe at War: Gathering Storm 1933–1939*, Vol. I, Chevron/Ian Allan, 2007, p.65.
159. Walter Musciano, *Messerschmitt Aces*, Arco, 1982, pp.90–91.
160. John Weal, *More Bf 109 Aces of the Russian Front*, Osprey Publishing, 2007, p.89.
161. Jerry Scutts, *Bf 109 Aces of North Africa and the Mediterranean*, Osprey Publishing, 1994, p.54.

162. Lexikon-der-Wehrmacht.de/Personnenregister/H/HuyWD.htm
163. Mike Spick, *Luftwaffe Fighter Aces*, Ivy Books, 1996, p.231.
164. Donald L. Caldwell, *The JG 26 War Diary*, Vol. II, Grub Street, 1988, p.478.
165. Martin Bowman, *German Night Fighters Versus Bomber Command 1943–1945*, Pen & Sword, 2016, p.233.
166. Peter Hinchcliff, *Schnaufer: Ace of Diamonds*, Tempus, 1999, p.257.
167. de-metapedia.org/viki/weissenberger_theodor. Also, cyber.breton.pagesperso-orange.fr
168. Andrew Johannes Mathews; John Foreman, *Luftwaffe Aces – Biographies and Victory Claims*, Vol. I, Red Kite, 2014, pp.61–62.
169. David T. Zabecki, *The German War Machine in World War II*, ABC Clio, 2019, p.329.
170. Christer Bergström; Vlant Antipov; Claes Sundin, *Graf and Grislowski: A Pair of Aces*, Eagle Editions, 2003, pp.259–260. Also, Zabecki, p.329.
171. Christer Bergström, *Bagration to Berlin: The Final Air Battles in the East 1944–1945*, Burgess Hill, 2008, pp.91–98.
172. Neil Page, *Day Fighter Aces of the Luftwaffe 1943–1945*, Casemate Publishers, 2020, p.19.
173. John Weal, *More Bf 109 Aces of the Russian Front*, Osprey Publishing, 2012, p.66.
174. *Der Spiegel*, 25 October 2019.
175. Hanna Reitsch, *The Sky My Kingdom*, Biddles Limited, 2009, pp.119–123.
176. James E. Mrazek, *Airborne Combat: The Glider War. Fighting Gliders of World War II*, Stackpole Books, 2011, p.56.
177. Lexikon-der-Wehrmacht.dc/Personenregister/S/StudenK.htm
178. Peter D. Antill, *Crete 1941: Germany's Lightning Airborne Assault*, Osprey Publishing, 2005, p.20.
179. Bob Carruthers, *German Paratroopers 1939–1945. The Fallschirmjäger*, Pen & Sword, 2013, p.105.
180. Lexikon-der-Wehrmacht.dc/Personenregister/B/BohlkeH.htm
181. Derek R. Mallett, *Hitler's Generals in America: Nazi POWs and Allied Military Intelligence*, University Press of Kentucky, 2013, p.43.
182. Mallett, p.42.
183. Lars Hellwinkel, *Hitler's Getaway to the Atlantic: German Naval Bases in France*, Seaforth Publishing, 2014, p.158.
184. Joseph Balkowski, *From Brittany Beachhead: The 29th Infantry Division at Brest August-September 1944*, Stackpole Books, p.288.
185. Lexikon-der-Wehrmacht.de/Personenregiste/K/KorteH.htm
186. Lexikon-der-Wehrmacht.de/Personenregister/S/SchulzKL.htm
187. Lexikon-der-Wehrmacht.de/Personenregister/H/HeykinRv.htm
188. Lexikon-der-Wehrmacht.de/Personenregister/E/ErdmannW.htm
189. Lexikon-der-Wehrmacht.de/Personenregister/N/NeckerHv.htm
190. *Di Zeit*, 20 November 1987.
191. Anthony Beevor, *Berlin. The Downfall 1945*, Viking-Penguin Books, 2008, p.236.
192. Lexikon-der-Wehrmacht.de/Personenregister/M/MullerFW.htm
193. George Psychoundakis, *The Cretan Runner: His Story of the German Occupation*, John Murray, 1955, pp.177–178.

NOTES

194. Hermann F. Meyer, *Von Wien nach Kalavryta. Die blutige Spur der 117.Jäger-Divisio durch Serbien und Griechenland* (Translated into Greek), Labyrinthos, 2004, p.87.
195. Mark Mazower, *Inside Hitler's Greece. The Experience of Occupation*, Yale University Press, 1993, p.214.
196. Andrew Borowic, *Destroy Warsaw! Hitler's Punishment Stalin's Revenge*, Praeger, 2001, p.179.
197. *Deutsche Welle* (in Polish), 5 September 2019.
198. Jochen Böhler, *Prelude to a War of Extermination: The Wehrmacht in Poland* (in German), Fischer Taschbuch Verlag, 2006, p.241.
199. Mark C. Yerger, *Allgemeine-SS: The Commands, Units and Leaders of the General SS*, Schiffer Publishing, 1997, p.28.
200. Andrew Ezergailis, *The Holocaust in Latvia 1941–1944: The Missing Center*, Historian Institute of Latvia/US Holocaust Memorial Museum, 1996, p.239.
201. Wolfram Wette, *The Wehrmacht: History, Myth and Reality*, Harvard University Press, 2009, p.115.
202. Christopher R. Browning, *Ordinary Men: Reserve Police Battalion 101 and the Final Solution in Poland*, Harper/Collins, 2017, p.23.
203. Robert S. Wistrich, *Who's Who in Nazi Germany*, Routledge, 2001, pp.142–143.
204. Vasyl Markus, Encyclopedia of Ukraine, Vol. 2, 1988, encyclopediaofukraine.com/KochErich.htm
205. Michael T. Kaufman, 'Erich Koch dies in Polish prison; The Nazi war criminal was 90', *The New York Times*, 15 November 1986.
206. encuclopediaofukraine.com/KochErich.htm
207. *The New York Times*, 15 November 1986.
208. Richard Rhodes, *Masters of Death: The SS-Einsatztruppen and the Invention of the Holocaust*, Vintage Books, 2002, p.257.
209. Ibid., pp.274–275.
210. Norbert Frei, *Adenauer's Germany and the Nazi Past: The Politics of Amnesty and Integration*, Columbia University Press, 2002, p.165 and p.173.
211. Adrian Weale, *Army of Evil: A History of the SS*, Caliber, 2012, p.308.
212. Rhodes, p.4.
213. Ibid., p.272.
214. Ibid., p.113.
215. Robert Wistrich, *Who's Who in Nazi Germany*, Routledge, 1995, p.185.
216. Norbert Frei, *Politics of the Past*, Beck, 1996, p.195.
217. Christopher Browning, *The Origins of the Final Solution: The Evolution of Nazi Jewish Policy*, University of Nebraska Press, 2004, p.663.
218. Christian Ingrao, *Believe and Destroy. Intellectuals in the SS War Machine*, Malden, 2013, p.226.
219. Michael Bryant, *Eyewitness to Genocide: The Operation Reinhard Death Camp Trials 1955–1966*, University of Tennessee Press, 2014, p.28.
220. Rhodes, p.275.
221. Michael Miller, *Leaders of the SS and German Police*, Vol. I, James Bender Publishing, 2006, p.362.
222. battle-of-arnhem.com/wilhelm-bittrich-the-chivalrous-ss-general

223. Michael Miller, *Leaders of the SS and German Police*, Vol. I, James Bender, 2006, p.132.
224. *The New York Times*, 24 June 1954.
225. Mark C. Yerger, *Allgemeine-SS: Commands, Units and Leaders of the General SS*, Schiffer Publishing, 1997, p.51.
226. Allan Mitchell, *Nazi Paris: The History of an Occupation 1940–1944*, Berghahn Books, 2013, p.159.
227. Peter Longerich, *Heinrich Himmler*, Oxford University Press, 2012, p.631.
228. *Time* magazine, 5 May 1958.
229. Yerger, p.103.
230. *Frankfurter Allgemeine*, 30 August 2010.
231. Cornelius Ryan, *The Last Battle*, Collins, 1966, p.398.
232. Antony Beevor, *Berlin: The Downfall 1945*, Viking-Penguin, 2002, p.387.
233. Ryan, pp.394–396.
234. Anton Joachimsthaler, *The Last Days of Hitler*, Broekhampton Press, 1999, pp.293–294.
235. Michael Miller, *Leaders of the SS and German Police*, Vol. I, James Bender, 2006, p.155 and p.159.
236. Charles Hamilton, *Leaders and Personalities of the Third Reich*, Vol. I, James Bender Publishing, 1984, p.138.
237. Ian Kershaw, *Hitler: A Biography*, W.W. Norton & Company, 2008, p.950.
238. Arthur H. Mitchell, *Hitler's Mountain: The Führer, Obersalzberg and the American Occupation*, MacFarland, 2007, p.59.
239. Richard Evens, *The Third Reich at War*, Penguin Group, 2008, pp.159–163.
240. specialcamp11.co.uk/Vizeadmiral%20Helmuth%20Bringmann.htm
241. Hamilton, p.166.
242. Kershaw, p.925.
243. Traudl Junge, *Until the Final Hour: Hitler's Last Secretary*, Arcade Publishing, 2004, p.201.
244. James P. O'Donnell, *The Bunker*, Da Capo Press, 2001, p.311 and p.321.
245. Anton Joachimsthaler, *The Last Days of Hitler: The Legends, the Evidence, the Truth*, Brockhampton Press, 1995, p.285 and p.294.
246. Joachimsthaler, p.226.
247. V.K. Vinogradov, *Hitler's Death: Russia's Last Great Secret from the Files of the KGB*, Chancer Press, 2005, p.62.
248. Vinogradov, p.58.
249. Interview to Luke Harding. *The Guardian*, 2 May 2005.
250. CIA/FOIA (foia.cia.gov)
251. *Sydney Morning Herald*, 4 May 2005.
252. Junge, p.201. Also, *The New York Times*, 9 August 2004.
253. independent.co.uk/news/obituaries/walter-frentz-550169.html
254. The Associated Press, 9 August 2004.
255. Heinz Linge, *With Hitler to the End*, Skyhorse Publishing, 2009, p.10.
256. Junge, p.107. Also, Linge, p.209 and p.212.
257. Kershaw, p.952.
258. Michael Miller, *Leaders of the Storm Troops*, Vol. I, Helion & Company, 2015, p.24.

NOTES

259. Hamilton, p.161.
260. Peter Hoffmann, *Hitler's Personal Security. Protecting the Fuhrer 1921–1945*, Da Capo Press, 2000, pp.50–51.
261. Mark Felton, *Guarding Hitler. The Secret World of the Führer*, Pen & Sword Military, 2014, p.34.
262. Kershaw, p.954 and p.957. Also, Joachimsthaler, p.210 and p.212.
263. Hamilton, p.141.
264. David Irving, *Hitler's War* (Translated into Greek), Govostis, 2003, p.725, p.963 and p.1008. Also, Kershaw, pp.901–902 and p.923.
265. Phil Carradice, *Hitler and his Women*, Pen & Sword Military, 2021, p.142.
266. Junge, p.201.
267. Carradice, p.143.
268. Joachimsthaler, p.281. Also, Kershaw, p.881.
269. Joachimsthaler, p.281.
270. John Toland, *Adolf Hitler*, Bantam Doubleday Dell Publishing Group, 1976, p.733.
271. O'Donnell, pp.271–274.
272. forum.axishistory.com/26 April 2004.
273. *The New York Times*, 17 September 1997.
274. Hamilton, p.141.
275. John Hooper, 'Obituary: *Traudl Junge*', *The Guardian*, 14 February 2002.
276. Irving, p.1030.
277. O'Donnell, p.271 and p.291.
278. liverpoolecho.co.uk/woman-who-worked-for-nazis-10757448
279. Pierre Galante; Eugene Silianoff (Ed.), *Voices from the Bunker: Hitler's Personal Staff Tells the Story of the Führer's Last Days*, Anchor, 1990, p.1 and p.3.
280. O'Donnell, p.291.
281. Junge, p.219.
282. findagrave.com/memorial/12465553/heinrich-hitler
283. rbth.com/history/333453/hitler's-nephews-in-ussr
284. Len Deighton, *Winter: A Novel of a Berlin Family*, Knopf, 1987, p.464.
285. Milan Hauner, *Hitler: A Chronology of his Life and Time*, Macmillan, 1983, p.181.
286. Toby Thacker, *Joseph Goebbels: Life and Death*, Palgrave Macmillan, 2010, p.149.
287. Hamilton, p.110.
288. *The Washington Post*, 1 July 2018.
289. David Wingeate (Attn.: Correct spelling) Pike, *Spaniards in the Holocaust: Mauthausen. Horror on the Danube*, Routledge, 2000, p.380.
290. warfarehistorynetwork.com/wwii-concentration-camps-the-horriic-discovery-at-buchenwald/
291. company7.com/bosendorfer/mauthausen/ziereis_testimony.html
292. ww2gravestone.com/xavier-ziereis-commandant-mauthausen-concentration-camp/
293. Tomaz Jardim, *The Mauthausen Trial – American Military Justice in Germany*, Harvard University Press, 2012, p.46.
294. Israel Gutman, *Encyclopedia of the Holocaust*, Macmillan, 1995, p.400.
295. Herlinde Pauer-Studer; David J. Vellemann, *Rudolf Höss and Eleonore Hodys*, Palgrave Macmillan, 2015, pp.112–114.

296. Hermann Langbein, *People in Auschwitz*, University of North Carolina Press, 2004, p.311 and p.412.
297. *The Guardian*, 31 August 2013.
298. Stevan Paskuly (Ed.), *Rudolf Höss: Death Dealer. The Memoirs of the SS Commandant at Auschwitz*, Da Capo Press, 1996, p.39.
299. Paskuly, pp.179–180.
300. capitalpunishmentuk.org/nazigirls.html
301. Geoffrey P. Megargee, *Encyclopedia of Camps and Ghettos 1933–1945*, The US Holocaust Museum/Indiana University Press, Vol. I, 2009, p.1479.
302. *The Times*, 15 December 1945.
303. bergenbelsen.co.uk/PAGES/TrialTranscript/Trial_Day_029.html
304. forum.axishistory.com/viewtopic.php?t=151855
305. Michael D. Miller; Andreas Schulz, *Gauleiter: The Regional Leaders of the Nazi Party and their deputies*, Vol. I, R. James Bender Publishing, 2012, pp.149–150.
306. Memorial Book for the Dead of the Mauthausen Concentration Camp, New Academic Press (Vienna), 2016, p.56 and p.57.
307. Joshwa Green, *Justice at Dachau: The Trials of an American Prosecutor*, Broadway Books, 2003, p.209. Also, expostfacto.nl/dtrr/dtfiles/us423.htm
308. Ernst Klee, *Das Personenlexikon zum Dritten Reich: Wer War Was Vor und Nach 1945* (In German), Fischer-Taschenbuch Verlag, 2007, p.13.
309. forum.axishistory.com/viewtopic.php?t=151855
310. Trials by the US Army Courts in Europe 1945–1948, File Number US423, Case Number 000-50-5-23 (US vs Kofler et al).
311. Juliette Pattinso, *Behind Enemy Lines: Gender Passing and the Special Operations Executive in the Second World War*, Manchester University Press, 2007, p.157.
312. Jerzy Pindera; Lynn Taylor; Liebe Mutti, *One Man's Struggle to Survive in KZ Sachsenhausen 1939–1945*, University Press of America, 2004, pp.71–72.
313. Michael J. Bazyler; Frank M. Tuerkheimer, *The Hamburg Ravensbrück Trial. Forgotten Trials of the Holocaust*, NYO Press, 2014, p.148.
314. Jewishvirtuallibrary.com/Sauchsenhausen Trial (October 1947).
315. Donald Bloxham, *The Final Solution: A Genocide*, Oxford University Press, 2009, p.253.
316. Peter Longerich, *Heinrich Himmler*, Oxford University Press, 2012, p.485.
317. *Time* magazine, 21 October 1966.
318. Yitzak Arad, *Bełzec, Sobibór, Treblinka: The Operation Reinhard Death Camps*, Indiana University Press, 1987, p.191.
319. Juliet Golden, *Remembering Chełmo. Archaeological Ethics*, Rowman Altamira, 2006, p.189.
320. David Lester, *Who Committed Suicide? Suicide and the Holocaust*, Nova Publishers, 2005, pp.11–12.
321. Robert Melvin Spector, *The Konzentrationlager. World without Civilization*, Vol. I, University Press of America, 2004, p.360.
322. Yitzak Arad, *Bełzec, Sobibór, Treblinka: The Operation Reinhard Death Camps*, Indiana University Press, 1987, p.182.
323. P. R. Reid, *Colditz: The Full Story*, Pam Macmillan, 2011, p.347.
324. Mark Mazower, *Hitler's Empire: How the Nazis Ruled Europe*, Penguin Press, 2008, p.382.

NOTES

325. Longerich, p.547.
326. *International Herald Tribune*, 26 July 1974.
327. jewishvirtuallibrary.org/ernst-lerch
328. Hannah Arendt, *Eichmann in Jerusalem: A Report on the Banality of Evil*, Penguin, 1992, p.15.
329. Martin Winstone, *The Dark Heart of Hitler's Europe: Nazi Rule in Poland and Under the General Government*, Bloomsbury Publishing, 2014, p.241.
330. Theresienstadt Lexikon: Karl Rahm. Also, ghetto-theresienstadt.de/pages/r/rahmk.htm
331. Holocaust Encyclopedia, US Holocaust Memorial Museum (encyclopedia.ushmm.org/content/en/article/Theresienstadt)
332. Christian Zentner; Friedmann Bedürftig, *The Encyclopedia of the Third Reich*, Macmillan, 1991, p.292.
333. Tom Segev, *Soldiers of Evil: The Commandants of the Nazi Concentration Camps*, Berkeley, 2002, p.137.
334. Segev, p.153.
335. Gusen-memorial.org/en/The-Concentration-Camp-Gusen/Camp-Commandant-Karl-Chmielewski
336. Michael Bar-Zohar, *The Avengers*, Hawthorn Books, 1969, p.254.
337. Wittmann, pp.233–234.
338. Henry Friedlander, *The Origins of Nazi Genocide: From Euthanasia to the Final Solution*, University of North Carolina, 1995, p.242.
339. Jefferson Chase, 'Remembering the 'forgotten victims' of Nazi 'euthanasia' murders', Deutsche Welle, 26 January 2017.
340. Heyde, Werner, *Who's Who in Nazi Germany*, Routledge, 2001, p.107.
341. Ute Deichmann, *Biologists under Hitler: Expulsion, Careers, Research*, Harvard University Press, 1992, p.x (Prologue).
342. Charles Hamilton, *Leaders and Personalities of the Third Reich*, Vol. I, 1984, p.138.
343. George J. Annas, *The Nazi Doctors and the Nuremberg Code*, Oxford University Press, 1995, p.106.
344. Patricia Heberer; Jürgen Matthäus (Ed.), *Atrocities on Trial: Historical Perspectives on the Politics of Prosecuting War Crimes*, University of Nebraska Press, 2008, p.136.
345. Hamilton, p.138.
346. Ernst Klee, *Das Personnenlexikon zum Dritten Reich*, Fischer Taschenbuch Verlag, 2005, p.71.
347. William Shirer, *The Rise and Fall of the Third Reich*, Simon & Schuster, 1960, p.981.
348. David Cesarani, *Final Solution: The Fate of the Jews 1933–1945*, St Martin's Press, 2016, p.286. Also, Paul J. Weindling, *Nazi Medicine and War Crimes to Informed Consent*, Palgrave Macmillan, 2004, p.302.
349. Michael H. Kater, *Doctors Under Hitler*, University of North Carolina Press, 1989, p.73.
350. Nikolaus Wahsmann, *KL: A History of the Nazi Concentration Camps*, Farrar Straus & Giroux, 2015, p.59.
351. Klee, p.278.

352. Ibid.
353. Rolf Casteli et al, *Geschichte der Kinder-Und Jugendpsychiatrie in Deutschland in den Jahren 1937 bis 1961,* Vandenhoeck & Ruprecht Gmbh & Co, 2003, p.520.
354. *Die Welt*, 13 November 2005.
355. Steve Fielding, *Pierrepoint: A Family of Executioners*, John Blake Publishing, 2008, p.203 and p.287.
356. *The Times*, 15 December 1945.
357. *Der Spiegel*, 9 December 2013.
358. newworldencyclopedia.org/entry/guillotine
359. *The New York Post*, 14 June 2017. Also, nypost.com/2017/06/14/hitlert's-chief-executioner-invented-his-own-guillotine
360. Thomas E. Beam; Linette R. Sparacino (Ed.), *Military Medical Ethics*, Vol. II, DIANE Publishing, 2003, p.436. Also, Alexander Cockburn; Jeffrey St Clair, *Whiteout: The CIA, Drugs and the Press*, Verso, 1998, pp.148–149.
361. Klee, p.35.
362. Robert Jay Lifton, *The Nazi Doctors from Hell: Medical Killing and the Psychology of Genocide*, Basic Books, 1986, p.275. Also, Vivien Spitz, *Doctors from Hell: The Horrific Account of Nazi Experiments on Humans*, Sentient, 2005, p.265.
363. Anna Hájková, *The Last Ghetto. An Everyday History of Theresienstadt*, Oxford University Press, 2020, p.135.
364. Judith Baumel et al, *Holocaust Encyclopedia*, Yale University Press, 2001, p.411.
365. Hamburger Abendblatt, Issue 92, 20 April 1979, p.2.
366. Mauthausen-memorial.org/en/History/The-Mauthausen-Concentration/Camp–19381945/Prosecution-of-the-Perpetratprs-in-the-Courts
367. *The Times*, 15 December 1945.
368. Capitalpunishment.org/Hameln.htm
369. Ibid.
370. *The Times*, 15 December 1945.
371. Lore Shelley, *Auschwitz: The Nazi Civilization*, University Press of America, 1992, p.33.
372. Nanda Herbermann, *The Blessed Abyss: Inmate # 6582 in Ravensbrück Concentration Camp for Women*, Wayne University Press, 2000, p.15.
373. *The Times*, 'The Belsen Trial', 18 September 1945.
374. *The Times*, 15 December 1945.
375. First Belsen Trial, bergenbelsen.co.uk
376. *Der Spiegel*, 18 April 1947.
377. Michael J. Bazyler; Frank M. Tuerkheimer, *Forgotten Trials of the Holocaust*, New York University Press, 2015, p.141.
378. Bazyler and Tuerkheimer, p.143.
379. Capitalpunishment.org (Chapter 8, Female Concentration Camp Guards, PDF)
380. Capitalpunishment.org/Hameln.htm
381. Capitalpunishment.uk.org/nazisgirls.html
382. Ibid.
383. Female Nazi War Criminals, capitalpunishment.org
384. Daniel Patrick Brown, *The Female Auxiliaries Who Assisted the SS Running the Nazi Concentration Camp System*, Schiffer Publishing, 2002, p.288.
385. Brown, p.185.

NOTES

386. *Der Spiegel*, 30 November 1975.
387. Gizela Bock, *Die Aufseherin Luise Danz. Genozid und Geschlecht: Jüdische Fraven im Nazionalsozialistischen Lagersystem* (in German), Campus Verlag, 2005, pp.71–77.
388. Joseph Lelyveld, 'Breaking Away', *New York Times Magazine*, 6 March 2005.
389. Douglas Martin, 'A Nazi Past. A Queens home life: An overlooked death', *New York Times*, 2 December 2005.
390. Geoffrey P. Megarger, *Gertrud Heise*, The United States Holocaust Memorial Museum Encyclopedia of Camps and Ghettos 1933–1945, Indiana University Press, 2009, p.1097.
391. Paul R. Bartrop; Eve E. Grimm, *Perpetrating the Holocaust: Leaders, Enablers and Collaborators*, ABC-CLIO, 2013, p.44.
392. *Los Angeles Times*, 2 May 1948.
393. The Encyclopedia of the Camps, United States Holocaust Museum, p.1459.
394. Alchetron. The Free Social Encyclopedia (alchetron.com/Joanna-Langfeld)
395. ewdocs.de/the-female-guard-the-case-of-johanna-langfeld
396. Bella Gutterman, *A Narrow Bridge to Life: Jewish Forced Labour and Survival in the Gross-Rosen Camp System 1940–1945*, Berghahn (Attn: Correct spelling) Books, 2008, p.101.
397. Susan Benedict, '*Maria Stromberg: A nurse in the resistance in Auschwitz*', Nursing History Review, 14 (1), 2006, pp.189–202.
398. Hermann Langbein, *People in Auschwitz*, University of North Carolina Press, 2005, pp.464–465.
399. *Zeit* Online, 7 November 2021.
400. *Der Spiegel*, 5 March 1990.
401. Ibid.
402. Airbornearnhem.nl/Willem Tiemens Archief.
403. paradata.org/uk/media/1911
404. Airbornearnhem.nl/Willem Tiemens Archief.

Italians

1. Flavio Giovanni Conti, *I Prigioneri du Guerra Italiani*, Il Mulino, 1986, p.62.
2. generals.dk/general/Lastrucci/Romolo/Italy.html
3. Winston Churchill, *Second World War* (transl. into Greek), Helliniki Morfotiki Hestia, Vol. II, p.77.
4. *Associated Press*, '*HMAS Sydney. Italian prisoners and captured Italian general*', 17 February 2012.
5. Bastian Matteo Scianna, *The Italian War on the Eastern Front 1941–1943: Operations, Myths and Memories*, Palgrave Macmillan, 2019, p.304.
6. regimental-books.com/we-were-the-rats-1st-edition
7. Richard Collier, *The War in the Desert*, Time-Life Books, 1977, p.15.
8. Antony Beevor, *The Second World War*, Little Brown & Company, 2012, p.181.
9. Major Kenneth Macksey, *Beda Fomm: The Classic Victory*, Ballantine Books, 1971, p.151.

10. *The Times*, 12 February 1941.
11. John Keegan; Kenneth Macksey, *Churchill's Generals*, Cassel Military, 1991, pp.194–195.
12. J. Harding, '*Appendix E; HQ Cyrenaica Command Intelligence Summary No. 6, 23 February 1941*', The National Archives, WO 169/1258.
13. *Time* magazine, 19 August 1940.
14. J.F.C. Fuller, *The Second World War 1939–1945. A Strategical and Tactical History*, Da Capo Press, 1993, p.102. Also, H.E. Rough, *Wavell in the Middle East 1939–1941. A Study of Generalship*, Bassey's, 1993, pp.182–183.
15. *Time* Magazine, 16 March 1942.
16. Ibid.
17. D.J.E. Collins; Bisheshwar Prasad, *History of the Royal Indian Navy 1939–1945. The Official History of the Indian Armed Forces in the Second World War*, Orient Longmans, 1964, p.58 and p.64.
18. '*Biography of Lieutenant General Pietro Piakentini (1898–1963), Italy*'/www.generals.dk
19. Neil Orpen, *East African and Abyssinian Campaigns. South African Forces in World War II*, Vol. 1, Purnell, 1968, p.320.
20. '*Nasi Guglielmo*' – Dizionario Storico Biographico della Tuscia (gentedituscia.it/nasi-guglielmo)
21. P. Maravigna, *Come Abiamo Perduto La Guerra in Africa* (in Italian), Tosi, 1949, p.191.
22. *The New York Times*, 4 February 1977.
23. Flavio Giovanni Conti, *Prigionieri Di Guerra Italiani Negli Stati Uniti 1942–1946* (Italian prisoners of war in the United States 1942–1946) (PhD thesis) Roma Tre University, 2010/2011.
24. James H. Burgwyn, *Mussolini Warlord: Failed Dreams of Empire 1940–1943*, Enigma Books, 2012.
25. '*Biography of Major-General Giulio Cesare Gotti-Porcinari (1888–1946), Italy*', www.generals.dk
26. Nikolaos Theotokis, *Airborne Landing to Air Assault. A History of Military Parachuting*, Pen & Sword, 2020, p.25.
27. John Strawson, *Hitler as Military Commander*, Sphere Books, 1973, pp.178–179.
28. Strawson, p.180
29. Ibid.
30. Philip Morgan, *The Fall of Mussolini*, Oxford University Press, 2007, p.15.
31. reccani.it/enciclopedia/Giovanni-Marinelli (Dizionario Biografico)
32. *The Telegraph*, 17 April 2009.
33. R.J.B. Bosworth, *Mussolini's Italy: Life Under Fascist Dictatorship 1915–1945*, Penguin Books, 2005, p.514.
34. A.T. Lane (ed.), *Bibliographical Dictionary of European Labour Leaders*, Vol. I, Greenwood, 1995, p.205. Also, Farrell, p.441.
35. Morgan, p.15.
36. John Gooch, *Re-conquest and Suppression: Fascist Italy's Pacification of Libya and Ethiopia 1922–1939*, Journal of Strategic Studies, Band 28, near 6, 2005, p.1009.
37. John Hooper, 'Urbano Lazaro: The partisan who arrested Mussolini', *The Guardian*, 28 February 2006.

NOTES

38. Sir Colin Coote, Mussolini, in: Lord Longford; Sir John Wheeler-Bennett (Ed.), *The History Makers*, Sidgwick & Jackson Limited, 1973, p.319.
39. *Time* magazine, 7 May 1945.
40. reccani.it/enciclopedia/achille-starace (Dizionario Biographico)
41. John Michaud, '*Takes: Death of a dictator 1945*', *The New Yorker*, 20 October 2011.
42. recanni.it/enciclopedia/guido-buffarini-guidi (Dizionario Biografico)
43. Hermann Frank Meyer, *Il Massacro di Cefalonia e la 1o Divisione da Montagna Tedesca* (in Italian), Gaspari, 2013, p.304.
44. memorial-archives.international/en/entities/show/546f72911759c02ca678cZc70
45. generals.dk/General/Vercellino/Mario/Italy.html
46. *Corriere di Saluzzo*, 8 November 2007.
47. Carlos Caballero Jurado, *Foreign Volunteers of the Wehrmacht 1941–1945*, Osprey Publishing, 2001, p.8.
48. Associazione Nationale Reduci dalla Prigionia dall' Intermento dalla Guerra di Liberazione a Loro Farmiglari (ANRP), La Porte della Memoria, 2/2013.
49. wrecksite.eu, SS Oria
50. Andrew Roberts, *The Storm of War. A New History of the Second World War*, Allen Lane, 2009, p.379.
51. Philip S. Jowett; Stephen Andrew, *The Italian Army 1940–1945*, Vol. I, Osprey Publishing, 2000, p.8.
52. Maurizio Brescia, *Mussolini's Navy: A Reference Guide to the Regia Marina 1930–1945*, Seaforth, 2012, p.227.
53. Lucio Ceva, '*Il Maresciallo Cavallero*' (in Italian), *Storia Militare*, III (19), 1995, pp.4–12.
54. Spencer Tucker, *Who's Who in Twentieth Century Warfare*, Routledge, 2002, p.101. Also, Pier Paolo Battistelli, *The Balkans 1940–1941. Mussolini's Fatal Blunder in the Greco-Italian War*, Bloomsbury Publishing, 2021, p.11.
55. Sevastiano Visconti Prasca, *Io Aggredito La Grecia* (I Invaded Greece) (in Italian) (Translated into Greek), Govostis, 1999, pp.23–24.
56. *Biography of Major General Bruno Malaguti (1887–1945), Italy*, generals.dk. Also, Gerhard Schreiberg, *I Military Italiani Internati nei Campi di Concentramento del Terzo Reich 1943–1945*, Ufficio Storico, Stato Maggiore Dell' Esercito, 1992, p.634.
57. *Biography of Major General Giorgio Carlo Calvi di Bergolo (1887–1977), Italy*, www.generals.dk
58. Paolo Alberini; Franco Prosperini, *Dizionario Biografico Uomini della Marina 1861–1946*, Ufficio Storico della Marina Militare, Nadir Media, 2016, pp.433–437.
59. Paolo Alberini; Franco Prosperini, *Uomini della Marina 1861–1946*, Dizionario Biographico, Officio Storico della Marina Militare, 2015, p.43.
60. Kerstin von Lingen, *Allen Dalles and Nazi War Criminals: The Dynamics of Selective Prosecution*, Cambridge University Press, 2013, pp.77–80.
61. Adrian Weale, *Army of Evil: A History of the SS*, NAL Caliber, 2012, p.205.
62. Michael Salter, *Nazi War Crimes: Intelligence and Selective Prosecution at Nuremberg: Controversies Regarding the Role of the OSS*, Routledge, 2007, pp.110–119.
63. Kerstin von Lingen, *Kesselring's Last Battle: War Crimes and Cold War Politics 1945–1960*, University Press of Kansas, 2009, p.84.

64. *Associated Press*, 22 September 1944.
65. *The Irish Times*, 19 October 2013.
66. Jane L. Carwood-Cutler, *International Humanitarian Law: Origins*, Brill/Nijhoff, 2003, pp.89–90.
67. Garwood-Cutler, pp.89–90.
68. Philip Rees, *Biographical Dictionary of the Extreme Right Since 1890*, Prentice-Hall, 1990, p.212.
69. Nicholas Farrell, *Mussolini: A New Life*, Phoenix, 2004, pp.449–450.
70. Von Lingen (*Kesselring's Last Battle*), pp.80–81.
71. Ibid., p.84.
72. *Biography of Major General Tito Agosti (1889–1946), Italy*, www.generals.dk
73. *Biography of Lieutenant General Enrico Adami-Rossi (1880–1963), Italy*, www.generals.dk
74. United Nations War Crimes Commission, *The Central Registry of War Criminals and Security Suspects* (*CROWCASS*), Allied Control Authority, Consolidated Wanted List, Folder 17247, 1 March 1947.
75. Philip Morgan, *The Fall of Mussolini,* Oxford University Press, 2007, p.16.
76. Peter Neville, *Mussolini,* Routledge, 2004, p.190.
77. Morgan, p.16.
78. Owen Pearson, *Albania in Occupation and War: From Fascism to Communism 1940–1945*, I.B. Tauris, 2006, p.430.
79. Owen Pearson, *Albania as Dictatorship and Democracy: From Isolation to the Kosovo War (1946–1998)*, I.B. Tauris, 2006, p.423.
80. *Time* magazine, 11 September 1939.
81. Antony Mockler, *Haile Selasie's War*, Olive Branch Press, 2003, p.165.
82. Michael B. Lentakis, *Ethiopia: A View from Inside*, Janus Publishing, 2006, p.61.
83. Philippo Focardi; Lutz Klinkhammer, 'The question of Fascist Italy's war crimes: The construction of a self-acquitting myth 1943–1948', *Journal of Modern Italian Studies*, 2004, pp.330, Biography of Major General 340.
84. *The Guardian*, 25 June 2001.
85. Blane Taylor, '*Italian war criminal Rodolfo Graziani*', warfarehistorynet.com, 21 February 2020.
86. Victoria Witkowski, '*Remembering fascism and the Empire: The public representation of myth of Rodolfo Graziani in Twentieth century Italy*' (thesis), European University Institute, 24 September 2001, p.136.
87. Efi Pedaliu, '*Britain and the 'hand over' of Italian war criminals to Yugoslavia 1945–1948*', *Journal of Contemporary History*, Vol. 39, No. 4, 2004, p.509 and p.529.
88. *The New York Times*, 4 April 1945.
89. Amedeo Osti Guerrazzi, *The Italian Army in Slovenia. Strategies of Anti-partisan Repression 1941–1943*, Palgrave Macmillan, 2013, pp.139–144.
90. *Italian crimes against Yugoslavia*, Yugoslav Information Office London, 1945, p.138.
91. Tomasso Di Francesco; Giacomo Scotti, *Sixty years of ethnic cleansing*, Le Monde Diplomatique, May 1999.
92. Gianfranco Cresciani, 'Clash of Civilizations', *Italian Historical Society Journal*, Vol. 12, No. 2, p.7.

NOTES

93. Pierre Kosmidis, *Italian war crimes and atrocities in Greece during World War II*, ww2wrecks.com (portfolio/Italian-war-crimes-and-atrocities-in greece-during-ww2)
94. *L' Unità* (Italian newspaper), 22 April 1944. Also, *L' Unità*, 23 August 1944.
95. Focardi and Klinkhammer, pp.330–348.
96. Ibid.
97. Rory Carroll, '*Italy's bloody secret*', *The Guardian*, 25 June 2001.
98. *The Guardian*, 25 March 2018.

Japanese

1. John Toland, *The Rising Sun: The Decline and Fall of the Japanese Empire 1936–1945*, Random House, 1970, pp.871–872.
2. Richard Frank, *Downfall: The End of the Japanese Empire*, Penguin Books, 1999, pp.319–320.
3. Mark J. Ravina, '*The apocryphal suicide of Saigō Takamori: Samurai, 'Seppuku' and the politics of legends*', The Journal of Asian Studies, 69 (3), 2010, pp.691–721.
4. The Pacific War Research Society (Ed.), *Japan's Longest Day – Surrender: The last 24 hours through Japanese eyes*, Kadansha International, 1973, pp.88–89.
5. trove.nla.gov.au/newspaper/article/971305
6. Michael Wert, *Samurai: A Very Short Introduction*, Oxford University Press, 2021, p.35.
7. *The San Bernandino Daily Sun*, 27 September 1945.
8. Steve Zaloga, *Kamikaze: Japanese Special Attack Weapons 1944–1945*, Osprey Publishing, 2011, p.12.
9. generals.dk/Okamoto/Kiyotomi/Japan.html
10. history.state.gov/historicaldocuments/frus1945v06/d360
11. '*The fate of Japanese POWs in Soviet Captivity*', National World War II Museum, New Orleans, 28 August 2020.
12. Andrew Roberts, *The Storm of War. A New History of the Second World War*, Allen Lane, 2009, pp.575–577.
13. Williamson Murray; Allan R. Millett, *A War to be Won. Fighting the Second World War*, The Belknap Press of Harvard University Press, 2001, p.525.
14. Eiji Takemae, *Inside GHQ: The Allied Occupation of Japan and its Legacy*, Continuum International, 2002, p.67.
15. Herbert P. Bix, *Hirohito and the Making of Modern Japan*, HarperCollins, 2000, p.541.
16. Douglas MacArthur, *Reminiscences of General of the Army Douglas MacArthur*, Bluejacket Books, 1964, pp.318–319. Also, Victor Sebestyer, *1946: The Making of the Modern World*, Pantheon Books, 2015, pp.96–100. Also, Bix, p.545.
17. John W. Dower, *Embracing Defeat. Japan in the Wake of World War II*, W.W. Norton & Company, 1999, p.51.
18. *International Military Tribunal for the Far East* (IMTFE) *Judgement*, Chapter III, pp.1001–1003.
19. B.V.A. Rolling; Antonio Cassese, *The Tokyo Trial and Beyond*, The Polity Press, 1993, p.76.
20. singaporecrimestrials.com/background

21. MacArthur, pp.318–319.
22. *The Washington Post*, 17 January 2014
23. David Lon Lu, *Agony of Choice: Matsuoka Yōsuke and the Rise and Fall of the Japanese Empire 1880–1946*, Lexington Books, 2002, pp.6–7.
24. 'Fourteen new lawyers: Class of 1900 in the University of Oregon pass examination', *The Sunday Oregonian*, 27 May 1900.
25. Timothy P. Maga, *Judgement at Tokyo: The Japanese War Crimes Trials*, University of Kentucky Press, 2001, p.134.
26. *BBC*, 15 June 2021.
27. pwencycl.kabudge.com/S/a/Sato_Kenryo.htm
28. thefreelibrary.com/Hashimoto%2c+Kingoro+(1890–1957)-a017065984
29. history.state.gov/historicaldocuments/frus1941v04/d320
30. Michael Hunt, *The World Transformed: 1945 to the Present*, Oxford University Press, 2013, p.86.
31. Louis G. Perez (Ed.), *Japan at War: An Encyclopedia*, ABC-Clio, 2013, p.114.
32. Roy Conyers Nesbit; Georges van Acker, *The Flight of Rudolf Hess: Myths and Reality*, Stroud History Press, 2011, p.132.
33. pwencyccl.kabudge.com/S/a/Sato_Kenryo.htm
34. The Pacific War Online Encyclopedia (pwencycl.kgbudge.com/O/k/Oka_Takazumi.htm
35. *The Telegraph*, 3 June 2004.
36. Paul E. Spurlock, 'The Yokohama War Crimes Trials: The truth about a misunderstood subject', *American Bar Association* (ABA), Vol. 36, 1950, p.387.
37. Major General Roger Pulvers, 'Okada: A rare leader who took the blame', *Japan Times*, 24 June 2007.
38. *Japan Times*, 24 June 2007.
39. Jonathan Watts, 'Japan guilty of germ warfare against thousands of Chinese', *The Guardian*, 28 August 2002.
40. BBC *Horizon*, 'Biology at war. A plague in the wind', 29 October 1984.
41. Hugh Deane, *The Korean War 1945–1953*, China Books & Periodicals, 1999, p.155.
42. Ken Dooley, 'The judgement at Yokohama: How a World War II crimes trial aided the search for RI flier's remains', *The Providence Journal*, 10 November 2020.
43. guampedia.com/u-s-navy-war-crimes-on-guam
44. George Wibur, 'Five Japanese Military criminals executed on Guam for atrocities', *Navy News*, 26 September 1947.
45. Paul Addison, '*Forgotten war-crimes trials*', World Press Review, 41 (7), July 1994, p.45.
46. executedtoday.com/2014/03/31/1949-dr-chisato-ueno
47. *Newcastle Morning Herald & Miners' Advocate* (NSW, Australia), 16 July 1947.
48. executedtoday.com/2015/01/17/1949-hiroshi-iwanami/
49. Anne Sharp Wells, *The A to Z of World War II: The War Against Japan*, Scarecrow Press, 2009, p.16.
50. *Malaya Tribune*, 23 February 1946.
51. John Toland, *The Rising Sun: The Decline and Fall of the Japanese Empire 1936–1945*, Random House, 1970, p.320.
52. forum.axishistory.com, 'Executions at Sugamo Prison'
53. *Time* magazine, '*Sequels: Forgiving neighbor*', 27 July 1953.

NOTES

54. Sharp Wells, p.16.
55. W.L. Cheah, 'An overview of the Singapore War Crimes Trials (1946–1948): Prosecuting lower-level accused', *Singapore Law Review*, Vol. No. 34, 10/2017.
56. *The Singapore Free Press*, 10 March 1947. Also, *The Straits Times*, 3 April 1947.
57. generals.dk/general/Kawamura/saburō/japan.html
58. *The Straits Times*, 2 March 1946.
59. Ibid., 16 April 1946.
60. *The Straits Times*, 16 August 1947. Also, Heng Wong, '*Double Tenth Trial*', Singapore Infopedia
61. Saburo Hayashi, *Kogun: The Japanese Army in the Pacific War* (Translated from the Japanese), The Marine Corps Association, 1959.
62. forum.axishistory.com/Lieutenant-General Adachi Hatazō
63. *Mercury*, 26 September 1945.
64. Rabaul R176 Trial Report. Also, Michael T. Smith, *Bloody Ridge: The Battle That Saved Guadalcanal*, Pocket, 2000, pp.224–225. Also, Smith, p.230.
65. *The Argus*, Melbourne, 6 June 1947. Also, *The Mercury*, 6 June 1947.
66. Labuan ML28 Trial Report.
67. David van Reybrouck, *Revolusi. Indonesia and the Birth of the Modern World*, De Bezige Bij., 2020, p.210.
68. *The Sydney Morning Herald*, 8 January 1946.
69. *The Sydney Morning Herald*, 3 May 2007.
70. Japanese War Crimes in the Pacific. Australia's Investigations and Prosecutions, National Archives of Australia, 2019, p.145.
71. James Boyd; Narrelle Morris, '*High standard of efficiency and steadiness: Papua New Guinea native police guards and Japanese war criminals 1945–1953*', The Journal of Pacific History, Vol. 50, No. 1, 2015, pp.20–37.
72. National Library of Australia (catalogue.nla.gov.au/catalog/565235)
73. Hank Nelson, 'Blood oath': A reel history, *Australian Historical Studies*, 24 (1991), p.429.
74. *The Canberra Times*, 16 January 1946.
75. Fred L. Borch, *Military Trials of War Criminals in the Netherlands East Indies 1946–1949*, Oxford University Press, 2017, p.36.
76. *Canberra Times*, 28 September 1950.
77. *Evening Standard*, 12 April 2012.
78. Arthur Cotterell, *Western Power in Asia: Its Slow Rise and Swift Fall 1415–1999*, John Wiley & Sons, 2009, p.247.
79. generals.dk/general/Yasuoka/Masaomi/Japan.html
80. Nikolaos Theotokis, *Airborne to Air-Assault. A History of Military Parachuting*, Pen & Sword Military, 2020, p.91.
81. Borch, pp.184–185.
82. Morten Bergsmo; Chean Wui Ling; Yi Ping (Ed.), *Historical Origins of International Criminal Law*, Vol. II, Torkel Opsahi Academic Publisher, 2014, p.134.
83. foreignaffairs.com/reviews/capsule-review/2018-02-13/Japanese-war-criminals-politics-justice-after-second-world-war
84. Takashi Yoshida, *The Making of the 'Rape of Nanking'. History and Memory in Japan, China and the United States*, Oxford University Press, 2009, p.64.

85. http://www.chinaww2.com/2029/03/17/nanjing–1948-the-reckoning
86. chinadaily.com.cn, 3 August 2015.
87. Suzannah Linton, *Hong Kong's War Crimes Trials*, Oxford University Press, 2013, p.99.
88. cambridge.org/core/book/abs/trials-for-international-crimes-in-asia/peoples-republic-of-china-lenient-policy-towards-japanese-was-criminals
89. Jacob Darwin Hambling, *Arming Mother Nature: The Birth of Catastrophic Environmentalism*, Oxford University Press, 2013, p.23.
90. Poslednie plenniki vtoroy mirovoy voyni. Dokumenti iz fondov TS KPSS o repatriatsii japonskih voennoplennih, Istorichesky archiv (in Russian) (The last prisoners of World War II. Documents from the CPSU Central Committee of the Japanese POW reparations. Historical Archives), 1993, p.72.
91. V.V. Romanova, 'From the Tokyo to Khabarovsk trials: The history of the preparation of the trial of Japanese war criminals', *Istoriya Meditsiny* (History of the Medicine), Vol. II, 2015, p.67.
92. Nick Kapur, *Crossroads: Conflict and Compromise after Anpo*, Harvard University Press, 2018, pp.79–80.
93. Mark Levene; Penny Roberts, *The Massacre in History*, Berghahn Books, 1999, pp.223–224. Also, Paul R. Bartrop; Samuel Totten, *Dictionary of Genocide*, Greenwood, 2008, pp.298–299.
94. *The New York Times*, 'Prince Asaka becomes Catholic', 18 December 1951.
95. *The Japan News*, 17 December 2022.
96. *Time*, 5 April 1948.

PART TWO – DETAINEES (II)

1. Steliu Lambru, '*Romanian prisoners in the USSR after World War II*', Radio Romania International, 25 August 2014.
2. Frank Gordon, '*Latvians and Jews between Germany and Russia*', Memento, 1990, p.81.
3. '*Social memory of the peoples of the world*', Bolashaq Academy, 31 May 2021. Also, *History and Destiny, Romanian prisoners in Kazakhstan*, Observatorul (Toronto), 15 January 2007.
4. '*Generals from Romania: Sănătescu, Constantin*', Generals.dk
5. '*Generals from Romania: Cosma, Gheorghe*', Generals.dk
6. Mark Axworthy; Horia Şerbanescu, *The Romanian Army of World War II*, Osprey Publishing, 1991, p.191.
7. John Erickson, *The Road to Berlin*, HarperCollins, 1985, p.397.
8. George Popescu, '*Divizia trădăta*' (4 Infanterie) (in Romanian), Radio Romania Actualităti, 18 December 2017.
9. '*Generals from Romania: Chirnoagă, Platon*', Generals.dk
10. Otto Kumn, *The History of the 7th Mountain Division 'Prinz Eugen'*, J. J. Fedorowicz, 1995, pp.9–10.
11. Hans Bergel, *The Dice of Life: Four Portraits of Important Transylvanians – Conrad Haas, Johan Martin Honigberger, Paul Richter and Artur Phleps* (in German), H. Meschendörfer, 1972, p.106.

NOTES

12. '*Generals from Romania: Sion, Alecu Ioan*', Generals.dk
13. '*Generals from Romania: Bălan, Grigore*', Generals.dk
14. '*Generals from Romania: Lăscar, Mihail*', Generals.dk
15. Archie Brown, *The Rise and Fall of Communism*, HarperCollins, 2009, p.140. Also, David Engel, *Facing a Holocaust: The Polish Government-in-Exile and the Jews 1943–1945*, UNC Press Books, 1993, p.71. Also, Stéphane Curtois; Mark Kramer, *Livre Noir du Communisme: Crimes, terreur, repression*, Harvard University Press, 1999, p.209.
16. Harvey Sarner, *General Anders and the Soldiers of the II Polish Corps*, Brunswick Press, 2006, p.10.
17. Final Report of the International Commission on the Holocaust in Romania (PDF), 11 November 2004.
18. '*Generals from Romania: Cosma, Gheorghe*', Generals.dk
19. Dénes Bernád, *Romanian Aces of World War II*, Osprey Publishing, 2003, p.16.
20. Institute and Museum of Military History (PDF), Budapest.
21. '*Malenki Robot – Hungarian forced labourers in the Soviet Union*', Wayback Machine.
22. Stephen R. Burant; Eugene K. Keefe (Ed.), *Hungary: A Country Study*, US Government Printing Office, 1990, pp.230–231.
23. hungarianfreepress.com/2019/01/21/general-gusztav-jany-world-war-ii-war-criminal/
24. Raphael Patai, *The Jews of Hungary: History, Culture and Psychology*, Wayne State University Press, 1996, p.730.
25. Michael Clodfelter, Warfare and Armed Conflicts: A Statistical Encyclopedia of Casualty and Other Figures 1492-2015, McFarland, 2017, p.456.
26. Grigorii F. Krivosheev, *Rossiia I SSSR v voinakh xx veka; Poteri vooruzhennykh sil/ statisticheskoe issledovanie* (in Russian), OLMA-Press, 2001, table 198, ISBN 5-224-01515-4
27. Gareth Stockey, *Gibraltar: A Dagger in the Spine of Spain,* Sussex Academic Press, 2009, p.152.

Pro-Axis puppet governments

1. Florian Thomas Rulitz, *The Tragedy of Bleiburg and Viktring 1945*, Northern Illinois University Press, 2015, pp.31–33.
2. N. Thomas; K. Mikulan; D. Pavelić, *Axis Forces in Yugoslavia 1941–1945*, Osprey Publishing, 1995, p.32.
3. Carlos Caballero Jurado, *Foreign Volunteers of the Wehrmacht 1941–1945*, Osprey Publishing, 1983, p.9.
4. Jurado, p.11.
5. Wilson Center Digital Archive, 14 November 1945.
6. Joso Tomasevich, *War and Revolution in Yugoslavia 1941–1945. Occupation and Collaboration,* Stanford University Press, 2001, p.765.
7. Florian Thomas Rulitz, *The Tragedy of Bleiburg and Victring 1945*, Northern Illinois University Press, 2015, p.62.

8. Vladimir Geiger, '*Review of Croatian History*', Croatian Institute of History, 8 (1), 2012, p.94.
9. Marko Attila Hoare, *Genocide and Resistance in Hitler's Bosnia: The Partisans and the Chetniks*, Oxford University Press, 2006 pp.20–24.
10. Misha Glenny, *The Balkans: Nationalism, War and the Great Powers 1804–1999*, Penguin, 2001, pp.497–500.
11. Tomasevich, p.326.
12. Christopher Pyle, *Extradition, Politics and Human Rights*, Temple University Press, 2001, p.133.
13. Walter R. Roberts, *Tito, Mihailović and the Allies 1941–1945*, Duke University Press, 1973, p.307.
14. Matteo J. Milazzo, *The Chetnik Movement and the Yugoslav Resistance*, John Hopkins University Press, 1975, p.182.
15. Jozo Tomasevich, *War and Revolution in Yugoslavia 1941–1945: The Chetniks*, Stanford University Press, 1975, p.427.
16. Thomas Fleming, *Montenegro: The Divided Land*, Chronicle Press, 2002, p.147.
17. Agnes Mangerish, *Albanian Escape – The True Story of US Army Nurses Behind Enemy Lines*, University Press of Kentucky, 2010, p.6.
18. *BBC* News, 13 December 2008.
19. Robert Elsie, *A Biographical Dictionary of Albanian History*, I.B. Tauris, 2012, pp.54–55.
20. Tomor Aliko, *Genocide of the Intellectual Elite of the Albanian Nation Under Communist Terror*, Shtypshkronja Maluka, 2007, p.97.
21. David H. Close, *The Origins of the Greek Civil War*, Routledge, 2013, p.62.
22. Mark Mazower, *Inside Hitler's Greece: The Experience of Occupation 1941–1944*, Alexandria Editions, 1994, p.45.
23. Markos Vallianatos, *The Untold History of Greek Collaboration with Nazi Germany 1941–1944*, Lulu.com, 2014, p.210.

Volunteers and collaborators (I)

1. ww2images.blogspot.com/2012/11/general-leclerc-and-captured-french-ss.html
2. Carlos Jurado, *Foreign Volunteers of the Wehrmacht 1941–1945*, Osprey Publishing, 1983, p.6.
3. David Littlejohn, *Foreign Legions of the Third Reich*, Vol. I, Bender Publishing, 1987, p.172.
4. *Signal* magazine, Issue No. 20, October 1943.
5. Robert O. Paxton, *Vichy France: Old Guard and New Order 1940–1944*, Alfred A. Knopf, 1972, pp.391–392.
6. Rey Warner, *Pierre Laval and the Eclipse of France*, Macmillan, 1968, p.387.
7. Charles Williams, *Pétain: How a hero of France became a convicted traitor and changed the course of history*, Palgrave Macmillan, 2005, pp.528–529.
8. Nikola Barber, *World War I: The Western Front*, Black Rabbit Books, 2003, p.53.
9. Hubert Cole, *Laval*, G.P. Putman's Sons, 1963, pp.210–211.

NOTES

10. Nico Wouters, '*Belgium*', in: David Stahel (Ed.), *Joining Hitler's Crusade: European Nations and the Invasion of the Soviet Union, 1941*, Cambridge University Press, 2018, pp.260–287.
11. *The New York Times*, 2 April 1994.
12. Carlos Jurado, *Foreign Volunteers of the Wehrmacht 1941–1945*, Osprey Publishing, 1983, p.9.
13. David Littlejohn, *The Patriotic Traitors*, Heinemann, 1972, p.155.
14. Luc Huyse, *Belgian and Dutch Purges after World War II* (2006_Belgian and Dutch Purge, pdf)
15. *Time* magazine, 23 February 1940.
16. *The Guardian*, 18 June 2023.
17. britishexecutions.co.uk/execution-content.php?=610&termRet
18. Jurado, p.8.
19. *Amarillo Globe*, 7 May 1946.
20. Luc Huyse, *Belgian and Dutch Purges after World War II* (2006_Belgian and Dutch Purges.pdf)
21. Jurado, p.8.
22. *Time* magazine, 5 November 1945.
23. capitalpunishment.org/Hameln.htm
24. *The Times*, 12 January 1946.
25. Eric Pleasants, *Hitler's Bastard. Through Hell and Back in Nazi Germany and Stalin's Russia*, Mainstream Publishing, 2003, p.228.
26. *The Times*, 30 January 1946.
27. *Daily Mirror*, 19 February 2021.
28. *Reading Eagle*, 3 November 1942.
29. *Daily Mirror*, 19 February 2021.
30. Sean Murphy, *Letting the Side Down. British Traitors in the Second World War*, The History Press, 2005, pp.45–48. Also, Daily Mirror, 19 February 2021. Also, capitalpunishmentuk.org
31. *Daily Express*, 30 August 2018.
32. Ibid.
33. Ibid.

Volunteers and collaborators (II)

1. Jurado, p.12.
2. Ibid., p.15.
3. Ibid., pp.15–16
4. Ibid., p.15.
5. Ibid., p.16.
6. Andreyev, Catherine, *General Vlasov and the Russian Liberation Army*, Cambridge University Press, 1987, p.370.
7. Jurado, p.21.
8. Brent Mueggenberg. *The Cossack Struggle against Communism 1917–1945*, McFarland, 2019, p.288.

9. Jurado, p.30.
10. Ibid., p.31.
11. Jozo Tomasevich, *War and Revolution in Yugoslavia 1941–1945. Occupation and Collaboration*, Stanford University Press, 2001, p.305.
12. Franz Menges, '*Hellmouth* (Attn. Correct spelling, two 'l') *von Pannwitz*', Neue Deutch Biographie (in German), 2001, pp.34–35.
13. Jurado, p.29.
14. Ibid., pp.15–16.
15. Jurado, p.30.
16. Jurado, p.31.
17. Jurado, pp.15–16.
18. David Marshall Lang, *A Modern History of Georgia*, Weidenfeld & Nicolson, 1962, p.260.
19. Jurado, p.17.
20. Christopher J. Walker, *Armenia: The Survival of a Nation*, Palgrave Macmillan, 1990, p.357.
21. Jurado, p.24.
22. Chris Bishop, *Waffen-SS Divisions 1939–1945*, Amber Books, 2017, p.160.
23. Stephen Dorril, *MI6: Inside the Covert World of Her Majesty's Secret Intelligence Service*, Simon & Schuster, 2002, p.288.
24. Richard Rashke, *Useful Enemies: America's Open-Door Policy for Nazi War Criminals*, Open Road Media, 2013, p.26.
25. *The New York Times*, 8 September 1960. Also, *The Guardian*, 26 July 2008.
26. *The Los Angeles Times*, 2 July 1987.
27. Jurado, p.25.
28. Ibid., p.25.
29. Ibid., p.26.
30. *The Guardian*, 24 May 2022.
31. *Time* magazine, 19 March 1965.
32. Ibid.
33. timesofisrael.com/latvians-march-to-honor-troops-who-fought-alongside-nazis
34. Eric Lichtblau, *The Nazis Next Door. How America became a safe haven for Hitler's men*, Houghton Mifflin Harcourt, 2014, p.225.
35. Jurado, p.32.
36. Ibid., p.30
37. Sugata Bose, *A Hundred Horizons. The Indian Ocean in the Age of the Global Empire*, Harvard University Press, 2006, p.141.
38. *Irish Sun*, 3 June 2020 (irishsun.com/news/265333522/now-russian-samurai-fought-for-japan-in-world-war-ii
39. Boris Egorov, *Russia Beyond*, 3 June 2020 (rbth.com/history/332269-russian-samurai-fought-for-japan
40. David Barret, *Chinese Collaboration with Japan 1932–1945. The Limits of Accommodation*, Stanford University Press, 2002, pp.109–111.
41. *The Taipei Times*, 8 June 2007.
42. Philip S. Jowett, *Rays of the Rising Sun*, Helios & Company, 2004, p.34.
43. B. V. A. Rolling; Antonio Cassesse, *The Tokyo Trial and Beyond*, Polity Press, 1993, p.76.

44. *The New York Times*, 19 January 1994
45. kajomag.com/fighting-for-japan-korean-and-formosan-soldiers-during-wwii
46. *The Taipei Times*, 26 August 2016
47. historyisnowmagazine.com/blog/2022/9/17/collaboration/the-forein-forces-who-helped-to-build-the-japanese-empire
48. Wibke Kristin Timmermann, '*Incitement in international criminal law*', International Review of the Red Cross, 88, 2006, p.28
49. Gregory S. Gordon, '*The forgotten Nuremberg hate speech. Otto Dietrich and the future of prosecution law*', Ohio State Journal, 75, 2014, p.571
50. Julian Jackson, *The Dark Years 1940–1944*, Oxford University Press, 2001, p.117
51. Frederic Spotts, *The Shameful Peace*, Yale University Press, 2008, p.70
52. *The Times*, 'Amery sentenced to death: A self-confessed traitor', 29 November 1945
53. M. A. Doherty, *Nazi Wireless Propaganda: Lord Haw-Haw and British Public Opinion in the Second World War*, Edinburg University Press, 2000, p.9 and p.13
54. *The New York Times*, 8 June 1966
55. *The Telegraph*, 12 January 2022
56. *The New York Times*, 7 June 1947
57. *Time* magazine, 29 December 1952
58. *The Pittsburg Press*, 14 October 1949
59. *The Los Angeles Times*, 21 July 1946
60. *The New York Times*, 2 July 1988
61. *The Washington Post*, 28 September 2006
62. *The Milwaukee Journal*, 27 October 1947
63. *The Baltimore Sun*, 9 December 1947

PART THREE – RELEASE AND REPATRIATION

1. Simon Rees, historynet.com/german-pows-and-the-art-of-survival/
2. Robert Quinn, *Independent*, 1 May 2015
3. weaponsandwarfare.com/2015/10/20/pows-a-comparison-of-mistreatment
4. S. P. McKenzie, *The treatment of prisoners of war in World War II*, The Journal of Modern History, 66 (3), pp.467-20
5. Franz-Karl Stanzel, '*German POWs in Canada. An autobiography-based Essay*', Canadian Military History, Vol. 27, Issue 2, article 19, 2018, p.14
6. National Archives, FO939/321668 Camp/Aliwal-Tidworth, Wiltshire
7. Stanzel, p.10
8. Tom Moseley, '*South Wirral High School's wartime past*', southwirral.wirral.sch.uk/news/south-wirral-wartime-history/
9. The National Archives, RG48/2009. Also, '*British Women*(Marriages)', Parliamentary Debates (Hansard), 439, House of Commons, 8 July 1947, col. 2013-2019
10. Toby Neal, '*Tales of the enemy who came to stay*', Shropshire Star, 25 July 2020.
11. Eric Brandreth, Harpenden History, No. 95 Batford POW camp, 1943–1948 (Harpenden-history.org.uk
12. Robert Quinn, *Independent*, 1 May 2015
13. Alan Rowlands, Trautmann: The Biography, Breedon, 2005, p.57

14. *Deutsche Welle*, 14 March 2019
15. *The Independent*, 19 July 2013
16. Stanzek, p, 14
17. Bill Carey, '*Former German soldier recalls life at the Crossville POW camp*', The Tennessee Magazine, July 2015
18. Story contributor: Patrick Barrett, bbc.uk/history.ww2peopleswar/stories/02/a8080102.shtml
19. Dingwall Sheriff Court, National Records of Scotland, Reference SC25/15/1946/1
20. egyptstudycircle.org.uk/Articles/QC233.pdf
21. Birgit Schneider, *From Demilitarization to Democratization: Demobilized Soldiers between the American Occupation and the German and Japanese States 1945–1955*, Oldenburg, 2012, p.329.
22. Frank Biess, *Homecoming: Returning POWs and the Legacies of Defeat in post-war Germany*, Princeton University Press, 2009, p.45.
23. Rüdiger Overmans, *Soldaten hinter Stacheldaht, Deutsche Kiriegsgefangene des Zweiten Weltkriege* (in German), Ullstein, 2000, p.246.
24. German POWs in Allied hands, worldwar2database.com, 27 July 2011.
25. G.I. Krivosheev, *Rossiia I SSSR v voinakh XX veka: Poteri vooruzhennykh sil/ Statisticheskoe issedovanie* (in Russian), OLMA-Press, 2001, Table 198.
26. Alexandra Olivotto, 'Romanian Prisoners in Kazakhstan' (in Romanian), *Cotidianul*, 14 April, 2006.
27. Nicholas D. Christof, 'Japan's blossoms soothe a POW lost in Siberia', *The New York Times*, 12 April 1998.
28. *New Zealand Herald*, 31 December 1945.
29. Nick Thorpe, 'Prisoner of war gets his life back', *The Guardian*, 19 September 2000.
30. *The Los Angeles Times*, 28 October 2000.
31. nationalpost.com/news/world/the-mystery-of-yang-kyoungjong-the-only-soldier-to-have-been-fought-on-the-three-sides-of-a-war
32. Antony Beevor, *The Second World War*, Dark Bay Books, 20123, p.1 (Introduction).
33. Steven Zaloga, *The Devil's Garden: Rommel's Desperate Defense of Omaha beach on D-Day*, Stackpole Books, 2013, p.60.

INDEX

1st Aircraft Regiment, Russian Liberation Army (Russia/Germany) 176
1st Cavalry Division (France) 162
1st Cossack Division (Germany) 175
1st Division, Russian Liberation Army (Russia/Germany) 173, 174, 175
1st Division, Ukrainian National Army (Ukraine/Germany) 176
1st Mountain Division (Romania) 142, 148
1st Night Fighter Wing (Germany) 38
1st Parachute-Panzer Division *Hermann Göring* (Germany) 44, 54
1st Special Naval Landing Force (Japan) 131
1st SS Panzer Division *Leibstandarte Adolf Hitler* 25, 30, 31
2nd Air Division (Germany) 43
2nd Alpine Division *Tridentina* (Italy) 98
2nd Armored Division (France) 161
2nd Armored Division (United States) 95
2nd Division, Ukrainian National Army (Ukraine/Germany) 176
2nd Grenadier Division *Vitorio* (Germany) 108
2nd Infantry Division *Sfortzesca* (Italy) 100
2nd Mountain Division (Germany) 26
2nd Mountain Division (Romania) 146
2nd Italian-Libyan Division (Italy) 90
2nd New Zealand Division 18
2nd South African Division 20
3rd Air Division (Germany) 35
3rd Alpine Division *Giulia* (Italy) 94
3rd Canadian Infantry Division 25
3rd SS Panzer Division *Totenkopf* (Germany) 167
4th Alpine Division *Monte Rosa* (Italy) 108
4th Armored Division (Japan) 138
4th Colonial Division (France) 30
4th Infantry Division (Germany) 24
4th Infantry Division *Parma* (Italy) 99
4th Mountain Division (Romania) 147
4th Parachute Division (Germany) 101
4th Seaforth Highlanders Regiment (Great Britain) 168, 190
4th SS Polizei Panzer Grenadier Division (Germany) 46
5th Air Division (Germany) 35
5th Infantry Division *Savona* (Italy) 93
5th Infantry Division (Japan) 116
5th SS Panzer Division *Viking* (Germany) 33, 167, 168, 178
6th Alpine Division *Alpi Graie* (Italy) 103
6th Infantry Division (Australia) 128
7th Air Division (Germany) 42
7th Armoured Division (Great Britain) 90, 91
7th Infantry Division (Germany) 23
7th Hussars Queen's Own Regiment (Great Britain) 90
7th Mountain Division (Germany) 26
7th Parachute Division (Germany) 16
7th SS Mountain Division *Prinz Eugen* (Germany) 68, 104, 152
8th Air Corps (Germany) 9
8th Cavalry Division (Romania) 146
9th Infantry Division (Australia) 129
9th Infantry Division (United States) 25, 34
9th Panzer Division (Germany) 26
9th Parachute Division (Germany) 45
10th Parachute Division (Germany) 44
11th Infantry Division *Brennero* (Italy) 113
11th Hussars Prince Albert's Own Regiment (Great Britain) 90

11th Night Fighter Wing (Germany) 37
12th Panzer Division (Germany) 17
12th SS Panzer Division *Hitlerjugend* (Germany) 31, 33
13th Battalion, Lithuanian Territorial Defense Force (Lithuania/Germany) 183
13th Panzer Division (Germany) 23, 27
14th SS Infantry Division (Germany) 176
15th Panzer Division (Germany) 18
15th Punjab Regiment (Great Britain) 92
15th Waffen-SS Grenadier Division (Latvia/Germany) 180
16th Infantry Brigade (Australia) 91
16th Infantry Division *Pistoia* (Italy) 95
16th Panzer Division (Germany) 17
17th Infantry Division *Pavia* (Italy) 93
16th SS Panzer Grenadier Division *Reichsführer* (Germany) 53, 54
18th SS Panzer Grenadier Division *Horst Wessel* (Germany) 30
18th Voksgrenadier Division (Germany) 9
19th Panzer Division (Germany) 17
19th Waffen-SS Grenadier Division (Latvia/Germany) 180
20th Panzer Division (Germany) 21, 26
21st Infantry Division *Granatieri di Sardegna* (Italy) 110
21st Panzer Division (Germany) 18
22nd Air Landing Division (Germany) 20, 45
24th Infantry Division (Germany) 24, 28
24th Infantry Division *Pinerolo* (Italy) 114
26th Panzer Division (Germany) 53
27th Infantry Division *Brescia* (Italy) 93, 106
27th SS Volunteer Grenadier Division (Belgium/Germany) 165, 166
32nd Infantry Division *Marche* (Italy) 101, 104
33rd Mountain Division *Acqui* (Italy) 97
33rd Waffen-SS Division *Charlemagne* (Germany) 161, 162
35th Infantry Division (Germany) 23
35th Infantry Division (United States) 29
36th Infantry Division (United States) 3, 11, 30
36th Infantry Division *Forli* (Italy) 98
36th Waffen-SS Grenadier Brigade (Germany) 20
37th Tank Battalion (United States) 28
38th Infantry Division (Germany) 15
44th Infantry Division (Germany) 22
48th Panzer Corps (Germany) 25
48th Infantry Division *Taro* (Italy) 100
52nd Infantry Division *Torino* (Italy) 105
56th Infantry Division *Casale* (Italy) 97
58th Fighter Squadron (Romania) 148
59th Infantry Division *Cagliari* (Italy) 97
59th Rifle Brigade (Soviet Union) 174
60th Infantry Division (Germany) 15
62nd Infantry Division (Germany) 23
62nd Infantry Division *Marmarica* (Italy) 93
68th Infantry Division *Legnano* (Italy) 97
77th Infantry Brigade (Japan) 125
80th Infantry Division (United States) 3
80th Infantry Division *La Spezia* (Italy) 94
89th Blackshirt Assault Legion *Etrusca* (Italy) 109
90th Infantry Division (United States) 39, 40
101st Airborne Division (United States) 4, 6, 8
101st Motorized Division *Trieste* (Italy) 94
103rd Counterintelligence Corps (United States) 5, 107
105th Infantry Division *Rovigo* (Italy) 94
109th Infantry Division (Japan) 11, 23, 24
117th Jäger Division (Germany) 46
121st Infantry Division (Germany/Spain) 151
131st Armoured Brigade *Centauro* (Italy) 106
133rd Fortress Division (Germany) 29
135th Armoured Brigade *Ariete* (Italy) 102, 105
151st Infantry Division *Perugia* (Italy) 97
153rd Infantry Division (Germany) 22
155th Infantry Division *Emilia* (Italy) 101
156th Infantry Division *Vicenza* (Italy) 94

INDEX

162nd Rifle Regiment (China/Japan) 185
163rd Infantry Division (Germany) 19
180th Infantry Division (Germany) 29
183rd Paratrooper Division *Ciclone* (Italy) 100
194th Glider Infantry Regiment (United States) 6
198th Infantry Division (Germany) 179
201st Luftwaffe Regiment (Germany) 89
202nd Coastal Division (Italy) 95
206th Coastal Division (Italy) 95
213th Coastal Division (Italy) 95
215th Coastal Division (Italy) 112
215th Infantry Regiment (Japan) 127
216th Coastal Division (Italy) 101
222nd Coastal Division (Italy) 101
237th Infantry Division (Germany) 27
333rd Artillery Battalion (United States) 30
334th Infantry Division (Germany) 162
337th Infantry Division (Soviet Union) 148
337th Volksgrenadier Division (Germany) 17
361st Infantry Division (Germany) 24
369th Infantry Regiment (Germany/Croatia) 153
374th Grenadier Regiment (Germany) 23
387th Infantry Division (Germany) 17
555th Infantry Division (Germany) 20
638th Infantry Regiment (Vichy France) 161, 162
643rd Infantry Battalion, Ukrainian National Army (Ukraine/Germany) 176
658th Infantry Battalion (Estonia/Germany) 178
659th Infantry Battalion (Estonia/Germany) 178
660th Infantry Battalion (Estonia/Germany) 178
709th Infantry Division (Germany) 25
812th Infantry Battalion (Armenia/Germany) 178
822nd Infantry Battalion (Georgia/Germany) 177
823rd Infantry Battalion (Georgia/Germany) 177

Army Group A (Germany) 10, 11
Army Group Africa (Germany/Italy) 25
Army Group B (Germany) 12
Army Group Center (Germany) 8, 14, 176
Army Group East (Italy) 105
Army Group H (Germany) 13, 16, 29
Army Group North (Germany) 7, 8, 10, 11
Army Group Ostmark 29
Army Group South (Germany) 10, 12, 15
Army Group Vistoula (Germany) 25, 47
Black Sea Fleet (Romania) 145, 147
Blue Division or División Azul (Spain) 150
Burma Area Army (Japan) 119
Cheshire Regiment (Great Britain) 3
Central China Area Army (Japan) 119
Eighteenth Army (Germany) 26
Eighteenth Army (Japan) 116
Eighth Army (Great Britain) 38
Eighth Army (Italy) 104
Eighth Army (United States) 117
Eleventh Area Army (Japan) 115, 122
Eleventh Army (Germany) 15
Eleventh Army (Italy) 105
Fifteenth Army (Germany) 14
Fifteenth Army (Japan) 128
Fifth Area Army (Japan) 132
Fifth Army (Italy) 102
Fifth Army (United States) 103
Fifth Panzer Army (Germany) 28
First Army (Germany) 12
First Army (Hungary) 148
First Area Army (Japan) 116, 117, 135, 188
First Parachute Army (Germany) 42
First Russian Army (Russia/Germany) 174
Forty-Sixth Army (Soviet Union) 149
Fourteenth Army (Japan) 119, 125, 126
Fourth Army (Germany) 14, 45
Fourth Army (Italy) 100
Fourth Army (Japan) 116
Fourth Army (Romania) 141, 142, 145, 146
Fourth Panzer Army (Germany) 14
Gando Special Force (Manchuria/Japan) 187

Horia, Closca and Crisan Division (Romania/Soviet Union) 143
I Air Corps (Germany) 35
II Air Corps (Germany) 36
I Canadian Corps 13
I Parachute Corps (Germany) 43
II Army Corps (Italy) 99
II Army Corps (Poland) 143
II Parachute Corps (Germany) 43
II SS Panzer Corps (Germany) 52
IV Army Corps (Germany) 22
IX Army Corps (Germany) 16, 18, 24
IX Mountain Corps (Germany) 29
L Army Corps (Germany) 22
LIII Army Corps (Germany) 25, 28
LIV Army Corps (Germany) 24
LVI Panzer Corps (Germany) 23
LIX Army Corps (Germany) 28
LXVII Army Corps (Germany) 9, 29
LXVIII Army Corps (Germany) 13
LXXXIX Army Corps (Germany) 17
Glider Pilot Regiment (Great Britain) 89
Kwantung Army (Japan) 120, 138
Luftflotte-2 (Germany) 9
Luftflotte-3 (Germany) 11, 16, 36
Luftflotte-6 (Germany) 8
Luftflotte-9 (Germany) 9
Ninth Army (Germany) 25
Ninth Army (Italy) 98, 105, 112, 113
Nineteenth Army (Soviet Union) 174
No. 6 Commando (Great Britain) 13
North China Area Army (Japan) 121
Panzer Army Africa (Germany) 35
Princess Louise Kensington Regiment (Great Britain) 170
Royal Warwickshire Regiment (Great Britain) 170
Second Army (Germany) 14
Second Army (Hungary) 148, 150
Second Army (Italy) 112, 113
Second Army (Japan) 120
Second Panzer Army (Germany) 12, 14
Second Shock Army (Soviet Union) 173
Seventh Army (Japan) 119
Seventeenth Army (Japan) 128, 129
Sixteenth Army (Germany) 24
Sixteenth Army (Japan) 122, 129, 132
Sixth Army (Germany) 8, 14, 26, 27
Sixth Army (United States) 137
Sixth Fleet (Japan) 131
Sonderverband 287 Regiment (Iraq/Germany) 184
Southern Expeditionary Group (Japan) 128, 138
Special Air Service or SAS (Great Britain) 3, 14
Special Purpose Division (Estonia/Germany) 178
SS Assault Brigade *Langemarck* (Belgium/Germany) 165
SS Handschar or 1st Croatian (Germany) 29
SS Ski Jäger Battalion *Norwegen* (Norway/Germany) 168
Tenth Army (Italy) 90, 91, 104
Third Army (Hungary) 149
Third Army (Romania) 141, 142, 147
Third Air Fleet or Air Command West (Germany) 36
Third Area Army (Japan) 135
Third Army (United States) 9
Third Panzer Army (Germany) 14
Thirty-Eighth Army (Japan) 133
Thirty-Second Army (Japan) 137
Thirty-Third Army (Japan) 128
Tudor Vladimirescu Division (Romania/Soviet Union) 142, 143
Twelfth Area Army (Japan) 115 135
Twelfth Area Army (Germany) 13, 14
Twelfth Army (Japan) 119
Twenty-Fifth Army (Japan) 116, 124, 131
Twenty-Fifth Tank Corps (Soviet Union) 174
Twenty-First Army (Great Britain/Canada) 25
Twenty-Eighth Army (Japan) 130
Twenty-Fourth Army Group (China/Japan) 187
V Army Corps (Great Britain) 152
V Army Corps (Italy) 194
V SS Mountain Corps 29
VI Air Corps (Germany) 36
VI Army Corps (Italy) 99
VI Army Corps (Romania) 146
VI SS Army Corps (Germany) 29
VIII Army Corps (Germany) 22, 26

INDEX

Waffen-SS Panzer Division *Das Reich* (Germany) 52
West Yorkshire Regiment (Great Britain) 168
XI Air Corps (Germany) 45
XI Army Corps (Germany) 21, 23
XII Army Corps (Italy) 95
XII Army Corps (United States) 53
XI SS Army Corps (Germany) 18
XIV Army Corps (Italy) 98, 99
XLIII Army Corps (Germany) 23
XV Mountain Corps (Germany) 27
XV SS Cossack Cavalry Corps 175
XVII Mountain Corps (Germany) 12
XVIII Mountain Corps (Germany) 22
XX Army Corps (United States) 26
XXII Army Corps (Italy) 91
XXII Mountain Corps (Germany) 13
XXV Army Corps (Italy) 99
XXX Panzer Corps (Germany) 14
XXXIII Army Corps (Germany) 19
XXXIX Panzer Corps (Germany) 17
XXXVIII Army Corps (Germany) 22
XXXXIV Army Corps (Germany) 27
XXXXIX Army Corps (Germany) 46

Aachen 55
Abe, General Nobuyuki 137
Abwehr (Germany's military information service) 151, 164
Abyssinia 91, 92, 93, 96, 111, 112
Adami-Rossi, Lieutenant General Enrico 109
Addis Ababa 92, 93, 111 **Addis Ababa massacre** 111
Adenauer, Konrad 31, 53, 196
Admiral Graf Spee (Pocket battleship) 16
Advisory Board on Clemency (ABC) 74
Afghanistan 177, 184
Afrika Korps 169
Agazio, Major General Alberto De 98, 108
Agosti, Colonel Tito 108, 109
Airmen's Trial 32
Aiud prison 144, 145, 146, 147, 148
Agarici, Captain Horia 148
Akerhus fortress 168
Aktuković, Andrija 154

Alamo Scouts 137
Alba forced labour colony 146
Alba Iulia prison 145
Albania 12, 97, 99, 105, 111, 152, 156, 157, 158, 159 **Albanian Fascist Party** 158
Albini, Umberto 96
Albrecht, SS Brigadier General Alwin-Broder 54
Alem Bekagn prison 111
Aldea, Lieutenant General Aurel 144, 145
Aldershot POW camp 8
Alexandra Barracks Hospital massacre 124
Alexandria 18, 21, 38
Algeria 37, 95 **Algiers** 163
Aliud prison 145
Aliwal POW camp 194
Alizoti, Fejzi 157 **Alizoti, Riza** 157
Allendorf POW camp 25
Alps 184 **Alps (Battle)** 109
Alsace 164
Altfuldisch, SS Lieutenant 65
Altshausen POW camp viii, 20
Amba Alagi 92
Ambon Island massacre 131
Amedeo, Prince of Savoia 90, 92, 93
Amery, John 169, 189
Amico, Divisional General Giuseppe 101, 104
Am Spiegelgrund psychiatric clinic 78
Anami, Korechika 115
Anders, Lieutenant General Władysław 143
Anderson, Jane 192
Ando, General Rikichi 116
Andoni, Vasil 157
Andrae, Major General Alexander 45
Andreoli, Brigadier General Giuseppe 9
Angelis, Major General Maximilian de 27
Angern, Lieutenant General Günther 17
Antonescu, Field Marshal Ion 23, 141, 143, 145, 147
Anzio 44
Arājs Kommando (Latvian auxiliary police force) 181, 182

239

Arājs, SS Major Victors 182
Araki, General Sadao 120, 121
Arbore, Major General Ioan 145
Ardeatine massacre 8, 9, 102, 103, 107
Ardennes 44
Arena, Brigadier General Francesco 98
Argentina 16, 39, 71, 107, 112, 153, 154, 165, 168
Arildskov, Max Johannes 167
Armenia 177, 178 **Armenian Legion** 177, 178 **Armenian Revolutionary Federation** 178
Armistice of Cassibile 31, 97, 100, 105, 106, 109, 110, 113
Armstrong, John Johnson 171
Arnhem (Battle) 53, 88, 89
Arnim, Colonel General Jürgen von 24, 25
Arps, Vice Admiral Theodore 33
Arsenescu, Colonel Gheorghe 148
Asaka, Prince Yasuhiro 133, 138
Asano Detachment 185
Asano, Rear Admiral Shimpei 124
Ashcan detention center 3, 5, 11
Aspheim, Olav 168
Athens 45, 114, 159, 160, 184
Aumeier, Hans 63, 64
Auschwitz-Birkenau concentration camp system 18, 32, 50, 63, 64, 69, 73, 75, 76, 77, 79, 81, 82, 84, 85, 86, 88, 107 **Auschwitz Trials** 62, 72, 73
Australia vi, 118, 129, 150, 169, 182, 191, 195, 196
Austria 3, 4, 5, 8, 9, 10, 12, 18, 23, 26, 29, 31, 35, 39, 44, 52, 55, 57, 60, 61, 65, 69, 70, 71, 72, 77, 80, 81, 84, 86, 88, 106, 142, 149, 152, 153, 155, 156, 175, 176, 190, 191, 192
Averoff prison 158, 159
Avramescu, General Gheorghe 143, 146
Axtheln, Major General Walther von 44

Babini, Divisional General Valentino 90
Babi Yar Massacre 15, 47, 49, 51
Badoglio, Field Marshal Pietro 95, 103, 112
Badsmandsstraaede Barracks 167
Bahs, General Žanis 179

Bairaktari, Muharrem 157
Baillie-Stewart, Norman 190
Bakos, Major General Georgios 158
Bălan, Brigadier General Grigore 143
Balbis, Captain Franco 103
Balck, Major General Hermann 24, 25
Baldescu, Major General Radu 145
Balli Kombëtar (Albania's National Front) 156, 157
Balotta, Lieutenant General Mario 105
Barberis, Divisional General Umberto 90, 91
Barbó, Brigadier General Guglielmo 100
Barcewo Prison 48
Barde, Brigadier General Konrad 17
Bardia 90, 91, 93 **Bardia (Battle)** 90
Bareuther, Second Lieutenant Herbert 36, 37
Barkmann, Jenny Wanda 83, 84
Bartram, Grethe 167, 168
Barzolescu, Major General Emanoil 146
Basović, Petar 155
Bataan (Battle) 122, 125 **Bataan death march** vii, 117, 122, 125
Batavia 118, 130, 131, 132
Bätcher, Lieutenant Colonel Hansgeorg 39
Bats, Major Wilhelm 39
Battaglione Azad Hindustan 185
Battisti, Lieutenant General Emilio 93, 94
Bauer, Colonel Victor 38
Baumanis, Captain Valdemārs 181
Baumbach, Colonel Werner 39
Baur, SS Brigadier General Johannes 56, 57
Baur, Maria 57
Bautzen Penitentiary 56, 88
Bavaria 4, 6, 8, 10, 11, 14, 16, 17, 25, 26, 28, 31, 36, 39, 44, 48, 52, 53, 55, 57, 58, 59, 61, 66, 69, 72, 84, 85, 107, 150, 159, 161, 165, 173, 191
Bayer, Lieutenant General Friedrich 22
Becker, Elisabeth 83, 84
Beda Fomm (Battle) 91
Beerbroke, 1st Lieutenant Franz-Josef 41
Beevor, Antony 197
Beilhard, Erna

INDEX

Beinjing 139
Beisfjord Massacre 18
Belgium vi, 24, 30, 31, 33, 42, 43, 44, 49, 89, 157, 161, 165, 167, 170, 171, 181, 188, 193, 195
Belgrade viii, 6, 12, 26, 27, 152, 155, 156
Belletti, Major General Pietro 948
Belomo, General Nicola 108
Below, Brigadier General Gerd Paul von 22, 23
Below, Major General Nikolaus von 55
Belzec concentration camp 69 **Belzec Trials** 7, 61, 72
Benthack, Brigadier General Hans-Georg 29
Berchtesgaden 8, 55, 56
Beregfy, Colonel General Károly 149
Bergen Belsen 71, 78, 80, 81, 86 **Bergen Belsen Trials** 7, 61, 64, 65, 72, 78, 82, 86
Berginau, Jane 86
Bergmann, Erika 88
Bergolo, Major General Giorgio Carlo Calvi di 106
Bergonzoli, Divisional General Annibale 90, 91
Berlin 2, 3, 6, 9, 16, 17, 18, 21, 23, 24, 26, 41, 54, 55, 56, 57, 58, 59, 67, 71, 80, 81, 86, 87, 105, 107, 118, 121, 169, 172, 173, 175, 180, 182, 189, 190, 191, 192 **Berlin** (Battle) 25, 55 **Berlin University** 177, 191
Berneville-Clay, 2nd Lieutenant Douglas 169
Bernigau, Jane 9
Berry, Kenneth 170
Bertone, Brigadier General Emmanuele Barbo 99
Bērziņš, Alfons 181
Best, Robert-Henry 190, 191
Bethlehem, Andrija 153
Biberstein, SS Lieutenant Colonel Ernst 49
Biçakçiu, Ibrahim 158
Biddle, Francis 2
Biglieri, Captain Giulio 103
Bikernikie Forest massacre 68
Bila Tserkva Massacre 49

Bingxuan, General Pang 187
Binz, Dorothea 81, 82
Bishop's Hill 64, 83, 84
Bitossi, Lieutenant General Gervasio 99
Bittrich, Waffen-SS Major General Wilhelm 52, 53
Black Hand (Črna Roka) 155
Blackshirts 102, 109, 110, 111, 112, 113
Blaskowitz, Colonel General Johannes 13, 14, 15
Blaschke, SS Brigadier General Hugo 57
Blei, SS Lieutenant August 65
Blobel Massacre 49
Blobel, SS Colonel Paul 48
Blücher (Heavy cruiser) 19
Blume, SS Colonel Walter 49, 50
Bochum Prison 73
Bock, Field Marshal Fedor von 10
Boeckh-Behrens, Lieutenant General Hans 22
Boege, Brigadier General Ehrefried-Oskar 24
Boenicke, Major General Walter 15, 16, 34
Bohemia and Moravia Protectorate 4, 5, 30, 52, 100, 173
Böhler, Jochen 47
Bois d'Erain 30
Böhlke, Lieutenant General Hellmuth 42
Böhm-Ermolli, Field Marshal Eduard 12
Böhme, Brigadier General Franz 12, 13
Bolšteins, Ludvigs 179
Boltenstern, Lieutenant General Walter von 22, 23
Bonin Islands 123, 124
Bono, Field Marshal Emilio De 96
Borchers, Major Adolf 40
Boremski, Captain Eberhard von 40
Bormann, SS Lieutenant General Albert 56
Bormann, Brigadier General Ernst 41
Bormann, Johanna 81, 82
Bormann, Martin 3, 6, 56, 58, 59
Borneo 116, 126, 129, 130, 131, 132
Bortmann, SS Captain Hans 68
Borussia Dortmund soccer club 179
Bose, Subbas Chandra 184

Bosnia-Herzegovina 27, 29, 109, 152, 155
Boston 171, 178 **Boston Federal District Court** 191
Bothe, Herta 86, 87
Böttcher, Walter 78
Bourantas, Nikolaos 160
Boyarsky, Lieutenant-Colonel Vladimir 173, 174
Bradenburg 47, 67, 68, 88
Bradenburger Commando 29
Braham Castle or No. 109 POW camp
Brandl, Therese 84
Brandt, Brigadier General Karl 55
Brandt, SS Brigadier General Karl 76
Brandt, SS Brigadier General Rudolf-Hermann 76
Brauchitsch, Field Marshal Walther von 7, 10
Brauer, Major General Bruno 41, 45
Braun, Eva 58
Braune, SS Lieutenant Werner 48, 49
Braunsteiner, Hermine 85, 86
Bray, Edgar 172
Bray, Sophia 172
Brazil 80, 182
Breitweiser, Arthur 63
Bremen 6, 29, 38, 49, 51
Bridgend 9, 19, 20, 34, 42, 53
Briganti, Divisional General Alberto 98
Bringmann, Vice Admiral Helmuth 56
British Army vi, vii, 3, 11, 13, 16, 20, 26, 38, 41, 43, 67, 70, 77, 78, 82, 86, 152, 164, 185 **British commandos** 70, 127 **British Free Corps** (BFC) 169, 189 **British Intelligence** 21 **British troops** 5, 8, 10, 16, 28, 33, 34, 35, 36, 38, 41, 42, 45, 48, 51, 53, 55, 56, 58, 59, 63, 6, 67, 68, 76, 78, 82, 84, 86, 88, 89, 92, 93, 94, 95, 108, 154, 163, 164, 168, 180, 190, 195, 197 **British Union of Fascists** 170, 171, 190
Brittany 34, 43
Brivonesi, Vice Admiral Bruno 105
Brown Nurses vi, 89
Bruchsal Prison 33
Brunetti, Major General Brunetto 93

Bruns, Brigadier General Walther 28
Bruns, Captain Curt 9
Bubani, Gjergj 158
Buchanan Castle 2
Bucharest 23, 24, 142, 143, 146, 147
Buchenwald concentration camp 61, 75, 76, 79, 105, 191
Buchler, SS Lieutenant-Colonel Philipp 55
Buchligen, Lieutenant-Colonel Kurt 40
Budapest 149, 150
Buenos Aires 16, 39, 154
Bulgaria 28, 141 **Bulgarian troops** 22
Bulge (Battle) 24, 30
Bullens, Brigadier General E.F. 125
Bunker 54, 55
Bunyachenko, Brigadier General Sergei 174
Burgdorf, Major General Wilhelm 54
Burgman, Herbert J. 190, 191
Burma 117, 119, 127, 135, 137, 185, 188
Burmese National Army 189
Burrel prison 158
Busch, Field Marshal Ernst 7, 8
Busse, Major General Theodore 24
Buttá, Major General 101
Butak, Mile 153, 154
Butka, Safet 157
Butyrka Prison 14, 23, 55, 60, 174
Butzbach Prison 75
Bydgoszcz Massacre 46
Byelorussia or Belarus 23, 24, 40, 49, 50, 51, 182
Bychov, Major Semyon 176

Caithness POW camp (No. 165) 33
Cambrea, Brigadier General Nicolae 142
Cambridge University 60, 171
Camp Clinton 25
Campioni, Admiral Inigo 103, 104
Canada vii, 1, 18, 20, 31, 35, 86, 155, 178, 181, 182, 187, 193, 194
Canton or Guangzhu 132
Caperdoni, Brigadier General Felice 101
Carabinieri Corps 94
Carinthia 9, 29, 30, 152, 190
Carlaont, Major General Dumitru 147
Caroline Islands 12

INDEX

Carp, Brigadier General Corneliu 1463
Caruso, Pietro 107
Caserta 9, 107
Casimir, Colonel Artur von 36
Castagna Major General Salvatore 93
Castaldi, Brigadier General Sabato Martelli 102
Caucasus 49, 146, 147, 174, 184
Cavallero, Field Marshal Hugo 104
Caviglia, Field Marshal Enrico 95
Celle 12, 34, 81, 86
Cephalonia 97, 102
Ceriana-Mayneri, Lieutenant General Carlo 101
Cerica, General Angelo 101
Chandler, Douglas 190, 191
Changi Jail vii
Channel Islands 34, 177
Charles, Lance Corporal William 170
Chelmno concentration camp 68
Chelmno Trials 7, 72
Cherbourg 25, 34, 176
Cherche-Midi Prison 16
Chirieleison, Major General Domenico 101
Chervinska, Liselotte 57
Chetniks 155, 156
Chiang Kai-shek 187
Chiappi, Lieutenant General Armellini 100
Chi Hoa prison 132
Chiminello, Major General Ernesto 97
China or People's Republic of China vii, vii, 116, 117, 120, 131, 132, 133, 135, 138, 139, 186, 196, 197 **Chinese military tribunals** 133
Chirnoagă, Brigadier General Platon 142
Chmielewski, SS Captain Karl 72
Christian, Brigadier General Eckhard 58, 59
Chuikov, Marshal of the Soviet Union Basily, 54
Churchill, Winston viii, 8, 172
CIA 57, 183
Ciano, Galeazzo 95, 96
Cigala-Fulgosi, Major General Alfonso 975
Cihoski, Lieutenant General H. 145

Ciupercă, General Nicolae 144, 146
Civitavecchia prison 109
Civitella massacre 54
Clade, Captain Emil 38
Cladestine Military Front 102, 103
Clark airfield 137
Class-A (or Grade-A) war criminals 138, 194 **Class-B** (or Grade-B) war criminals 132, 138, 194 **Class-C** (or Grade-C) war criminals 188, 194
Clauberg, SS Lieutenant Carl 75
Closius-Neudeck, Ruth 81, 83
Cluddley POW camp 194
Cristofini, Colonel Simon P. 162
Crottaglie POW camp 156
Colditz Castle or Oflag IV-C POW camp 69
Cold War 111, 112, 117
Cologne 7, 23, 35, 50, 51, 85, 189
Cologne University 50
Coltano POW camp 110, 113
Commissar Order 3, 14, 15
Commando Order 3
Como 92, 106, 110
Cona 91
Conant, Jabes B. 74
Conrath, Major General Paul 44
Constantinescu, Brigadier General Vladimir 144, 14
Constantinescu-Claps, Brigadier General C.S. 145, 147
Conti, SS Major Leonardo 74, 75
Conzaka, Brigadier General Ferante 101
Cooper, Thomas-Haller 170
Cora, Divisional General Ferdinando 90
Coroller-Danio, Jeanne 162, 163
Cortese, Guido 111
Courlander, New Zealand Army private Roy N. 170
Cosma, Major General Georghe 142, 146
Coturi, Lieutenant General Renato 99
Coty, René 53
Cramer, Major General Hans 21
Cramer, Major General M.C. 118
Cranz, Christel vii
Crasemann, Major General Eduard 53
Crebs, Major General Hans 54

Crete 20, 26, 29, 42, 45, 46, 103, 113 **Crete** (Battle) 41, 42, 60, 170 **Crete** (Fortress) 45
Crimea 19, 49, 50, 145, 146, 147, 148, 178
Crinis, Max de 74
Crinius, Second Lieutenant Wilhelm 37
Croatia 6, 26, 27, 98, 101, 104, 109, 112, 113, 141, 152, 153, 154 **Croatian Air Force Legion** 154 **Croatian Legion** 152 **Croatian prisoners** 153
Csataj, Colonel General Vitez Lajos Csatay de 149
Cukurs, SS Captain Herbert 182
Courland Peninsula 17, 22, 24, 29 **Courland Pocket** 181
Cuenca, Luis Lopez Gordon 151
Czechoslovakia viii, 40, 65, 71, 81, 145, 148, 151, 175, 176, 178 **Czech partisans** viii, 21, 173, 175 **Czech Republic** or **Czechia** 40, 52, 100
Czikszentsimon, Lieutenant General Geza Lakatos de 150

Dachau concentration camp 7, 22, 30, 32, 55, 61, 62, 65, 68, 72, 75, 77, 79, 80, 84, 105 **Dachau/ Mauthausen-Gusen Trials** 7, 62, 68, 77
Daigo, Vice Admiral Tadashige 131
Daily Mail (London) 192
Dalmazzo, Lieutenant General Renzo 105
Damaceanu, Major General Dimitru 144
Dálnok, Colonel General Béla-Miklos de 148
Dálnok, Lieutenant General Lajos Veress de 150
Dálnokfalva, Colonel General Károly-Bartha de 150
Dangić, Major Jesdimir 155
Danz, Luise 85
Daodice, Major General Giuseppe 114
Daranowski-Christian, Gerda 58, 59, 60
Darmand, Joseph 163
Dăscălescu, Lieutenant General Nicolae 145, 146
D'Aquino, Iva Toguri 191, 192
Déat, Marcel

Deboi, Lieutenant General Heinrich-Anton 22
Debrecen (Battle) 142, 150
Decker, Major General Karl 17
Deelen airfield 88
Defenders for the Motherland (Duch East Indies) 189
Defense of Canada Act 194
Degrelle, SS Colonel Léon 164, 165
Dehner, Major General Ernst 12, 13
Dehradun POW camp 90
Delmotte, Hans 75
Demestichas, Lieutenant General Panagiotis 159
Demining tasks 193
Denazification courts vii, 60, 189
Denmark viii, 4, 17, 25, 26, 33, 36, 161, 167, 181, 182, 190, 193
Dessloch Colonel General Otto 36
Devillers, Henri 164
Dianying, General Sun 186
Diekmann, SS Major Otto Weiding 52
Dietrich, SS Sergeant Kurt 64
Dietrich, Colonel General Josef Sepp 30
Dietrich, SS Colonel Fritz-Emil 32
Dieppe (Battle) 170
Dijk, Anna van 166
Ding-Schuler, SS Major Erwin-Oskar 75
Dinort, Brigadier General Oskar 35
Dirlewanger, Senior Colonel Oskar viii, 20
Distomo Massacre 46
Dodbiba, Socrat 158
Doctors' Trial 76, 79, 80
Dodecanese 97, 98, 104 **Dodecanese Campaign** 45
Dodo, Brigadier General Pietro 103
Doihara, General Keiji 119, 121
Domeniko massacre 114
Dönitz, Grand Admiral Karl 3, 5
Donnedieu de Vabres, Henri 2
Donovan, Major General L. 125
Doriot, Jacques 161
Dortemann, Captain Hans 37
Dosti, Hasan 157
Dostler, Major General Anton 9
Double Tenth Trial 127
Do-young, Lieutenant General Jang 188

INDEX

Dragalina, Lieutenant General C., 144
Drauz, Richard 32
Dreschhel, Margot 88
Dresden 17, 21, 67, 69, 78, 88
Drewes, Majo Martin 38
Dublin 18, 165, 190 **Dublin Castle** 18
Dubrovnik 98, 99, 104
Dujić, Momcilo 156
Dumitrache, Lieutenant General Ion 146, 147
Dumitrescu, General Petre 144, 147
Dupanloup, Brigadier General Francesco-Amilcare 109
Durić, Pavle 155
Dusmet, Brigadier General Davide 98
Düsseldorf 5, 7, 13, 15, 40, 41, 51, 59, 61, 72, 73, 81, 85, 86
Dutch East Indies (DEI) 118, 130, 131, 132, 188
Dyachenko, Lieutenant General Petro 176, 177
Džal, Colonel Franjo 154
Dzelzītis, Pēteris 180

East Germany or German Democratic Republic (GDR) 10, 56, 71, 78, 88, 196
Eastern Legions 177
Eberbach, Lieutenant Heinz-Eugen 28
Eberbach, Major General Heinz 28
Eberhard, SS Brigadier General Kurt 48
Eberhardt, Lieutenant General Friedrich-Georg 15
Eberl, Lieutenant Irmfried 68
Eden POW camp vi
Edvaldsson, Atli 179
Edvaldsson, Jóhannes 179
Eftimiu, Brigadier General Constantin 145
Eggers, SS Captain Reinhold 69
Egypt 18, 20, 21, 37, 38, 90, 93, 106, 195
Ehbert, Herta 86
Ehrich, Elsa vi, 85
Ehrlinger, SS Colonel Erich 51
Eichelberger, General Robert L. 117
Eichmann, SS Lieutenant Colonel Otto-Adolf 71
Eigruber, Waffen-SS Major General August 65

Einsatzgruppe Trial 49, 52
Eisenhöffer, SS Lieutenant 65
El Alamein 21, 93
El-Galiani, Rashid 184
Engelbrecht, Major General Erwin 19
England 8, 18, 25, 35, 38, 92, 93, 94, 101, 138, 170, 181, 182, 189, 190, 195
Entress, SS Captain Friedrich 77
Eppinger, Hans 75
Erdmann, Lieutenant General Wolfgang 16, 41, 42, 43
Eritrea 91, 92, 111
Esposito, Major General Giovanni 109
Estonia 4, 33, 50, 64, 178, 179 **Estonian Legion** 178
Euthanasia (Aktion T4) Program 55, 74, 75

Faber, First Lieutenant Armin 359
Falck, Colonel Wolfgang 39
Falco, Robert 2
Falaise Pocket 28, 33, 43
Falugi, Major General Giuseppe 95
Farinacci, Roberto 97
Faruse, Rear Admiral Takesue 126
Fascist Grand Council (Italy) 96, 110, 112 **Fascist Party** (Italy) 96, 97, 110, 111
Featherstone Park POW camp 25, 197
Fehn, Major General Gustav 27
Female POWs 88
Fendler, SS Major Lothar 51
Fenulli, Brigadier General Dardano 102
Ferdennet, Paul 189
Ferla, Lieutenant General Francesco La 94
Fermor, Major Patrick Leigh
Fermy, Major General Helmuth 12, 13
Feroleto, Lieutenant General Mario di 103
Ferrero, Brigadier General Ugo 99
Feuchtinger, Lieutenant General Edgar 26
Ficalbi, Brigadier General Gino 95
Fiebig, Major General Martin 27
Finland 33
Fischer von Weikersthal, Major General Walther 29

245

Flegel, Erna 57
Flemish Legion 164, 165
Flensburg 3, 5, 17, 37, 53, 69, 164, 190
Flensburg Government 3
Florence 53, 100, 109, 112
Flössenburg concentration camp 32, 100
Foertsch Major General Hermann 12, 13
Ford, Gerald 192
Formosa 184, 187
Fort de Châtillon 163, 189
Fort de Montrouge 164
Fort Dix POW camp 195
Forte Boccea prison 109, 110
Forte Bravetta prison 107, 108
Frakelj, Franc 155
France viii, 10, 11, 12, 14, 16, 17, 19, 22, 23, 24, 25, 28, 30, 31, 32, 34, 36, 38, 41, 52, 53, 57, 61, 81, 100, 118, 132, 138, 142, 161, 162, 163, 164, 165, 170, 171, 175, 176, 178, 181, 184, 188, 189, 193
Franco, Francisco 112, 113, 151
Francette concentration camp 113
François, 1st Lieutenant Jef 165
Frank, Anne 166
Frank, Hans 3, 4, 5
Frank, SS Lieutenant General Karl-Hermann 52
Frank, Olga 154
Frankfurt 9, 13, 25, 35, 41, 59, 68, 75, 182, 191
Franz, SS Lieutenant Kurt 71, 72
Frasheri, Mid'hat 157
Free Arab Legion 184
Free Corps Denmark 166, 167
Free French Army 30
Free India Legion 184, 185
Free Ukraine Brigade 176
Freiher von Bodenhausen, Major General Erpo 17
Freitag, Brigadier General Fritz 18
Frentz, Lieutenant Walter 57
Friar, Margaret 195
Frick, Wilhelm 3, 4
Fridrichsons, Kurts 180
Friedburg, Admiral Hans-Georg von 17
Frisius, Vice Admiral Friedrich 34
Fritzsche, Hans 3, 5, 6, 189

Frusci, Divisional General Luigi 90, 91
Fucuda, Captain Yoshio 133
Führer's Bunker 56, 57, 58, 59
Fujishige, Major General Mashatoshi 124, 125
Fuller, J.F.C. 8
Funk, Walter 3, 5
Fürhner, Irmgard 86, 87
Fushun war criminals' management center or Liaoning concentration camp 134, 186, 197

Gaeta fortress (prison) 54
Galbriati, Lieutenant General Enzo-Emilio 110
Gallina, Lieutenant General Sebastiano 90
Gambara, Lieutenant General Gastone 113, 114
Gandin, Divisional General Antonio 97
Garibaldi, Brigadier General Giuseppe 106
Gariboldi, General Italo 104
Garmaev, Urzhin 186
Gaulle, Charles de 31, 53
Gazzera, Divisional General Pietro 90, 92, 93
Gdansk or Danzig 62, 64, 67, 72, 73, 83, 84
Gdansk/Torun Stutthof Trials 7
Gebbhardt, SS Brigadier General 76
Geelkerken, Cornelis van 166
Gefolge (SS Women's Division) 81, 89
Geitner, Major General Kurt Ritter von 12, 13
Geloso, Divisional General Carlo 98
Geneva Conventions vii, viii, 3, 125, 194
Genzken, SS Major General Karl 79
Georgia 180, 181 **Georgian Legion** 177
Georgis, Divisional General Fedele de 93
German Navy 5, 21, 33, 34, 166, 168
German POWs vi, viii, 15, 75, 195, 196 **German intelligence services** 171 **German secret services** 23
Germany or Nazi Germany vi, vii, viii, 1, 2, 4, 8, 9, 15, 17, 18, 25, 26, 28, 29, 31, 33, 35, 36, 37, 38, 41, 42, 44, 45, 46, 48, 50, 53, 54, 55, 57, 60, 63, 67,

INDEX

68, 69, 71, 72, 73, 74, 75, 78, 81, 86, 87, 88, 100, 102, 105, 109, 111, 118, 120, 138, 141, 142, 144, 150, 152, 156, 159, 161, 163, 164, 165, 168, 169, 171, 172, 176, 180, 181, 182, 183, 189, 190, 194, 196
Gerstenmeier, SS Captain Wilhelm 62
Gesche, SS Lieutenant Bruno 54
Gestapo 4, 7, 12, 14, 76, 82, 83, 149, 164, 167, 168, 175, 177, 184
Geyer, Major General Hermann 18
Gheorghiu, General Ermil 144
Giãlak, Lieutenant General Gheorghe 146
Gihr, Brigadier General Gustav 24
Gillars, Milfred-Elizabeth 191
Gille, SS Major General Herbert 33
Gilliaert, General Auguste 92
Gilza, Major General Werner 17
Giorgio, Lieutenant General Umberto di 98
Giosmas, Xenophon 159
Girotti, Lieutenant General Mario 103
Glasenbach POW camp 142
Glaise-Horstenau, Edmund 6
Glattes, Captain Gerhard 19, 20ł
Globocnik, Major General Odilo 29, 30, 69, 70
Glodok prison 132
Goebbels, Joseph 6, 54, 56, 57, 60
Goebbels, Magda 60
Gomułka, Władysław 153
Görtz, Captain Hermann 18
Göring, Reich Marshal Hermann vi, 3, 5, 7, 8, 9, 44, 55
Gottardi, Luciano 96
Gott, Lieutenant General William 38
Gotti-Porcinari, Major General Giulio 95
Gotzamanis, Sotirios 159
Grabner, SS Lieutenant Maximilian 63
Graevenitz, Lieutenant General Hans von 27
Graf, Colonel Hermann 39
Grandes, General Agustin Muñoz 151
Grattarola, Major General Attilio 99
Grawitz, SS Mayor General Ernst-Robert 55
Graziani, Field Marschal Rodolfo 111, 112

Grazioli, Emilio 114
Great Bitter Lake POW camp 37, 90
Great Britain 1, 2, 17, 19, 20, 25, 26, 97, 109, 117, 150, 169, 171, 172, 189, 190, 193, 194, 195
Greim, Lieutenant Humbert 8
Greim, Field Marshal Robert Ritter von 7, 8, 15, 34, 47
Greece 12, 13, 27, 45, 46, 71, 105, 111, 113, 114, 157, 158, 170, 184 **Greek islands** 102, 104, 113
Gresse, Irma 81, 82
Grimm, SS Lieutenant Johannes 65
Grīnbergs, Emmanuels 180
Grislawski, Captain Alfred 39
Gröpler, Carl 79
Grossdeutschland Division 30
Gross Rosen concentration camp 75, 87
Groza, Petru 143
Grundmanis, Mārtiņs 180
Gruwell, Major General Ludwig 22, 35
Guam 118, 123, 124, 197
Guernsey 34, 176, 177
Guidi-Buffarini, Guido 96
Gulags or forced labour camps 60, 175, 177, 180, 185, 196
Gunsche, SS Major Otto 56
Gutheridge, William 172
Guzzoni, Lieutenant General Alfredo 100, 101

Haaland, Reidar 168
Haase, Werner 55
Haensch, SS Lieutenant Colonel Walter 49
Hahn, Major Hans 40
Hamburg vi, 4, 7, 9, 10, 13, 15, 16, 17, 24, 29, 30, 34, 36, 40, 43, 44, 47, 49, 57, 61, 66, 67, 68, 69, 70, 79, 81, 82, 83, 86, 182
Hamada, Lieutenant General Hitoshi 116
Hamanaka, Rear Admiral Kyosho 130
Hamelin Prison 30, 32, 33, 64, 65, 67, 78, 81, 82, 83, 168
Handloser, Colonel General Siegfried-Adolf 79
Hanke, Karle August 20, 21
Hanle, Reichsführer Karl vii

247

Hannsted POW camp 39
Hanover 12, 15, 24, 27, 35, 38, 42, 60, 70, 73, 79 **Hanover** military academy 144
Hansen, Lieutenant General Erick-Oskar 22, 23, 24
Hara, Vice Admiral Chuchi 124
Harbin 122, 186
Hartjenstein, SS Captain Friedrich 32
Hartmann, Colonel Erich 196
Haruhito, Prince Kan'in 138
Haruzo, Major Sumida 127
Harwek, Brigadier General M.H. 125
Hashimoto, Colonel Kingaro 120, 121
Hassel, Ulrich von 113
Hasselbach, SS Major Hanscarl 55
Hata, Field Marshal Shonruku 120, 121
Hatakeyama, Rear Admiral Koichiro 131
Hatoyama, Ichiro 121
Haug, Bishop Martin 74
Haussmann, Wolfgang 74
Havet, Lieutenant General Achille d' 95
Häzners, SS Major Vilis A, 181
Heidelberg 14, 37, 38, 178 **Heidelberg University** 38
Heidrich, Major General Richard 43
Heilmann, Brigadier General Sebastian-Ludwig 44
Hellmich, Brigadier General Heinz 173
Heim, Lieutenant General Ferdinand 24, 25
Heimburg, Vice Admiral Heino von 33
Heinz, Colonel General Walter 22
Heise, Gertrud 86
Helbig, Colonel Joachin 39
Hengkel, SS Captain Wilhelm 65
Hennecke, Rear Admiral Walter 34
Henneyey, Colonel General Gusztáv 150
Henning, Kai 167
Henriot, Philippe 163
Hérold-Paquis, Jean 189
Herzogenbusch concentration camp 72
Hess, Rudolf 2, 3, 5, 121
Hesse 13, 25, 26, 38, 41, 50 55, 70, 73
Heszlényi, Colonel General Joszef 149
Hewel, Walther 56
Heyking, Brigadier General Rüdiger 44
Heyde, SS Colonel Werner 75
Heydich, Reinhard 52

Higashikuni, Prince Naruhito 116, 138
High Command Case 7, 14 **High Command Trial** 9, 11, 13, 15
Hildebrandt, SS Major General 32
Hintermayer, SS Lieutenant Fritz 77
Himmler, Gudrun vii, 61 **Himmler**, Heinrich vi, viii, 6, 21, 30, 31, 33, 54
Himmler, Margarete vii, 61
Hippel, Lieutenant Colonel Theodor von 29
HIPPO Corps 167
Hirano, Colonel Kuratano 122
Hiranuma, Baron Kiichiro 120
Hirate, Captain Kaichi 122
Hirschfeld, Colonel Harald von
Hirt, SS Major August 75
Hitler, Adolf or Führer 2, 3, 4, 6, 8, 10, 11, 12, 22, 33, 41, 43, 54, 55, 56, 57, 58, 59, 60, 70, 74, 76, 153
Hitler, Heinrich 60
Hiran, Major General Toyoji 116
Hirohito, Emperor of Japan 116, 117, 120, 138
Hiroshima vii, 116, 120
Hirota, Lieutenant General Koki 119
Hiroyasu, Prince Fushimi 138
Hochbaum, Major General Friedrich 22
Hocker, SS Lieutenant Karl-Friedrich 69
HMS *Faulknor* 20 HMS *Firedrake* 20 HMS *Foxhound* 20
Hoffle, SS Major Hermann 30
Hoffmann, Erich 168
Hoffman, Major Werner 38
Hoheneck Fortress 88
Hohxa, Enver 156, 157
Holland or the Netherlands 4, 8, 13, 16, 17, 32, 33, 42, 45, 49, 72, 88, 89, 117, 118, 161, 165, 166, 177, 193
Holle, Lieutenant General Alexander 36
Hollidt, Colonel General Karl-Adolf 13, 14
Holocaust 70, 87
Holoway prison 190
Holzlöhner, SS Major Ernst 75
Homma, Lieutenant Masaharu 124, 125
Hong Kong viii, 126, 129, 134, 187
Honjo, General Shikeru 116
Honshu 121, 138

INDEX

Horthy, Admiral N. de Nagybánya 148, 149, 150
Horiuchi, Captain Toyoaki 131
Hoshino, General Naoki 120, 121
Hosokawa, Morihiro 116
Höss, Rudolf 88
Hössler, SS Lieutenant Franz 64
Hostages Case 7, 11 **Hostages Trial** 12, 13
Hoth, Colonel General Hermann 13, 14
Hoven, SS Captain Waldemar 76
Hudal, Roman Catholic Bishop Alois 107
Hüffmeier, Vice Admiral Friedrich 34
Hughes, Raymond Davies 190
Hungarian Army 149 **Hungarian POWs** 148, 196 **Hungarian troops** 142, 146
Hungary vi, vii, 1, 12, 15, 20, 26, 31, 52, 71, 141, 142, 143, 149, 150, 174, 197
Huth, Elfried 86, 87
Huy, Captain Wolf-Dietrich 37

Iceland 167, 179
Ichikaya 115
Ichikawa, 2nd Lieutenant Yokichi 123
Iida, Lieutenant General Shojiro 135
Igarashi, Yoshikuni 117
Il-kuon, Colonel Chung 188
Illing, Ernst 78
Imamura, General Hitoshi 129
Imperial Family (Japan) 133, 137, 138 **Imperial Military Academy** (Tokyo) 188
Inada, Lieutenant General Masazumi 122
India 92, 93, 184, 185
Indochina viii, 132, 133
Indonesia viii, 118, 130, 188 **Indonesian Archipelago** 116, 129
Infantes, General Emilio Esteban 151
Ionescu, General Emanoil 144
International Criminal Court 125
International Military Tribunal for the Far East 117, 118, 119, 120, 121, 133, 137
Iraq 143, 184
Ireland 165, 184, 190
Island Farm or Special Camp XI or Camp 198 9, 10, 11, 20, 25, 28, 34, 42, 53, 56

Isle of Wight 172
Isogai, Lieutenant General Rensuke 133
Israel 71
Ishii, Lieutenant General 122
Isogai, Lieutenant General Rensuke 134
Itagaki, General Seishiro 119, 121
Italian Air Force 92, 102 **Italian atrocities** 111, 114 **Italian Co-Belligerent Army** 94, 95, 101 **Italian East Africa** 92, 93, 111 **Italian Military Internees** 101, 102 **Italian partisans** 8, 71, 96 **Italian POWs** vii, viii, 102, 104, 109, 196 **Italian Royal Army** 90, 97, 104, 110, 113 **Italian Social Republic** 95, 96, 98, 99, 100, 101, 105, 108, 109, 110
Italy or Kingdom of Italy or Fascist Italy vi, vii, 8, 9, 30, 31, 33, 42, 43, 44, 53, 54, 60, 61, 71, 90, 91, 92, 93, 95, 96, 98, 99, 100, 101, 102, 103, 104, 106, 107, 108, 109, 111, 112, 113, 114, 118, 141, 152, 156, 157, 169, 170, 176, 177, 184, 185, 189, 191
Ito, Lieutenant Colonel Toroji 123

Jabs, Lieutenant-Colonel Hans-Joachim 38
Jackson, Philip (British Army private) 171
Jahr, Lieutenant General Arno 17
Jais, Brigadier General Maximilian 28, 29
James, Leslie 59
Janums, SS Colonel Vilis 180
Jany, Colonel General Gusztav 149
Japan or Empire of Japan vi, vii, viii, 111, 115, 117, 118, 131, 134, 138, 141, 170, 189, 197
Japanese Army or Imperial Japanese Army 115, 116, 119, 122, 123, 125, 126, 127, 129, 131, 133, 134, 137, 138, 185, 186, 188 **Japanese Goebbels** 118 **Japanese Navy** or Imperial Japanese Navy 115, 119, 120, 123, 126, 130, 137, 138, 185, 186 **Japanese POWs** vi, viii, 116, 117, 134, 135, 196, 197 **Japanese Surrendered Personnel** (JSP) 117 **Japanese troops** 116, 132

249

Jasenovac concentration camp 155
Java 129, 131, 132
Jeckeln, SS Lieutenant General Friedrich 47
Jensen, SS Major Frederik 169
Jersey 34, 177
Jerusalem 86
Jeschonnek, Colonel General Hans 16
Jews 10, 14, 15, 16, 18, 31, 45, 47, 48, 49, 50, 51, 63, 64, 68, 69, 70, 71, 73, 74, 75, 76, 77, 79, 87, 107, 149, 153, 154, 159, 163, 166, 178, 179, 181, 182, 183
Jevdevic, Dobroslav 156
Jilava prison 144, 145, 146, 147, 148
Jinghuei, General Zhang 186
Job, Oswald-John 171
Jodl, Colonel General Alfred 3, 9
Jost, SS Brigadier General Heinz 50
Josten, SS Lieutenant Heinrich 63
Joyce, Margaret Cairns 190 **Joyce, William Brook** 190
Junge, Traudl 59, 60
Jungfernhoff concentration camp 68
Jürss, Ulla 88

Käärmann, Alfred 179
Kähler, Rear Admiral Otto 34
Kahrs, SS Major Sophus 168
Kaindl, SS Colonel 67
Kalacinski, Wanda 83, 84
Kalavryta Massacre 46
Kalējis, Konrāds 182
Kalinin, 1st Lieutenant Feoktist 195
Kaltenbach, Frederich-Wilhelm 191
Kaltenbrunner, Ernst 3, 4
Kamianets-Podilsky Massacre 47
Kaminski, Bronislav 174, 175
Kanayan, General Drasatmat 178
Kaniyaki, Lieutenant Nakamura 126, 127
Kappler, SS Lieutenant-Colonel Herbert 107, 108
Kaserović, Lieutenant-Colonel Dragutin 155
Kaso, Vice Admiral Abe 124
Kassel-Wehlheiden prison 182
Katayama, Lieutenant Paul Hideo 130
Katsimitros, Major General Charalambos 159

Katyn massacre 143
Kawane, Major General Yoshitaka 122
Kawapuchi, Lieutenant General Kiyotake 126
Kawashima, Princes Yoshiko or Jin Bijui or Mata Hari of the Far East 139
Kay, José-Estelle 151, 171
Kaya, General Okinori 120, 121
Kazoku 121
Keitel, Field Marshal Wilhelm 3, 7, 8
Këlcyra, Alibey 157
Kempetai (Japan's military police) 116, 127, 130
Kempka, SS Lieutenant Colonel Erich 58
Kenya 92, 93
Kesselring, Field Marshal Albert 7, 8, 9, 95, 106, 107
KGB 179
Khabarovsk POW camp 116, 135
Khalkyn Temple (Battle) 186 **Khalkyn Gol River** (Battle) 186
Khan, Major General Nawaz 185
Kharkov 98
Kiani, Major General Mohammad Zaman 185
Kido, General Koichi 120, 121, 121
Kiebon, Charles van der 165
Kieffer, SS Major Hans 31, 32
Kiel 5, 19, 29, 34, 37, 75, 76
Kimura, General Heitaro 119
King Michael I (Mihail I) of Romania 24, 141, 143
King Paul of the Hellenes (Greece) 45
Kinzel, Major General Eberhard 17
Kirin Provincial Army 186
Kirschner, Captain Joachim 27
Kita, General Seiichi 135
Kitano, Lieutenant General Masaji 122, 123
Kitashirakawa, Prince Nagahisa
Kiyoshi, Major General Kawashima 135
Kjelstrup, SS Major Finn 169
Klein, Anna 81
Kleinheistercamp, Major General Matthias 18
Kleinkamp, Vice Admiral Gustav 34
Kleist, Field Marshal Ludwig Evald von 8, 10, 11

INDEX

Kline, SS Major Fritz 77
Klingerhöffer, SS Major Waldemar 48, 50
Klosterkember, Brigadier General Bernhard 29
Kluge, Field Marshal Gunther 12
Knöchen, SS Colonel Helmut 31
Knöchlen, SS Captain Fritz 30
Kobus, Lieutenant General Arthur 17
Koch, Erich 48
Koch, SS Colonel Karl-Otto 85
Koch, Ilse 76, 85
Koch, Pietro 108
Koiso, General Kuniaki 120
Koizumi, Lieutenant General Chikachiko 115
Kokobu, Lieutenant General Shishichiro 131
Koller, Major General Karl 35
Kollmer, SS Lieutenant Colonel Joseph 63
Konatkwitz, Maria
Königsberg (Light cruiser) 16
Kono, Lieutenant General Takeshi 124, 125
Konoe, Fuminaro 116
Kononow, Major General Ivan N. 175
Konte, Brigadier General Hans 43
Koppe, Major General Wilhelm 69, 70
Korea 116, 120, 121, 126, 137, 187, 188 **Korean** Peninsula 188 **Korean War** 74, 188
Korne, Brigadier General Radu 144, 145
Kosevski Rog massacre 153
Köstlin, Captain Beate 41
Köstring, Major General Ernst-August 24, 25, 173
Kotta, Costaq 158
Kotohito, Prince Kan'in 133
Kournovo 114
Krakau, Lieutenant General August 26
Krakow 40, 62, 63, 64, 70, 79, 84, 85, 86 **Krakow prison** 87 **Krakow-Plaszow concentration camp** 86
Kramer, SS Lieutenant Colonel Joseph 64
Krasnov, Lieutenant General Pyotr N. 175

Kraus, SS Major Franz-Xaver 63
Krause, SS Captain Karl Wilhelm 33
Krebsbach, SS Lieutenant Eduard 77
Kreipe, Major General Heinrich 20
Kremer, Johann 79, 80
Kroch, Brigadier General Hans 43
Krotoff, 2nd Lieutenant Serge Hermann
Krüger, Else vii, 59
Krüger, Major General Friedrich-Wilhelm 29
Krupp von Bohlen und Halbach, Gustav 3
Kryeziu, Ismet 158
Kryssing, Christian P. 167
Kubiliūnas, Lieutenant General Petra 183
Küchler, Field Marshal Georg von 8, 10, 11, 13
Kullmer, Major General Arthur 23
Kummetz, Rear Admiral Oskar 19
Kunz, SS Major Helmut 57
Künze, Major General Walter 12
Kvaternik, Field Marshal Slavko 154
Kyroda, Lieutenant General Shigeroni 126
Kuomintag 133, 134, 135, 139, 186, 187, 197
Kurtaisi forced labour camp 180, 181
Kuznica Zelichowska 99
Kyoungjpng, Yang 197
Kyushu 126 **Kyushu Imperial University** 122

Laak, Aleksander 178
Labonne, Roger Henri 161
Labuan 116, 129 **Labuan trials** 129
Lachert, Hildgard
Lagrou, René 165
Lammerding, SS Lieutenant General Heinz 52
Landsberg Prison 13, 14, 15, 30, 32, 33, 48, 49, 50, 51, 56, 62, 67, 68, 72, 76, 77, 79
Landstormen 167
Langsdorff, Captain Hans 16
Lang Son massacre 132
Lanz, Major General Hubert 12, 13
Lascăr, General Mihail 143. 144
Lastrucci, Brigadier General Romolo 90

251

Latvia 7, 15, 17, 22, 29, 32, 47, 50, 68, 176, 178, 179, 180, 181, 182, 183 **Latvian Legion** 179, 180, 181, 182
Laurence, sir Geoffrey 2
Laval, Pierre 163, 164
Lay, Robert 3, 6
Leclerc de Hauttecloque, General Philippe 161
Leeb, Field Marshal W. R. von 10, 13
Légion de Volontaires Française (LVF) 161
Legions of the East 173
Leggio, Colonel Felice 97
Lehmann, Colonel General (Judge) Rudolf 13, 15
Leigh, Vera 32
Lemke, Brigadier General Max 44
Leningrad 11, 26, 51, 151, 165, 168, 173, 179, 180
Leone, Divisional General Adolfo de 90, 91
Le Paradis 30
Lepoglava prison 153, 155
Lerch, SS Major Ernst 69
Lester, Major General J.A. 125
Le Suire, Major General Karl von 46
Lethbridge POW camp 20
Leyser, Major General Ernst von 12, 13
Lezaky Massacre 52
Libya 18, 20, 91, 93, 106, 112
Libohova, Ekrem 156
Lidice Massacre 52
Liddel Hart, Basil 8
Liebenschel, SS Lieutenant Colonel Arthur 63
Liechtenstein 174
Liepāja massacre 181
Lileikis, Aleksandras 183
Lindhurst, Elisabeth 57
Lindemann, Colonel General Georg 24, 25, 26
Linge, SS Lieutenant Colonel Heinz
Linnas, Karl 178, 179
List, Field Marshal Wilhelm 7, 10, 159
Lithuania 10, 51, 183 **Lithuanian Activist Group** 183 **Lithuanian Territorial Defense Force** 183
Litomerice 71

Lobe, SS Colonel Kārlis 180
Loerzer, Colonel General Bruno 36
Logothetopoulos, Konstantinos I. 159
Löhr, Colonel General Alexander 26, 34
Lom, Johan van 166
London 2, 8, 21, 25, 26, 28, 34, 35, 42, 43, 44, 94, 95, 150, 165, 170, 171, 172, 181, 189 **London District Cage** 26, 28, 42, 43, 47 **London Olympics** (1908) 113
Lordi, Brigadier General Roberto 102
Lorentz, Captain Günther 19, 20
Lorenzen Jørgen 167 **Lorenzen Group** 167
Lorient basketball club 181
Loritz, SS Colonel Hans 68
Lorković, Mladen 153
Los Baños prison 125
Lossberg, Brigadier General Bernhard von 26
Lublin 7, 47, 62, 67, 70, 85
Lugli, Brigadier General Enrico 99, 100
Lubyanka Prison 6, 24, 57, 58, 94, 174, 175
Ludendorff Bridge 11
Luftwaffe 8, 11, 13, 16, 26, 27, 34, 35, 36, 37, 38, 40, 41, 55, 58, 60, 78, 80
Lukašević, Major Vojslav 155
Lund, Anna 167
Lüneburg (031 Interrogation and POW Camp) 6, 7, 9, 49, 61, 76, 77, 82
Lupé, Monsignor Mayol de 162
Lupka, Elisabeth 84, 85
Lüntzow, Vice Admiral Friedrich 34
Luxemburg 3, 5, 11, 29
Luykx, Albert 165
Lviv 12, 51

MacArthur, General Douglas 117, 125, 137, 138
McCloy, John J. 74
McLardy, (British Army private) George F. 171
Macelariu, Rear Admiral Horia 147
Machui, General Iwane 119
Mackensen, Colonel General Eberhard von 107
Madrid 155, 192

INDEX

Maidstone Prison 18
Maindiff Hospital 2
Major, Colonel General Jenő 150
Maestre Prison 8
Mafalda, Princess of Savoy 105, 107
Magdalene College (Cambridge) 60
Maglakelidge, Shalva 177
Majdanek concentration camp vi, 47, 67, 69, 80, 81, 85 **Majdanek Trials** 7, 62, 72
Málaga 165, 169
Malaguti, Major General Bruno 105
Malaya 117, 119 **Malayan Voluntary Army** 189 **Malaysia** 189
Malmalson prison 146
Malmedy massacre 30
Malyshkin, Major General Vasily F. 174
Manado 118, 130, 131
Manchester City soccer club 195
Manchukuo Imperial Army 185
Manchuria or Manchukuo 116, 119, 122, 135, 138, 185, 186, 187, 188, 197
Mandić, Nikola 153
Mandl, Maria 84
Manella, Divisional General Enrico Pitassi 90, 91
Manila 118, 125, 126 126 **Manila Bay** 125 **Manila massacre** 124 **Manila trials** 124, 188
Mannerini, Lieutenant General Alberto 94
Manoliu, Major General Gheorghe 144, 147
Manstein, Field Marshal Erich von 7, 9
Manus Island 129, 130
Manzabotto massacre 53
Manziarly, Constanze 60
Marciani, Lieutenant General Giovanni 95
Maria, Brigadier General Paolo De 109
Mariana Islands 123
Marinelli, Giovanni 96
Marion, General Charles 162, 163
Marschall, Elisabeth 81, 82
Marschall, Admiral of the Fleet Wilhelm 34
Marshal Islands 123

Martini, Lieutenant-Colonel Enrico 106
Martinsen, Captain Knud Børge 167
Masao, Lieutenant General Baba 129
Masayaki, Lieutenant-Colonel Oishi 127
Mascherpa, Rear Admiral Luigi 97, 103, 104
Mattaliano-Hodys, Eleonore 63
Matsuoka, Yosuke 118
Maurice, SS Colonel Emil 58
Mauthausen-Gusen concentration camp complex 61, 65, 66, 72, 73, 80, 87 **Mauthausen-Gusen Trials** 66, 72, 77
Mäzler, Major General Kurt 107
Mborja, Tefik 158
Meier, Karl H. 165
Melenthin, Brigadier General Friedrich von 26
Melenthin, Major General Horst von 26
Mendes-France, Pierre 31, 53
Mengele, SS Captain Joseph 88
Mešić, Ademaga 154
Messe, Field Marshal Giovanni 94
Meyer, SS Brigadier General Kurt 31
Meyer, SS Captain Theodor 72
MI5 (British intelligence service) 172 **MI6** (British intelligence service) 178
MI19 Interrogation Center 47
Michalsen, SS Major Georg 69, 70
Mihailović, General Draza 155
Mikasa, Prince Takahito 138
Mikosch, Major General Hans 23
Mikson, Evald 179
Milan 96, 97, 98, 100, 101, 109, 110, 191
Milch, Field Marshal Erchard 7, 8, 13
Milice Française 163
Military Scientific Research Institute 77
Mills-Roberts, Lieutenant Colonel Derek 13
Minami, General Jiro 120, 121
Minnitti, Lieutenant Tito 112
Mischi, Lieutenant General Archimide 110
Mitrovica, Rexhep 156
Mittelbau-Dora concentration camp system 62, 63, 65, 68, 73, 80, 81 **Mittelbau-Dora Trials** 72, 80
Miyazaki, Colonel Aritsune 123

Mociulschi, Major General Leonard 144, 148
Möckel, SS Lieutenant-Colonel Karl-Ernst 63
Model, Field Marshal Walter 7, 11, 16, 47
Mohneke, Elfriede 86, 87
Mohneke, Brigadier General Wilhelm 23, 24, 59
Moisiu, Alfred 156 **Moisiu, Spiro** 156
Mokotow Prison 46, 47, 48
Molat concentration camp 113
Mölders, Colonel Werner 19, 36
Möller, SS Squad Leader Kurt 62
Mondino, Lieutenant General Umberto 99
Mondorf-les-Baines 3, 8, 11
Mongolia 138, 185 **Mongolian Army** 185
Montagna, Major General Renzo 110
Montano, Lieutenant Massimo 103
Montelupich Prison 63, 64, 85
Montenegro 98, 99, 101, 109, 112
Montezemolo, Colonel Lanza di 102, 103
Montgomery, Field Marshal Bernard 17
Monticello POW camp 92
Moran, Frederick A. 74
Morell, Theodore 55
Morimasa, Field Marshal Nashimoto 138
Morotai Island 129, 130
Mory, Carmen-Castro 83
Moscow 5, 6, 8, 10, 11, 14, 21, 23, 24, 41, 50, 55, 56, 57, 58, 60, 67, 71, 94, 121, 148, 149, 151, 173, 174, 175, 179, 181, 183, 186, 197 **Moscow Declaration** 10
Mosley, Sir Oswald 190
Moss, Captain Stanley 20
Mossad 71, 182
Mösser, SS Lieutenant Hans 62, 63
Mountjoy Prison 18
Mourer, Jean-Pierre 164
Mrugowsky, SS Colonel Joachim 76
Mukai, 2nd Lieutenant Toshiaki 134
Müller, Major General Friedrich-Wilhelm 45

Multke, Luftwaffe cadet Guido 35
Munich 5, 7, 8, 10, 11, 13, 19, 22, 24, 30, 33, 35, 36, 37, 43, 47, 50, 55, 56, 57, 58, 60, 61, 62, 71, 73, 78, 79, 87, 150, 162, 164, 191 **Munich University** 50, 56
Muñoz, Jose Martin 151
Münster 12, 16, 34, 38, 44, 80, 180, 194
Munt, Albert 172
Murer, Brigadier General Alberto 100
Murra, Divisional General Vincenzo della 90, 91
Muslim-Caucasian Legion 177
Mussert, Anton 165, 166
Mussolini-Ciano, Edda 95, 96
Mussolini, Benito or Duce 93, 95, 96, 98, 99, 100, 101, 104, 106, 109, 110, 112
Muto, Lieutenant General Akira 119
Myrdacz, General Gustav von 158
Mysen concentration camp 64
Mytchett Place 2

Nagano, Marshal Admiral Osami 118, 119
Nagasaki vii, 116
Nagybaczon, Colonel General Vilmos Nagy de 150
Nagylak, Lieutenant General Vitez Jënö Rátz de 149
Nakajima, Colonel Ikke 188
Nakajima, General Kesago 133
Nanjin or Nankin 133, 134, 186, 187 **Nanjin massacre** 119, 134, 138
Naruhiko, Prince Higashikouni 121
Nasarenko, 2nd Lieutenant Ignatz 195
Nasi, Divisional General Guglielmo Ciro 90, 93
National Revolutionary Army (China) 186
National Socialist Movement (Holland) 165
Naumann, SS Brigadier General Erich 48, 49
Natzweiler-Strutthof concentration camp 32, 75, 80
Naumann, Werner 59
Navratil, Lieutenant General Miroslav 154

INDEX

Nayashi, Lieutenant General Yoshinide 126
Necker, Brigadier General Hanns-Horst 44
Nehradun POW camp 92
Nerger, Captain Karl-August 21
Neuengamme concentration camp 16, 27, 29
Neuengamme Trials 61
Neurath, Konstantin von 3, 5
Neururer, Otto 61
New Bilibid prison 126
New Zealand vi, 170, 197
Niederhagen concentration camp 32
Niedermayer, Brigadier General Ritter von 177
Nikitchenko, Ion 2
Nikolai, Colonel Walter 23
Nikolescu, General Constantin 147
Nishi, Lieutenant-Colonel Toshihide 135
Nishio, General Toshizo 137
Nitsche, Hermann-Paul 78
NKVD agents 23, 143, 146, 174, 175, 183 **NKVD Special Camp No. 7** 21
Noda, 2nd Lieutenant Tsuyoshi 134
Nojaki, Major General Seiji 131
Noreika, Captain Jonas 183
Normandy or D-Day 11, 12, 21, 31, 43, 52, 194, 197
North Africa vi, 12, 20, 38, 42, 90, 91, 103, 104, 105, 112, 162, 171, 184
North African Legion 184
North Caucasian Legion 177
Norway viii, 16, 18, 19, 33, 36, 45, 64, 161, 164, 167, 168, 193 **Norwegian Campaign** 16, 19 **Norwegian Legion** 168
Nosske, SS Lieutenant Gustav 50, 51
Nuremberg 3, 4, 5, 6, 11, 12, 13, 14, 15, 39, 48, 49, 50, 51, 55, 57, 67, 75, 76, 80, 107, 111 **Nuremberg** (International Military Tribunal) 2, 5, 6 **Nuremberg Prison** 3, 70 **Nuremberg Trials** 3, 4, 5, 6, 10, 47, 55, 59, 75, 118, 178, 182, 189
Nyeri POW camp 92

Oberg, SS Major General Carl 53
Ochota Massacre 46
Odessa 143, 144, 146 **Odessa Massacre** 48
Office of Strategic Services (OSS) 57
O'Grady, Dorothy 172
Ohlendorf, SS Brigadier General Otto 48, 50
Oie, Colonel Satoshi 125
Oka, Vice Admiral Takazumi 120, 121
Okada, Lieutenant General Tasuku 122
Okamoto, Lieutenant General Kiyotomi 116
Okamura, General Yasuji 133, 134, 137
Okawa, Shumei 118
Okazaki, Lieutenant General Seisaburo 132
Okinawa (Battle) 137
Okuma, Lieutenant Commander Kaoru 123
Oldham POW camp 194
Olschanesky, Sonya 32
Omari, Bahri 157
O'Neill, Sergeant Major Richard-Anthony 78, 81
Onesti forced labour colony 148
Onishi, Vice Admiral Takijiro 115
Operation Ache 97
Operation Barbarossa 11, 15
Operation Market Garden 16
Opitz, Friedrich 67
Oria (Steamboat) 102
Orlando, Lieutenant General Taddeo 94
Orlowski, Alice 85
Oshima, Lieutenant General Hiroshi 120, 121
Oslo 18, 19, 47, 168
Ostoji, Zaharije 155
Ott, SS Lieutenant Colonel Adolf 49, 50
Ozols, Lieutenant Karlis A. 182

Pacific War 115, 116, 129
Padule massacre 53
Pāis, Vice Admiral Nicolae 144
Palau Island 123, 126
Palwan 125
Panay massacre 120, 125
Pancrac Prison 52
Pankhurst prison 190
Pannwitz, Lieutenant General Helmuth von 175, 176

Paoli, Pierre 164
Papen, Franz von 3, 5, 6
Papua New Guinea 118, 123, 129
Paradies, Ewa 83, 84
Pareschi, Carlo 96
Pariani, General Alberto 111
Paris 16, 31, 32, 36, 53, 83, 156, 162, 163, 164, 184, 189
Parker, John 2
Parpaglia, Divisional General Pino 90, 92
Pascolini, Lieutenant General Etelvoldo 93, 94
Paternion interrogation center 30, 70
Pauls, SS Sergeant Johann 64
Paulus, Field Marshal Friedrich von 8, 22, 94
Pauly, SS Colonel Max 67
Pavelić, Ante 152, 153
Pavolini Alessandro 97
Peck, David W. 74 **Peck Panel** 51, 74
Pečovnik massacre 153
Pedrazzoli, Lieutenant General Gino
Peenemünde rockets installation 16, 190
Peiper, SS Colonel Joachim 30, 31
Peltz, Brigadier General Dietrich 35
Penendick, Helmut 80
Peng, General Ye 186, 187
Penlington, Wanda 172
Pentoville prison 165, 171
People's Liberation Army (China) 186
People's Tribunal (Budapest) 149, 150
Përmeti, General Akif 157
Perón, Juan 153
Perro, SS Lieutenant Oskars 181
Perrot, Jean-Marie 162
Perotti, Brigadier General Giuseppe 103
Pervizi, Major General Prenk 156
Pescatori, Major General Armando 90
Petacci, Clara 96
Pétain, Marshal Philippe 163
Peters, Dorothea 191
Peters, Lieutenant Andries-Jan 166
Petrovicescu, Brigadier General Constantin 145
Petersen, SS Colonel Heinrich 30
Pfeffer, Major General Max 22
Phalange Africaine 162, 184
Philipp, Landsgrave of Hesse 105, 106

Philippines 118, 119, 124, 127, 137, 188
Phleps, Major General Artur 142, 143
Piacentini, Divisional General Pietro 90, 92
Piazzale Loreto 96
Piazzoni, Lieutenant General Alessandro 99
Pierrepoint, (Public executioner) Albert 32, 64, 65, 67, 78, 81, 83, 151, 171, 189
Piletić, Colonel Velimir 156
Pister, SS Colonel Rudolf 68
Pitesti prison 147
Plagge, SS NCO Ludwig 63, 64
Platon, Rear Admiral Charles 162
Plechavičius, General Povilas 183
Plungé massacre 183
Pohl, SS Lieutenant General Oswald 67
Pokorny, Adolf 80
Poland vi, 7, 10, 11, 19, 21, 29, 40, 45, 46, 47, 48, 51, 6, 64, 65, 67, 68, 69, 70, 71, 76, 80, 81, 83, 84, 85, 87, 98, 104, 105, 143, 159, 163, 175, 176, 180, 183 **Polish Home Army** 47, 183 **Polish resistance** 88
Poniatowa concentration camp 47
Pons, Sjoerd 165
Popescu, Lieutenant General David 144
Popovici, Brigadier General Ioan 145
Posen POW camp 98
Posthuma, Folkert 165
Poulo Island prison 132
POW Camp No. 99 56
POW massacres 30
Poznan 76
Prasca, General Sebastiano Visconti 104
Prague 10, 21, 52, 71, 174
Prem Nagar POW camp 92
Priebke, SS Captain Erich 107
Prinz Albrecht Strasse Prison 21
Prinz Eugen (Heavy cruiser) 56
Procida prison 110
Propaganda broadcasters 189
Prun, Lieutenant General Luigi Barbasetti di 98
Puaud, Colonel Edgar 162
Pucheu, Pierre 163
Pugliese, Umberto 106

INDEX

Puppet governments (pro-Axis) 152
Purins, Colonel Jānis 179
Putlos POW camp 181
Pyawbwe Battle vii

Qia, General Xi 186
Quandt, Lieutenant Harald 60
Quasimodo, Major General Santi 110
Quirino, Elpidio 125, 126
Quisling, Vidkun 168
Qvist, SS Major Arthur 168, 169

Rab concentration camp 113
Rabaul 118, 129, 130, 134
Racoviță, General Ioan-Mihail 144, 145, 146
Radescu, Lieutenant General Nicolae 143
Rădulescu, General Edgar 144
Radetzky, SS Major Waldemar 51
Raeder, Admiral Erich 3, 5
Rahm, SS Major Karl 71
Rainefarth, Waffen-SS Lieutenant General Heinz 47
Rainer, SS Major General Friedrich 69, 70
Rāis, Vice Admiral Nicolae 145
Rallis, Georgios 159 **Rallis, Ioannis** 159
Ramal (Ayalon) Prison 71
Ramcke, Major General Bernhard 41, 43
Rāmnisu Sārat prison 147
Rappard, Brigadier General Fritz-Georg 23
Rasch, SS Brigadier General Otto 48, 51, 52
Rattenhuber, SS Major General Johann 70, 71
Raubal, Lieutenant Leo-Rudolf 60
Ravensbrück concentration camp 21, 63, 66, 67, 81, 82, 83, 84, 85, 86, 88
Ravensbrück Trials 7, 61, 66, 67, 72, 83, 87
Ravenstein, Lieutenant General Johannes von 18, 19
Rebane, SS Colonel Alfonse 178
Recklinghausen POW camp vi, 89
Red Army viii, 5, 6, 8, 10, 14, 17, 18, 21, 22, 23, 24, 28, 33, 40, 41, 46, 48, 54, 55, 57, 58, 60, 61, 63, 67, 76, 79, 80, 93, 98, 99, 100, 105, 134, 135, 141, 143, 145, 146, 148, 151, 152, 156, 162, 173, 174, 175, 176, 177, 179, 180, 181, 183, 185, 186, 188, 190, 191, 195, 196, 197
Reder, SS Major Walter 53, 54
Regina Coeli prison 106
Reich Chancellery 54, 56, 57, 58, 59
Reich Security Office 3 **Reich Security Service** 70
Reichenau concentration camp 87
Reichenau, Field Marshal Walter von 12
Reimann, Irene 89
Reineque, Lieutenant General Hermann 13, 15
Reinhardt, Colonel General Georg-Hans 13, 14
Reinhart, Johann 78
Reitsch, Hanna 41
Rendulic, Colonel General Lothar 12, 13
Renicci di Anghiari concentration camp 113
Renucci, Marta 162
Repatriation of Axis POWs 193, 194, 195, 196, 197
Reverberi, Lieutenant General Luigi 98
Reynolds, Major General R.B. 125
Rheinbach Prison 33
Rhine River 11, 165, 175
Ribbentrop, Joachim von 3, 4
Ricagno, Lieutenant General Umberto 93, 94
Ricci, Lieutenant General Renato 110
Richert, Brigadier General Johann-Georg 23
Richthofen, Field Marshal Wolfram von 7, 8, 9, 34
Riga 47, 68, 179, 180, 181, 182 **Riga University** 181
Rinkel, Fred-William 87, 88
Ritter von Leeb, Field Marshal Wilhelm 7
River Plate (Battle) 16
Roatta, General Mario 112, 113, 114
Robotti, Lieutenant General Mario 113, 114
Rodenschatz, Major General Karl 55
Rohd, Werner 32
Roma (Battleship) 105

Romania vi, vii, 1, 22, 23, 24, 28, 77, 141, 142, 143, 144, 145, 146, 148 **Romanian POWs** 143, 196 **Romanian troops** 27, 48, 141, 142, 174
Romberg, Hans-Wolfgang 80
Rome 9, 54, 90, 91, 92, 93, 94, 95, 96, 98, 99, 100, 101, 102, 103, 104, 105, 106, 107, 109, 110, 111, 112, 113, 114, 156, 157, 171, 185, 191
Rommel, Field Marshal Erwin 12, 24
Roncalia, Lieutenant General Ercole 99
Roques, Lieutenant General Karl von 13, 15
Rose, Major General Gerhard 79
Rosenberg, Alfred 3, 4
Rosetti, Brigadier General R.R. 145
Rossi, Lieutenant General Carlo 99
Rossi, General Ezio 105
Rossmann, First Lieutenant Edmund 40
Rothkirch, Major General Edwin Graf 28
Röthricht, Major General Edgar 28
Röttiger, Wilhelm 79
Rowden, Diana 32
Royal Albanian Army 158
Royal Air Force (Great Britain) 35, 37, 148, 190
Royal Danish Army 166
Royal Navy (Great Britain) 16, 18, 20
Rožman, Archbishop Gregorij 155
Royal New Zealand Air Force 10
Rucels, Lieutenant-Colonel Jānis 180
Rudolph, Francis 181
Rühl, SS Captain Felix 51
Rühr 17, 29, 89 **Rühr Pocket** 25, 44
Rumbula massacre 15, 47, 181, 182
Rundstedt, Field Marshal Gerd 7, 10, 11, 12
Rupnic, General Leon 154
Russia 10, 11, 12, 23, 36, 40, 42, 44, 49, 50, 87, 104, 105, 142 **Russian White Army** 186 **Russian Liberation Army** (RLA) 173, 174, **175 Russian partisans** 37 **Russian People's National Army** 174
Ryan, Russel 86
Ryuji, Lieutenant General Kajitsuka 135

Saalbach, Fritz 195
Saburo, Lieutenant General Kawamura 127
Sahgal, Major General Prem 185
Saigon 118, 132, 133, 138 **Saigon Trials** 132
Saik, Lieutenant General Hong 124, 187
Sakai, Lieutenant General Takashi 134
Sakaibara, Rear Admiral Shigematsu 124
Salagan, Leontin 145
Salaspils concentration camp 182, 183
Salinas, Major General Gioacchino 110
Salmouth, Colonel General Hans von 13, 14
Salvequart, Vera 81, 83
Salvi, Brigadier General Constantino 100
Salzburg 3, 8, 33, 38, 39, 49, 54, 56, 142, 153, 154, 192
Samurai 115, 119
San, Aung 189
Sănătescu, Lieutenant General Constantin 142, 146
Sandberger, SS Colonel Martin 49, 50
San Francisco Federal District Court 191
San Francisco prison 104
San Savino, Francesco Jacomini Di 111
Sant'Anna di Stazzema massacre 53
San Vittor prison 100
Santakan POW camp 129
Sardinia 92, 101, 105, 110
Šarić, Archbishop Ivan 155
Sarkandaugava concentration camp 180
Sato, Lieutenant General Kenryo 120, 121
Sato, Major General Shunzi 135
Sauberzweig, Major General Karl-Gustav 16, 29
Sauschenhausen concentration camp 32, 67, 68, 69, 75, 76, 80
Scattaglia, Major General Nazzareno 93
Scattini, Major General Arturo 9
Schack, Major GUNTHER 39
Schacht, Hjalmar 5, 6
Schädle, SS Lieutenant Colonel Wilhelm 54
Schäffer, Konrad 80
Schalburg Korps 157
Schellenberg, SS Brigadier General Walter 33

INDEX

Schenck, SS Lieutenant Colonel Ernst-Günther 55
Schilling, SS Lieutenant Claus 77
Schirach, Baldur von 3, 5
Schleinitz, Lieutenant General Siegmund Freiherr von 24
Schlemann, Major General Alfred 42
Schlieben, Lieutenant General Karl-Wilhelm von 24
Schmalz, Lieutenant General Wilhelm 54
Schmidt, Carlo 74
Schmidt, Captain Dietrich 37, 38
Schmidt, Lieutenant General Gustav 17, 23
Schmidt, SS Captain Heinrich 80, 81
Schmidt, Lieutenant General Joseph 36
Schmidt, Colonel General Rudolf 14, 15
Schmitt, Lieutenant General Arthur 20
Schnaufer, Major Heinz-Wolfgang 38
Schniewind, Admiral Otto 13
Schokken POW camp 98, 100, 105
Schörner, Field Marshal Ferdinand 8, 10, 11
Schräder, Admiral Otto von 15, 16
Schreiter, Ida-Bertha 81, 83
Schröder, Colonel General Oskar 79
Schroeder, Emilie-Christine 58, 59
Schroer, Major Werner 37
Schubert, Sergeant Friedrich 45, 46
Schubert, Lieutenant Hans 49, 50
Schurch, Theodor (British Army private) 171
Schwarzhuber, Lieutenant Colonel Johann 66
Schwerin, Major General Gerhard von 30
Scott-Ford, Duncan 171
Scuero, Lieutenant General Antonio 104
Shearer, 2nd Lieutenand William 169
Shedai, Mohammad Iqbal 185
Shigemitsu, Mamoru 121
Shimada, Admiral Shigetaru 120, 121
Shiratori, General Toshio 120
Shozi, Major General Toshinari 132
Schultz, SS Brigadier Erwin 51
Schultz, Brigadier General Harald 24, 43, 44
Schümers, SS Brigadier General Karl 46

Schutzstaffel or SS vii, viii, 3, 4, 29, 47, 49, 50, 51, 58, 74, 81, 82, 87, 88, 89, 99, 102, 103, 105, 106, 107, 109, 168, 175, 181, 183
Schwartz, Carola 170
Securitate (Romania's security services) 148
Seibert, SS Colonel Willi 49
Seidl, SS Lieutenant Colonel Siegfried 71
Seidler, SS Captain Fritz 61
Seltic soccer club 179
Selvester, Captain Tom 6
Semaška, Major Jonas 183
Serbia 112, 150, 152, 155, 156
Seyss-Inquart, Arthur 3, 4
Shanghai POW camp 122
Shin Bet 71
Shiyi, General Zhang 186
Shuxwan, Lieutenant General Xiao 186, 187
Shozo, Lieutenant General Sakurai 130
Siberia 116, 146, 177, 180, 186
Sicily 94, 95
Sidi Barani 91
Sighet prison 145, 146
Signal (German propaganda magazine) 162
Simon, SS Lieutenant General Max 53, 54
Simon Wiesenthal Center 86, 88
Singapore 119, 125, 126, 127, 129
Sion, Major General Alecu-Ion 143
Škirpa, Kazys 184
Skorzeny, SS Lieutenant-Colonel Otto 95
Slovakia 20, 97, 141, 145
Slovenia 70, 110, 111, 112, 152, 153, 155
Slovenian Home Guard 152, 154
Slovenian prisoners 153
Smiley, Colonel David 157
Smyslovsky, Brigadier General Boris A. 174
Snow, Brigadier General Conrad E. 74
Sobibor concentration camp 68, 69, 73
Sobibor Trials 7, 61, 67, 68, 72
Sommer, SS Master Sergeant Martin 61
Sonnemann, Emmy vi, 60
Sook Chin massacre 124, 127

259

Soprokköhida prison 150
South Korea or Republic of Korea (ROK) 188 **South Korean army** 188
Soviet military tribunals 133 **Soviet troops** 6, 57, 60, 73, 82, 84, 86, 87, 98, 143, 179, 180, 195 **Soviet Union or USSR** vi, vii, 1, 2, 14, 15, 22, 23, 24, 27, 40, 48, 49, 50, 56, 57, 93, 98, 107, 135, 141, 142, 144, 147, 148, 151, 153, 164, 173, 176, 177, 178, 179, 184, 186, 196
Spain or Francoist Spain 39, 60, 106, 112, 113, 150, 151, 153, 164, 165, 169, 188, 192, 195
Spandau Prison 2, 5, 121
Spanish Civil War 151 **Spanish POWs** 151
Spannlang, Mathias 61
Spassky POW camp 141
Spatocco, Lieutenant General Carlo 99
Specchia-Normandia, Vice Admiral Carlo 106
Speer, Albert 3, 5
Specht, Major General Karl-Wilhelm 22
Special Operations Executive (SOE) 20, 31, 32, 157
Speidel, Major General Wilhelm 12, 13
Sperrle, Field Marshal Hugo 7, 10, 11, 13, 34
Sporrenben, SS Lieutenant General Jakob 47
SS Mobile Killing Squads 47, 48, 49, 51, 52, 71
Stahel, Major General Reiner 22, 23, 47
Stalag XVIII POW camp 70
Stalin, Joseph viii, 143, 173, 196
Stalingrad 8, 10, 14, 17, 20, 22, 23, 25, 33, 46, 60, 141, 142, 143, 145, 146, 149, 152, 156
Stapleton, Irma 172
Statspolitiet 168
Staubin Prison 69
St. Cathrerin's College (Cambridge) 130
St. Petersburg 151
Stecker, Major General Karl 23
Șteflea, Lieutenant General Ilie 144
Stepinac, Archbishop Aloysius 155
Straube, Major General Erich 42

Streicher, Julius 3
Stromberger, Maria 88
Stroop, SS Lieutenant General JURGEN 46
Stryi pow camp 155
Student, Colonel General Kurt 25, 42, 45
Stulpnagel, Major General Otto 15, 16
Stumpf, Colonel General Hans-Jürgen 34, 35
Sturm, Lieutenant General Alfred 41, 42
Stuttgart 5, 26, 27, 30, 31, 50, 51, 58, 60, 142
Stutthof concentration camp 83, 84, 86 **Stutthof Trials** 62, 64, 72, 87
Suga, Lieutenant-Colonel Tatsuji 116
Sugamo prison 115, 119, 120, 121, 122, 123, 124, 125, 129, 130, 131, 133, 134, 137, 138,
Sugiyama, Field Marshal Hajime 115
Suk-won, Colonel Kim 188
Sumatra 116, 131
Sun-yup, Colonel Baik 188
Supreme Commander for the Allied Powers (SCAP) 117, 118, 121, 137
Süssmann, Lieutenant General Wilhelm 41, 42
Susumu, Captain Hoshi 129
Suzuki, Lieutenant General Teiichi 120, 121
Sweden 167, 168, 169, 180
Switzerland vi, viii, 35, 41, 96, 106, 116, 155, 184, 189
Symond, British Army private Henry A. 170
Szálazi, Ferenc 148, 149
Sztójay, Colonel General Döme 149

Tachibana, Lieutenant General Yoshio 123, 124
Tada, General Hayao 121, 139
Tagasago Volunteers 187
Taiwan 116, 184, 197
Tajima, Lieutenant General Hikotaro 124, 125
Takaatsu, Lieutenant General 135
Takahashi, Admiral Sankichi 137
Takakuwa, Captain Takuo 129
Takasaki, Lieutenant Commander Masamitsu 130

INDEX

Takeda, Prince Tsuneyoshi 138
Tallinn 4, 178, 179
Tanade, Lieutenant General Moritake 131
Tanaka, Captain Gunkichi 134
Tanaka, Lieutenant General Hisakazu 134
Tanaka, General Shizuichi 115
Tantoei POW camp 129
Targu Ocna forced labour colony 148
Tartu concentration camp 179
Tataranu, Lieutenant General Nicolae 144
Tbilisi 177, 181
Telera, Lieutenant General Giuseppe 91
Teodorini, Major General Corneliu 144
Teramoto, Lieutenant General Kumaichi 115
Terboven, Lieutenant Josef 18
Terenzo Monti massacre 53, 54
Terezin Ghetto 80
Teruzzi, Lieutenant General Attilio 110
Tessari, General Arrigo 109
Tettau, Major General Hans von 28
Tetto, Brigadier General Ettore Del 110
Tezno massacre 153
Thailand 116, 135
Theresienstadt ghetto / concentration camp 71, 73, 75
Thernes, SS Lieutenant Colonel Anton 62
Thessaloniki or Salonica 27, 46, 114, 159
Thilo, SS Lieutenant Heinz 75
Thorpe, 2nd Lieutenant Robert E. 123
Thoma, Major General Wilhelm Ritter von 17, 21
Thumann, SS Lieutenant Anton 67
Tiber battalion 113
Tippelskirch, Major General Kurt von 24, 25
Tirana 105, 111, 156, 157, 158
Tirpitz (Battleship) 34
Tito, Josip Broz 6, 26, 27, 114, 152, 155, 175, 191
Tobruk 18, 91
Tocci, Terenzio 157
Togliatti, Palmiro 109
Togo, Shigenori 121
Toichi, Lieutenant General Sasaki 134
Tōjō, General Hideki 115, 119, 120
Tokketai (Japan's naval police) 130

Tokyo 106, 115, 116, 117, 118, 120, 121, 122, 123, 124, 125, 126, 130, 135, 137, 138, 188 **Tokyo Bay** 116
Tokyo trials 118, 120, 121, 132, 138
Tomas, (Hungarian army private) Andras 197
Tomasevich, Joso 153
Topp, Vice Admiral Karl 34
Torgau prison 177
Tornow, Sergeant Fritz 58
Toulon 28, 100, 178
Tower of London 2, 20
Toyoda, Admiral Soemu 137
Tracchia, Major General Ruggero 93
Trautmann, Sergeant Bernd 194, 195
Trawnik concentration camp 47
Treachery Act 171
Treblinka concentration camp 69, 71, 73
Treblinka Trials 7, 61, 68, 72
Trenkel, Captain Rudolf 40
Trent Park POW camp 21, 25, 26, 28, 31, 34, 35, 42, 43, 44
Trezzani, Lieutenant General Claudio 92
Trinity College (Dublin) 184
Trionfi, Brigadier General Alberto 99
Tröger, Lieutenant General Hans 27, 28
Tromara, Kol 157
Tronnier, Brigadier General Louis 22, 23
Truk 123, 124
Truman, Harry S. 125, 193
Tsaritsani 114
Tsolakoglu, Lieutenant General Georgios 159
Tsuchihashi, Lieutenant General Yutsu 133
Tsukada, Lieutenant General Rikichi 137
Tsunenori, Prince Kaya 138
Tsushima garrison 126
Tunisia 8, 21, 25, 29, 94, 95, 162, 169, 184
Turin 30, 33, 90, 94, 99, 103, 104, 105, 106, 112 **Turin University** 185
Turkey 90, 106, 156
Tzideng concentration camp 132

U-39 (U-boat) 20 *U-63* (U-boat) 19
U-230 (submarine) 28
Uchiyama, Lieutenant General Isamu 122

Uckermarck concentration camp 83
Wembley stadium 193
Uemura, General Mikio 116
Ueno, Chisato 124
Ugolini, Colonel Augusto 93
Ukraine 12, 15, 17, 41, 47, 48, 49, 50, 51, 70, 98, 164, 177 **Ukrainian Liberation Army** 176 **Ukrainian National Army** 176
Umezu, General Yoshijiro 120, 121
Un, Lieutenant General Prince Yi 188
Unger, Second Lieutenant Willy 38
Unit 731 (Biological weapons research) 138
United Nations 111 **United Nations Commission of War Crimes** 111, 114
United States 1, 2, 25, 47, 76, 86, 88, 91, 92, 97, 111, 117, 118, 143, 157, 176, 178, 179, 181, 182, 183, 184, 188, 191, 193, 195, 197
US Army vi, vii, 5, 10, 14, 25, 26, 27, 31, 33, 39, 44, 47, 53, 54, 59, 71, 87, 89, 117, 118, 120, 142, 176, 177, 182, 187, 197 **US Army Air Force or USAAF** 16, 19, 27, 120, 148 **US Army Historical Division** 9 **US Navy** 123 **US Pacific Fleet** 123 **US troops** 4, 8, 12, 14, 25, 31, 33, 36, 40, 41, 46, 47, 52, 56, 57, 58, 59, 63, 65, 71, 76, 84, 106, 109, 120, 149, 154, 159, 169, 171, 174, 178, 180, 191 **USS *Missouri*** (Battleship) 116, 120, 121
Ural Mountains' concentration camps 179
Urbanchich, Lyenko 191
Ustaše or Ustaša 152, 154, 155
Usuki, Lieutenant Kishio 127
Utz, Lieutenant General Willibald 26
Uxbridge RAF air base 190

V-1 (Flying bomb) 21
Vac (Theresian) prison 149, 150
Văcăresti prison 145, 147
Vaccaneo, Brigadier General Alessandro 99
Vajna, Gábor 149

Valvo, Captain Francesco 90
Vecchi, General Cesare Maria De 112
Vechtel, First Lieutenant Bernhard 38
Veliky Novgorod 40, 151
Velter, Captain Kurt 37
Vercellino, Divisional General Mario 100
Verona 50, 96, 104, 105, 111 **Verona Trial** 96, 103, 110, 112
Vetter, SS Captain Helmut 77
Viannos massacre 45
Via Tasso prison 102
Vichy France 4, 162, 163, 184, 189
Victor-Emmanuel III King of Italy 95, 101, 105, 106, 107
Victor, SS Colonel Hermann 76
Vienna 5, 30, 40, 52, 54, 71, 78, 85, 154, 169, 190
Vietina, Rear Admiral Maximiliano 90, 91
Viktring POW camp 152, 153
Vilvoorde POW camp vi, 89
Vinca massacre 53
Vinters, Edgars 181
Virgilio military hospital 112
Vittel POW camp 100
Vladimir prison 11, 14, 23, 177
Vlasov, General Andrey 25, 173, 174, 175, 176
Vockamer von Kirchensitytenbach, Major General Friedrich-Jobst 24
Voikovo Prison 8 Camp (No. 48) 8, 22, 23, 24, 47
Volga Tarta Legion 177
Volkenrath, Elizabeth 81, 82
Volkenrath, SS Lance Corporal Heinz 82
Vorkuta POW camp or gulag 22, 67, 80
Vörös, Colonel General János 149
Voss, Vice Admiral Hans-Erich 56
Vrioni, Kemal 158

Wachi, Lieutenant General Takaji 122
Waffen-SS 7, 23, 29, 31, 55, 65, 74, 101, 143, 151, 156, 158, 161, 164, 167, 169, 170, 175, 177, 178, 184, 194, 196
Walasek, Teofil 78
Waldberg, Joseph R. 165

INDEX

Wales 9, 19, 20, 25, 34, 35, 42, 53, 181
Wallon Guard 165 **Wallon Légion** 164
Wandsworth prison 171, 189, 190
Wang Kemin 185
Warlimont, Lieutenant General Walter 13
Warsaw 23, 36, 46, 47, 48, 62 **Warsaw Ghetto** 46 **Warsaw Uprising** 7, 47, 175
Warzecha, Admiral of the Fleet Walter 34
Washington D.C. federal district court 191
Wasicky, SS Captain Erich 77
Watanabe, Captain Kenzo 129
Weichs, Field Marshal Maximilian von 7, 8, 12
Wehrmacht 3, 14, 23, 24, 33, 45, 46, 47, 52, 53, 58, 70, 89, 101, 158, 161, 164, 166, 169, 170, 173, 174, 175, 176, 177, 180, 196, 197
Weidling, Major General Helmuth 23, 24
Weil, Lilly
Weiss, SS Lieutenant Colonel Martin-Gottfried 62
Weltz, Georg-Auhust 80
Wendler, Eberhard 194
Wenyue, General Bao 186
Werfft, Colonel Peter 39
Wehl Prison 9, 53
West Germany or Federal Republic of Germany (FRG) 7, 10, 19, 30, 31, 47, 51, 52, 53, 54, 60, 70, 72, 73, 74, 75, 79, 81, 85, 86, 88, 107, 182, 191
Wewak 129
White Movement 175
Wiedbaden 11, 15, 26, 44, 70
Wigan or No. 50 POW camp 194
Wilke, Lieutenant General Gustav 44
Wilke, Major Wolf-Dietrich 19, 36
Wilton Park POW camp 94, 95
Winkelmann, SS Major Adolf 69
Wirths, SS Major Edward 75
Wisliceny, SS Captain Dieter 71
Witzleben, Field Marshal Erwin von 12
Wladimirowsa Prison 24
Wöhner, Lieutenant General Otto 13, 15
Wola Massacre 46

Wolff, SS Lieutenant General Karl-Friedrich 106
Wolfheze 88
Wolf, Joanna 58, 59
Wolf, SS Lieutenant General Karl-Friedrich-Otto 69, 106, 107
Wolfenbutter prison 78
Wolf's Lair 55, 59
Wolff, Major General Ludwig 35
Wolfrum, 1st Lieutenant Walter 39
Wölstein POW camp 100
Wolter, SS Major Waldemar 65
Woodford viii
Woods, Master Sergeant Joch C. 78, 79
Wünsche, SS Lieutenant General Max 33
Wüfel, Second Lieutenant Otto 40

Yahara, Colonel Hiromichi 137
Yalta viii, 174 **Yalta Agreement** 173, 176
Yamada, General Otozo 135
Yamada, Lieutenant General Seiichi 116
Yamaguchi, Lieutenant Akuni 127
Yamamoto, Admiral Isoroku 119
Yamamoto, Captain Kazaharu 123
Yamashita, General Tomoyuki 119, 124, 125
Yamashita Standard 125
Yanagawa, Lieutenant General Heisuke 133
Yasuoka, Lieutenant General Masaomi 131
Yokohama 118, 191 **Yokohama trials** 120, 121, 122, 123
Yokohama, Lieutenant General Isamu 122
Yokohama, Lieutenant General Shizuo 126
Yol POW camp 91
Yolanda, Princess of Savoy 106
Yoshimoto, General Teiichi 115
Yugoslavia 6, 11, 12, 13, 26, 27, 29, 49, 77, 97, 98, 99, 103, 104, 109, 111, 112, 114, 152, 153, 154, 155, 156, 175, 176, 184, 191 **Yugoslav guerrillas or partisans** iii, 152, 153, 154
Yundao, General Ren 187

Zagreb 26, 153, 154, 155
Zallari, Mihal 158
Zaloga, Steven 197
Zambon, Major General Bortolo 106
Zaryanov, Major General I.M. 118
Zedelgem POW camp 181
Zelewski, SS Lieutenant General Erich 47
Zhytomy Massacre 49
Ziereis, SS Colonel Franz 61, 66
Zimmer, Emma 81
Zoddel, Erich 78
Zoller, SS Captain Viktor 65, 66
Zuckschwerdt, Rear Admiral Adalbert 33, 34
Zucca, Rita-Louisa 191
Zutter, SS Captain Adolf 65, 66